Radical Reads

101 YA Novels on the Edge

Joni Richards Bodart

The Scarecrow Press, Inc.
Lanham, Maryland, and London
2002

SCARECROW PRESS, INC.

Published in the United States of America
by Scarecrow Press, Inc.
4720 Boston Way, Lanham, Maryland 20706
www.scarecrowpress.com

4 Pleydell Gardens, Folkestone
Kent CT20 2DN, England

British Library Cataloguing in Publication Information Available

Library of Congress Cataloging-in-Publication Data

Bodart, Joni Richards.
   Radical reads : 101 YA novels on the edge / Joni Richards Bodart.
      p. cm.
   Includes bibliographical references and indexes.
   ISBN 0-8108-4287-4 (alk. paper)
   1. Teenagers—Books and reading—United States. 2. Young adult fiction,
American—Bibliography. I. Title.

Z1037 .B65 2002
028.5'35—dc21   2001057705

♾™ The paper used in this publication meets the minimum requirements of
American National Standard for Information Sciences—Permanence of
Paper for Printed Library Materials, ANSI/NISO Z39.48-1992.
Manufactured in the United States of America.

This is for the people who inspired it,
the librarians and teachers who struggle to put
the very best of young adult literature onto their shelves
and into the hands of the teens who need it most,
with the hope that it will make that process easier for you

And for the teens who read these books—
Find the lessons in experiences, real or virtual, and use them
to become the best that you can be,
because…
"The moving finger writes; and having writ,
Moves on: nor all your piety nor wit
Shall lure it back to cancel half a line,
Nor all your tears wash out a word of it."
(Edward Fitzgerald, *The Rubaiyat of Omar Khayyám*, st. 71, 1859.)

📖 Contents 📖

SECTION THREE: *Give A Boy a Gun* to *Nobody Else Has to Know*

SECTION FOUR: *On the Fringe* to *Swallowing Stones*

SECTION FIVE: *The Taking of Room 114* to *Wringer*

📖 Acknowledgments 📖

Every time I finish a book, I look back at the long, hard road that got me to the end, and see all the people that contributed in many ways to that book's birth. And now it's time to do it again, and share with you the people that have been with me all the way.

First of all, Shirley Lambert of Scarecrow Press was delighted to have the chance to push the envelope a little, doing a book on the darker, more controversial side of YA literature, and encouraged me to get right to it! (And then she was patient when it took longer than either of us expected.)

Beth Wrenn-Estes compiled and input reviews and awards lists, helped with the title selection, and wrote the rough draft of the appendices as the capstone project for her MLS at the University of Denver. I would have been dead in the water without her contribution to getting this book started and off the ground.

Cathi MacRae, editor of *Voice of Youth Advocates*, and her staff, Linda Benson and Judy Briles, also contributed by sending mountains of reviews to Beth to organize, with others, into the biggest looseleaf notebook I have *ever* seen—almost a *foot* thick!

Patty Campbell, best grrrlfriend, not only helped select titles, she helped me stay on track during the last push to the finish line, and stay sane and focused from beginning to end. Witty, wise, and wonderful, I am so lucky to have her as a friend and colleague. Don't know what I'd do without you, babe!

Floyd (Laff) Lafferty also contributed to my sanity and good humor, compiled the bibliographical data for each title, including all the formats available for each, and input pages and pages of entries for me, cutting in half the time necessary to finish the book. He and Patty are both tireless encouragers ("Come on, Joni, you can do it!") as well as fantastic friends.

Members of the YALSA-BK Listserv unknowingly contributed their comments, picks and pans, while I lurked, took notes, found books, and added or deleted new titles. Thanks everyone, I know I would have missed some gems without your help!

And finally, many heartfelt thanks to Dana Richardson, fellow librarian, great friend, ex-student, fellow Siamese enthusiast, and ukulele player extraordinaire! I'd like to tell the world what you did, but you're right, it might get us both fired. The world will have to wonder, but you know why I have to say I couldn't have done it on time without you!

Thank you, thank you, one and all!

📖 Introduction 📖

What's a Radical Read, and
Why This Book Was Written

Radical young adult fiction is edgy, raw, and relevant to the young adults who read it. Teens struggling with pressures and issues in today's society have found that these radical young adult novels can help them work through their own problems because they can recognize and identify with the characters in the novels. There are no easy answers or pat endings in these books, and many characters don't live happily ever after. They are called dark, bleak, gritty, depressing, and hard to read. This harsh realism is one of the reasons adults find these titles controversial. Those trying to protect youth from the realities of life today reject them immediately.

Radical young adult fiction deals with incest, teenage pregnancy, substance abuse, sexual and physical abuse, mental and physical illness, dysfunctional families, homosexuality, gangs, homelessness, manipulation, prejudice, suicide, peer pressure, violence, and murder. Central characters can be quite mature, and even those who are not are complex and multidimensional. Plot lines are also complex, and may include perspectives from several characters, nonlinear or nonsequential sections or chapters, ambiguous endings, or several story lines layered or woven together. According to Eliza Dresang, in her groundbreaking book, *Radical Change: Books for Youth in the Digital Age*, these books break boundaries in many ways—in format, in topic, in treatment, in letting youth speak for themselves, and in giving voice to those who were previously unheard. They challenge the reader, and show how much their authors respect their audience. They are no longer just "fiction for teens," sneered at as lesser stepchild of "good literature," as the "problem novels" of the '60s and '70s were—there are no smug, pat answers here. Radical YA fiction is frequently more complex and better written than many adult bestsellers. It is an area of literature that has finally come of age, and deserves to be promoted for the contribution that it makes to the thoughts and lives of those who read it.

But controversial titles are frequently difficult to support in either school or public libraries. Librarians' "silent censorship" keeps them off the shelves, and out of the hands of the kids who need them most. And that point is where this book began, as an effort to make these wonderful, valuable, and controversial titles more accessible to teens and the professionals who work with them. The entry on each book has information that will be useful in helping encourage teens to read that title (bibliographic information, reading and interest level, classes for which the title would be appropriate, an annotated list of characters, a booktalk, and ideas on how to write a book report or booktalk) and teachers or librarians defend it (why the book is considered radical, controversial subjects or risks in the book, its strengths, awards it has won and lists it has been put on, and a list of review citations, with brief excerpts from some of them.) Appendices give additional information on dealing with challenges and censorship attempts.

Titles were selected based on their format and their content, following to some extent the three criteria set out by Dresang, which are:

- *Radical form and format*, including graphics used in new ways, words and pictures working together more closely, nonlinear or nonsequential organization and format, and multiple layers of meaning
- *Radical perspectives*, including multiple perspectives, both visual and verbal, previously unheard voices, and youth who speak for themselves
- *Radical boundaries*, including subjects, groups or communities, and settings that were previously forbidden or omitted, characters portrayed in new and complex ways, and ambiguous or unresolved endings

Two people contributed to the selection process, Beth Wrenn-Estes, who is the director of collection development for Denver Public Schools, and Patty Campbell, editor, writer, and YA literature critic extraordinaire. The list started at about 250, and was gradually cut down to 150, where it stayed for several months, as we tinkered with it, trying to get in as many recent titles as possible. Then it was decided that we had to take it down to 100, an extremely painful process that none of us enjoyed, and which resulted in 101 titles in the final list.

Then I started writing, while Beth began her research on reviews and awards for each of the titles. When looking at reviews, we looked first for a *Voice of Youth Advocates* review, then for ones in the other major selection tools. It was not an exhaustive search, and you may be able to find reviews in other sources. Since we wanted to support the books, we didn't include any negative reviews. In fact, too many negative reviews meant some books were dropped. Nor was the search for awards exhaustive; state awards were not included because there are so many and there was no way we could be sure we'd gotten all of them. In addition, it's important to remember that some of these titles, ones published in late 2000 or 2001, were too new to have been considered for awards and lists by the time this book went to press. By the time you are reading this, that situation will probably have changed because many of these books are most deserving of honors.

As for my comments on the risks and strengths of each book, those of you in less-conservative communities may think I have been overly cautious about what people might object to. I decided to err on the side of caution and mention anything I thought might be considered objectionable. However, I suspect that I probably omitted things in some entries that someone else would have included. After all, "controversial" is a personal thing.

You may notice that almost all of the titles in this book are given a middle school reading level. That is because the words in these books are easier for younger adolescents to read than some of the content is. Many of them should be discussed when used with younger kids to make sure that students are able to cope with that content.

I have listed three interest levels, MS, YHS, OHS, which correspond to sixth to eighth grades, ninth and tenth grades, and eleventh and twelfth grades. You may or may not agree with me about either reading or interest levels. You know your community, I don't. Go with what works for you. Before putting any of these books in your collection, *read them*! Find out if a title is likely to create a hot-button issue *before* you put it in your collection. Pick your battles!

The appendices should give you information on why and how censorship happens, and how to deal with the censors. There are also lists of where you can go for help in combating censorship in your community, including both print and electronic sources. But be aware, this information is just a place to start, not all that you could or should do. Again, know your community, and take the action appropriate for it.

Well, that's how it came about. Our job is over—at last! We've spent almost three years on this book, now it's your turn! We all hope it will be helpful to you and useful for your students.

📖 Tips for Writing Effective Book Reports 📖

1. Write down everything you will need to know about the assignment when the teacher tells you about it. Ask questions if you are not sure about something.

2. Go to the school or public library or a bookstore and get at least two or three books. Look in the library catalog for books on subjects you will like reading about or ask a librarian for help. Most bookstores have a subject arrangement. Ask one of the salespeople for help in finding the subject or subjects you are interested in. You should select more than one book in case you don't like the first one you picked out. It is very hard to enjoy reading or to write effectively about a book that you really don't like or that doesn't hold your attention.

3. Read a little bit every day and take notes on what you read as you go along. You need to jot down the characters' names and a brief description of each of them, a summary of the plot line, and any important scenes or ideas from the book (with the page numbers so you can find them again).

4. Try to plan a special time to read, and make sure you have something to take notes with and that you are not too tired. If you read when you're very tired, you might easily miss something important.

5. Organize your notes. Use a separate sheet for each topic in your book report, and keep them in order in one place so you will know where to find them. Putting them with the book is always a good idea.

6. Write your first draft using these four sections: a brief plot summary; the author's main idea or ideas, including why you think the author wrote the book; a discussion about the characters and the setting, with an evaluation of their realism and believability; and your own opinion of the book, why you either liked it or didn't like it, what kind of a person you think might like it, and to whom you would recommend it.

7. Check with your teacher to see if you are on the right track and doing what he or she expects you to do. Be sure to find out if you need to include any other information about the book or about the author.

8. Revise and edit your first draft. Check the spelling of all the words in your draft, and make sure that your grammar is also correct. At this point you may also want to change what you have written in the body of the report if you have thought of a better way to explain what you want to say or if you have thought of something else to add.

9. Make your final draft and proofread it to be sure there are no mistakes. Don't forget to put your name and class information on the top sheet, and be sure if your paper is handwritten that your writing is clear and easy to read.

10. Turn in your paper on the due date.

These ideas are partially based on *Scholastic's A+ Junior Guide to Book Reports* by Louise Colligan (Scholastic, 1989, $2.50), which has much more information and also helpful forms in it that you can use to make sure that your book reports are easier to write and easier to make an A on.

Richard Peck, who is a well-known and prolific writer for teens, has ten questions to ask yourself about a novel, which could also give you book report ideas.

- What would this story be like if the main character were of the opposite sex?
- Why is the story set where it is?
- If you were to film this story, what characters would you eliminate if you couldn't use all of them?
- Would you film this story in black-and-white or color?
- How is the main character different from you?
- Why or why not would this story make a good TV series?
- What one thing in the story that's happened to you?
- Reread the first paragraph of chapter 1. What's in it to make you read on?
- If you had to design a new cover for the book, what would it look like?
- What does the title tell you about the book? Does it tell the truth?
- Are there characters in the book who wear disguises of some kind, and if so, what are they, and why do they wear them?

📖 Tips for Writing Effective Booktalks 📖

1. A booktalk is not a book report, but a kind of commercial for a book that persuades the listener to read it. Therefore, it doesn't tell the ending and doesn't evaluate the book in any way. It just tells a little about the plot and the characters and stops without telling what happened next. In addition, a book report is mainly something that you write and the teacher reads (although you may be asked to read it in class as well), but a booktalk is usually spoken. It is really talking about the book. It is basically the kind of thing you'd say to a friend when you've just finished a book you really liked and want to make sure that your friend reads it too.

2. Never talk about a book that you didn't like—how could you convince someone else to read it if you didn't like it?

3. Never talk about a book you haven't read all the way through—you might miss something crucial, or your teacher might ask you to talk with him or her privately about the end of the book. Plus, in a booktalk, you are introducing your audience to the people in the book, and if you haven't read the book, you won't know who they are—they'll be strangers, not friends.

4. There are four basic kinds of booktalks based on what you thought was exciting in the book.

Plot summary is the first kind. You just summarize the plot, leading up to an exciting and climactic moment and stopping without telling what happened. The last sentence for a talk like this could be "To find out what happened next, read. . . ."

Character description is another kind of booktalk, one that is based on talking about one or two or more of the main characters in the book. You can pretend that you are one of the characters and write your talk in the first person, or you can just describe the characters in the third person. The more characters you use, the less you can say about each one of them because you don't want to make your talk too long.

If you are writing about a book that is a collection of short stories or is written in an episodic style (the main character might have a series of adventures or problems to deal with, each one contained in one or two chapters), you can use the **short story/scene** kind of booktalk. This talk simply tells the whole story or scene (or one adventure or problem) from beginning to end. The last few sentences of the talk let the audience know that there are other adventures or stories that they will miss if they don't read the book.

If the author of your book has a unique writing style or if the book itself has a mood about it, mysterious, scary, or suspenseful, then you will want to write a **mood-based** booktalk. This kind of talk lets your audience know what to expect from the book and sometimes includes an excerpt from it that demonstrates the author's writing style. In order to communicate the mood, you'll need to use your voice, including variations in pitch, pace, and rhythm, to convey the mood.

5. A booktalk shouldn't be too long and usually lasts between two and four minutes, depending on how much of the book you have to tell to convince your audience to read it. This means that you will have to leave out either most or all of the details about the book and just put into your talk what is absolutely necessary.

6. Take notes while you read your book, including the names of the characters and the page number of any special scene or quote you want to use in your talk.

7. Make your first sentence exciting so that it will hook your audience immediately. Start in the middle of the action, and be sure to include more action than description, because most audiences find action more interesting. Once you have gotten your audience's attention with your first sentence, they will be more willing to listen to what else you have to say.

8. Time your talk after you've written it, while you are practicing, to make sure that it isn't too long, no more than four minutes. Be sure that you do practice and that you practice not only what you are going to say but also the way you're going to stand, how you will handle the book itself and your notes on it, and whatever gestures you will use. If you don't practice everything at once, you will be more likely to forget something you really wanted to say when you deliver your talk. Make sure you also practice projecting your voice so everyone in the room can hear you.

9. Don't memorize your talk! Use slightly different words when you practice so that if you forget the exact words you have written down, you will have some other familiar words to fill in. This means that you shouldn't look at your notes too much while you practice after the first two or three times you read it aloud. This will force you to find different words to use.

10. Wear comfortable clothes. I always make sure that I have pockets in my skirt or pants so I have somewhere to put my hands to keep from waving them around. And remember to speak slowly, because you may be nervous and more likely to speed up without realizing it. But most of all, remember to have fun! That's one of the main purposes of booktalks—to have fun sharing books you've enjoyed with other people who will enjoy them too.

And there's also an extra bonus to doing booktalks. People are more afraid of getting up in front of a crowd and talking than anything else. If you learn how to do this, while you are learning how to give booktalks, you'll have an advantage over all of them!

There is more information about how to write and present booktalks in my book *Booktalk! 2* (H. W. Wilson, 1985, $32.00). Most public and school libraries have copies of this book. In addition, your librarians may be willing to share their own hints on how to do booktalks.

📖 Guide to Abbreviations 📖

READING AND INTEREST LEVELS

MS   Middle School, sixth through eighth grades

YHS   Younger High School, ninth and tenth grades

OHS   Older High School, eleventh and twelfth grades

📖 SECTION ONE 📖
Am I Blue? to *Burning Up*

AM I BLUE? COMING OUT FROM THE SILENCE. Bauer, Marion Dane. HarperCollins, 1995. $5.95. 273 p. ISBN: 0-06-440587-7. Short story collection, Realistic fiction. Reading level: MS, YHS. Interest level: MS, YHS, OHS. Sex education, Psychology, English, Creative writing, Sociology, Ethics, Filmmaking, Drama.

SUBJECT AREAS
activism; homosexuality; love; illness, physical; rites of passage; peer pressure; prejudice; abuse, physical; minorities, black; school; death and dying; family relationships; self-knowledge; friendship.

CHARACTERS
"Am I Blue?" by Bruce Coville
Vince: a teen who's trying to figure out if he's gay or not
Melvin: Vince's fairy godfather, who's the first of his kind

"We Might as Well All Be Strangers" by M. E. Kerr
Alison: a sixteen-year-old Jewish girl who's just told her mother she's gay
Grandmother: she knows firsthand what prejudice is like

"Winnie and Tommy" by Francesca Lia Block
Winnie: she's seventeen and in love with Tommy
Tommy: he wants to be in love with Winnie, but....

"Slipping Away" by Jacqueline Woodson
Jacina: with a black father and a white mother, she knows all about prejudice
Maria: she has questions that Jacina can't answer

"Honorable Shepherds" by Gregory Maguire
Lee, Pete: two teens who are beginning their first gay relationship
Violet Cabbage: their film teacher, in whose class they met

"Running" by Ellen Howard
Terry: she's never had a boyfriend, and is intrigued by Sheila, Heather's lesbian
  friend
Heather: Terry's older stepsister who just got back from Europe

"Three Mondays in July" by James Cross Giblin
David: he's attracted to men and worries about being gay
Allen: an older gay man, he understands what David is going through

"Parents' Night" by Nancy Garden
Karen, Roxy: they are in love and have decided to come out to their parents

"Michael's Little Sister" by C.S. Adler
Michael: he's not quite ready to admit he's gay
Walt: a gay soccer and drama star, he understands Michael's confusion

"Supper" by Leslea Newman
Meryl: a Jewish teen who wonders why she doesn't like boys

"Holding" by Lois Lowry
Will: when his father's partner Chris dies, Will spends a week with his dad
Jon: Will's best friend who doesn't know Will's "mom" was a man

"Blood Sister" by Jane Yolen
Selna: she's a huntress and a warrior
Marda: she's Selna's best friend and blood sister

"Hands" Jonathan London
Lon: he's a high school student and budding poet
Ray Hiller: one of Lon's teachers, he is a poet and also gay

"50% Chance of Lightning" by Cristina Salat
Robin: she wrote an article about being gay for her school paper
Malia: she's Robin's best friend

"In the Tunnels" by William Sleator
Bay, Dang, Tran: three guerrilla soldiers on a dangerous mission
Boy: the narrator, a young man who loves Bay

"Dancing Backwards" by Marion Dane Bauer
Thea, Cindy: roommates at a Catholic girls school who are accused of being gay

BOOKTALK
What's it like being gay or lesbian? What's it like to have a parent or a friend who is? Have you ever wondered if you are gay or lesbian? Let the teens in these stories show you their lives from the inside out—you may discover you all have more in common than you'd thought.

Vince meets his fairy godfather in "Am I Blue?," finds out about the great gay fantasy number three, and makes a wish to make it come true.

In "We Might as Well All Be Strangers," Alison discovers her grandmother knows a lot more about prejudice and acceptance than she had ever imagined.

Lee and Pete, in "Honorary Shepherds," use their film project to express their love for each other and their admiration for their teacher who helps them redefine themselves, even as she is dying of cancer.

Will's dad and Chris have been together since Will was three, but Will's never admitted to his best friend that his dad's gay in "Holding."

You'll also meet Tommy, Terry, David, Michael, Meryl, Lon, Thea, Cindy, and many more; teens all wondering about their sexuality, struggling with the probabilities and possibilities in their lives, and not wanting to go through that process alone.

What's it like being gay? Listen to these stories and find out.

MAJOR THEMES AND IDEAS
- Most people see and believe what they choose to, rather than dealing with reality.
- Prejudice feels the same, no matter its source.
- You are a unique and special individual—be proud of it!
- People frequently are most angry about what they fear the most or understand the least.
- Even if you need to lie to other people until you can tell them the truth, don't ever lie to yourself.
- Understanding and love can come from the most unexpected sources.
- Real friends are those who accept you completely, no matter what. Never forget to value them or to let them know how much their friendship means to you.
- Sometimes your family is the people with blood ties to you, sometimes it is the people you choose to create your family with you. Both kinds can be equally valuable and supportive.
- When you have questions you can't answer, sometimes someone who's "been there, done that" can help.
- Prejudice is *not* logical.
- Focus your attention on those who build you up, not tear you down.

- Unfortunately, there will always be those who hate. However, it is far more important to remember that there will also always be those who love.

BOOK REPORT IDEAS

1. Several of the stories are about teens asking themselves, "Am I gay? Am I a lesbian?" Compare and contrast how their families react to or help with their decision.
2. In the title story, the third gay fantasy comes true. Speculate on what might happen if that actually occurred at midnight tonight, and how the world might change or stay the same as a result.
3. In a number of stories, sympathetic adults help teens realize that they are gay. Discuss how those teens' lives were changed as a result of that supportive interaction.
4. Choose the story that had the greatest emotional or psychological impact or the greatest personal significance for you and explain why you chose it and what it means to you.

BOOKTALK IDEAS

1. Choose two or three stories that have a common theme and introduce the character in each based on that theme.
2. Do a series of one sentence mini-plot summary talks to introduce six to eight of the stories.
3. Focus your talk on the idea of outsiders, with an "us/them" perspective, and use it to introduce the book as a whole. Material from the introduction and the authors' notes might be useful to you in doing this.
4. Become a character in one of the stories, and in first person introduce characters or situations from some of the others.

RISKS

- Discusses teen and adult homosexuality positively and without prejudice.
- Portrays homosexuality as a biological or genetic fact of life rather than an intellectual choice.
- Includes racially mixed teens.
- Teens shown sleeping together, both with and without sexual contact.
- Language is realistic but vulgar.
- Teens are sexually active.

STRENGTHS

- Realistic characters that teens can understand and identify with.
- Gives a variety of perspectives, ideas, and relationships.
- Lets teens who are wondering about their sexuality know that it's okay to do so.

- Includes authors who are and are not homosexual, yet all of whom are open and understanding.
- Lets teens know that they are not alone in being homosexual or in having friends or family members who are.
- Portrays gay adults as positive role models.
- Positive portrayal of homosexuality.
- Variety of stories will appeal to teens in many different situations.

AWARDS
Gay, Lesbian, Bisexual & Transgendered Book Award, 1995 (ALA)
Best Books for Young Adults, 1994 (ALA)
Quick Picks for Reluctant Readers, 1994 (ALA)
Popular Paperbacks, "Lesbian and Gay Tales," 1997 (ALA)

REVIEWS
"Teen years are years of questions, many of them about sex and personhood. One's own fears or doubts can be seen reflected in any of these stories, and, while fiction, help resolve how to live, or how to live with someone. . . . this [collection] has a consistently high quality; there isn't one [story] that isn't well-written, involving, and with characters that live. Just about every library serving YAs should have *Am I Blue?*" —*Voice of Youth Advocates*, 8/94, W. Keith McCoy.

"Wonderfully diverse in tone and setting, the stories cut across color and class lines. . . . With stories that go beyond struggle and stereotype to show individuality, pride and affection, this is an important book that should be in every YA collection." —*Booklist*, 1994, Stephanie Zvirin.

"These stories. . . . will help such young people realize that they are not alone, unique or abnormal in their sexual orientation." —*Kirkus Reviews*, 6/15/94.

"While all the pieces center on themes of coming to terms with homosexuality, they are also stories of love, coming of age, adventure, and self-discovery. A powerful commentary about our social and emotional responses to homosexuality and our human need for love and acceptance." —*Horn Book*, 1994.

📖 📖 📖

ARE YOU ALONE ON PURPOSE? Werlin, Nancy. Houghton-Mifflin, 1994. $16.00. 204p. ISBN: 0-395-67350-X. Fawcett Juniper, 1996. $4.50. 184p.

ISBN: 0-449-70445-9. Reading level: MS. Interest level: MS, YHS. English, Psychology, Sociology.

SUBJECT AREAS
family relationships; illness, physical; handicaps, physical; school; rites of passage; self-knowledge; peer pressure; religion, Jewish; secrets; minorities; friendship; problem parents; racism.

CHARACTERS
Alison Shandling: a fourteen-year-old girl who believes that her role in life is to be normal and not to worry her parents

Adam Shandling: Alison's twin brother is autistic and the focus of their parents' attention

Harry Roth: the school bully, a year older than Alison, he has teased her for years about her brother

Betsy Shandling: the twins' mother who spends much of her time focused on her son

Jake Shandling: Harvard mathematics professor, who invented the Shandling Sphere, and is the twins' father

Rabbi Avi Roth: Harry's father, who has withdrawn into himself since his wife's death, and almost ignores his son

Paulina de la Silva: Alison's best friend, she understands about Adam and doesn't mind being around him

BOOKTALK
Sometimes it seemed to Alison that she had been alone for a long, long time. Ever since everyone realized that Adam was different, damaged, and she was normal. He was the autistic twin, the one their mother paid all her attention to, defending him, fighting all his battles for him. Alison was the one who was always good, didn't make trouble, went to school and did her homework. But everyone knew about Adam, and so Alison was never just herself, she was always Adam's sister—even to her best friend, Paulina.

Alison had done her share of defending Adam, too, especially when Harry Roth, the rabbi's son and the school bully, jeered at her about her brother. But she hadn't told her parents about him, so they had no clue about what might happen when the rabbi introduced his son to the Shandlings after Saturday morning services. "Yeah," Harry sneered, "I've met the retard *and* his sister." There was a shocked silence in the synagogue social hall, and his father grabbed Harry by the arm and dragged him away.

Alison's mother never forgot that moment. Months later, when the rabbi refused to let Adam go to Hebrew school, she lost her temper. "I wish your son was even more handicapped than mine!" That was the same day that Harry had a diving accident at camp, broke his back, and ended up in a wheelchair. That was the day that changed all of their lives in ways none of them could have ever predicted.

When Harry came home from the hospital eight months later, he was the same angry, jeering bully he'd been before—or was he? Alison wanted to find out.

MAJOR IDEAS AND THEMES

- Hiding your pain doesn't make it go away.
- People are not always who they appear to be.
- Bullies may be trying to protect themselves by hurting people and shoving others away from them.
- A good offense may not be the best defense.
- Coincidences can change lives.
- Keeping the world at a distance doesn't mean you won't be hurt.
- Good things can come of even the worst tragedies.

BOOK REPORT IDEAS

1. What is the meaning of the title? Who was alone in the book, and why? How did different characters deal with being alone? How is being alone on purpose different from being alone accidentally?
2. How did Harry's view of himself and of his father change after his accident? How did the accident change how he felt about Alison?
3. Discuss how Alison might have felt about Harry after his accident if she had not heard her mother say she wished he were more handicapped than Adam. Explain why that is one of the pivotal scenes in the book.
4. Show how Alison changed in her understanding of herself during the course of the book.
5. Compare how Alison and Adam were treated by their parents, and show how that treatment affected each one of them. How do you think that treatment will change in the future, based on the ending of the book?

BOOKTALK IDEAS

1. Focus your talk around the scene in the rabbi's office when Mrs. Shandling confronts him about Adam going to Hebrew school.
2. Write your talk in first person, first from Alison's point of view and then from Harry's, as they describe each other, either before or after the accident.
3. Focus your talk on the idea of being good to someone who has hurt you.

RISKS

- Portrays anti-Semitism.
- Language is realistic but vulgar.
- Shows prejudice or persecution of teens who are different.
- Teen characters show lack of respect for parents.

STRENGTHS

- Problems in both main families are worked through in realistic and positive ways.
- Positive portrayal of paraplegic teen coping with his handicap.
- Strong multidimensional characters who show growth and insight.

AWARDS

None

REVIEWS

"Harry and Alison's tentative beginnings and tender friendship will strike a familiar chord with young people who cope with feelings of alienation from family and peers on a regular basis." —*Voice of Youth Advocates*, 10/94, Marian Rafal.

"Werlin exhibits an understanding of the emotions of adolescents and writes a complex, compelling story of families struggling to be whole." —*Horn Book*, 1/2/95, M.V.K.

"Her characterizations are superb, and her smooth writing and refined plot will make this ultimately uplifting story very popular." —*Booklist*, 1994, Karen Simonetti.

📖 📖 📖

ASYLUM FOR NIGHTFACE. Brooks, Bruce. HarperCollins, 1996. $13.95. 137p. ISBN: 0-06-027060-8. HarperTrophy, 1999. $4.95. 160p. ISBN: 0-06-447214-0. Realistic fiction. Reading level: MS. Interest level: MS, YHS. English, Art, Ethics.

SUBJECT AREAS

religion; family relationships; problem parents; ethics; rites of passage; self-knowledge; friendship.

CHARACTERS

Zimmerman: a fourteen-year-old boy who has "fallen in love with God and Creation"
Luke Mark John: founder of the Faith of Faiths
Marcos: Zimmerman's best friend who's now in jail

Zimmerman's parents: they were concerned about their son's "bleached lifestyle" until they converted to the Faith of Faiths

William and Ellen Erskine, the McCortys: other members of the Faith of Faiths

Mason Farwell: he owns Kollectible Kards

Allen Thomassen: Farwell's partner, he created the Rack of Stars

Drake Jones: a genius who created comic strips and cards featuring each of his superheroes, including Nightface

BOOKTALK

Zimmerman isn't your average fourteen-year-old. He's in love with God and with His Creation. And his beliefs are his own, and he doesn't go around shouting about them or trying to convert anyone. But his parents are concerned about what they call his "bleached life." They actually seem to be acting more like teenagers than their own son—pot and hash parties and always wine with every meal. Zimmerman's refusal to join in, his determination to live his own life, worries them, and they try to talk Zimmerman into doing something, anything, wrong.

However, all that changes when they come back from a vacation in Jamaica, where they've converted to the Faith of Faiths. They pray loudly and frequently. They no longer drink or party. And they apologize to Zimmerman constantly for not understanding his faith before.

Zimmerman just ignores them as much as he can, just as he has for years, until the day he discovers that their plans for the Faith of Faiths now include their plans for him.

MAJOR THEMES AND IDEAS

- Religion is a way of letting us love ourselves.
- The more you look at the intricacies of this world, the more obvious it becomes that it wasn't an accident. It was designed.
- All love is, in essence, love of God.
- People see in others only what they choose to see.
- Being true to oneself is more important than anything else.
- The design of Nature reflects the Mind of God.

BOOK REPORT IDEAS

1. Compare the ways his parents see Zimmerman before and after their conversion, and discuss how their views do and do not reflect Zimmerman's own understanding of himself.
2. Analyze Zimmerman's friendship with Marco, showing why they became friends and what each gets from the relationship.
3. Discuss the character of Drake Jones and explain why the author made him such a major character in the book.

4. Explain the symbolic meaning of Nightface and the scene that appears on his card.
5. Zimmerman finds God through examining the pattern and design of the natural world. Give examples of some of the things that convince him that Creation is deliberate rather than accidental, and explain why they were so convincing.
6. Zimmerman's parents, prior to their conversion, spend a large amount of time trying to get him to sin. Analyze the concept of sin in the book, including what it is from the point of view of both Zimmerman and his parents, before and after their conversion.

BOOKTALK IDEAS
1. Zimmerman has long dialogues with himself. Use quotes from these to introduce him and his situation.
2. Write your talk in first person as Marcos and let him introduce Zimmerman.
3. Focus your talk on two scenes, one in which Zimmerman's parents are trying to get him to sin, and one where they are apologizing to him, ending with a hint of what they might want him to do to be more like them.

RISKS
- Parents use illegal drugs and encourage their son to do so as well.
- Parents encourage their son to steal.
- Presents two different, but equally unconventional, views of religion.

STRENGTHS
- Provides many topics for class discussion, especially around the idea of what is sin, and taking control of yourself and your beliefs.
- An intellectual teenager is portrayed positively.
- Ambiguous of incomplete resolution allows reader to create various possible endings.
- Discussion defining religion and spirituality is from several perspectives.

AWARDS
None

REVIEWS
"The problem for readers of this fine novel will be with Zimmerman's highly sophisticated thoughts. . . . Brooks gives much to consider in this slim, thought-provoking novel which will be treasured by YAs who are emotionally mature."
—*Voice of Youth Advocates*, 10/96, Susan R. Farber.

"This quickly philosophical novel has much to commend it. . . . Brooks provides a provocative look at love, acceptance, and the search for asylum." —*School Library Journal*, 6/96, Luann Toth.

"Spare but provocative novel. . . . The different views of Christianity and the juxtaposition of divergent geniuses provide an interesting perspective on religion within the context of a specific (albeit peculiar) contemporary family. —*Horn Book*, 9-10/96, M.B.S.

ⅢⅢ

BABYLON BOYZ. Mowry, Jess. Simon and Schuster, 1999. 188p. ISBN: 0-689-80839-9. Simon and Schuster, 1999. $8.00. 188p. ISBN: 0-689-82592-7. Realistic fiction. Reading level: MS. Interest level: MS, YHS. Ethics, Sociology, English, Psychology.

SUBJECT AREAS

substance abuse; abuse, sexual; intimidation; unwed mothers; friendship; illness, physical; family relationships; rites of passage; eating disorders; homosexuality; prejudice; gangs; violence; survival; minorities, black; minorities, oriental; racism; poverty; homelessness; peer pressure; sex and sexuality; death and dying; school.

CHARACTERS

Dante: his mother was a crack addict who died when he was born, and he has a damaged heart that might last, if he's lucky, till he's thirty
Pook: tall, gorgeous, athletic, he lives with Dante and his father because his parents kicked him out when they learned he was gay
Wyatt: he weighs over 300 pounds, with an attitude to match, and lives with his little brother and mother downstairs from Pook and Dante
Mrs. Brown: Wyatt and Cheo's mother, who runs the American Cafe next door to their apartments
Radji: a homeless boy whom Dante invites to stay at his place
Air Touch: a crack dealer who loses his gun and his dope
Shara: a girl at school that Dante has a crush on
Jinx: a crack addict trying to get clean
Kelly: a Korean boy in the same class as Dante, Pook, Wyatt, and Jinx, he deals in a variety of things
Mr. Pak: Kelly's father, who runs a small liquor store

BOOKTALK

Life ain't always like some of you may live it the easy way—sometimes life sucks, and sometimes it ain't fun at all. And that's the way it is for these three homies, the Babylon Boyz.

Take Pook, tall, gorgeous, athletic, and gay. Always fighting for who he is, always wanting to get outta Babylon and be a doctor.

Take Dante, who's never had a chance. His mom was heavy into crack when she was pregnant with him and died when he was born—born with a bad heart. If he's really good, no smoke, no alcohol, no excitement of any kind, he might live till he's thirty. His only chance at a normal life is a heart transplant, and they just don't exist in Babylon.

Take Wyatt, over 300 pounds of flab with a 300-pound attitude to back it up. Don't mess with him—or with Pook or Dante—he sneaks his gun into school everyday, and you don't want to know how.

For these brothers, life is not fun. Life is not easy. Every day they fight the dealers in the street and the jocks at school. These are the good guys, Pook, Wyatt, and Dante, but what will happen when they witness a crack dealer's arrest and end up with his gun and the briefcase he threw out of the car just before the cops caught up with him? It could be money—money for a new heart, a medical education, a new start. It could be crack, crack that they could sell, if they knew who they could sell it to without getting killed. But either way, that briefcase is guaranteed to be danger.

What will they do with it? Is it a way out of Babylon or just something else to keep them trapped there?

MAJOR THEMES AND IDEAS

- Family and friends are the most important things in life.
- Take care of your own.
- No one promised life would be fair—and lots of the time, it isn't. But there are all kinds of ways to fight back.
- You don't have to have blood between you to be family.
- There are choices in life; you just have to look for them.
- Don't lie to your friends—you need them too much.
- You always choose. Even choosing not to makes a choice, and is a decision.
- You have to live with the results of your choices. You are responsible for them, no one else is.
- Friends can help you make the right choices.
- Everyone needs to love and be loved in return.
- Focus and determination can take you a lot farther than just wishing for something to happen.
- You are the only one who can change your life, because no matter how it feels sometimes, you are the only one in control of it.

BOOK REPORT IDEAS

1. Two of the main themes in the book are hope and making choices. Give several examples of each and discuss why you chose those incidents and how each of them contributed to the plot.
2. Speculate about what will happen to the Babylon Boyz after the book ends. Where will they be in five years—still stuck in Babylon, or out of that trap and on their way? Support your ideas with quotes from the book and your understanding of their personalities.
3. Several people die in the book. Could these deaths have been avoided if those people had made different choices? Why or why not?
4. Dante, Pook, and Wyatt all want to get out of Babylon for different reasons. How realistic is it to think that they will succeed? What will have to take place for them to escape?
5. Compare and contrast the different family situations of the four main characters, Dante, Pook, Wyatt, and Radji. How are each of these characters a product of those families, and what have they done as a result?
6. Dante, Pook, and Wyatt each had problems that made them different. Discuss how they dealt with these things on a daily basis and how their lives and their friendship were changed because of them.

BOOKTALK IDEAS

1. Choose one of the three main characters and let him introduce the story and the other characters in first person.
2. Focus your talk on the scene when Air Touch is beaten and Pook and Dante steal the drugs and the gun.
3. Use the first scene in the book, on the playing field, to introduce the main characters, the three boys, Radji, and Air Touch.
4. Center your talk around the choices the boys had to make, for example, whether to dump the drugs or try to sell them, whether to befriend Radji and Jinx or ignore them, whether to look for a way out of Babylon or give in to despair, letting different characters talk about them and revealing the plot a little at a time.

RISKS

- Graphic depiction of crime, delinquency, and drug dealing.
- Includes the rape of a minor and resulting pregnancy, and detailed scene of childbirth.
- Language is realistic, graphic and vulgar.
- Corrupt policemen beat up a drug dealer.
- Parents seem to be unaware of their children's illegal or delinquent activities.
- School faculty and administration are not in control of the student body.
- Violence, from several different groups in book, is depicted graphically.

- Homosexual and heterosexual characters are sexually active.

STRENGTHS
- Offers hope of escaping from a difficult and potentially lethal situation.
- Gritty and realistic portrayal of life in an inner city, ghetto environment.
- Strong, fast-moving plot grips the reader from the first pages.
- Unexpected and powerful ending shows growth in the characters and the possibility of more choices in the future than they had originally seen.
- Strong and realistic characters who exemplify the quintessence of friendship, loyalty, ethical behavior, and kindness.
- Shows how we all have choices even when it appears that we don't.
- Shows strong family connections in Dante's and Wyatt's family, and among the Babylon Boyz themselves.
- Powerful message about the dangers of drugs, from dealing to becoming addicted to the birth defects that they can cause.
- Pook is a strong, positive example of a young gay man.
- Language used makes it very accessible to teens, especially ones in situations similar to the ones in the book .
- Portrayal of sexual activity is not graphic, and is tastefully and realistically done.

AWARDS
None

REVIEWS
"Plot takes over and delivers riveting action. . . . While it's sometimes difficult to read about this subject matter, toning it down would have sadly compromised the story's realism. Instead, Mowry has delivered a realistic. . . . tale of urban hopes and dreams." —*Voice of Youth Advocates*, 6/97, Florence M. Munat.

"With its realistic, gritty dialogue, violent deaths, and semi-explicit sex scenes, this is definitely a book for mature teens. . . . readers will find authentic, unforgettable characters and descriptions that make the boys and their community come alive." —*School Library Journal*, 9/97, Beth Wright.

"Mowry injects new life into one of YA fiction's standard formulas: the alternative family under attack from a hostile world." —*Booklist*, 1997, Bill Ott.

"Mowry's depiction of the boys at home and at school is unerring as they struggle in the predacious environment. He doesn't sugar-coat reality." —*Kirkus Reviews*, 4/15/97.

📖 📖 📖

BAD. Ferris, Jean. Farrar, Straus, & Giroux, 1998. $16.00. 182p. ISBN: 0-374-30479-3. Realistic fiction. Reading level: YHS. Interest level: YHS, OHS. English, Psychology, Sex education.

SUBJECT AREAS
family relationships; crime and delinquency; friendship; rites of passage; self-knowledge; abuse, sexual; abuse, physical; unwed mothers; minorities, blacks; minorities, Hispanics; prejudice; intimidation; racism; secrets; problem parents; lying and deceitfulness; survival; rites of passage.

CHARACTERS
Dallas Carpenter: she's caught with a gun in her hand robbing a store and goes to the Girls' Rehabilitation Center when her father refuses to let her come home

Mr. Carpenter: Dallas's father who resents his daughter for being too much like her flighty mother, and is unable to either love or accept her

Ray: Dallas's boyfriend

Pam: Dallas's best friend prior to going to GRC

Sonny: Pam's boyfriend

Dahlia: Dallas's roommate at juvie, a white supremacist

Connie: one of the day counselors at GRC

Kate: a teacher at GRC, she encourages Dallas to read

Damaris: she arrives at GRC badly beaten and very quiet

Shatasia: Dallas's roommate at GRC, she's seventeen and the mother of Sharly, who's almost two

Toozdae, Lolly, Sylviana, Valencia, Andrette, Roma: other girls in GRC

Mary Alice (Malice): one of the night counselors, she is abusive to the girls, both verbally and physically

Barbara, Soledad, Nolan: other teachers and counselors at GRC

BOOKTALK
Even though I knew how angry he was with me, and how much he hated what I'd been doing, I never thought he'd send me away. After all, he was my father! But after I spent three weeks in Juvie, without any visitors at all, at my hearing, when the judge said she'd send me home on probation because it was my first offense, my father said no. He couldn't control me, and I had no respect for his authority, and he didn't want me back at all. He knew I'd just get in trouble again, and he didn't want to deal with it. GRC was the only place for me to go.

I'd nearly gone nuts in Juvie for three weeks, how was I going to deal with six months of being locked up? And do I really want to be rehabilitated, anyway? Even if I'd fallen in this time, I'd never been caught before, and skating on thin ice, taking chances, was the only excitement, the only rush I ever got. How could I live without it? I may have to go to GRC, but I *don't* have to change!

MAJOR IDEAS OR THEMES

- Sadly, parents are not required to love their children.
- You can always choose to change.
- Secrets sometimes need to be told.
- An angry, vindictive, or vicious person in a position of power can be very dangerous.
- Changing habits is slow and difficult, but if you are determined to change, you can.
- Sometimes you can learn as much, or more from books than you can from people.
- Friendship can help make any situation better.
- Betrayal is always painful, not matter who does it.
- For some people, violence is just not possible.
- You need to stop and evaluate who you are and where you are every so often. You may have changed without really realizing it.

BOOK REPORT IDEAS

1. Trace Dallas's process of change while she was in GRC, and compare who she was on the first and last pages of the novel.
2. Discuss the character of Mary Alice, the effect she had on the girls in GRC, and the appropriateness of her being employed there.
3. Focus on Dallas's father, showing how he changed or didn't change during the time span of the book. Speculate on what his and Dallas's relationship might be like in the future, and why.
4. Explore the idea of rehabilitation, how or why it takes place, and what influences impact on the rehabilitation process.
5. Discuss the characters of Ray, Pam, and Sonny, and how the robbery was set up. Explain why or why not you think Dallas was set up to take the fall from the beginning.

BOOKTALK IDEAS

1. Write a character description booktalk, letting each of the main characters introduce herself. Be sure to include counselors as well as inmates.
2. Introduce Dallas from Shatasia's point of view or let her tell about Dallas's first few days in GRC.
3. Using plot summary technique, tell the story up to Dallas's first day at GRC. Focus on her feelings as well as her actions.
4. Focus your talk on the scene in the courtroom when Dallas realizes her father will not take her back, and the final scene between them before she leaves for GRC.

RISKS

- Teen narrator engages in criminal activity and delinquency.

- Cold, uncaring father rejects his daughter over and over.
- Language is realistic but vulgar.
- Sadistic adult preys on incarcerated teen girls.
- Graphic portrayal of emotional, physical, and sexual abuse.
- Gang activity, drug use, teen sexuality and unwed mothers all vividly portrayed.

STRENGTHS

- Gives a realistic picture of a juvenile detention center.
- Author interviewed teens in detention centers prior to writing book.
- Counselors demonstrate positive ways to cope with problems and escape the cycle of delinquency and detention.
- Realistic ending doesn't solve all the problems, and allows readers to speculate on what might happen next.

AWARDS

Best Books for Young Adults, 2000 (ALA)
Quick Picks for Reluctant Readers, 1999 (ALA)

REVIEWS

"Ferris conducted a series of interviews with inmates at a rehabilitation center in preparation of writing *Bad*. The voices of Dallas, the other girls, and the counselors ring true. An insightful and nonjudgmental novel, this is also an absorbing, quick read." —*Voice of Youth Advocates*, 2/99, Marcia Mann.

"Dallas's story gives readers an excellent opportunity to see the many angles involved in such issues as peer pressure, family failings, rehabilitation, personal growth, and societal expectations. Ferris researched her topic well and the authenticity she invests in a novel will draw in both avid and reluctant readers." —*School Library Journal*, 12/98, Francisca Goldsmith.

"The resolution is tentatively optimistic, yet grounded." —*Horn Book*, 1/2/99, J.M.B.

"Ferris explores some causes of juvenile crime, as well as techniques and psychology of rehabilitation. . . . offers no easy resolutions, leaving Dallas at the end wiser but not particularly repentant and with the memory of how exciting wrongdoing can be. —*Booklist*, 10/1/98, John Peters.

"The author puts together an abrasive, volatile, and abused set of characters. . . . subtly and skillfully divines slim hope and a glimmer of choice from the necessarily weighted stories of the girls on the inside, making for a compelling read." —*Kirkus Reviews*, 9/1/98.

☐ ☐ ☐

BAT 6. Wolff, Virginia Euwer. Scholastic, 1998. $16.95. 230p. ISBN: 0-590-89799-3. Scholastic, 2000. $4.99. 230p. ISBN: 0-590-89800-0. Listening Library, 2000. $4.99. ISBN: 0-872-8223-5. (abridged audiotape) Bantam Books-Audio, 2000. $22.00. ISBN: 0-553-52663-4. (unabridged audiotape) Historical fiction. Reading level: MS. Interest level: MS. English, History, P. E.

SUBJECT AREAS
sports; friendship; prejudice; poverty; minorities, Asian; self-knowledge; revenge; ethics; anger; family relationships; racism; school; war; problem parents; grief and mourning; rites of passage; illness, mental.

CHARACTERS
Bear Creek Ridge Bat 6 Roster
Shadean: Pitcher—she's always wanted to pitch Bat 6
Tootie: Catcher—she's the first to meet Aki and ask her to be on the team
Aki: First base—she's back in town after four years in an internment camp
Kate: Second base—she thinks her family's new fridge is the most important thing that year, but she's wrong
Ellen: Shortstop—she wants everyone to forget the war
Daisy/Loose Lips: Third base—she's Lorelei's friend even though their fathers don't speak
Little Peggy: Right field—she's Aki's best friend and the best player on the team
Lorelei: Center field—she's different because her father refused to fight in the war
Susannah: Left field—even though her family has more money than most, she's friendly and popular
Vernell: Manager and sub—easily confused, she likes being manager instead of playing
Mr. and Mrs. Porter: she's the coach and he's her assistant

Barlow Road Bat 6 Roster
Ila Mae: Pitcher—pitching and winning the Bat 6 games are the most important things in her life
Audrey: Catcher—an arithmetic whiz, she coached Shazam
Wink: First base—she's tall, skinny, smart and the best slider on the team
Brita Marie: Second base—first to meet Shazam
Alva: Shortstop—her mother told a shameful secret about Shazam
Darlene: Third base—she has the fastest overhand in the history of Barlow
Hallie/Beautiful Hair: Right field—champion base stealer and hitter
Shazam: Center field—a natural athlete whose father was killed in the war

Manzanita: Left field—a good player with good judgment

Lola and Lila: Managers and subs—twins, who really wanted to play until Shazam took their place

Mr. Rayfield, Dotty Rayfield: he's the coach and his daughter is the first base coach

Other characters

Keiko Makami: Aki's mother, a 1930 Bat 6 MVP, whom the Bear Creek mothers welcome back to town

Billie Shiamatsu: first grader at the Barlow Road school

Louella: one of the original softball players from the first team in 1899

Mr. and Mrs. Utsumi: an elderly couple who lives next to Hallie and her family in Barlow

The McHenrys: they run the general store in Bear Creek, and are always ready to help their neighbors

Floy: Shazam's mother, who hasn't recovered from Pearl Harbor

Mrs. Winters: the sixth-grade teacher in Barlow

BOOKTALK

If only. . . . If only. . . . They all said it. There had been clues, signs, but they'd been ignored or misunderstood. But the Bat 6 game was everything, the most important event for sixth-grade girls, and this was the fiftieth game.

Forty-nine years before, in 1899, the women of Barlow Road and Bear Creek Ridge, at the end of the Oregon Trail, decided the rivalry between their towns had gone on long enough. They planned a ladies softball game and picnic, and the men from both towns showed up and made friends. Over the years, the games continued, and eventually, it became traditional for the sixth-grade girls teams to play against each other. It was the only game they played, and they could only be on the team for one year. For the nine girls on each of the teams, it was the most important year of their lives.

But in 1949, the Bat 6 game had an unexpected finish. A tragic finish. There was one girl on each of the teams who was different, new that year, an unknown quantity.

Aki was Japanese, and her family had just come back to town after being released from internment camp where they'd lived for years. She hadn't lived on Bear Creek Ridge since she was in the second grade. Her mother had been a Bat 6 girl in 1930, the MVP that year, and everyone in Bear Creek Ridge was delighted that the Japanese American families they'd missed for so long were back in town. The Ridgers were certain Aki would be able to help the Bat 6 team win. She was short, and a left-hander, great for first base, and could hit harder than almost anyone on the team. She had the potential to be a MVP, too. For her, the war was over.

Shazam wore dresses that looked like they'd been made out of tablecloths and shoes from a church rummage sale. She lived with her grandmother, out by the Barlow gravel pit, because her father died at Pearl Harbor and her mother couldn't take care of her. She had dreams about the fires, the gas masks, and the horror she'd seen when the bombs dropped. She'd been in Pearl Harbor and had seen it all firsthand. What she didn't remember, her mother told her about, over and over—how her father died on the *Arizona*, how the bombs looked and sounded when they exploded, and how it was all the fault of the Japanese that she didn't have a husband and Shazam didn't have a father. Shazam hated the Japs who killed her father, and even the Japanese Americans who lived in Barlow. The only time she didn't think about getting revenge for her father's death was when she was playing baseball. For her, the war would never be over.

The teams didn't know each other, hadn't met before they started the game. There was no way for anyone to know what would happen because of the two new girls, and the collision course they were on. Or was there? There were signs, there were clues, if only someone could have put them together. . . . If only. . . .

But the girls of the 1949 Bat 6 teams want to tell their own story, in their own way, their own words. Listen to what Aki, Shazam, and their teammates have to say, and then ask yourself, could there have been a different ending?

MAJOR THEMES AND IDEAS

- Lessons well learned, whether they are good or bad, are hard to unlearn and forget.
- Crises and other major events are built gradually, one step at a time, no matter how sudden or explosive they seem.
- Children learn anger and hatred from their parents the same way they might learn love and kindness—through constant repetition and reinforcement.
- Being a team member means helping out the others that need it.
- A game is just that—a game. It's not supposed to be life or death.
- Sometimes speaking up against an injustice is necessary. Keeping silent may result in tragedy.
- Mental confusion and mental illness are sometimes difficult to discern in time to prevent tragedy.
- Guilt for something that isn't your fault is useless, but frequently happens anyway.
- Sometimes good things can happen as a result of a tragedy.
- Once you have been forced to see and acknowledge a reality you'd prefer to deny, it's hard to close your eyes to it again.
- You may never know why tragedies happen.
- Some people break under pressure, others grow. Either way, it is their choice and their responsibility, not anyone else's.

BOOK REPORT IDEAS

1. Almost everyone on both teams felt guilty about what happened during the game. Discuss whether you think that guilt was appropriate or not and why.
2. If the Bat 6 girls or their parents had spoken up about Shazam's prejudiced remarks about the Japanese, how would things have changed, and how would they have stayed the same? In other words, was tragedy of one kind or another inevitable?
3. Reread the entries by Shazam and speculate about the kind of person she might turn out to be as a teen and as an adult, given her state of mind as a sixth grader.
4. Discuss the good things that resulted from the tragedy, and how they changed lives in both towns.

BOOKTALK IDEAS

1. Write your talk in two parts, one from each team, letting three or four of the girls on each team introduce themselves and the Bat 6 team. Be sure to have team members introduce Shazam and Aki, foreshadowing the conflict, as was done in the opening chapters.
2. Write the talk in third person, describing the game's history and importance to the towns and hinting at how the two new players will influence and change everything.

RISKS

- Format may make story hard to follow for some readers.
- Shazam is racist and prejudiced.

STRENGTHS

- Draws a powerful and frightening portrait of prejudice.
- Multidimensional characters grow and gain insight.
- Readable sports novel for girls.
- Strong historical setting gives clear picture of culture/society of the late 1940s.
- Sends a clear antiwar message.

AWARDS

Children's Notables, 1999 (ALA)
Jane Addams Children's Book Award, 1999

REVIEWS

"Wolff paints a picture of small town America in the forties that shows its beliefs, attitudes, and values, including the effects of the GI Bill, having a child out of wedlock, racial and religious prejudice, and the consequences of being a conscientious objector." —*Voice of Youth Advocates*, 6/98, Bill Mollineaux.

"The period details and use of the vernacular are right on the money. . . . Wolff delves into the irreversible consequences of war and the necessity to cultivate peace and speaks volumes about courage, responsibility, and reconciliation, all in a book about softball." —*School Library Journal*, 5/98, Luann Toth.

"Demonstrate[s] that wars may end, but the passions they foster—if unexamined—can make victims of the survivors. . . . an extraordinarily artful portrait of a moment in American history that challenged our comfortable assumptions about who we were and what we believed." —*Booklist*, 5/1/98, Michael Cart.

"Reveals. . . . the lingering after effects of war. . . . The questions she raises about war, race, and cherished beliefs are difficult and honest and a welcome antidote to more romanticized versions of the years following the 'last good war.'" —*Horn Book*, 7-8/98, N.V.

📖 📖 📖

BEE & JACKY. Coman, Carolyn. Front Street Press, 1998. $14.95. 96p. ISBN: 1-886-91033-2. Puffin, 1999. $4.99. 108p. ISBN: 0-141-30637-8. Reading level: MS. Interest level: MS, YHS. English, Sex education.

SUBJECT AREAS
family relationships; incest; secrets; dysfunctional family; war; handicaps, physical; self-knowledge, anger, violence.

CHARACTERS
Bee Cooney: thirteen years old, she watches her older brother and remembers
    the games they used to play
Jacky Cooney: Bee's brother, at seventeen, he is pulling away from his family
Ann Cooney: Bee and Jacky's mother
Phil Cooney: Bee and Jacky's father, a Vietnam vet struggling to cope with his
    disabilities

BOOKTALK
The weekend started and finished with Jacky's startling announcements, "I'm not going. You can't make me." He would spend Labor Day weekend at home, not at his grandparents house.

Bee was stunned at her brother's decision. She couldn't imagine her grandparents' house and the woods behind it without Jacky. She stayed home, too, not wanting to see the woods where they'd played war games. Bee was always the wounded soldier, Jacky always the one who saved her. But there was a darker side to their games that Bee had forgotten until she woke up very late that night to find Jacky lying on top of her.

MAJOR THEMES AND IDEAS
- War wounds everyone in a family, not just the soldier who came back with visible and invisible scars.
- Sometimes anger is just a cover-up for fear.
- Routine helps some people cope with great change or great trauma.
- Solitude may be the only place where we can meet and conquer our fear.
- Understanding precedes forgiveness.

BOOK REPORT IDEAS
1. Jacky shows his anger toward his father in several scenes. Discuss these scenes and what Jacky was trying to say that he could only express as anger.
2. Explain why you believe everything came together and then exploded on this weekend. What hints does the author give of the underlying factors that contributed to the events in the book?
3. The novel ends with Jacky's decision to leave the family. Discuss why he felt that way, and what each family member contributed to his decision.
4. While Jacky shows his fear as rage, Ann covers hers with routine and positive platitudes. Show how the author expresses Ann's fear and her method of controlling it.
5. Explain your understanding of the hallucination Bee has about her body. What is the significance of the fire that burns her up inside?
6. Explore the idea of incest. How and why did it happen with Bee and Jacky? What function did it perform?

BOOKTALK IDEAS
1. Write a first person talk, letting Bee tell her own story.
2. Focus your talk on the war games Bee and Jacky played, giving hints that there are things about them that Bee doesn't recall.

RISKS
- Language is realistic and vulgar.
- Shows sexual contact between siblings.
- Child shows violent anger towards parents.
- Flashbacks and hallucinations challenge readers.
- It is difficult to understand while easy to read.

STRENGTHS
- Writing style is strong and spare.
- Bee's emotions are clearly and graphically portrayed.

- Flawed characters struggle to survive and succeed.
- Ambiguous ending is not without hope.

AWARDS
None

"Stark portrayal of a war-ravaged family. . . . arresting in its honesty. . . . a must-read for teachers and librarians." —*Voice of Youth Advocates*, 12/98, Cynthia L. Blinn.

"Brilliantly written novel. . . . this is neither an easy book to read nor does it suggest any neat resolutions. What Coman does offer, masterfully, is honesty, compassion, and even a glimmer of hope." —*School Library Journal*, 9/98, Miriam Lang Budin.

"This is a fierce, intriguing novel, not easily forgotten; it is also an extremely convoluted story that many readers (including adults) will find easy to read but difficult to grasp." —*Booklist*, 10/1/98, Stephanie Zvirin.

ᨏ ᨏ ᨏ

THE BEET FIELDS: MEMORIES OF A SIXTEENTH SUMMER.
Paulsen, Gary. Delacorte Press, 2000. $15.95. 176p. ISBN: 0-385-32647-5. Realistic fiction. Reading level: MS. Interest level: YHS, OHS. English; Sex education; Creative writing.

SUBJECT AREAS
rites of passage; working; runaways; cooking; friendship; self-knowledge; sex and sexuality; problem parents; homeless; poverty.

CHARACTERS
"the boy": the unnamed narrator who recounts his sixteenth summer
"the farmer's wife": a cruel, cold woman
"the farmer": he hires the boy to work the beet fields
"the old man": the oldest of the Mexican laborers working the beet fields, who befriends the boy
Bill Flaherty: a wheat farmer with a small field of beets
Alice Flaherty: Bill's wife
Lynette Flaherty: their daughter
Jacobsen: a dishonest sheriff's deputy

"the Hungarian": he picked up the boy when he was hitchhiking
Hazel: an old woman who gave the boy a ride
Taylor: he hires the boy to run the Tilt-a-Whirl at the carnival
Bobby: Taylor's brother, who does the geek show
Ruby: Taylor's wife, who's the hootchy-kootchy dancer

BOOKTALK
It was 1955, and he was sixteen and on his own. He'd run away when his drunken mother had crawled into his bed to do more than sleep, and the first job he got was working in the beet fields, thinning beets.

The beets taught him the boredom of mindless repetitious labor, and the Mexicans he worked beside taught him the value of belonging to a group and of friendship.

And after the beet fields, there were the wheat fields and endless, exhausting work with never enough sleep.

When the wheat fields were behind him, he learned about betrayal and death and mourning.

And finally, he learned to be a carney—tough, cynical, out to make a buck any way he could. And just when he thought he'd learned it all, Ruby taught him that he hadn't.

MAJOR THEMES AND IDEAS
- Facing your fear takes away its power over you.
- You cannot pay for what is offered in friendship.
- When you become a member of a group, you become responsible for making a contribution to it.
- There are different kinds of crazy. It's important to know which kinds will hurt you and which won't.
- Sometimes bad things happen and there isn't much you can do about them except go on.
- You learn something from everyone you know—things you need to know and things you never wanted to know.
- The more you learn about surviving on your own, the closer you get to being a man.
- You'll remember your first sexual experience for your whole life.

BOOK REPORT IDEAS
1. During his sixteenth summer, the boy learned many things. Discuss the ones you think were most important and why.
2. Having the deputy steal his money changed the boy's journey drastically. Explain how different his experiences might have been if he had been able to keep that money.

3. Choose the scene you think you will remember best and explain why you chose it.
4. Speculate what happened to the boy in the time period between the last two chapters.

BOOKTALK IDEAS

1. Focus your talk on the time the boy spent in the beet fields with the Mexicans.
2. Center your talk on several of the lessons the boy learned and how he learned them.
3. Write your talk in first person, as the boy.
4. Highlight the different roles the boy had, from migrant worker to farmhand to carney shill and so on.

RISKS

- Language is realistic but vulgar.
- Frank descriptions of the coarseness of life in a carnival.
- Portrays a variety of unappealing adults.
- Sex and sexuality discussed openly.

STRENGTHS

- Terse powerful, poetic style conveys much in simple words.
- Easy, brief read, attractive to reluctant readers.
- Ambiguous, abruptly truncated ending leaves room for individual and group reflection and speculation.
- Allows the reader into the mind and soul of a sixteen-year-old boy.
- Speaks directly to male teens.

AWARDS

Booklist Editors' Choice, 2000
Best Books for Young Adults, 2001 (ALA)

REVIEWS

"Paulsen says this is his story, one that he has waited twenty years to tell honestly in fiction. It comes alive with fully realized characters. . . . portrays the roller coaster of emotions a boy of sixteen experiences as he tries on every possible look and attitude on the way to manhood." —*Voice Of Youth Advocates*, 2000, Mary Arnold.

"While sensual scenes and occasionally gritty language may make this novel problematic for adults, there is not a 15-year-old boy around who would not find that this poetic, powerful novel speaks to his soul." —Amazon, 2000, Patty Campbell.

"The story is gritty and unblinking. . . . Paulsen's ability to put readers behind the boy's eyes—so they can feel what's going on as well as see it—that makes this novel exceptional and so heartbreakingly real." —*Booklist*, 2000, Ilene Cooper.

📖 📖 📖

BLACKWATER. Bunting, Eve. HarperCollins, 1999. $15.95. 146p. ISBN: 0-060-27838-2. HarperCollins, 2000. $4.95. 146p. ISBN: 0-064-40890-6. Realistic Fiction. Reading level: MS. Interest level: MS, YHS. English, P. E., Ethics.

SUBJECT AREAS
death and dying; secrets; lying and deceitfulness; ethics; family relationships; self-knowledge; friendship; manipulation; grief and mourning.

CHARACTERS
Brodie Lynch: he has a terrible secret
Alex: Brodie's twelve-year-old cousin who shares the secret
John Sun: Brodie's best friend
Pauline Genero: a girl at school Brodie has a crush on
Otis McCandless: older than Brodie, he thinks he's a lady's man
Hannah: she and her father live near the Blackwater River
Raoul: the police chief
Jenny and David Lynch: Brodie's parents, a local minister and his wife
Mrs. Raud: she saw Pauline and Otis on the Toadstool that morning

BOOKTALK
It was an accident, a silly, unnecessary accident. Two kids were playing around near a dangerous river, fell in, and drowned. Another kid saw them and tried to save them, but failed. The whole town called him a hero.

But was he a hero? What had really happened on the Toadstool that summer morning? Who had been there? And who watched and saw it all? Were the deaths really an accident, or is there someone who is hiding something, something deadly?

MAJOR THEMES AND IDEAS
- Truth is best, even when it hurts.
- Tell the truth right away—it's easiest then.
- You can lie by keeping silent, just as you can by saying what isn't true.

- Accidents happen. It's best to admit them right off and deal with the consequences.
- Sometimes even witnesses don't see the whole truth.
- If you know something is wrong, don't let anyone talk you into doing it, no matter what.
- "To thine own self be true. . ."—Shakespeare.
- The longer you wait to tell the truth, the bigger the lie gets, the more people know about it, and the harder it is to tell the truth.

BOOK REPORT IDEAS

1. Examine Brodie's character and ethics, and explain why he let Alex manipulate him into telling a lie, rather than telling the whole truth immediately.
2. Speculate on what you think might happen to Brodie and Alex after the book ends, and how the people in the town and the kids at school will treat them.
3. Discuss the idea of telling the whole truth vs. omitting part of it to make yourself look better, and what insights about this you have gained from the book.
4. Discuss what happens to Brodie when he realizes someone knows his secret.

BOOKTALK IDEAS

1. Write a first person talk as Brodie.
2. Focus your talk on the idea of secrets.
3. Use a note like the one Brodie found as a prop, and end your talk by opening the envelope and showing the note to your audience.

RISKS

- Two characters lie to an entire town and profit from it.
- One character corrupts another.

STRENGTHS

- Strong ethical message.
- Main character persuaded to tell the truth.
- Shows supportive functional family.
- Shows that keeping quiet is a lie, just as an untruth is.
- Quick read about a major ethical question.
- Ending can stimulate class discussion.

AWARDS

Quick Picks for Reluctant Readers, 2000. (ALA)

REVIEWS

"[This] complex novel is an exciting blend of physical and psychological action and conflict. . . . also focuses on friendship, family, and forgiveness. . . . an engrossing tale with likable, realistic characters." —*School Library Journal*, 9/99, Janet Hilburn.

☐ ☐ ☐

BLOOD AND CHOCOLATE. Klause, Annette Curtis. Delacorte Press, 1997. $16.95. 272p. ISBN: 0-385-32305-0. Laurel-Leaf Books, 1999. $4.99. 264p. ISBN: 0-440-22668-6. Recorded Books, Inc., 1997. ISBN: 0-788-72758-3. (unabridged audiotape) Recorded Books, Inc., 1998. $49.00. ISBN: 0-788-71056-7. (abridged audiotape) Fantasy, Horror. Reading level: YHS. Interest level: YHS, OHS. English, Sociology.

SUBJECT AREAS

manipulation; supernatural and occult; peer pressure; family relationships; cultural identity; love; school; dating and social relations; self-knowledge; rites of passage; prejudice; sex and sexuality.

CHARACTERS

The Pack
Vivian Gandillon: she's a teenage werewolf who falls in love with a "meat-boy," a human
Esmé Gandillon: Vivian's widowed mother
Bucky: one of the older males, one of Esmé's age-mates
Uncle Rudy: one of the oldest males, Vivian and her mother live with him
Rafe: he wants Vivian to be his mate; and is the leader of The Five, Vivian's age-mates in the pack
William and Finn Wagner: twin werewolves, also members of The Five
Gregory Wagner: the twins' older brother, who is part of The Five
Ulf: he is also a member of The Five
Astrid: Ulf's mother, who doesn't get along with Esmé
Gabriel: in his mid-twenties, he's looking for a mate and wants to be the pack leader
Jean: one of the older males
Orlando Griffin: the oldest member of the pack
Rolf and Renata Wagner: parents of Gregory and the twins
Aunt Persia Devereux: the pack's healer
Raul and Magda Wagner: he is Rolf's brother
Jenny Garnier: a young widow with a baby
Lucien Dafoe: Rafe's father, who drinks too much
Tomas: he joined the pack after the Ordeal

The Humans
Aiden Teague: he writes poetry about werewolves and intrigues Vivian
Peter Quincy/Quince: Aiden's best friend
Kelly: she'd like to be Aiden's girlfriend
Mr. Antony: art teacher and sponsor of the school literary magazine
Jem: an artist and a friend of Aiden's
Bingo: one of Aiden's friends
Mr. and Mrs. Teague, Ashley: Aiden's parents and little sister

BOOKTALK

What's it like to run wild and free in the forests of the night? To feel your human body change into a beautiful sleek wolf's body? What's it like to be feared and hunted, and to see your friends and family killed in cold blood? What's it like to live in fear of being discovered as something more than human—a werewolf?

Vivian knows how all those things feel because she is a werewolf. Her pack came from Europe in the 1600s and lived in the hills of West Virginia until a year ago, when two girls were killed and one of the pack members was accused of their deaths. The pack was burned out of their homes, and some of them, including the pack leader, Vivian's father, were killed. Now they live in the Maryland suburbs and quarrel among themselves as the younger males compete to become the new pack leader.

But Vivian wants nothing to do with the power struggle, or the age-mates who also compete for her attention. She has done the unthinkable, the impossible—she has fallen in love with a "meat-boy," a human. A human who writes hauntingly real poems about being a werewolf, and the power and sensuality of changing from human to wolf. Vivian is certain that Aiden is the one person who can accept her as a human and as a wolf, the soulmate she's been hungering for and hasn't found among her pack-mates.

Is Vivian really in love with her true mate, or are the other members of the pack right when they tell her she's just fooling herself? Can a human and a werewolf find love and mate for life?

MAJOR THEMES AND IDEAS

- Hiding what you are, especially to gain the acceptance of others, is difficult.
- Loving someone who is not your kind is dangerous.
- Know and accept who you are. Don't try to run away from it.
- Don't ever endanger the pack.
- Sometimes a leader must rule with brains and teeth.
- The Law is The Law, even when you don't like it.
- We must face the consequences of our actions, even if they were unintentional.

- You can't force someone to love you. You have to let them go.
- Betrayal always hurts.

BOOK REPORT IDEAS
1. In this book, a girl is attracted to a boy who is not her kind, whom she can never have. Describe some instances in real life when this happens.
2. Discuss what Vivian meant when she said accepting Gabriel would pay her debt to her father.
3. Explain the title, what it means in the book and what it means to you.
4. Were you surprised when you found out who the renegade wolf was? Explain what foreshadowing events led you to figure it out before it was revealed.
5. Discuss how the renegade set up Vivian, including how she got human blood all over herself after she showed herself to Aiden.
6. This book is about two species of two societies that cannot live too close together, because the weaker one hates and fears the stronger. Give some examples of this situation in the real world.
7. Discuss what this book says about making assumptions about other people before you understand all the facts. Which people made this mistake and what were the results?

BOOKTALK IDEAS
1. Use a silver pentagram as a prop for your talk.
2. Write a character description talk, having Aiden describe Vivian and vice versa.
3. Focus your talk on the idea of the pack and its rules, and how Vivian violates them.
4. Write your talk as if it were a newspaper account of one or more of the killings.
5. Write your talk as if it were a romance story.
6. Write your talk from the perspective of one of the members of the pack who's concerned about Vivian. This person could be one of the minor members who isn't named in the book.

RISKS
- Contains supernatural characters who consider themselves superior to humans.
- Tone of the story is sensuous and lush.
- Pack's violence is portrayed graphically and in detail.
- Language is realistic yet vulgar.
- Pack members murder each other and humans.
- In the pack, males make the rules and females obey them.

STRENGTHS
- Shows strong, supportive pack/family relationships.
- Heroine is willing to put others' needs before her own.
- Multidimensional characters that are believable even though some of them are supernatural creatures.
- Shows love and caring between two incompatible individuals who try to protect rather than destroy each other.
- Deeply convincing blend of fantasy and reality.
- Rich imagery and language can be felt, tasted, and smelled as well as read.
- Portrays werewolves as different from humans, but not evil or menacing.

AWARDS
Booklist Editors' Choice, 1997
Best Books for Young Adults, 1998 (ALA)
Quick Picks for Reluctant Readers, 1998 (ALA)
Popular Paperbacks/Romance, 2000 (ALA)
Selected Audiobooks for Young Adults, 1999 (ALA)

REVIEWS
"Another superb title from a rising author. Teenage girls will understand Vivian's desire for popularity, her rebellion against her mother and other adults, her feeling of invincibility, and her wish to be a part of a group. This book should appeal to horror fans and even [to] those who are not." —*Voice of Youth Advocates*, 8/97, Beverly Youree.

"Poetically describes the violence and sensuality of the pack lifestyle, creating a hot-blooded heroine who puts the most outrageous riot grrls to shame. . . . a masterpiece of adolescent angst wrapped in wolf's clothing, and its lovely, sensuous taste is sure to be sweet on the teenage tongue." —Amazon, 1997, Jennifer Hubert.

"This violent, sexy novel is a seamless, totally convincing blend of fantasy and reality that can be read as feminist fiction, as smoldering romance, as a rites of passage novel or as a piercing reflection on human nature. Klause's imagery is magnetic, and her language fierce, rich, and beautiful. . . . powerful, unforgettable novel for mature teens." —*Booklist*, 1997, Stephanie Zvirin.

"Extrapolating brilliantly from wolf and werewolf lore, Klause creates a complex plot, fueled by politics, insanity, intrigue, sex, blood lust, and adolescent longings, and driven by a set of vividly scary creatures to a blood-curdling climax." —*Kirkus Reviews*, 6/1/97.

"Klause allows her werewolves all the unbounded heat and urgency of prime adolescence in this supernatural gothic romance that's sweaty (and bloody) enough for a sultry summer night." —*Horn Book*, 1998.

"Klause's representation of the pack as a microcosm of society reveals the fragile nature of human behavior and emotions. . . . the character's growth and development drives the plot, which sustains and creates moods that move readers from excitement to despair to hope." —*School Library Journal*, 8/97, Molly S. Kinney.

📖 📖 📖

THE BODY OF CHRISTOPHER CREED. Plum-Ucci, Carol. Harcourt, 2000. $17.00. 256p. ISBN: 0-152-02388-7. Hyperion, 2001. $6.99. 331p. ISBN: 0-786-81641-4. Realistic fiction. Reading level: MS, YHS. Interest level: MS, YHS, OHS. English, Psychology, Sociology, Ethics.

SUBJECT AREAS
crime and delinquency; school; peer pressure; runaways; gossip; mystery and suspense; prejudice; secrets; problem parents; sex and sexuality; friendship; family relationships; dysfunctional families; lying and deceitfulness.

CHARACTERS
Torey Adams: sixteen years old, and the narrator of the story, he feels obligated to solve the mystery of Chris Creed's disappearance
Christopher Creed: the weirdest kid in Steepleton, until he suddenly vanishes without a trace
Ron and Sylvia Creed: Chris's very strict and controlling parents
Ryan and Renee Bowen: Torey's friends, and children of the local police chief
Leandra: Torey's girlfriend
Ali McDermott: a friend of Torey's who lived on the same street as Chris and knew more about him and his parents than anyone else
Bo Richardson: from the wrong side of the tracks, the boondocks, his bad rep hides his good side from almost everyone
Susan Adams: Torey's mother, who's a lawyer
Glen Ames: the high school principal, who knows more about his students' lives than they realize

BOOKTALK
The e-mail flashed across the screen, the button signaling an attachment brightly lit.
"Dear Alex Healey,

"My name's Victor Adams and I am betting that you are going to know all about everything I have to say in this letter. If you don't, then just delete it, blow it off, and chalk it up to another Internet nutcase.

"But if you know what I'm talking about, you'll also know it's true. People lie and they love their lies, live with their lies. But what I have to say here isn't a lie. It's a truth I have to live with every day of my life, like it or not. And it's the reason I'm spending my senior year at a boarding school, away from the friends I grew up with, the teams I played on, the town I lived in.

"That town couldn't handle what happened to Chris Creed, and I couldn't handle it either. Chris was a joke, a dork, the kid that everyone loved to hassle, to pick on, to beat up. And I was part of everyone. But then when we were all juniors in high school, he vanished. No blood, no body, no clues or signs or anything. He was just gone, except for the strange e-mail he sent to the high school principal just before he vanished.

"Folks say I killed him, I saw him dead, and I'm on this giant denial trip. But that's not true. Chris Creed isn't dead—he's alive, I'm sure of it. He's alive somewhere, and I am going to find him.

"Read the file I've attached, and talk to the people who know what really happened. They've read it, and will vouch for every word. I swear the following account contains no lies. It is one hundred percent accurate. People can love their lies, tell their lies, believe their own lies until hell pays a visit. But this whole story is true. That's the point of it.

"Read it, and get back to me. You've got my address. The rest is up to you. Torey Adams"

What happened to Chris Creed? What is Torey Adams so afraid of? Why does everyone in his hometown think he killed Chris, and why can't he stop searching for the loser he and his friends beat up on so often?

MAJOR THEMES AND IDEAS
- The truth may be less important than the impact it has on people.
- Sometimes families who look normal from the outside are actually very dysfunctional and damaging to their members who see what's happening from the inside.
- A bad reputation doesn't mean someone isn't gentle or caring with those they love.
- When something bad happens in a town, it's usually the outsiders who are blamed.
- Kids in difficult or dysfunctional situations do what they need to do to survive, even if some of those things are illegal or mean they end up with a bad reputation.
- Acting tough may be a cover-up for fear or insecurity.
- Walking a mile in someone else's shoes doesn't always lead to understanding them.

- People, including parents, are capable of an almost infinite amount of denial.

BOOK REPORT IDEAS

1. Ali tells Torey, "It's more dangerous to have a slightly weird family than a totally weird family." Discuss what you think she meant by that, and what family or families she's talking about.
2. Analyze the character of Mrs. Creed, and discuss why she reacted so violently to Chris's disappearance. Show how her actions were one of the reasons for Chris's disappearance.
3. There are several dysfunctional families in the book. Discuss the impact of that dysfunction on all the kids in these families.
4. Torey is obsessed with getting in touch with Chris Creed. Explain why you think he can't give up and go on with his life.
5. Discuss why or why not you believe Chris Creed to be dead. Support your discussion with quotes from the book.
6. Lying and secrets are major topics in this book. List the various secrets characters kept and lies they told, and explain what their purposes were, and what effect they had.
7. Discuss whether Chris was or was not able to start over and create a new, nongeeky persona for himself. Support your comments with quotes from the book.
8. Speculate on whether any of the main characters ever see Chris again, and when, where, and how that meeting might occur.

BOOKTALK IDEAS

1. Have several people talk about Chris's disappearance and what they think really happened. Be sure to sketch in the plot of the book in their comments.
2. Let one of the characters narrate the booktalk, describing Chris and leading up to his disappearance.
3. Focus your talk not only on Chris's disappearance, but also on the conflict between the boons and the townies.

RISKS

- Language is realistic but sometimes vulgar.
- Most of the parental characters are dysfunctional, in one way or another.
- Teens are sexually active.
- Several characters are in adulterous situations.
- Sexual activity is somewhat graphically depicted.
- Characters who are different or easy to dislike are persecuted.
- Most adult characters are lying about or hiding something from their children and/or from the town.

STRENGTHS

- Graphic depiction of how dysfunctional parents can harm their children.
- Excellent portrayal of the negative effects of peer harassment.
- Strong characters, who develop and gain insight and maturity during the book.
- Teen characters are not stereotypes, but realistic portrayals of kids who are both good and bad, searching for solutions and answers in the best ways that they can.

AWARDS

Best Books for Young Adults, 2001 (ALA)
Michael A. Printz Award, Honor Book, 2001 (ALA)

REVIEWS

"Conversations sound as if they were recorded in any high school hallway. . . . The open-ended conclusion will have readers talking and discussing long after reading. . . . will inspire debate about how preconceived notions can color the manner in which people relate to each other. . . . will help teens challenge prejudices that they often are unaware exist." —*Voice of Youth Advocates*, 2000, Teri Lesesne.

"Offers mystery, a psychic, an Indian ghost, and an interesting perspective on how cruel people can be to one another. Plum-Ucci knows her audience and provides her readers with enough twists, turns, and suspense to keep them absorbed." —*School Library Journal*, 2000, Kim Harris.

"A complex, credible look at alienation, compassion, loyalty, and cruelty among young and other adults." —*The Bulletin of the Center for Children's Books*, 4/00, JMH.

📖 📖 📖

BOYS LIE. Neufeld, John. Dorling Kindersley Publishing, Inc., 1999. $16.95. 165p. ISBN: 0-789-42624-2. Realistic fiction. Reading level: MS. Interest level: MS. English, Sex education, Ethics.

SUBJECT AREAS

stereotyping; gossip; peer pressure; self-knowledge; fear; abuse, sexual; anger; sex and sexuality; school; secrets; bullying; intimidation; manipulation; family relationships.

CHARACTERS

Gina: after being attacked in a New York swimming pool, she and her mother have moved to California to start over

Gina's mother: a single mom, she's concerned about her daughter's safety

Ben Derby: tall and attractive, he has a crush on Jennie

Felix Maldanado: a friend of Ben's, he was the first boy to notice Gina

Jennie Johnson: is in several of Gina's classes, she's the first person to make friends with her.

Mr. Derby: Ben's father, who owns a restaurant

Valerie: she's engaged to Ben's dad

Irene: Felix's mother, who works for Ben's dad

MacNulty Love: in Gina's class, he's an all-American type, but also the shortest kid in class

Eddie Phipps: a friend of Felix's who calls himself a stud, and was also quick to notice Gina

Sally Johnson: Jennie's mother who makes friends with Gina's mother

Raquel: Felix's sister who warns him not to go along with Eddie's plan

BOOKTALK

I'm Gina and this is my story.

It all came crashing back on me that Saturday afternoon when that little boy splashed water in my face. The pool in New York, and the boys who'd surrounded me, splashing, holding me under the water, grabbing, grasping, feeling me. Suddenly, there on the beach, all I could do was crouch down and scream. And scream. And scream.

It was all over school the next week, but the story had changed. I hadn't been attacked; I'd been raped. And saying it wasn't true didn't help things at all. Boys looked at me differently. So did girls. My mother and I had moved from New York to California so we could start over. We couldn't move again.

I'm Ben and this is my story.

I was uncomfortable when Felix and Eddie started talking about how hot and stacked Gina was. They were sure she was experienced, even before we found out she's been raped. Once Eddie knew that, he was determined to have sex with her, and lose his virginity as fast as possible. In fact he cooked up a plan for all three of us to get it on with her. We'd make friends with her; get her to trust us, and then pounce. He was sure she'd want to have sex again, with a body like hers, so Felix and I decided to go along.

What's going to happen? Will Felix's plan work? Will Ben get over his uneasiness about what might happen? Do boys always lie?

MAJOR THEMES AND IDEAS

- Lies have consequences.
- Going along with what you know is wrong is never a good idea.
- Getting over an emotional trauma is usually a long and difficult process.

- Lies hurt. So does name-calling.
- Rape isn't about sex. It's about power, and it's *never* the victim's fault.
- When bullies are confronted about their actions, they usually run away.
- Standing up and telling the truth, revealing others' lies, makes you stronger than they are.
- When you fight someone who's "playing dirty pool," fight back fairly. It makes you look good and makes them look worse.
- Accepting yourself for who you are is the best thing you can do for you.

BOOK REPORT IDEAS

1. Lying is a major theme in this book. Discuss how different characters use lying for their benefit, and why.
2. When telling someone else's secrets turns into gossip, truth can turn into fiction very quickly. Show how that happened in several instances in the book and explain the effect of the gossip on the person it was about.
3. Gina changed a great deal by the end of the book. Analyze her thoughts and actions after the scene with Eddie at her house, and explain what actions and ideas helped her change.
4. Examine Mac Love and his relationships with Gina and the other kids at school, and discuss what made him react or take action in several different situations.
5. Compare the way different characters saw Gina (her mother, Jennie, Ben, Felix, Mac, and others) with the way she saw herself. How did others' opinions of her impact her self-image?

BOOKTALK IDEAS

1. Write your talk as if you were gossiping about Gina. "Hey, have you heard about that new girl, Gina? You won't believe what [insert character's name] just told me!"
2. Write your talk as if you were Gina's mother, worrying about her daughter. Remember there's a lot she doesn't know about, and include only her perspective.
3. Use the title as a refrain in your talk. Briefly set up a scene, then say, "But we all know, boys lie." Do this several times, perhaps using the swimming pool scene, and then several scenes that hint at the danger to Gina.

RISKS

- Young girl is sexually harassed.
- Portrayal of attempted rape.

STRENGTHS

- Accurate portrayal of teens.
- Gina finally believes in herself enough to fight back.

- Sympathetic male character offsets the rapist.

AWARDS
Quick Picks for Reluctant Readers, 2000 (ALA)

REVIEWS
"Many moral lessons and messages throughout this novel that are valuable to young adults." —*Voice of Youth Advocates*, 10/99, Erica Thorsen.

"A sensitive, realistic novel about an all-too-common rite of passage. Young teens will relate to Gina and probably recognize themselves or their school mates in the other characters. Short, quick-moving chapters, coupled with the subject matter, make this a sure winner." —*School Library Journal*, 3/99, Barbara Auerbach.

"Present[s]. . . . important, thought-provoking issues; teen mixed emotions about sex, the definition of "rape," and personal responsibility and ethical behavior versus peer pressure...may be useful for educators as a stepping-stone to discuss the dangers and implications of stereotyping, both in fiction and in life." —*Booklist*, 2/15/99, Shelle Rosenfeld.

ᙙᙙᙙ

BREAKING BOXES. Jenkins, A. M. Delacorte Press, 1997. $14.95. 182p. ISBN: 0-385-32513-4. Laurel-Leaf Books, 2000. $4.99. 192p. ISBN: 0-440-22717-8. Realistic fiction. Reading level: MS. Interest level: MS. English, Ethics, Sex education.

SUBJECT AREAS
homosexuality; self-knowledge; family relationships; friendship; prejudice; school; substance abuse; peer pressure; rites of passage; sex and sexuality; secrets; problem parents; gossip; suicide.

CHARACTERS
Charlie Calmont: a sophomore in high school and a loner, he lives with his older brother

Trent Calmont: Charlie's older brother, he works full-time to support himself and Charlie

Brandon Chase: a rich kid who becomes Charlie's friend

Luke Cattington, David Carlson: they and Brandon hassle Charlie

Mr. Payton: high school vice-principal who puts Charlie and Brandon in On-Campus Suspension

Megan Dunlop: Charlie's ex-girlfriend, and a junior

Matt: a friend of Trent's

Katie Garret: she's been dating Luke, but really likes Charlie

BOOKTALK

Hi. My name's Charlie. I'm a loner, don't have too much to do with other people. I guess it started when I was a little kid and couldn't invite kids to my house after school cause my mom was almost always drunk, and I didn't want anyone to know. I was almost glad when she died—I thought I'd magically become like everyone else and have friends to do things with. But it didn't happen. I was still alone.

I live with Trent, my older brother. He's cool, not like a parent, but I know I still have rules I have to stick to. But he doesn't hassle me and I don't hassle him. To tell the truth, I don't really hassle anyone. Most things just roll off my back—there's not a lot I care enough about to get upset. But Luke Cattington is one person who knows how to press my buttons. He's a Richie Rich, and loves to give me grief about almost anything.

That's how I ended up getting to know Brandon. It was just three weeks into my sophomore year, and Luke and his rich jock friends had been riding me pretty heavy. I tell Trent at breakfast that I'm gonna have to fight them. I've swallowed all that I can. It's time to spit in their faces. Like I said, Trent's cool. He just asks if the office has his work number. They do.

It goes down about like I thought it would, except that it's Brandon, not Luke, who grabs me by the shoulder, which is when things go from verbal to physical. It's over pretty quickly, though, and we get hauled to the office and then into On-Campus Suspension for four days.

Even though we aren't supposed to be talking, Brandon and I say a few things to each other, and I begin to realize he doesn't have as much in common with Luke as I thought he did. I began to wonder if maybe we could be friends, if maybe this was another chance for me to stop being a loner.

MAJOR THEMES AND IDEAS

- Money doesn't always make life better or easier.
- You might as well not run and hide from an angry parent. It just makes them madder when they do find you.
- You can't change your parents; you can only make sure you survive them.
- Caring about people and things is like walking a tightrope. If you care too much, you'll get dragged down. If you don't care at all, you shut yourself up in a box, all alone.
- If you don't have anyone to teach you how to care about someone else when you're young, it's difficult to learn later on. But it's not impossible.

- Everyone is the sum of all of his or her parts. Sexual orientation is only one of those parts.
- Love outlasts temper tantrums and overreactions.
- Learning someone's secrets changes how you see them only if you define them as those secrets, and nothing more.

BOOK REPORT IDEAS
1. Discuss the comment Brandon makes on page 139, "Which is worse, smacking a kid around or telling him he's not worth shit?" Explain, in detail, which you think is worse and why.
2. Charlie thinks Trent treats him differently than a parent would. Show how this is and is not true, citing examples from the book.
3. Compare Charlie's and Brandon's home lives, being sure to include both feelings and experiences.
4. Luke is a bully, harassing Charlie about who he is and what he doesn't have. Speculate on why he does it and how he will treat Charlie after the book ends, and after both Katie and Charlie have confronted him.

BOOKTALK IDEAS
1. Let Charlie tell his own story, introducing himself, Trent, and Brandon.
2. Focus your talk on the beginning of Brandon and Charlie's friendship, when what they had in common was not wanting to go home.

RISKS
- Teens are sexually active.
- Teens abuse alcohol.
- Homosexuality portrayed as a positive lifestyle.
- Language is realistic, but vulgar.
- Parents are distant and controlling.
- Examines teen depression with suicidal thoughts.

STRENGTHS
- Homosexual character portrayed as much more than his sexual orientation.
- Shows strong, close relationship between brothers.
- Safe sex practices are recommended.
- Characters are able to recover from abusive, alcoholic parent.
- Demonstrates the strength of a close friendship.

AWARDS
Delacorte Prize for First Young Adult Novel, 1998
Quick Picks for Reluctant Readers, 1998 (ALA)

REVIEWS

"The book's focus on accepting the risks of friendship and learning to care for others is sensitively handled. The major characters have depth and the dialogue flows well. The conversations contain a variety of obscenities, but they fit the situations and the characters. . . . the conflicts Charlie faces in opening himself up to others make for a powerful reading experience." —*Voice of Youth Advocates*, 12/97, Susan H. Levine.

"Dialogue. . . . rings true, and Jenkins delivers a devastatingly accurate portrayal of adolescent males. Charlie and Brandon are believable and likable, with Trent's affection for his brother credibly drawn. But the boys are also realistically flawed. . . . the combination makes this book both thoughtful and compelling." —*Booklist*, 9/15/97, Debbie Carton.

"The use of profanity and explicit talk about sex is realistic for these teenage boys, and the novel doesn't overplay the problems of alcoholism, neglect, and abuse; Trent's gayness is similarly taken in stride." —*Horn Book*, 9-10/97, L.A.

"Alternately heart-warming and heart-breaking." —Amazon, 1997.

"Articulates with appreciable clarity the emotional risks of opening up to others." —*Kirkus Reviews*, 1997.

ﻡﻡﻡ

BREAKING RANK. Randle, Kristen D. Morrow, 1999. $15.95. 160p. ISBN: 0-688-16243-6. Avon Books, 2001. $4.95. 272p. ISBN: 0-380-73281-5. Realistic Fiction. Reading level: MS. Interest level: MS, YHS. English, Vocational education.

SUBJECT AREAS

friendship; peer pressure; school; prejudice; gangs; love; lying and deceitfulness; rites of passage; secrets; self-knowledge; working; manipulation; intimidation; gossip.

CHARACTERS

Casey Willardson: she agreed to work with Baby because it was the right thing to do
Thomas Fairbairn/Baby: Lenny's brother and Crown Prince of the Clan
Mr. Hall: head counselor at Feynman High, and the originator of the Great Idea
Skyler, Monkey, Lauce, Kovacs, Marsh, Tully, Holt, Kelle: members of the Clan

Lenny, Shelly, Edmund: they started the Clan and are its Masters
Rowena: Baby and Lenny's mother
Chase and Mrs. Willardson: Casey's parents
Joanna: Casey's best friend

BOOKTALK

The Clan were, well, the Clan. They never spoke to anyone, never looked anyone in the eye, never laughed. They were all male; they wore all black; and each wore a tiny, beaded braid at his left temple. They went to school, but did nothing. They took no notes, said nothing when questioned by teachers, turned in no homework, took no tests. The Special Ed classes were crowded with Clan members. Since they spoke to no one but each other, no one in town knew why they dressed and acted as they did, and they were both feared and hated. The Clan had existed for twelve years when all that changed.

Baby didn't really think about what would happen when he took the aptitude test instead of just sitting and looking at it. He just wanted to see if he knew the answers. He did, and his high scores sparked a series of events that would change him, the Clan, and even the whole town in ways no one ever expected.

When you're Clan, *that* is your life. You don't take tests, get into honors classes or get scholarships to colleges. You especially don't get involved with nice girls who also do those things. But Baby, the Crown Prince of the Clan, does. This is about what happens afterwards.

MAJOR THEMES AND IDEAS

- School isn't the only place to get an education.
- Arrogance can lead to mistakes, and even to tragedy.
- Loving someone and wanting what's best for them doesn't always mean you understand them or know what their best is all about.
- Going along with the crowd even when you don't like what they're doing is wrong and usually cowardly.
- People hate and fear what they don't understand, which frequently leads to violence.
- It's important to let others, especially those you love, be themselves, and honor them for it.
- Be true to yourself, even when it's painful.
- Seek out your gift, what resonates for you, what you can use to give back to life and to humanity.
- The more you learn, the more you see that all of life is part of a connected organic whole.

BOOK REPORT IDEAS

1. Education is a main theme of the book. Compare the education Baby gets from the Clan to the education he and Casey get at school.
2. Characters speculate at the end of the book on the Clan's future. Explain whether or not you agree with these speculations, and what characteristics of the Clan might cause its demise.
3. In the book, violence is the response to those who hate and fear the Clan. Discuss the assumptions the Cribs and the Clan make about each other and how those assumptions escalated into violence.
4. Compare the situation in this book to other similar ones, such as *The Outsiders*, in which two groups of teens from different social classes clash and erupt into violence.
5. Speculate on what will happen after the end of the book, including the characters of Baby, Casey, Lenny, and Rowena. Will the Clan exist in another five years? Why or why not?
6. Discuss what Baby says to Monkey on page 15 of the hardcover edition, "You step outside, you stay outside." Why is this rule so important to the Clan?

BOOKTALK IDEAS

1. Tell the story in first person, as Baby.
2. Write your talk from two points of view, introducing the story from Casey's and Baby's perspective and focusing on their first meeting.
3. Use a woman's black and yellow bracelet as a prop for your talk. Consider dressing as a Clan member also.

RISKS

- Clan members see no value in public education.
- High school cliques clash violently.
- Includes demeaning comments about girls/women.
- Language is realistic, with mild obscenities.
- Clan dress and actions are quite similar to different gangs or individuals blamed for actual school shootings.

STRENGTHS

- Interesting portrayal of civil disobedience.
- Shows how incorrect assumptions about others can lead to violence and tragedy.
- Supports the value of education, whether in or out of school.
- Strong, realistic characters teens can identify with.
- Encourages readers to find their own path in life, their "road with a heart."
- Speaks out against cliques, especially jock-oriented ones.
- Characters grow and attain insight.

- Realistic language reflects how teens speak today.
- Ambiguous ending encourages discussion and speculation about what happens next.

AWARDS
Best Books for Young Adults, 2000 (ALA)

REVIEWS
"Randle has written a poignant and timely story that explores the nature of alienated high school cliques similar to the 'Trench Coat Mafia.' She takes readers inside the Clan, showing the pain and defensiveness that some young people suffer at the hands of the majority." ——*Voice of Youth Advocates*, 12/99, Chris Crowe.

"Reminiscent of *The Outsiders* and *West Side Story*, Randle's novel is compelling reading. Romance, gang in-fighting, and high school classroom and social scenes are realistically detailed. . . . Powerful writing and a suspenseful, action-driven story will grab teen readers." —*School Library Journal*, 5/99, Gail Richmond.

"Modern insightful Romeo and Juliet story is a rare and notable contribution. . . . alternating points of view and Randle's taut, poetic prose provide remarkable character depth and complexity. . . . gritty, smart, and realistic. . . . a story of morality without judgment, this will encourage teens to look beyond appearances and deep within their own hearts." —*Booklist*, 5/1/99, Shelle Rosenfeld.

�☐�☐�☐

BREATHING UNDERWATER. Flinn, Alex. HarperCollins, 2001. $15.95. 263p. ISBN: 0-060-29198-2. Realistic fiction. Reading level: YHS. Interest level: YHS, OHS. Sex education; English; Ethics; Creative writing.

SUBJECT AREAS
dating and social life; violence; abuse, physical; therapy; self-knowledge; bullying; family relationships; anger; racism; abuse, mental; prejudice; peer pressure; writing; friendship; love; abuse, sexual; justice; legal system; fear; school; sports; rites of passage; problem parents; secrets; lying and deceitfulness; substance abuse.

CHARACTERS

Nick Andreas: at sixteen, he's ordered into therapy for abusing his girlfriend; he used to have the reputation of being one of the coolest guys in school

Caitlin McCourt: Nick's girlfriend

Deborah Lehamn: the judge who hears the case between Caitlin and Nick

Mr. Andreas: Nick's only parent, his abusive father, a wealthy self-made man who constantly tells Nick he's a loser

Mrs. McCourt: Caitlin's mother

Tom Carter: he's Nick's best friend, but he doesn't know about what Nick's father does to him, or why he abused Caitlin

Mario Ortega: he teaches Nick's family violence class

Kelly Steele, Leo Sotolongo, Tyrone/Tiny Johnson, A.J./Psycho, Ray DeLeon: members of Nick's family violence class

Mr. and Mrs. Carter: Tom's parents who treat Nick like one of the family because he's there so much, but who are not accepting of anyone outside their social circle

Liana Castro: a girl Tom dates, despite his parents' disapproval

Saint O'Connor: star quarterback, Tom's new best friend and Caitlin's new boyfriend

Miss Higgins: Nick's honors English teacher, who sees more of Nick than he knows he's revealed

Derek Wayne: he's in choir with Caitlin and is smart and geeky

BOOKTALK

The Nick everyone saw was one of the really cool kids at school. Rich, popular, smart, handsome, he played on the football team and drove a classic '67 red Mustang convertible. He had a charmed life—everyone wanted to be Nick.

The Nick no one saw was an angry, resentful loser, who frequently missed school when his father's abuse got too obvious. His father may have given Nick his car, but he also told his son, over and over, that he was a failure, a loser, never good enough at anything. Nick hasn't seen his mother since he was five, and he and his father live alone with a series of housekeepers. Nick avoids his father as much as possible, and worries about what will set him off.

Then just after school starts, he sees Caitlin, and thinks "dream girl." His friend Tom helps him meet her, and they start dating. Nick is in love for the first time, but the only examples he has of love are the memories of his parents. Which Nick will he show Caitlin, the one everyone knows, or the one that no one does?

MAJOR THEMES AND IDEAS

- Hitting people, even once, no matter what the reason, is wrong.
- Sometimes it's a good thing when life kicks you in the butt so you'll take a good look at the messes you've made.

- Exploring the past brings out feelings that cause us to become insecure, controlling, or violent.
- What happens to you at home is the cornerstone of your other relationships.
- Control freaks are frequently also violent.
- People interpret your behavior differently from the way you do, and may see patterns you are denying or blind to.
- Abusive behavior is both physical and mental.
- It's important to acknowledge your emotions, and find positive ways of dealing with them.
- You're not a loser because someone calls you that, over and over. You become a loser when you tell that to yourself, over and over. So, figure out how to turn off both those voices, and be a winner.
- You can't respect yourself if you're letting someone beat you up, whether they use their words, or their fists, or both.

BOOK REPORT IDEAS
1. Discuss the meaning of the title, and the scenes in the book that helped you find that meaning.
2. Explain why you think Miss Higgins didn't call social services about Nick being abused, when there were two years of evidence she and a previous teacher had recorded.
3. There are several turning points in this book when Nick gained new insight about himself. Discuss them and the insights he gained.
4. Speculate on what Nick will be like in the future, including his friendship with Tom, his relationship with his father, and his relationship with women.
5. Examine the scenes in the Family Violence Class, and show how Mario helped its members gain new insight about themselves and their actions.
6. Describe the most important thought or idea that you take away from this book and explain why you chose it.
7. At one point, Nick describes Caitlin as strong. Give examples of her strength and of her love for Nick.
8. Explain why you think Caitlin told Tom about Nick and his father.
9. Explain why recalling and remembering pain helps cure it, and why the judge wanted Nick to keep a journal.
10. In a way, abusers are not hitting or hurting the person they abuse, but someone else. Who is it, and why?

BOOKTALK IDEAS
1. Have Caitlin describe Nick, first his love, then his abuse, and her confusion about what to do.
2. Focus your talk on Nick's initial meeting with Caitlin, contrasting that with a date when he was angry or controlling, asking at the end, which Nick was real.

3. Center you talk on the courtroom scene, being sure to include Nick's fear of his father, closing with a few words about his first journal entry.
4. Include the poem Nick wrote on March 29 as part of your talk, using it to show how he isolated himself, even from his best friend.

RISKS
- Portrait of a long-term abusive father.
- Shows graphic dating violence.
- Language is realistic but vulgar.
- Depicts harassment and stalking behavior.

STRENGTHS
- Format makes book more visually accessible—typeface of journal sets it apart.
- Multiple story lines, in past and present, create complexity.
- Multidimensional characters that teens quickly identify with.
- Powerful, unflinching look at abusers and those they abuse.
- Realistic portrait of how abusive behavior is a generational issue.
- Shows the insidiousness of controlling behavior escalating to obsession and violence.
- Shows the level of denial present in an abuser's mind.
- Analyzes an abusive relationship and how it destroys both people in it.
- Example of how therapy can help people change if they want to.

AWARDS
None

REVIEWS
"The messages in this unsparing novel of teenage love turned dangerous are powerful, on target, and almost too painful to read—exactly why this highly recommended book should be required reading for all teenagers. It is a road map to warning signs, consequences, and the very real hope of redemption if the cycle of abuse is. . . . caught and treated in time." —*Voice of Youth Advocates*, 6/01, Beth E. Anderson.

"Flinn tackles the difficult task of making us understand, if not sympathize with, the motivation of a violent young man. . . . This extraordinarily moving novel is highly relevant reading for all young men in our violence-prone society." —Amazon, 2001, Patty Campbell.

"An open and honest portrayal of an all-too-common problem." —*School Library Journal*, 2001, Joel Shoemaker.

📖📖📖

BRUISES. DeVries, Anke. Stacey Knecht, translator. Front Street Press, 1996. $15.95. 168p. ISBN: 1-886-91003-0. Laurel-Leaf Books, 1997. $4.50. 168p. ISBN: 0-440-22694-5. Realistic fiction. Reading level: MS. Interest level: MS, YHS, OHS. English, Psychology.

SUBJECT AREAS
abuse, physical; friendship; problem parents; self-knowledge; family relationships; anger; dysfunctional families; fear; violence; secrets; rites of passage; other countries; intimidation.

CHARACTERS
Judith Van Gilder: beaten by her mother, she believes she deserves to be abused
Dennis Van Gilder: Judith's little brother
Connie Van Gilder: she adores Dennis, but beats Judith
Uncle Ben: Dennis's father who no longer lives with them
Mr. Buckman: Judith's teacher who worries about her
Diana: a friend of Judith's who sits next to her in class and asks embarrassing questions
Michael: Dyslexic and older than the other students, he's determined to discover Judith's secret
Aunt Elly and Uncle Bob: Michael lives with them and his three cousins, Michele, David, and Frank
Mr. and Mrs. Van Klavern: they live in the apartment below the Van Gilders
Nico: he's dating Judith's mother
Dirk and Helen: Michael's father and his girlfriend

BOOKTALK
There was trouble ahead. Judith could tell by the way the front door slammed shut, by her mother's footsteps on the stairs.

Her body tensed, her eyes darted around the room. Was everything in its place? That was the most important thing, not attracting attention.

But it was too late, and only minutes later, Judith huddled on her bed, covering her face while her mother beat her, again. Sometimes she just used her hands, but this time it was the metal tube from the vacuum cleaner. It hurt so much she couldn't even cry. She thought the beating would never end, but suddenly, it was over. Her entire body hurt and the welts on her back and legs burned like fire. But she'd hidden her face in her pillow so it wasn't bruised. She'd have to wear a long-sleeved sweater, but she could go to school tomorrow.

Judith has never known any life but this. She doesn't know why her mother screams at her for even the smallest mistakes, but never touches her little brother

Dennis. She only knows it must be her fault; she must deserve it. She's afraid to tell anyone what is going on, but gradually people around her are beginning to notice that something is wrong, and questions begin to arise from teachers, day-care workers, neighbors, and friends.

But as the beatings continue and get worse and worse, Judith begins to wonder if her mother will go too far one day and kill her. Is there anyone who can stop the abuse and keep that from happening?

MAIN THEMES AND IDEAS
- If someone hits you or hurts you, it's never your fault.
- Some secrets aren't meant to be kept.
- Abuse can be mental or physical; either way, it's still abuse.
- Sometimes minding your own business and not getting involved is the wrong thing to do.
- Being open and honest about a disability may mean you won't be teased about it.
- If you laugh at yourself first, when others laugh, they're laughing with you, not at you.
- Sooner or later you've got to stand up for yourself.

BOOK REPORT IDEAS
1. This book is set in the Netherlands where child abuse laws differ from those in the United States. Discuss how the book would be different if it was set in this country.
2. Speculate on what happens to Judith after the book ends. Where does she go and who does she stay with? What happens to her mother and brother? What about her relationship with Michael and his family?
3. Compare and contrast the ways in which Michael and Judith were abused, and how that abuse affected their lives and personalities.
4. Discuss the reasons why Connie abused her daughter, and whether or not she ever really loved Judith.
5. Michael was drawn to Judith almost immediately. Explain what he saw in her, besides her resemblance to Steffie, that could be the reason for that attraction.
6. Explain why none of the adults close to Judith ever took any decisive action upon seeing her bruises and other signs of abuse.

BOOKTALK IDEAS
1. Tell the story from Michael's perspective as he gets to know Judith.
2. Write your talk from both Michael's and Judith's perspectives, letting each of them introduce themselves and tell a little about their story.
3. Focus your talk on one scene when other characters in the book wonder about Judith's puzzling actions or explanations designed to hide her abuse.

RISKS
- Scenes of physical abuse are graphic and detailed.
- Abusive parent is neither discovered nor punished.
- People see evidence of abuse and ignore it or accept Judith's lies about it.
- Description of mental abuse by a distant, nonemotional parent.

STRENGTHS
- Multidimensional characters who mature and gain insight during the book.
- Ambiguous ending leaves major issues unresolved.
- Story is told from multiple points of view.
- Strong portrayal of the power of friendship.
- Detailed portrait of a centered, functional, loving family group in stark contrast to the two abusive parents.
- Open ending leaves room for individual speculation and group discussion.
- Wrenching descriptions of the guilt felt by an abused child.
- Excellent, nonjudgmental description of a learning disability and how to cope with/live with it.

AWARDS
Best Books for Young Adults, 1996 (ALA)
Quick Picks for Reluctant Readers, 1996 (ALA)

REVIEWS
"Plot is generally tightly knot and engaging. . . . characterization is strong. . . . gripping story will hold [the reader's attention]." —*Voice of Youth Advocates*, 6/96, Donna L. Scanlon.

"A searing novel—sometimes painful to read, impossible to put down. . . . In terrible, stark detail, de Vries describes Judith's abuse; the writing is taut, immediate, and emotionally charged." —*Kirkus Reviews*, 1996.

"In spite of the grim subject and graphic descriptions of abuse, the novel is not relentlessly dark as it explores the human frailties that affect relationships." —*Horn Book*, 1996.

"The technicolor horror of Judith's bruised life will not fade easily." —*School Library Journal*, 1996.

THE BUFFALO TREE. Rapp, Adam. Front Street Press, 1997. $15.95. 188p. ISBN: 1-886-91019-7. HarperCollins, 1998. $11.00. 192p. ISBN: 0-064-40711-X. Realistic fiction. Reading level: YHS. Interest level: YHS, OHS. English, Ethics.

SUBJECT AREAS
crime and delinquency; legal system; justice; fear; survival; friendship; bullying; abuse, physical; intimidation; manipulation; death and dying; suicide; family relationships.

CHARACTERS
Sura: at thirteen, he's the only white kid in the Hamstock Juvenile Detention Center; he got caught clipping hoodies
Coly Jo: Sura's patchmate in Spalding, who's twelve years old
Hodge, Boo Boxfoot: on their third year at juvie, they are bullies who control other inmates' lives
Mister Rose: the cottage counselor for Spalding
Mister Tully: he runs gut drill and has ugly eyes
Nurse Rushing: white and pretty, she's usually nice
Petey Sessoms: one of the strongest kids at juvie
Deacon Bob Fly: Sura's Path Mentor
Mazzy: Sura's mother, a dancer
Miss Denton: the teacher at juvie
Dean Petty: he has a huge paddle he uses on the boys who get into trouble
Strum Lister: he can beat anyone in the crying game
Long Neck: Sura's patchmate after Coly is sent to solitary

BOOKTALK
If you're gonna survive in Hamstock, you gotta have a patchmate. Hamstock isn't like most juvie detention centers—it's worse. Most places let you go when you make reform. At Hamstock, you stay 'til they decide to let you go, and that can be a long while. There are two things to remember at Hamstock. The first is to stay low and don't get carped. The second is watch out for Hodge and Boo. They're on their third clip, and they know the halls and shadows and the tricks in the shadows. They crib stuff from the other kids, send them up the buffalo tree, or beat them up to keep them in line. No one ever reports them 'cause they don't want to get more grief.

But Coly Jo just couldn't stand it that Boo always wore the coonskin cap he cribbed from Coly Jo the second night he was here. Every time Boo looked at Coly Jo, he sneered. And about six weeks later Coly Jo just couldn't take it any more, and in the middle of a field hockey game, he went for his cap. He didn't get the cap, but he got the tail. And that night, Boo and Hodge got him. Coly Jo changed after that.

What did they do to Coly Jo? It was worse than beating him up, worse than the buffalo tree, worse than anything you can imagine.

Take a turn in Hamstock and find out just how close to hell juvie can really be.

MAJOR THEMES AND IDEAS
- Stand up for your friends—you have to have someone to watch your back.
- Adults can't or don't always protect you, even when that's their job.
- When the mind has too much trauma to deal with, the body shuts down to give it time to heal.
- If you get caught doing something, do your time and when you get out, *don't* go back to what you were doing before.
- Bullies always know who the best targets are, and they will do anything to shame you and break your spirit—*anything*! Looking bad or sad makes you vulnerable and ripe for attack.
- Sometimes it's hard to talk to someone you love—all the questions and answers get all tangled up inside, and silence is the only result.
- Be careful who you show yourself, your real self to—you never know how that person will react.
- Sometimes protecting yourself is more important than the truth.
- If people don't see you as a person, your death doesn't touch them.
- Life in prison and life out of prison are two different things, and the adjustment period between them can be hard.
- Too much degradation can lead to suicide.
- Survival is possible, even in the harshest of environments.

BOOK REPORT IDEAS
1. Discuss Sura's Smooth Seven, and whether they would work in your neighborhood.
2. Speculate on what might have happened to Sura and Coly Jo if they had reported the incident when Coly was urinated and defecated on. How would the guards, the other boys, and Hodge and Boo have reacted?
3. Look at the alliances boys made and how those alliances helped them survive.
4. Discuss the buffalo tree and how it influenced life at Hamstock.
5. Examine the sentences various boys received for various crimes and compare the severity of the sentence at Hamstock with the seriousness of the crime. How many sentences seem reasonable, and how many don't?
6. Discuss the guards and other staff, showing how some helped the boys and how others made their sentences infinitely worse.
7. Examine the relationship Boo and Hodge had with the guards and staff and explain how it came about.

8. Chronicle what happened to Coly from the time he arrived at Hamstock, showing the steps of his "descent into hell."

BOOKTALK IDEAS

1. Focus your talk on Sura and Coly and how they worked together to survive.
2. Use a coonskin cap, or the tail from one, as a prop.
3. Include some of the boys' crimes and their sentences in your talk.
4. Write your talk as if it were one of Sura and Coly's late-night conversations.

RISKS

- Language is realistic, but contains slang and obscenities.
- Portraits of bullies and persecution.
- Characters discuss sexuality and masturbation.
- Child abuse, violence, and suicide shown in graphic detail.

STRENGTHS

- Strong realistic narrator's voice involves the reader from the beginning.
- Characters teens will identify with easily.
- Graphic, gritty picture of prison for juveniles is reflective of reality, at least for some inmates.
- Realistic language, including slang specific to juvie, makes the dialogue seem like actual conversations.
- Shows how friendship and alliances can help individuals survive.
- Ending leaves hope, but not without memories of the horror the characters have survived.

AWARDS

School Library Journal, Best Books of the Year, 1997

REVIEWS

"He writes sympathetically of African American teens, capturing the rhythm of their words and even, on the page, the motion of their young bodies [and their] flowing, juicy language. . . . One of the novel's strengths is its demonstration that these youths incarcerated for criminal activity possess little sense of having done anything wrong. . . . if the narrator's sexual precocity at twelve is jarring, the frankness of these young men's nightly, lonely masturbating feels believable and right." —*Voice of Youth Advocates, 8/1/97,* Richard Gercken.

"Rapp's prose is powerful, graphic, and haunting. . . . creates a vivid, memorable sense of place and strong characters. The world that Rapp portrays is often ugly, disturbing, and brutal, which makes Sura's struggles all the more poignant. . . . this is a story that should have wide YA appeal. An outstanding novel of redemption and survival." —*School Library Journal*, 6/97, Edward Sullivan.

"Although the brutality is unremitting, the book is hard to put down. The action plays out under Sura's watchful, cagey eyes, and his tone of bravado relieves the harshness without resorting to sentimentality. . . . his toughness of spirit. . . . inspires and makes the reading of this novel a transcendent experience." —*Horn Book*, 7-8/97, N.V.

"The creative, at times poetic, use of language is challenging, demanding that readers become immersed in the richly realized, dark look at an American subculture. The tension-filled plot will also draw in readers and maintain their interest throughout." —*Booklist*, 9/1/97, Susan Dove Lempke.

📖📖📖

BURGER WUSS. Anderson, M.T. Candlewick Press, 1999. $16.99. 192p. ISBN: 0-763-60680-4. Candlewick Press, 2001. $5.99. 192p. ISBN: 0-763-61567-6. Humor, Realistic fiction. Reading level: MS, YHS. Interest level: MS, YHS. English, Vocational education, Sociology, Ethics.

SUBJECT AREAS
working; revenge; dating and social life; friendship; bullying; intimidation; anger; cooking; gossip; love; rites of passage; self-knowledge; secrets; stereotypes; sex and sexuality.

CHARACTERS
Anthony: he's determined to get revenge on Turner, a girlfriend-stealing bully
Mike: the manager of O'Dermott's, a fast food burger franchise
Diana Gritt: Anthony's ex-girlfriend
Turner: he stole Diana from Anthony
Rick, Jenn: Anthony's friends who also work at O'Dermott's
Shunt: cynic and cook at O'Dermott's

BOOKTALK
Turner was big, big and mean. The first time Anthony saw him, he was lying on top of Anthony's girlfriend, Diana. They were both drunk and laughing. Anthony turned and walked out of the party.

Diana had been the one perfect thing in Anthony's life, and now she was gone. He wanted revenge in the worst kind of way, and the first step was getting a job at O'Dermott's, a burger franchise where Turner worked. He knew there was an opening—his friends Rick and Jenn who also worked there, told him Diana had quit.

Snowing the manager was easy and Anthony was hired. He wasn't sure how to get his revenge, but then Turner provided the inspiration he needed, first by getting Anthony beaten up by the guys from Burger Queen, O'Dermott's arch-rivals, and then by tricking Anthony into turning the whole restaurant into a toxic waste dump for hours.

And what was the plan? Will it involve a troll, a disguise, a kidnapping, ransom letters, humiliation, and doing to Turner all the things he'd hate most in the world? It was elaborate, and not the easiest plan to pull off. But it was beautiful, and huge and ornate—and inescapable. It would hurt Turner in many, many spots at once. It was perfect.

No more Mr. Nice Guy—Anthony was going for the throat. "I will make you *cry*, Turner," he vowed. "I will make you *cry!*"

Can a burger wuss really take down someone who's older, meaner, bigger, but not necessarily smarter? Is revenge served hot or cold at O'Dermott's? Find out in *Burger Wuss*.

MAJOR THEMES AND IDEAS
- Carrying out a plan for revenge may be more difficult than coming up with it.
- "Revenge is a dish best served cold."
- Frequently, when you work in a uniform, you aren't treated as a person but as a machine.
- If you want to know how someone feels about you, ask them. Just make sure you're really ready to hear what they have to say.
- A sense of humor is one of the best things you can share with someone you love.
- You might be your own worst enemy.

BOOK REPORT IDEAS
1. Revenge is one of the major themes of this book. Discuss Anthony's Plan, the results he expected, and the actual results, and whether or not you believe it was a success.
2. In the end, Anthony thinks that the rivalry between Burger Queen and O'Dermott's escalated because he and Shunt stole the troll. Decide whether you agree or disagree, and explain why.
3. Rick and Anthony discuss love several times, defining it in several ways. Discuss how realistic their perspectives were and why.
4. Examine Shunt's role in the plot, and the function he played.
5. Compare Anthony at the beginning and end of the book, showing how he has changed and why.
6. Discuss what might have happened if Anthony had blamed Diana, not Turner, for betraying him.

BOOKTALK IDEAS

1. Write your talk in first person, as Anthony, focusing on Diana's betrayal and his plan for revenge.
2. Emphasize the Burger Queen/O'Dermott's rivalry in your talk.
3. Build your talk around the idea of revenge, and who wants revenge for what.

RISKS

- Language is realistic yet vulgar.
- There are several grotesque or revolting scenes.

STRENGTHS

- Tone is clever and satirical.
- Stereotypical characters poke fun at themselves.
- Story line is nonsequential, adding complexity to the plot.
- Funny spoof of the fast-food business, teen love, and adolescent angst.
- Humor is dark and intelligent.

AWARDS

None

REVIEWS

"Humor is off-beat, on-target, and age appropriate. Anderson. . . . deftly employs current adolescent speech patterns. Hardly shallow, this cultural parody includes [many voices, and] there is intricate scheming on multiple levels, including Anthony's adolescent perception of himself." —*Voice of Youth Advocates*, 12/99, Cynthia L. Blinn.

"Hugely funny, fast-paced romp through teen angst." —Amazon, 1999, Brangien Davis.

"Savaging young love, male adolescence, and with tender attention to detail and wildly funny results. . . . Anderson plots this with the precision of a fast-food marketing campaign, but his hero is more human than high concept. Did somebody say MacSatire?" —*Kirkus Reviews*, 1999.

📖📖📖

BURIED ONIONS. Soto, Gary. Harcourt, 1997. $17.00. 160p. ISBN: 0-152-01333-4. HarperCollins Children's Books, 1999. $11.00. 149p. ISBN: 0-064-

40771-3. Realistic fiction. Reading level: MS. Interest level: YHS, OHS. English.

SUBJECT AREAS
prejudice; minorities, Hispanic; working; death and dying; crime and delinquency; rites of passage; self-knowledge; friendship; family relationships; revenge; gangs; death and dying; poverty; survival; substance abuse.

CHARACTERS
Eddie: he dropped out of college when his cousin was murdered
Angel: a friend of Jesus' who wants Eddie to avenge his cousin's death
Lupe: another friend of Jesus'
Dolores: Jesus' mother and Eddie's aunt who also wants revenge for her son's death
Mr. Stiles: he hired Eddie to do yard work
Mrs. Rios: Eddie's next-door neighbor
Norma: a girl Eddie knew in high school
Jose Dominguez: a friend of Eddie's who's in the Marines
Samuel: Lupe's little brother who's into sniffing glue
Coach: he works at the local playground

BOOKTALK
I live in the part of Fresno where fences sag, paint blisters on houses, and swamp coolers squeak like squirrels. The old sit on porches, fanning themselves, watching the young guys work on their cars, and mothers push strollers of fretful, crying babies.

There isn't much for me to do except eat, sleep, watch out for drivebys, and remember all the men in my family who are gone. I dropped out of City College right after Jesus, my cousin, was killed, just because he told another guy he had yellow shoes. The guy just turned around and stuck a knife into his chest. My father, my uncles, my best friend from high school, and now my cousin, all are dead. It seems like I am surrounded by the dead, and by the living who expect me to avenge their deaths. But I don't want to—there has been more than enough killing, and I will not be a part of making it continue.

I live alone, stencil house numbers on the curbs to get by, and refuse to answer the phone so I can avoid my aunt, who wants me to avenge my cousin's death, and I watch my back because even though I never ran with the gangs or *vatos locos*, it still pays to be careful and quick as a rabbit. And now I also have to avoid Angel, who wants me to help him kill Jesus' murderer, and Samuel, who wants to mess with me for reasons of his own.

It seems that no matter what I do, even when I think I am doing the right thing, life jumps up when I'm not looking and slaps me down. Isn't there any way out of this life? Any way I can be like other people, with a home, a job, a family, food on the table, and money in my pocket? Or am I stuck in the barrio with sadness of its buried onions forever?

MAJOR THEMES AND IDEAS
- Sometimes it seems like no matter how hard you try, you can't get ahead.
- Sometimes you get the help you need and sometimes you don't.
- Fighting solves very little.
- If you don't look honest, people seldom believe you when you say you are.
- Poverty is like a deep rut—very hard to get out of.
- Once you get caught in the cycle of violence, it's difficult to escape.
- Not all wars are fought overseas. Some are fought in our own neighborhoods.

BOOK REPORT IDEAS
1. Discuss the concept of buried onions—what does Eddie mean when he says they are responsible for making everyone sad?
2. Discuss who killed Jesus, and explain why you think Angel did or didn't do it.
3. Many of the characters are trapped by poverty, drugs, and violence. Explain how this cycle reoccurs over and over, from one generation to another, and why.
4. Speculate on what happens after the book ends. Is Eddie able to get out of Fresno, or will he be caught once again by the buried onions?
5. Gangs are everywhere in this book. Discuss the gang culture as it is seen here and how boys are drawn into gangs.
6. Discuss the hopeless tone of the book, and the idea that Eddie gets knocked down every time he gets ahead a little. How did this make you feel, and what would your response be to that kind of situation.

BOOKTALK IDEAS
1. Use an onion as a prop for your talk.
2. Focus your talk on one of Eddie's problems and his attempts to resolve it.
3. Let Eddie tell his own story, in first person.
4. Center your talk on the losses in Eddie's life and the helplessness he feels.

RISKS
- Graphic descriptions of violence.
- Shows the activities of gangs for both children and teens.
- Language is realistic but includes obscenities.

STRENGTHS
- Gives realistic picture of gang life for Hispanics.

- Strong narrator's voice involves readers immediately.
- Unflinching portrayal of the cycle of poverty.
- Unresolved ending leaves room for individual and group reflection.
- Dark, gritty tone enhances the starkness of the setting and the plot.

AWARDS
Best Books for Young Adults, 1998 (ALA)
Quick Picks for Reluctant Readers, 1998 (ALA)
Selected Audiobooks for Young Adults, 2001 (ALA)

REVIEWS
"A beautiful, touching, and truthful story about one young man struggling to keep the dignity and not bend to the will of the glue-sniffing locals . . . resorts to neither stereotypes nor clichés, portrays a young man fighting against society to make a place for himself in the world. . . . Soto's best fiction yet." —*Voice of Youth Advocates*, 10/97, Katie O'Dell Madison.

"Provides readers with strong images through the eyes and voice of Eddie. . . . Additionally, the author stirs more senses with his descriptions of smells and sounds. . . . Soto's descriptions are poetic, and he creates deep feelings of heat and despair. A powerful and thought-provoking read." —*School Library Journal*, 1/98, Mary M. Hopf.

"In what could be the most somber of the 'dark books' of 1997, Gary Soto writes of the inexorable no-exit circumscription of life in the Fresno barrio. . . . this is the story immortalized in Langston Hughes' *Harlem*, where a dream deferred can dry up, or explode. . . . We talk a lot about the need for more 'boys' books'; here is one for young men." —*Horn Book*, 1-2/98, R.S.

⊞⊞⊞⊞

BURNING UP. Cooney, Caroline B. Delacorte Press, 1999. $15.95. 192p. ISBN: 0-385-32318-2. Laurel-Leaf Books, 2001. $5.50. 240p. ISBN: 0-440-22687-2. Recorded Books, Inc., 1999. ISBN: 0-788-73190-4. (unabridged audiotape) Realistic fiction. Reading level: MS. Interest level: MS, YHS. English, Ethics, American history.

SUBJECT AREAS
family relationships; friendship; racism; prejudice; minority/black; problem parents; divorce and separation; school; gossip; self-knowledge; mystery and suspense; secrets; lying and deceitfulness.

CHARACTERS

Macey Clare: a fifteen-year-old whose curiosity about an old burned out barn changes her life

Lindsay, Grace: Macey's best friends

Putnam and Leandra Macey: Macey's maternal grandparents who love to cook and eat

Cordilia and Alec Clare: Macey's overworked parents

Austin: he lives with his grandparents, across the street from the Maceys

Henry and Monica Fent: Austin's grandparents

Mr. and Mrs. Demitroff: the burned out barn is on their property

Graff: the school media specialist who organized the Saturday group

Vanita, Davonn, Chamique, Isiah: black teens who go to the Church of the Good Shepherd, in the ghetto area of the city

Reverend Warren: the minister of the church

Wade Sibley: in 1959, he was a science teacher and the first black man in town

Mr. Collins, Stella Miller, Vinnie Raspardo, Alice Yinsow: they were all involved in the 1959 fire in one way or another

BOOKTALK

There was no doubt they wanted to stop her—the old barn that burned in 1959 was not something they were comfortable talking or thinking about. But Macey refused to stop. She wanted to know why it had started, if it had been arson, who had lived there, and what had happened to him. And her questions got even more intense after two things happened. She learned that Wade Sibley, a science teacher, had been the first black person to move into the pink and white Connecticut town. And Macey was in a fire herself.

Four kids went to Good Shepherd, a black ghetto church, that Saturday to help paint the Sunday School classrooms: Macey, her best friends Grace and Lindsay, and Austin, who lived across the street from Macey's grandparents. They teamed up with four black kids from the church and started painting. But it was hot and the paint smelled awful, so Venita and Macey opened a door to the outside. Minutes later they smelled smoke and ran to tell the others. But the fire was too quick, and Macey's long luxurious hair caught fire. If Austin hadn't quickly yanked off his t-shirt to smother the flames, Macey would have been badly burned. And none of them would've survived, trapped by the fire behind a padlocked door, if the fire engines hadn't been so close and gotten there so quickly.

A black teacher in 1959 and black church in 1997—somehow they were connected. But the deeper Macey looked, the more anger and denial she found, and the more unhappy she got about the ugly little secrets she was discovering from her grandparents, from Austin's grandparents, from her own parents, and also from the townspeople who had lived there thirty-eight years ago.

And finally Macey begins to realize that while doing something wrong is evil, so is ignoring that wrong, covering it up, or just being indifferent to it. Who were the evildoers in 1959? Who are they today?

MAJOR THEMES AND IDEAS
- Giving someone your old things while you enjoy new ones can be like saying they don't deserve nice new things.
- Calling someone names hurts and keeps on hurting.
- Some segregation isn't obvious, but that doesn't make it any less wrong.
- Some friendships take years to build; others take only minutes.
- People deny or hide what makes them uncomfortable, but that doesn't make it any less true.
- Find your true colors and let them show in your life.
- Sometimes anticipation can be fun, but having to wait to get your fair share can be difficult and even ugly.
- Going where you aren't wanted can be dangerous and even deadly.
- Evil isn't all action; indifference can be evil as well.
- Ignoring what's wrong is just as bad as doing wrong.

BOOK REPORT IDEAS
1. Discuss the connections between the fire in the past and the one in the present, showing the significance of each.
2. The dust jacket says this book explores, "the destructiveness of hatred, the evil of indifference and the power of accepting love and responsibility." Show how and when each of these things are depicted in the book, by which character, and in what situations.
3. Covert vs. overt segregation is a theme in the book. Give several examples of them and discuss each.
4. The end of this book could be called "The Beginning." If you were to write a sequel describe what happens to each of the main characters and their relationships to each other.

BOOKTALK IDEAS
1. Have Macey tell her story in first person.
2. Use old photos or newspaper stories as props for your talk.
3. Focus your talk on the two fires, the one in 1959 and the one in the church, leading up to the idea that they were deliberately set.

RISKS
- Two generations in a segregated town deny and cover up a racist crime.
- Dysfunctional and overworked parents are distant from their children.
- Austin and Macey's relationship seems far too young for fifteen-year-olds.

STRENGTHS

- Shows racism in the past and in the present.

- Graphically depicts the insidious nature of covert racism.
- Accurate picture of the steps to follow in historical research.
- Complex, multilayered characters teens can identify with.
- Ambiguous ending leaves room for individual and group speculation.
- Contrasts racism in the '50s and today, showing differences and similarities.
- Contrasts overt and covert racism and shows how both are destructive.
- Graphically depicts the evil of denial and indifference and shows how their impact can linger across generations.

AWARDS

Quick Picks for Reluctant Readers, 2000 (ALA)

REVIEWS

"Although the background on race relations sometimes threatens to overwhelm Macey and Austin's story, the plot moves along and stays right on track in this complex and thought-provoking novel. . . . deep and well-written characters." —*Voice of Youth Advocates*, 2/99, Hillary Theyer.

"This story line is strong. Clever phrasing and likable central characters enliven the story. The emotions are palpable, and the topic is important." —*School Library Journal*, 2/99, Joel Shoemaker.

"What Cooney handles best—and what readers will like most—is the tentative boy-girl relationship between Macey and Austin, and the portrayal of the sort of questioning and fervor that propels some teens to look beyond themselves and their families to larger issues." —*Booklist*, 12/98, Stephanie Zvirin.

"Cooney. . . . has risen to new heights of suspenseful storytelling with this wise and compassionate story. Teens will be riveted by the gradual revelation of the mystery, and inspired by Cooney's clear message that young people—as well as their elders—can be caught up in the apathy of 'doing nothing' about evil." —Amazon, 1999, Patty Campbell.

📖📖📖

⚏ SECTION TWO ⚏
Chinese Handcuffs to *Forged by Fire*

CHINESE HANDCUFFS. Crutcher, Chris. Greenwillow, 1990. $12.95. 202p. ISBN: 0-688-08345-5. Dell, 1996. $4.99. 220p. ISBN: 0-440-20837-8. Realistic fiction. Reading level: YHS. Interest level: YHS, OHS. P. E., Psychology, Sociology, Ethics, Sex education, English, Creative writing.

SUBJECT AREAS
abuse, physical; abuse, sexual; child abuse; animals; suicide; family relationships; self-knowledge; bullying; rites of passage; fear; crime and delinquency; death and dying; ethics; friendship; grief and mourning; love; lying and deceitfulness; peer pressure; problem parents; secrets; school; substance abuse; unwed mothers; writing; elderly.

CHARACTERS
Dillon Hemingway: he makes his own way in life, passionately believing in doing the right thing, even if he's the only person who knows that it is right

Preston Hemingway: Dillon's older brother, who shot himself in front of Dillon two years before

Dad: Dillon's father, who lives so deeply inside himself that he has driven away his wife and daughter

Mom: Dillon's mother, who lives on the other side of town with her daughter

Christy Hemingway: Dillon's little sister

Stacey Ryder: the girl Dillon has been in love with his whole life, she has always been in love with Pres

Jennifer: Dillon's friend, they are deeply connected from the moment they meet, but she has many secrets she hides from him

Mr. Caldwell: the high school principal, whom Dillon delights in tormenting any way he can

Coach Kathy Sherman: the girls' basketball coach, she helps both Dillon and Jennifer deal with their pasts and presents

Dr. Newcomb: a college professor specializing in child abuse and sexual victims and offenders

BOOKTALK

My name is Dillon Hemingway, and I'm seventeen years old. But I was only nine when Stacy caught me with Chinese handcuffs. We were at the carnival and she came up to me and shoved a woven straw cylinder stuck on the end of her index finger at me. "Stick your finger in!" I did, and discovered that I couldn't get away. No matter how hard I pulled, the cylinder just got tighter and tighter. "Chinese handcuffs," Stacy said. "Neat, huh? You have to know the secret to get out. The gypsy lady said it was the secret of life."

Well, that gypsy knew what she was talking about. The way to escape *was* one of the secrets of life—at least, of my life. In order to get my finger out of that straw tube, I had to push my finger into it, not try to pull it out. The harder I tried to get away, the more I pulled against the tube, the tighter I was trapped. The only way to get my finger out of that tube was to quit trying to escape and release the pressure.

Now I'm caught in another version of Chinese handcuffs—only the finger in the other end of the cylinder belongs to my brother Pres, who's dead. He shot himself in front of me one Saturday morning at dawn two years ago. He said he wanted to get some target practice—I didn't realize the target would be his head.

But I'm not the only one struggling to get out of an impossible situation. Jennifer is, too. She's the main lady in my life, but even though we're best friends, she's never let anything romantic get started. I couldn't figure out why 'till she told me about her Chinese handcuffs: about how first her father and now her stepfather sneak into her room late at night and molest her. She can't remember the first time it happened—she was too young, maybe only three or four. She told twice—once on her father, when she was in second grade and the teacher talked about what to do when people touch you in ways you don't like. Her mother kicked him out, but then, just a few years later, she married T.B. and it started all over again. And T.B. warned Jennifer not to tell, because if she did, he'd make her look like a fool, and then he'd kill what she loved the most. But finally she couldn't stand it any longer, and told again. And everything T.B. had predicted came true. He got out of it, made Jennifer look like a liar, and then he ran over her dog with the car. Jennifer never told again—that is, until she told me. And she made me promise never to tell anyone else, no matter what. She was scared T.B. would do more than just beat up on her mother. He might also start doing the same things to her little sister that he was doing to her. She was caught, and she couldn't get out.

Chinese handcuffs—you can't pull away, you have to give in. Can Jennifer discover how to escape? Can I?

MAJOR THEMES AND IDEAS

- No matter what the experience, never walk away empty-handed, never walk away without the lesson.
- You are not responsible for what other people do or say or think. You are responsible for yourself, and only yourself.
- Fear is fool's respect.
- The only way you can create change is to change yourself.
- Controlling yourself frees you. Trying to control people or situations outside yourself just gets you stuck and out of control.
- All you really have are your responses, your responses to yourself, and your responses to what comes in from outside.
- You can't win wars with other people. The only war you can win is the one between your ears.
- Kids have an unalienable right to unconditional care, and parents who don't give it are breaking a spiritual law.
- It's easier to live with your mistakes than to hide them or ignore them.
- If you tell the truth, especially a hard truth, people will respect you for it, whether or not they agree with it.

BOOK REPORT IDEAS

1. This book has a series of flashbacks that explain the characters' actions in the present. Compare Dillon's and Jennifer's flashbacks, and show how what happened in the past helped create the people they are now.
2. Dillon wrote letters to Pres. But was he really the person the letters were for? What function did they play in Dillon's life?
3. Speculate on what Jennifer, Dillon, and Stacy might be like five or ten years from now, and support your ideas with excerpts from the book.
4. Discuss what other instances of being caught in Chinese handcuffs might be, when someone has to do what seems wrong to get out of the situation.
5. There are several different kinds of problems in the book. Select the one that interested or affected you most, and explain why it did.

BOOKTALK IDEAS

1. Let each of the four main characters, Dillon, Jennifer, Pres, Stacey, tell their story from their own perspective.
2. Dillon's letters to Pres are a big part of the story. Pretend that Pres is responding to them, and let him write the talk.
3. It is Jennifer's situation that finally brings things to a head for Dillon. Write your talk from her point of view, either in first or third person.

RISKS

- T.B. is a sexual predator, a character who is evil to the core.
- Jennifer's mother does not protect her, her little sister, or herself.

- Stacey gets pregnant deliberately, in an attempt to draw Pres closer to her.
- Multiple instances of violence: Pres and Dillon deliberately kill Charlie the Cat, Pres commits suicide in front of his brother, Jennifer is raped by her father and stepfather.
- Several characters use drugs of various kinds.
- Pres is handicapped as a result of his drug use.
- Language is realistic and sprinkled with vulgarities.
- Dillon is less than respectful of the high school principal.
- Dillon is willing to kill T.B., or to kidnap Jennifer and her sisters, and flee to Canada.
- Adults are not portrayed as strong or positive, in all but a few instances.

STRENGTHS
- Realistic discussion of the long-term effects of sexual abuse of children.
- Realistic depiction of an intelligent and crafty rapist, and the inability of the system to help his victim.
- Coach Sherman's philosophical and down-to-earth discussions with Dillon.
- Strong characters who grow and mature and are able to cope with the situations they find themselves in.
- Several story lines that all tie together, enabling the reader to look at several different interacting situations.
- There are no pat answers to the problems presented—resolutions are appropriately lifelike.

AWARDS
Best Books for Young Adults, 1990 (ALA)
Margaret A. Edwards Award, 2000 (ALA)
100 Best Books for Teens, 2000 (ALA)

REVIEWS
"Crutcher draws the reader into the story. . . . characters think and grow, and it is through this cultivation of the inner life that we become involved with them. There may be too many harrowing incidents crammed into it, but *Chinese Handcuffs* is a rewarding novel, tough, topical, compelling, and well written. Encourage your older YAs to read it." —*Voice of Youth Advocates*, 6/89, Randy Brough.

"Crutcher's special kind of no-nonsense compassion comes through in the voices of the teenage narrators and in the few adult advocates they find. There's genuine brutality and evil. . . . but there's a fascinating and believable kind of triumph as well—both of spirit and of practical survival. . . . triumph of loyalty and risk over brutality and weakness." —*ALAN Review*, 1997, Susannah Sheffer.

⊞⊞⊞

CRAZY JACK. Napoli, Donna Jo. Delacorte Press, 1999. $15.95. 134p. ISBN: 0-385-32627-0. Laurel-Leaf Books, 2001. $5.95. 134p. ISBN: 0-440-22788-7. Thorndike Press, 2000. $20.95. 183p. ISBN: 0-786-23047-9. (large print) Recorded Books, Inc., 2000. ISBN: 0-788-74159-4. (unabridged audio) Fantasy. Reading level: MS. Interest level: MS, YHS. English, Creative writing.

SUBJECT AREAS
rites of passage; self-knowledge; problem parents; love; working; abuse, physical; occult and supernatural; family relations; death and dying; grief and mourning; illness, mental.

CHARACTERS
Jack: his life is simple and happy until his father disappears and the neighbors begin to call him crazy.
Father: Jack's father who loves to gamble
Mother: Jack's mother who struggles to make ends meet
Flora: Jack's best friend and sweetheart
Flora's Father: a cheese maker, he is kind to Jack and his mother
Flora's Mother: she loved well, but far too briefly
William: the man Flora plans to marry
The Giant: he loves his gold and has a terrible craving for fresh meat, preferably human

BOOKTALK
We all know the story of Jack and the Beanstalk, how Jack traded his last cow for a handful of magic beans; planted a beanstalk; stole the Giant's hen, harp, and gold; and chopped down the beanstalk while the giant was on it, sending him crashing to his death, while Jack and his mother lived happily ever after. That story is, and isn't, this one, and it begins long before that one did.

It begins when Jack is nine and finally old enough to help his father plant their fields. But a drought has come to this part of England, and season after season they watch as the seedlings wither away to nothing. Jack's father has always loved to gamble, and has won more frequently than lost. Now, however, his luck has dried up, and then with one final wager, he loses everything. Jack doesn't understand his father's desperation, and jokes about finding the pot of gold at the end of the rainbow and solving all their problems. That night his father climbs the sheer cliff near their home and disappears into the fog that covers its top.

Jack climbs as high as he dares calling for his father to come back. No gold is worth losing him. His father gives no sign of hearing his son, as he steps off the cliff into the foggy, white air. Jack's father is gone and Jack is left behind to regret his foolish words.

Seven years later, Jack has more than words to regret. His guilt and grief have changed him, and now he's called Crazy Jack. Every year on the anniversary of his father's disappearance, he throws himself at the cliff, trying to climb it, giving up only when he passes out from pain and exhaustion. He has no friends, and even his sweetheart refuses to marry a madman.

How can this end up with Jack living happily ever after? Follow Crazy Jack to the foot of that cliff, and find out.

MAJOR THEMES AND IDEAS
- Sooner or later, gamblers lose.
- Words, once spoken, can never be unsaid.
- Sometimes blessings come from the most unexpected sources.
- All we truly need is food on the table, a roof over our heads, and each other.
- Without love, laughter, songs, simple pleasures, life is dull, gray, and colorless.
- Grief and quietness can be seen as madness.
- Magic exists in many forms.
- Use what life gives you to create a better world.

BOOK REPORT IDEAS
1. Describe the traditional elements in the story and compare them with the more modern twists the author uses. Is the outcome of the story changed in this version? If so, how?
2. Discuss what you consider to be the main theme of the book, which stretches from the beginning of the book to its end. What message is the author attempting to convey?
3. The story has both realistic and fanciful elements. Compare and contrast them, showing how they support and further the story.
4. Explain the role of rainbows in the book and show what they symbolize. In addition, show the ways colors or lack of colors are used, and what they symbolize.

BOOKTALK IDEAS
1. Focus your talk on the first section of the book when Jack is a boy.
2. Let Flora tell the story, revealing how much she loves Jack but how frightened she is by how he has changed.
3. Include parts of the original fairy tale in your talk.
4. Use seven painted beans as a prop. You can use real dried beans, or jelly beans, just as long as they are the right colors.

RISKS

- Supernatural or magical elements—fairies, enchanted beans, hen, gold, harp are included.
- Portrayal of spousal abuse.

STRENGTHS

- Masterful retelling of an old fairy tale.
- Shows how little we really need in life and the true complexity of simplicity.

AWARDS

None

REVIEWS

"Jack finally learns to. . . . integrate the imaginative and practical sides of his own nature. The subtle highlighting of the need to work hard, yet appreciate the beauty in life unfolds throughout the story. This novel is richly detailed and well-crafted, with every image as carefully planted as one of Jack's beans." —*Voice of Youth Advocates*, 12/99 Karen Herc.

"This beautifully written novel offers something for everyone—romance, adventure, fantasy. . . . and an appealing protagonist struggling to make sense of what's really important in life." —*Booklist,* 10/1/99, Kay Weisman.

"The world Napoli creates is at once well-known and strange, as if she is telling the truth, at last, about the story's origins, and pointing the way to its later exaggerations. Her locale is one where magic works, but not too well, and where dark and psychologically truthful lives give meaning to the events of a childhood tale." —*Kirkus Reviews*, 1999.

📖📖📖

DANCING ON THE EDGE. Nolan, Han. Harcourt, 1997. $16.00. 244p. ISBN: 0-152-01648-1. Penguin Putnam, Inc., 1999. $5.99. 244p. ISBN: 0-141-30203-8. Realistic fiction. Reading level: MS. Interest level: MS, YHS. English, Creative writing, Psychology, P. E.

SUBJECT AREAS

dysfunctional families; problem parents; illness, mental; dance; grief and mourning; secrets; family relationships; lying and deceitfulness; elderly; manipulation; death and dying; suicide; poetry; therapy; racism.

CHARACTERS

Miracle McCloy: brought up to believe she's special, her father's disappearance
    when she's ten changes her whole life
Dane McCloy: Miracle's father, a novelist who hasn't been able to write since
    his wife's death
Gigi McCloy: Dane's mother, a medium, who raised Miracle
Casey and Toole Dawsey: Miracle's aunt and uncle who try to help her cope
    with Dane's disappearance
Granddaddy Opal: Gigi's ex-husband who refuses to put up with her "hocus
    pocus"
Mrs. Hewlett: she owns the gift shop where Gigi holds her séances and meets
    with her clients
Miss Emmaline Wilson: a black woman with a beautiful voice, she's a friend of
    Opal's
Mr. Eugene Wadell: a friend of Gigi's who's also a spiritualist
Dr. DeAngelis: the psychiatrist who works with Miracle after the fire

BOOKTALK

Miracle always knew she was special and different—her grandmother, Gigi, had told her so, because she'd been born after her mother had been declared dead. But no one told her the whole story about her, her mother, or her father. He was a writer and one day just disappeared. Miracle was ten when it happened, and Gigi told her he'd melted. It seemed impossible—how could he just melt? Candles melted, not people. But there his clothes were, collapsed in the middle of the floor as if he'd disappeared from inside them—melted.

And Miracle began to wonder if she was going to melt, or if she'd been the one who made him disappear. She had saved all his things, including all the bottles with candles in them that he lit when he read to her from the book he was writing. Sometimes she missed him so much, she'd sit in the center of all those lit candles, and wish so hard, over and over, that she could just melt and be with her mommy and daddy wherever they were.

And then, one day, she did.

MAJOR THEMES AND IDEAS

- You make yourself who you are. No one else can do it for you.
- What people don't understand, they usually fear.
- People who love you don't crush your hopes and dreams, but help you achieve them.

- Never measure yourself by someone else's yardstick, just your own.
- Frequently children blame themselves for things that go wrong around them, even when it's not their fault, if they don't have adults around them who will tell them the truth.
- People see what they want to see, not what is real. They also don't see what they don't want to acknowledge.
- Sharing your pain can help you heal.
- If you don't tell someone what you want, you give them the power to choose for you, instead of making the choice yourself.
- Sometimes children act out the very thing adults try to keep hidden from them.

BOOK REPORT IDEAS
1. Describe how constantly being told she was a miracle baby affected Miracle's life.
2. Discuss the idea of being invisible and how Miracle decided that she was.
3. Explore the idea of a child acting out what the adults in the family are hiding from them. Explain whether or not this makes sense to you and why.
4. Decide what the most important idea or thought in the book was, describe it, and explain why you chose it.
5. Analyze Gigi and explain why she did and said the things she did.
6. Speculate on what will happen in Miracle's future and what obstacles might lie in the way of her achieving her goals.
7. Discuss what dancing did for Miracle, even before she found out about her mother.

BOOKTALK IDEAS
1. Focus your talk on the idea of Dane melting and how that made Miracle feel.
2. Use Gigi's activities as a medium as a frame for your talk.
3. Have different characters describe Miracle, and then have Miracle describe herself.

RISKS
- Characters support themselves by pretending to do magic and helping people contact the dead.
- Manipulation of a child by an adult caretaker.
- Adults who have responsibility for a child don't care for it.

STRENGTHS
- Multidimensional characters that grow and gain insight.
- Shows the positive effects of therapy with a skilled professional.
- Shows the steps into and out of mental illness.

- Looks at the effects unreasonable expectations can have on a child who knows they can't be met.
- Powerful story line draws readers in quickly.
- Ending leaves room for individual and group reflection and speculation.

AWARDS
National Book Award for Young People's Literature, 1997
Best Books for Young Adults, 1998 (ALA)
Booklist Editors' Choice, 1997
School Library Journal, Best Books of the Year, 1997

REVIEWS
"Characters are well-drawn and have warmth in spite of [their] problems."
—*Voice of Youth Advocates,* 1997, Patricia Morrow.

"Nolan dives into the mind of an emotionally disturbed girl in an intense, exceptionally well-written novel. . . . While the characters initially seem like stereotypical Southern eccentrics, Nolan skillfully disclosed their true natures, allowing them to blossom." —*Kirkus Reviews*, 1997.

"A compelling novel with well-realized characterizations." —*Horn Book*, 1998.

ᘓᘓᘓ

DARE, TRUTH, OR PROMISE. Boock, Paula. Houghton-Mifflin Company, 1999. $15.00. 170p. ISBN: 0-395-97117-9. Realistic fiction. Reading level: MS. Interest level: MS, YHS. English, Sex education, Drama.

SUBJECT AREAS
homosexuality; friendship; love; working; cooking; family relationships; school; secrets; sex and sexuality; prejudice; drama; religion; problem parents; self-knowledge; rites of passage.

CHARACTERS
Louie: smart, self-confident, she runs the Comedy Club at Woodhaugh High School and likes to quote poetry
Willa: she wants to be a chef and just started at Burger Giant
Kevin: the manager of the Burger Giant
Joan, Kelly, Simone, Deirdre: other Burger Giant employees
Jolene: Willa's mother
Bliss: Willa's sister

Gary: Bliss's boyfriend

Sid: he runs the pub where Willa and Jolene live, and is a good friend of Jolene's

Mo: performer at the Comedy Club and is one of Louie's closest friends

Tony and Susi Angelo: Louie's parents

Marrietta, Nic: Louie's sister and brother

Cathy: Willa's ex-girlfriend

Father Campion: Louie's parish priest

BOOKTALK

Willa fell in love the moment she walked into the Burger Giant and saw Louie up to her elbows in coleslaw. But then she knew she was gay. It didn't hit Louie until a few weeks later, watching Willa at a fencing match. Suddenly she knew that for the first time in her life, she was in love.

But parents and friends and churches all tried to separate them. Life became layers of secrets, secret meetings, and brief moments alone together. Louie and Willa were sure of their love, but everyone else tried to keep them apart. Are they strong enough to fight everyone who opposes them, or will they be forced apart?

MAJOR THEMES AND IDEAS

- Falling in love is a life-changing thing.
- Love just happens. You don't plan for it; it comes from the outside and changes everything.
- A broken heart's a broken heart, whether it's gay or straight.
- Love is never evil in the eyes of God. Hatred is.
- Accepting yourself for who you are may be difficult, but it's necessary, and worth it.
- Love comes from God and to turn away from genuine love is like turning away from God.
- Being gay is not a choice or a lifestyle, it's simply who you are.

BOOK REPORT IDEAS

1. Discuss the process the three parents went through in accepting their daughters' homosexuality and explain whether or not you feel it was realistic, and why.
2. Explain and contrast the different views of homosexuality in the book, and compare them to your own view.
3. Describe your own concept of love and falling in love. Is "love at first sight" real?
4. Discuss how realistically Louie, Willa, and Cathy are portrayed as gay teens trying to come to grips with the fact of their homosexuality.

BOOKTALK IDEAS

1. Write your talk in first person, from either Willa's or Louie's perspective or from both.
2. Focus your talk on both girls' reactions when they met for the first time.
3. Write your talk as a description of a love story, revealing only at the end that it's a story about two girls.

RISKS

*   Portrays an intimate, sexual relationship between two girls.
*   Teens are seen as sexually active.
*   Language, while realistic, contains obscenities.
*   Priest does not condemn homosexuality.

STRENGTHS

*   Multiple perspectives lend depth and complexity to the story.
*   Powerful love story has much to say about *any* kind of love, gay or straight.
*   Homosexuality presented nonjudgmentally.
*   Realistic characters teens can identify with.
*   Positive ending gives hope for the future.
*   Realistic portrayal of families learning that one of their members is gay.

AWARDS

New Zealand Post Children's Book Award, 1998.
Lambda Literary Awards, 2000

REVIEWS

"Louie's parish priest stands out for his open, embracing view of love. The differing voices of family and friends show a realistic slice of personal views. The casual and breezy writing rings true, accurately reflecting the age and maturity of the young women . . . there is a strong sense of place and time." —*Voice of Youth Advocates,* 10/99, Marian Rafal.

"Both Louie and Willa are nicely articulated, and . . . the emotions ring true . . . sexuality is sensitively yet realistically portrayed. Boock's courageous confrontation of the issues of homosexuality and religion, unique characters, and a talent for truth set this novel apart." —*School Library Journal,* 11/99, Jennifer A. Fakolt.

"The descriptions of the girls' attraction and longings are authentically rendered. Lesbian readers will see themselves, and straight readers will see what gay teens already know—that the feelings of young love are the same for everyone." —*Horn Book,* 9-10/99, J.M.B.

ᚋᚋᚋ

DEEP WATERS. Herman, John. Philomel, 1998. $17.99. 198p. ISBN: 0-399-23235-4. Reading level: MS. Interest level: MS. P. E., English, Ethics.

SUBJECT AREAS
sports; peer pressure; manipulation; self-knowledge; friendship; secrets; death and dying; bullying; revenge; rites of passage; intimidation; mystery and suspense; crime and delinquency.

CHARACTERS
Andy Schlesinger: small and skinny, he's good at running and swimming
Brad: one of Andy's bunkmates, he's good at sports, is a bully, and is very competitive
Tim: also Andy's bunkmate, he's the bunk nerd, fat, soft-looking, and wimpy
Dave: tall, friendly, he's kind of a whiner and bunks next to Andy
Ralph Dowdy: tent 10's bunk counselor
Tony Snow: Andy's swimming counselor, he's smart, into science and nature, and is older than the other counselors
Johnny Marsh: he's the coolest and most handsome counselor and the hero of the swimming area
Julian Pascal: an excellent swimmer who can't play basketball because he's lame, he and Andy become friends
Marsha Peters: also a swimming counselor for the girls, beautiful, nice and engaged to Tony
Carly: Andy's girlfriend, she's taller and older than he is, and a leader among the girls

BOOKTALK
I've written this book like it was a story, but it isn't. It really happened to me two years ago, and it has changed every moment of my life since then. Maybe there are patterns in life you can't escape. Maybe things happen for a reason. Maybe they just happen. I don't know. Maybe if I'd done something sooner, it would have been different—and maybe that's not true. But what I do know is that there's no way to turn back time and fix what went wrong. It's broken and it will always be broken. And I have to find a way to live with that.

That summer I was looking forward to being at Camp Winasauku. My older brother Doug had told me all about it.

The other guys in my tent were fairly okay, and even though I was short and skinny, I was good at running and swimming. But I was lousy at basketball, which is why Dowdy, our tent counselor, fixed it so that I could swim instead.

That may have been the turning point that started it all. That's the reason I got to know Tony and Johnny and Marsha. That's the reason Julian and I got to be friends. It was Julian who told me that even though Marsha and Tony were engaged, she and Johnny had gone together last summer. I couldn't imagine dumping someone like Johnny, who was the best swimmer and diver, the all-around best counselor, and handsome on top of it all, for someone like Tony. Tony was okay, a good teacher and into science, a nice guy, and an okay counselor, but Johnny was Johnny.

I wonder what would've happened if we hadn't started trying to get Johnny and Marsha back together, but I'll never know. All I know is what we did, what happened because of it, and what I'll have to live with for the rest of my life.

MAJOR THEMES AND IDEAS
- Bullies want to be the best, but they're afraid they can't be, and don't dare let anyone know it.
- Once a pattern of events has been set in motion, it can be difficult or impossible to stop.
- You are not responsible for what anyone else says or does. We are all free to make our own decisions in life, and are the only ones responsible for the results of those decisions.
- Sometimes you can judge a book by its cover—but not always.
- You can't go back and change what you did in the past, you just have to deal with the results.
- Just because you know the difference between right and wrong doesn't mean you'll always choose right.
- You are the sum total of all you do and think.

BOOK REPORT IDEAS
1. Discuss what Andy told the camp director and the effects that his confession had.
2. Manipulation is a major theme in this book. Discuss who manipulated whom and why.
3. Explain the significance of Andy's dream of falling.
4. Analyze Marsha and explain why she broke up with Johnny and started dating Tony.

BOOKTALK IDEAS
1. Write a plot summary booktalk leading up to Andy's discovery that Marsha and Johnny went together the previous summer.
2. Focus your talk on the mystery of why Marsha dumped Johnny and the plan to get them back together.

RISKS
- Language is realistic but vulgar.
- Manipulative characters' manipulations go unpunished.

- Brief nudity in some scenes.

STRENGTHS
- Poses a variety of ethical questions.
- Ambiguous ending allows for in-depth analysis and group discussion.
- Strong, multidimensional characters gain insight from their problems.

AWARDS
None

REVIEWS
"In the end, the reader is left with Andy's examination of morality and what he can live with, or more correctly, what choice he could not live with. The world will never look the same to him, and maybe not to the reader, either. The sinister cover art, short chapters, and engrossing story will attract, hold, and remain with readers." —*Voice of Youth Advocates*, 4/99, Judy Ehrenstein

"Documents Andy's coming of age and understanding by slowly peeling back layers that will keep teens turning pages while questioning their own morals and motivations . . . chronicles a teen Everyman and his painful discovery of a world that has lost its shine." —Amazon, 1998, Jennifer Hubert.

"Grim and fascinating, the novel explores morality through Andy's rich inner conflict rather than contrived plot twists. In the end . . . the disturbingly vivid pictures it reveals about humanity will leave readers, like Andy, 'uncomfortable—disgusted and curious at the same time.'" —*Booklist*, 9/15/98, Roger Leslie.

"Dark coming-of-age novel. . . . The sense of impending doom and the implication that there's more going on than Andy is revealing keep the reader engaged to the end." —*Horn Book*, 1998.

📖📖📖

A DOOR NEAR HERE. Quarles, Heather. Delacorte Press, 1998. $13.95. 231p. ISBN: 0-385-32595-9. Laurel-Leaf Books, 2000. $4.50. 240p. ISBN: 0-440-22761-5. Thorndike Press, 2000. $21.95. 323p. ISBN: 0-786-22884-9. Realistic fiction. Reading level: MS. Interest level: MS, YHS. English, Psychology.

SUBJECT AREAS
substance abuse; problem parents; divorce; child abuse; family relationships; survival; rites of passage; self-knowledge; secrets; school; love.

CHARACTERS
Katherine Graham: she takes care of her three younger siblings because her father's gone and her mother stays drunk

Douglas: at fourteen, a year younger than Katherine, he's a genius at fixing things

Tracey: thirteen years old and very self-centered

Alisa: a third grader looking for a door into Narnia

Suzanne Donovan/Mom: their alcoholic mother who seldom gets out of bed

Dale/Dad: their father who left ten years ago

Ophelia: their stepmother

Chandler, Miranda: Dad and Ophelia's children

Edith Barnes: Alisa's teacher

Mr. Dodgson: the religion teacher

Miriam Haley: the elementary school principal

BOOKTALK
The harder Katherine tried to make it work, the more difficult it got. Her mother never had been much of a mother, so she and her brother and sisters had been forced to learn to take care of themselves. Their mom always drank a lot, but until a couple of months ago she had a job, so she just couldn't go to bed and stay there. After she got fired, she quit doing anything but drinking and sleeping. Bills didn't get paid, things around the house didn't get fixed, and because Katherine was fifteen and the oldest, she ended up being the one trying to keep them all together, and not let anyone know how bad things had gotten.

Their parents had been divorced for ten years, and their dad had a new wife and kids. Katherine knew that if it had just been her and Tracey and Douglas, they could have lived with them. But all three of them were determined not to leave Alisa behind. She'd been born two years after the divorce, when their mom was dating a lot of men. No one knew who her father was, and the three older kids had brought her up a lot more than their mom had. They wouldn't give her up, and she was the reason they were trying to make it on their own.

But Katherine found out the hard way that the lies they'd constructed so carefully were no more than a house of cards, just waiting for a gust of wind to topple it over. The morning the pipes under the sink broke, and she sliced open her hand making everyone's lunches, and Alisa wrote her letter to C.S. Lewis, who wrote *The Chronicles of Narnia*, was the morning that house of cards began to fall apart.

MAJOR THEMES AND IDEAS
- It's difficult for kids to survive without parents or other care-giving adults.

- Lies can backfire on you in ways you never anticipated or imagined.
- Keeping your family together may be the most important thing in life.
- Sometimes the best thing to do is not the easiest or most comfortable.
- Desperation frequently leads to mistakes.
- It's usually best to tell the truth even when it's painful.
- When you betray someone, you can't expect them to continue to treat you with love and respect. But sometimes they do anyway.

BOOK REPORT IDEAS
1. Both Dale and Suzanne are examples of dysfunctional parents. Discuss which one was the more negative parent and explain why.
2. Examine the character of Mr. Dodgson and the role he played in the book, and show how the children's perceptions of him changed over time.
3. Alisa believed Narnia and Aslan were real. Mr. Dodgson told her and Katherine that he believed that Aslan was real. Explain the differences and the similarities between their statements of belief.
4. Loyalty, trust, and faith are major themes of the book. Explain how the main characters (the four children, their parents, Ms. Haley, and Mr. Dodgson) do and do not show these traits.

BOOKTALK IDEAS
1. Write your talk as a newspaper or TV press release.
2. Have each of the children introduce themselves and the situation. Be sure to take their ages and personalities into consideration, and let Katherine speak last, focusing on her determination to keep her family together.
3. Use the first chapter of the book as your talk, showing that despite Katherine's efforts her situation is spinning out of control.

RISKS
- Parents are alcoholic, neglectful, promiscuous, distant, uninvolved, and adulterous.
- Teens smoke.

STRENGTHS
- Multidimensional characters that teens can identify with.
- Realistic ending doesn't sugarcoat what has happened.
- Realistic portrayal of children trying to survive essentially alone.

AWARDS
Best Books for Young Adults, 1999 (ALA)

REVIEWS

"The story is a crusade for survival and a desperate attempt to avoid separate foster homes. . . . It is a sad, powerful and compelling first novel that ends on a note of hope." ——*Voice of Youth Advocates*, 10/98, Diane Tuccillo.

"All four children are quirky, memorable characters, and readers will root for them from beginning to the end. Heartbreaking and beautifully written." —*School Library Journal*, 11/98, Miranda Doyle.

"A painful, authentic story of a family whose children are left in limbo. . . . it remains hopeful because of the children's sheer tenacity and deep love and support for one another. Quarles refuses to compromise her novel with an unrealistically happy ending: although adults eventually take charge, life is only a little better for everyone concerned." —*Booklist*, 9/1/98, Frances Bradburn.

ꙮꙮꙮ

DOVEY COE. Dowell, Frances O'Roark. Atheneum, 2000. $16.00. 192p. ISBN: 0-689-83174-9. Realistic fiction. Reading level: MS. Interest level: MS, YHS. English, Ethics, Sociology.

SUBJECT AREAS

legal system; family relationships; self-knowledge; ethics; mystery and suspense; love; rites of passage; secrets; death and dying; crime and juvenile delinquency.

CHARACTERS

Dovey Coe: a twelve-year-old girl charged with murder
Caroline Coe: Dovey's big sister
Parnell Caraway: son of the richest man in town, he has a streak of mean in him, and is determined to marry Caroline
Homer Caraway: Parnell's father who owns the dry goods store in town
John Coe: Dovey's father, a jack-of-all-trades
Ames Coe: Dovey's thirteen-year-old brother
Mrs. Coe/Mama: Dovey's mother who's trying to make her into a young lady
Wilson Brown: he's sweet on Dovey
Thomas G. Harding: Dovey's lawyer
Sheriff Douglas: the law in Indian Creek
Judge Young: the judge at Dovey's trial
Tobias Jarrell: the prosecuting attorney

BOOKTALK

I didn't kill Parnell Caraway, no matter what I said about him or even to him; I didn't touch one hair on his scheming, weasly head! And all those folks in town who're acting like Parnell was some kinda saint just cause he's dead—I don't know what's got into them. There ain't a person in Indian Creek, 'cept maybe his family, who didn't believe Parnell was the meanest, vainest, greediest man who ever lived. Seventeen years old and rotten to the core. But just 'cause I couldn't stand him doesn't mean I killed him. I might have thought of it a time or two, but I didn't do it.

But telling the truth didn't make any difference to Sheriff Douglas, he still arrested me and said I had to go to trial. The way everyone saw it, I had to have killed Parnell.

Now I got a little time before the trial, so if you'll have a seat on the porch here, I'll tell you how this whole mess came about, and you can decide how you'd vote if you were on my jury: for Dovey Coe or against her.

MAJOR THEMES AND IDEAS

- Money alone won't make you happy or satisfied.
- Part of a parent's job is to raise their children to make their own decisions about what's right or wrong, even if the parent doesn't agree with it.
- If you see yourself as rich and someone else sees you as poor, that's their problem not yours.
- Don't get mad at someone for failing to see you as more than a pretty face when you use your beauty to get what you want.
- Speaking before you think can be dangerous.
- Hard times show you who your friends really are.
- Sometimes there are good reasons for keeping secrets.

BOOK REPORT IDEAS

1. Discuss the concept of truth as it is seen in this book. Include not only the final truth that Dovey decided not to share, but also other instances when someone decided either to lie or keep quiet.
2. Compare the Coes and the Caraways, including the values and ethics each set of parents taught their children.
3. Speculate on what might have happened if Amos had confessed. Explain whether or not you think he would have been tried for Parnell's death or sent away as Dovey believed he would.
4. Several characters, at different times, spoke in haste only to repent later on. Had they thought before speaking, how might their story have been different.

BOOKTALK IDEAS

1. Focus your talk on the first page of the book when we learn how Dovey feels about Parnell, and then briefly describe the scene in the store, ending with Dovey's realization that he's dead.
2. Center your talk around the relationship between Parnell and Caroline, and on how angry Dovey was about it, and how determined she was to stop it.
3. Let Dovey introduce the story just as she does in the book.

RISKS

- Language is realistic but vulgar.
- Family decides to keep their knowledge of a crime secret.
- Negative assumptions are made about a handicapped child.

STRENGTHS

- Dialect and characters' voices are realistic.
- Central characters are strong and independent.
- Powerful portrait of a supportive, functional family.
- Demonstrates that happiness comes from within, not from money.
- Fast moving plot has an unexpected ending.

AWARDS

Edgar Allen Poe Award, 2001

REVIEWS

"Feisty voice of the female narrator carries this story. . . . positive messages about family pride, self reliance, and inner beauty. Dovey's strength of character alone is worth the read." ——*Voice of Youth Advocates*, 2000, Nick Spencer.

"Dowell has created a memorable character in Dovey. . . . Her need to protect her deaf brother, Amos, and Caroline (and even her daddy) from smarmy Parnell is funny, painful, and ultimately terrifying. . . . this is a delightful book, thoughtful and full of substance." —*Booklist*, 5/1/00, Frances Bradburn.

"Dovey's fresh, clear voice in southern dialect cuts through the social behavior of the locale and time period to speak the truth. . . . this fabulously feisty heroine will win your heart." —*Kirkus Reviews*, 2000.

"An impeccably drawn heroine, complete with southern dialect, sturdy self-esteem, and down-home wisdom." —Amazon, 2000, Emilie Coulter.

DOWNSIDERS. Shusterman, Neal. Simon and Schuster, 1999. $16.95. 246p. ISBN: 0-689-80375-3. Simon and Schuster, 2000. $4.99. 256p. ISBN: 0-689-83969-3. Library Reproduction Services, 2000. $29.95. 336p. ISBN: 1-581-18071-3. (large print) Science fiction, satire. Reading level: YHS. Interest level: YHS, OHS. English, History, Government, Sociology.

SUBJECT AREAS
friendship; family relationships; humor; cultural identity; problem parents; war secrets; survival; self-knowledge; rites of passage; love; politics; fear; mythology; prejudice.

CHARACTERS
The Downsiders
Talon Angler: a fourteen-year-old Downsider who is intrigued by the Topside
Railborn Skinner: a Downsider who hates Topsiders and needs to learn compassion
Gutta: Talon and Railborn's partner who calls things as she sees them
Pidge Angler: Talon's little sister who is very ill
Skeet Skinner: Railborn's father

The Topsiders
Lindsay Matthais: a Topsider who is moving to New York to live with her father
Todd Matthias: Lindsay's stepbrother whom Lindsay can't stand because he is cruel and conscienceless
Mark Matthias: Todd's stepfather and Lindsay's father, he has spoiled his son and ignored his daughter
The Champ/Reginald Champlain: an eighty-seven-year-old man who lives in the shell of an abandoned city pool, which connects the Topside and the Downside, while he lives between them
Becky Peckerling: a girl Lindsay goes to school with who is determined to be her friend

BOOKTALK
We've all heard the urban legends about New York City—about the alligators in the sewers, the homeless who live in forgotten subway tunnels, the rats that grow as large as dogs—but what if they weren't legends? What if they were true?

Robert Gunderson is about to find out. He's nineteen years old, homeless, and ready to die, when he jumps down onto the subway tracks under Grand Central Station and walks down a long dark tunnel. But when he's finally facing the train, he can't do it, and leaps to one side, clinging to a steel beam as the train rushes by.

Three figures appear out of the darkness and a boy demands to know his name. When he tells them, a flashlight comes on, and he sees instead of the dirty, homeless, vicious tunnel-rats he'd expected to see, something entirely different. The three kids, a girl and two boys, aren't dirty at all. Their hair is shaved around their ears, but long everywhere else, hanging down their backs. Their clothing is made of hundreds of bits of patchwork, and they wear metallic cuffs on their wrists and ankles. Even their flashlight is strange—its face is oblong instead of round, and the shaft swirled with red and green patterns. It looks ancient and almost holy.

Robert Gunderson does not know it but he is about to enter another world, a world that exists far below the New York streets where he spent much of his life. It's called the Downside, and Robert Gunderson will spend the rest of his life there.

What is the Downside? Why do its residents hate and fear those who live on the surface? Slip through a sewer grate, into the maze of tunnels underneath New York City, and find out.

MAJOR THEMES AND IDEAS
- We all take our own worlds for granted most of the time because they are familiar to us. It takes an outsider to help us rediscover their beauty.
- People frequently see what they choose.
- Little of value is achieved without effort and sacrifice.
- A secret that could make people think less of themselves is a secret better kept than told.
- What's right and logical in one culture is inexplicable in another.
- Determination to do the right thing and creative thinking can overcome most obstacles.
- Asking "what if?" is futile. Instead concentrate on dealing with what *is*.
- Cultures do change, but they must do it in their own time and at their own pace.
- The way we die is the way we are remembered—which may be when we are at our worst, rather than our best.
- Every culture has skeletons in its closet that it wants to keep hidden.

BOOK REPORT IDEAS
1. Compare the Topside and the Downside to two actual cultures or subcultures that live very close together but do not interact.
2. Re-create the legends Beach and his followers created, and show how they defined Downside culture.
3. Speculate on how long it will take for the Downsiders to rebuild their culture to the extent that they will be able to interact with the Topsiders, and explain the rationale for your reasoning.
4. Compare the ethics of the Topside and the Downside.
5. Describe members of each culture from the other culture's perspective.

6. If you could choose to be either a Topsider or a Downsider, which would you choose? Describe the characteristics of the culture that were the reason for your choice.

BOOKTALK IDEAS
1. Use the scene of the first faller as the focus of your talk.
2. Center your talk on the differences between the two cultures.
3. Use a sock as a prop for your talk, or wear your watch on your ankle.
4. Describe Lindsay and Talon and have them introduce each other.

RISKS
- Some of the parents are distant and uninvolved in their children's lives.
- Portrayal of teen substance abuse.
- U.S. culture and ethics described negatively.

STRENGTHS
- Views cultures from both the inside and the outside.
- Incorporates urban legends and historical fact into the story.
- Examines how we perceive people from other cultures, when we know nothing about that culture, and when we have had a chance to experience it firsthand.
- Shows how cultures grow, develop, and change.
- Multidimensional characters teens can identify with.
- Shows power of love, friendship, and courage.
- Mixture of satire and fantasy.

AWARDS
Best Books for Young Adults, 2000 (ALA)
Quick Picks for Reluctant Readers, 2000 (ALA)

REVIEWS
"Shusterman has invented an alternate world in the Downside that is both original and humorous. . . . His city detail is dead-on, especially his description of the subway smell. . . . this novel will be read by more than just fantasy and science fiction fans." —*Voice of Youth Advocates*, 8/99, Jennifer Hubert.

"A good deal of sophisticated social satire, as Topside is seen through naive underworld eyes. . . . this is an exciting and entertaining story that will please fans of adventure, science fiction, and fantasy." —*School Library Journal*, 7/99, Bruce Anne Shook.

"Twines suspense and satire through this ingenious tale. . . . the pace never flags." —*Kirkus Reviews*, 1999.

📖📖📖

DREAMLAND. Dessen, Sarah. Viking, 2000. $15.99. 280p. ISBN: 0-670-89122-3. Realistic fiction. Reading level: MS. Interest level: MS, YHS, OHS. Sex education, English, Art, Photography.

SUBJECT AREAS

dysfunctional families; abuse, physical; abuse, substance; friendship; illness, mental; secrets; runaways; dating and social life; stereotypes; sports; peer pressure; lying and deceitfulness; anger; therapy; family relationships; writing; survival.

CHARACTERS

Caitlin O'Koren: her life changes when her perfect sister runs away
Cass O'Koren: she runs away with her boyfriend instead of going to Yale
Adam: Cass's boyfriend
Margaret O'Koren: Cass and Caitlin's mother, she falls apart when Cass leaves
Jack O'Koren: Cass and Caitlin's father, he's a university Dean of Students, and is rather distant and controlling
Boo and Stewart Connell: the O'Korens' next-door neighbors and college professors
Rina Swain: Caitlin's best friend who's gorgeous, rich, and loyal
Rogerson Biscoe: the guy Caitlin falls for
Bill Skerrit: football quarterback and Rina's boyfriend
Chelsea Robbins, Eliza Drake, Lindsay White, Kelly Brandt, Melinda Trudale: members of the cheerleading squad
Jack: another of Rina's boyfriends
Bobbi Biscoe: Rogerson's mother, a real estate agent
Rogerson Biscoe Sr.: Rogerson's father, a corporate executive
Corina and Dave: Rogerson's friends who become Caitlin's also
Dr. Marshall: Caitlin's doctor at Evergreen Care Center

BOOKTALK

Cass was an athlete, Prom Queen, Homecoming Queen, popular, smart, and the best at anything she did. And at eighteen, only a few weeks from going to Yale, she ran away on her little sister's sixteenth birthday, and Caitlin's life changed forever. Her parents were still as focused on Cass as they always had been, and she was just as invisible. Her best friend, Rina, persuaded her to try out for cheerleader, and even though Caitlin hated cheerleading as much as Rina loved it, they both made the squad. Her mother immediately started organizing Caitlin's life the way she had Cass's. For a while, the hole Cass had left in the family began to close, but as it did, the hole inside Caitlin began to grow. She'd always felt overshadowed by Cass, and had hoped for a chance to find her own way. Becoming a Cass substitute wasn't finding her own way.

Then she met Rogerson—older, puzzling, handsome, magnetic, *dangerous* Rogerson. Someone outside her circle, outside her life. Someone Cass would never have dated. Someone Cass would never have fallen for and stayed with, even after she knew she shouldn't. But that's exactly what Caitlin did. She was finally finding her own way, but was she on the right path or the wrong one?

MAJOR THEMES AND IDEAS

- Don't lose yourself in meeting other people's expectations.
- It's hard to live in someone's shadow, unable to step away and make your own shadow.
- It's never okay for someone to hit you, and it's never your fault.
- Friendships are made up of differences and similarities, knowing each other's flaws and weaknesses and being comfortable with them.
- Knowing people too well when they don't want to be known can be dangerous.
- Avoiding your problems only makes them worse.
- Wanting to be someone else doesn't work. You have to figure out who you are and how to be that person.
- In order to like yourself and your life, you have to accept everything that is in your past, both good and bad.
- Peace is being able to love and accept yourself.

BOOK REPORT IDEAS

1. Compare Cass and Caitlin, showing how they were alike and different. Be sure to include the letters they wrote to each other and their relationships with their parents.
2. Analyze Rogerson's background and personality, showing why he was an abuser and looking at the odd quirks in his personality and behavior, including the contrast between his gentleness and his violence toward Caitlin. Was there a pattern to his violence that wasn't dependent on her actions?
3. Caitlin retreated to a dreamland for much of the book. Discuss what caused her to do it and how she got there.
4. Examine the examples of friendship in the book and how those friendships were formed and nourished.
5. Look at the role photography played in the book and how it helped Caitlin retain her sense of self.
6. Speculate on what might have happened if Caitlin had told her parents the first time Rogerson hit her. Base your comments on what has happened in the book up to that point and the relationships between Caitlin and Rogerson and Caitlin and her parents at that time.

7. Looking at the book as a whole, decide what its most important theme is, and explain your rationale for your choice.

BOOKTALK IDEAS

1. Use a black and white photo of a girl, torn up and pieced together as a prop for your talk. Other props could be a toy shovel, a Barbie doll, or a camera.
2. Write your talk as Caitlin, and describe Rogerson and her relationship to him, ending with a description of the scene when Caitlin saw Rogerson's father abuse him, as a foreshadowing of her abuse. (Do *not* include her abuse in your talk. That needs to come as a surprise to the reader.)
3. Do a plot summary booktalk ending when Caitlin walked out of the party with Rogerson.

RISKS

- Depicts an intimate and physically/mentally abusive relationship.
- Single father is mentally and physically abusive to his son.
- Shows the effects of mental illness.
- Parents are distant and uninvolved.
- Shows teen drug abuse and sexuality.
- Manipulation of one character by another.

STRENGTHS

- Characters survive their crises and are able to learn from them.
- Frighteningly accurate picture of an abusive relationship.
- Shows the strengths of women's friendships.
- Vivid description of what goes on in the mind of a victim of abuse.
- Characters teens can identify with.
- Powerful, intense writing style involves the reader from the beginning.
- Characters are multidimensional, even the abusers.
- Shows how damaged relationships have to be rebuilt slowly.
- Characters realize they have to accept all aspects of themselves to find wholeness and peace.

AWARDS

Best Books for Young Adults, 2000 (ALA)
Booklist Editors' Choice, 2000

REVIEWS

"Dessen masterfully traces the evolution of an abusive relationship in yet another breathtaking novel. . . . She evokes the various masquerades of love through the couples in the novel. . . . In examining the question of how much must be sacrificed to maintain a romantic relationship, Dessen has created a compassionate novel that examines how wrong love can go." —*Voice of Youth Advocates*, 10/00, Diane Masla.

"Intense, exhausting tale. . . . Dessen's characters are familiar but not entirely typecast, which adds flavor to their interactions. . . [Caitlin's] descent and recovery come in believable stages, and though Rogerson is definitely the villain here, the author gives readers reason to spare a dash (a very small dash) of sympathy for him, too." —*Kirkus Reviews*, 2000.

"A subtle and compelling work. . . . a story rich with symbolism, dark scenes of paralyzing dread, quirky. . . . memorable characters, and gleams of humor. With . . . . consummate skill and psychological depth. . . . she explores the search for self-identity, the warmth of feminine friendships, and the destructive ways our society sets up young women for love gone wrong." —Amazon, 2000, Patty Campbell.

📖📖📖

DRIVE. Wieler, Diana. Groundwood Books, 1998. $15.95. 246p. ISBN: 0-888-99347-1. Groundwood Books, 1998. $5.95. 246p. ISBN: 0-888-99348-X. Realistic fiction. Reading level: MS. Interest level: MS, YHS. Music, English, Creative writing.

SUBJECT AREAS
sports; working; self-knowledge; family relationships; rites of passage; secrets; music; lying and deceitfulness; sex and sexuality; substance abuse; writing.

CHARACTERS
Jens Frieson: an eighteen-year-old with the drive to succeed
Daniel Frieson: a sixteen-year-old with a $5000 problem
Jack Lahanni: car dealership owner who gave Jens more than one chance
Karl Frieson: Jens and Daniel's father, "The Window Man"
Mariette Friesan: Jens and Daniel's mother who has a terrible secret
Mozen Kruse: the record producer Daniel owes money to
Chris Butler: a football player from a nearby town, he egged Jens into a fight
    that changed his life

BOOKTALK
Jens couldn't believe it: one minute he had a truck, a job, and an apartment; the next he had nothing. And shortly after that, his songwriting, blues playing, younger brother showed up with a $5000 problem. But Jens had drive—he

hadn't been a wide receiver and the chocolate sales king in his high school for nothing. He talked Daniel's record producer into giving them two weeks to come up with the money, got the crate of tapes Daniel had agreed to sell, forgot to return the truck to the car dealership he'd just been fired from, and conned their parents into letting him and Daniel go on a camping trip.

But they weren't going camping—they were going on the road. Jens had sold chocolate and cars, he could sell his brother's tapes too. And he did. Daniel was to blues guitar what Jens was to sales. Jens was stunned—Daniel was brilliant. However, not even brilliance could cover up the problems between them, the anger Daniel has felt since Jens kicked him out of their room years before, and the terrible secret that was the reason Jens rejected his own brother. It was a secret that had eaten Jens up inside for years and when they were on the road, just the two of them, it was a secret that nearly killed them both.

MAJOR THEMES AND IDEAS

- Being a family isn't always about sharing the same blood.
- Hurting someone else because you're in pain doesn't help either of you.
- Parents aren't perfect; they just do their best. Sometimes that's enough, but not always.
- If you want something badly enough and are willing to work for it, you can usually get it—but not always.
- Facing up to your mistakes is essential. It helps you restore your self-respect and others' respect in you.
- Figure out what your talent is and go for it—use your bliss.
- Some truths don't really need to be told.

BOOK REPORT IDEAS

1. Discuss the relationship between Jens and Daniel, both before and after Jens learned his mother's secret. Include how it changed on the road and how it might be in the future.
2. Marietta's secret and her preference for Daniel controlled the relationships in the family to a great extent. Explain how the family might have been different had she told her sons the truth earlier, before Jens could find it out on his own.
3. Explain why Jen's drive is important to him. Show how he uses it to define and protect himself.

BOOKTALK IDEAS

1. Let Jens tell his own story of how he went from chocolate king to car salesman to tape salesman, leading up to their going on the road.
2. Focus your talk on the two fights Jens had and how they changed his life. Lead up to, but don't reveal, his mother's secret.

3. Use a tape of blues music as a soundtrack, with a tape cover similar to Daniel's as a prop.

RISKS
- Sexual scene between a woman and a sixteen-year-old boy.
- Promiscuity leads to questions about a boy's biological father.
- Teens are shown drinking.

STRENGTHS
- Shows power of forgiveness.
- Characters mature and gain insight.
- Portrays parents that love and support their sons.
- Strong family and sibling ties endure in spite of conflict.

AWARDS
McNally Robinson Book for Young People Awards, 1998

REVIEWS
"Wieler uses metaphors and imagery to orchestrate this tale of coming-of-age and acceptance. . . . delicately deal[s] with issues of teenage sexuality and the realization that good parents are capable of making bad choices. . . . In the end, there is great comfort in realizing that you can go home again." —*Voice of Youth Advocates*, 7/99, Cheryl Karp Ward.

"An intense story of two young men testing themselves against the world— together and alone. Older teens, and particularly fans of Rob Thomas's *Rats Saw God*, will be entranced, intrigued, and enlightened." —Amazon, 1999, Patty Campbell.

"A tight, mesmerizing story with many complex threads, including undercurrents of violence and barely suppressed angst. . . . Gritty language and sexual situations abound but are never gratuitous." —*Booklist*, 5/1/99, Debbie Carton.

📖📖📖

EIGHT SECONDS. Ferris, Jean. Harcourt Brace, 2000. $17.00. 192p. ISBN: 0-152-02367-4. Realistic fiction. Reading level: MS. Interest level: MS, YHS. English, P. E., Sex education.

SUBJECT AREAS

homosexuality; sports; friendship; prejudice; peer pressure; family relationships; bullying; anger; love; rites of passage; stereotypes; self-knowledge; secrets.

CHARACTERS

John Ritchie: an eighteen-year-old high school junior because of his sixth grade heart surgery, he wants to be a rodeo bull rider

Bobby Bryant: John's best friend who goes to rodeo school with him as a roper

Marty, Caroline: John's older sisters

Kelsey: John's girlfriend who wants to get married

Sally, Clemmie: John's younger sisters

Russ Millard: a bully who picks on John and wants to be a pro bull rider

Mom: John's mother who always seems to expect him to be a problem

Dad: John's father who encourages John to do anything he wants to and offers to send him to rodeo school

Kit Crowe: a bull rider, he rooms with Bobby, John, and Matt at rodeo school and is openly gay

Matt Strauss: a university student, he wants to be a roper

Tyler Thompson: the owner of the rodeo school

BOOKTALK

The summer I was eighteen was the best and worst summer of my life. It was the summer I learned to ride rodeo bulls, the summer I met Kit, and the summer that my life changed forever.

It was just a few weeks into the summer when Dad surprised me by sending me to rodeo school. Bobby, my best friend, was going too, but so was Russ, a bully who lived to pick fights, and I was one of his favorite targets. I can fight as good as anyone, but I just don't enjoy it as much as Bobby and Russ do. Mom's all the time getting on me about needing to just walk away, but sooner or later Russ's smartass mouth gets to me, and all I can see is a red haze and that's it.

I was just hoping that at rodeo school Russ would find a new target and stay away from me. And he did, Kit, another bull rider like Russ and me, and one of my roommates. But Kit was cool and smart and didn't let Russ egg him into a fight; although he did stand up for himself. Kit was different from anyone I'd known—handsome, cool, sure of himself. I couldn't believe we were actually getting to be friends.

You know, before I went to rodeo school, I didn't think eight seconds was all that long. That was before I knew just how endless it seemed when you're on the back of a bull or facing a friend, when you've just found out exactly why he's always seemed so different from everyone else.

MAJOR THEMES AND IDEAS

- Labeling people makes you stop seeing them as individuals.

- Analyzing and agonizing over something can make it seem a lot more complex than it really is.
- When someone hassles you, and you stay cool and smart and don't let him make you angry enough to fight, you're the real winner.
- Not everything is forgivable, sometimes sorry isn't enough.
- Understanding yourself is far more difficult than understanding someone else.
- Bullies prefer to stick their knives in your back—it's safer that way.
- Trust, once broken, is difficult and sometimes impossible to rebuild.
- Actions really do speak louder than words.
- Some things cannot be forgiven.

BOOK REPORT IDEAS
1. Compare the fights that John gets into and explain why he fought them, especially the two final ones with Kit and Russ.
2. Analyze John's personality and character, and explain why he reacted so violently and intensely to the gossip about his being gay.
3. Analyze Kit, his beliefs and his actions, and explain why he was so absolute in his rejection of John at the hospital. It is likely they will meet in the future, either at rodeos, in town, or at college. Describe how you think Kit would act.
4. When Kit's sister tells him that guys who hate gays are really wondering about their own orientation, he says it BS, that some guys are just haters. Discuss your own opinion on this and the emotions behind it.
5. While Bobby can accept that Kit, a stranger, is gay, he is horrified about the rumors that John, who has always been his best friend, is also. Discuss how you think he will react when he discovers the rumors are true.
6. Speculate about what John's senior year will be like at home and at school, whether he will share his secret in either place, and what will happen if he does.

BOOKTALK IDEAS
1. Have characters introduce themselves and/or talk about each other to set up the plot and situations. John, Bobby, Kit, Matt, and Russ can all show different perspectives of the story.
2. Write a first-person talk as John, leading up to his discovery that Kit is gay.
3. Focus your talk on the idea of feeling different and how everyone feels different in one way or another.

RISKS
- Portrayal of homosexual teen.
- Shows homophobic characters, dialogue, and actions.

STRENGTHS

- Strong, positive gay role model is a main character.
- Realistic portrayal of a teen coming to grips with his own homosexuality.
- Ambiguous and unexpected ending, leaving opportunity for group discussion or individual speculation.
- Homosexuality is only one aspect of complex multidimensional characters.
- Strong portrayal of friendship.
- Portrait of a close-knit, healthy family.
- Engrossing, fast-moving plotline involves readers from the beginning.

AWARDS

None

REVIEWS

"Ferris scores again. . . . creating a suspenseful plot with powerful characters. As a story of coming to terms with homosexuality, [it] is strong, but will appeal to a much wider audience. Its focus is realizing one's identity and on how one looks at the world, rather than concentrating on specific details of sexuality." —*Voice of Youth Advocates*, 10/00, Erin Pierce.

"Compassionately shares the challenges of gay teens, both those comfortable with who they are and those just discovering their true feeling. . . . explores quite eloquently what it means to really accept oneself and one's friends. . . . one of the best novels on this theme." —*Booklist*, 1999, Roger Leslie.

"More substantial then the typical teenage problem novel because of its subtle characterizations and unusual western setting." —*Horn Book*, 2001.

📖📖📖

THE EMPRESS OF ELSEWHERE. Nelson, Theresa. DK Ink, 1999. $17.95. 278p. ISBN: 0-7894-2498-3. Puffin, 2000. $5.99. 288p. ISBN: 0-141-30813-3. Realistic fiction. Reading level: MS. Interest level: MS. English, Psychology.

SUBJECT AREAS

animals; friendship; death and dying; illness, mental; self-knowledge; love; family relationships; secrets; elderly; handicaps, physical; rites of passage; grief and mourning; lying and deceitfulness.

CHARACTERS

James Henry Harbert, Jr./Jim Junior: the narrator of the story, he's eleven years old, and lives in East Texas, near Houston

Mary Alice Harbert/Mary Al: Jim Junior's seven-year-old sister, she's the one who first makes friends with the Empress

Mrs. Luly Kate Monroe: a wealthy recluse who lives across the street from the Harberts

J.D. (Joy Dolores) Monroe: Mrs. Monroe's granddaughter who curses, bites, and says she is "untamable," but who slowly makes friends with Jim Jr. and Mary Al

James Henry Harbert: Jim Junior and Mary Al's dad, who is currently out of work due to a back injury

Maggie Harbert: Jim Junior and Mary Al's mom, who does Mrs. Monroe's hair and nails

Jasper: Mrs. Monroe's chauffeur who is very tall, bald, and cannot speak

BOOKTALK

The first time Jim Junior saw the Empress, she was sprinting out of the Monroe mansion with her crown tipped over one ear and her tail in the air. It was the beginning of the second worst day of his life, a day he wasn't going to forget anytime soon. His best friend had just moved to Houston, and he was shoveling the last of the dirt clods over the body of his dog, Ranger, who'd been the best dog a boy could ever have. Mary Al, Jim Junior's little sister, had found him that morning and Jim had to get him buried before the neighbors started to complain. And as he stood there in the hot East Texas sun, sweat pouring all over him, struggling not to cry about Ranger, all hell broke loose.

Before he really knew what was happening, Jim Junior was knocked flat by a whole pack of wild-eyed girls chasing something with goldy-brown fur. It looked like one of those yippy little dogs wrapped up in a dress. But then whatever it was ran up in a tree and started throwing green acorns down at them. Turns out it was a monkey that belonged to Mrs. Monroe, and the girls had accidentally let it go. That monkey had good aim, and it didn't take but a few acorns to chase those girls away. But Mary Al was made of stronger stuff, and a fool for any kind of animal anyway, so she stayed right where she was, trying to talk that monkey out of the tree. Nothing she said made any difference to the monkey until she started crying. Seems like the monkey couldn't stand to see someone cry, so she was down from that tree in a flash, chittering and chirping and playing with her hair.

Mary Al wasn't real happy when Jim Junior told her they had to take the monkey back, but she finally agreed. And that was when they met Mrs. Monroe and Jasper, her chauffeur, which started the whole summer in a totally different direction. Mrs. Monroe took a shine to Jim Junior and Mary Al, and hired them to "tame" both the monkey and J.D., her wild and uncontrollable granddaughter, who bit and cursed and was angry with everyone and everything.

It was J.D. who got all of them thinking about the island in the middle of the lake in back of Mrs. Monroe's house, and about time travel, and about being able to fix things back the way they should've been. And it was also J.D. who got all three kids involved in the very worst day of their lives, the day they heard a big redheaded cop say the six most awful words in the English language, "Your parents are on their way."

How did they get from facing Mrs. Monroe that first morning to facing that cop and eventually their parents? Come to Elsewhere, meet the Empress, and find out.

MAJOR THEMES AND IDEAS
- Secrets are frequently easier to deal with once everyone knows what they are.
- Sometimes talking about what hurts you can help lessen that pain.
- Sometimes grief looks more like anger or emptiness than sorrow.
- It's important that you accept the consequences of your actions.
- Accidents are just that, accidents. They are no one's fault, and no one needs to feel guilty.
- Life is what it is, and sometimes it may feel both illogical and unfair. Control what you can, and learn to live with what you cannot.

BOOK REPORT IDEAS
1. Discuss the idea of being able to go back and "fix things the way they should have been." Is it ever possible to repair the past, and if so, explain how you think someone could do it.
2. Contrast the person J.D. was before her father's death and the one she was when Jim and Mary Al meet her, and explain how her actions are a result of her recent experiences.
3. There are different definitions of "right" and "wrong" in the book. Discuss several instances of each, and explain why you think the characters' actions in each situation were either appropriate or inappropriate.
4. Examine the character of Mrs. Monroe, explaining why she acted as she did toward each of the other characters.

BOOKTALK IDEAS
1. Let the Empress herself introduce the characters and the story.
2. Have J.D., Jim, and Mary Al each introduce themselves and the plot. Make sure you show clearly how different each of them is from the others, in their words and their emotions.

RISKS
- Child is traumatized after witnessing the death of a parent.
- Shows physical/verbal acting out.

- Grandmother is withdrawn, cold, and emotionless.
- Children break the law to rescue an animal.
- Portrays lying and manipulative child.

STRENGTHS
- Strong friendship helps characters learn to cope with life.
- Multidimensional characters grow and gain insight.
- Shows a healthy, supportive nuclear family.
- Handicapped character is completely accepted by the other characters.
- Sibling relationship is very strong and supportive.

AWARDS
None

REVIEWS
"All the characters are superbly drawn. . . . Nelson has perfect pitch for the speech of the east Texas hill country, and writes so well that she masks the fact that this is a familiar story about the hostile child who is lonely and needs only love." —*Voice of Youth Advocates*, 2/99, Richard Gercken.

"By turns comic and heartrending, the story is propelled along by Jim's distinctive East Texan narration and populated by a cast of memorable characters, most particularly Jim and Mary Al's honest and hardworking parents, who have passed on to their children the decency and courage to help a friend in need." —*Horn Book*, 1-2/99, Terri Schmitz.

"In a tidy but not shrink-wrapped resolution, Nelson employs several understanding adult characters to help J.D. release most of her pent-up anger and to work the story around to an upbeat ending. . . . a supporting cast that is energetically drawn from top to bottom will keep readers engaged." —*Booklist*, 9/1/98, John Peters.

📖📖📖

EVERY TIME A RAINBOW DIES. Williams-Garcia, Rita. HarperCollins, 2001. $15.95. 166p. ISBN: 0-688-16245-2. Realistic fiction. Reading level: MS. Interest level: YHS, OHS. Sex education, English, Art.

SUBJECT AREAS

abuse, sexual; love; animals; school: dating and social life; grief and mourning; cultural identity; friendship; family relationships; self-knowledge; sex and sexuality; working; art; minorities, Caribbean.

CHARACTERS

Thulani: mourning his mother's death, he sits on the roof with the doves he's taken care of for two years

Truman and Shakira: his brother and sister-in-law with whom Thulani lives

Ysa: Thulani helps her when he sees her being raped

Mr. Dunleavy: a tenant in the apartment building Thulani lives in

Jenine Desravines: she goes to Thulani's school

Julie: Janine's friend who likes Thulani

Eula: Truman and Shakira's daughter

Yong Moon: he sells the best produce in the neighborhood and hires Thulani to work for him after school

Tant Rosie: Ysa's great-aunt

BOOKTALK

Thulani couldn't stop thinking about her, the girl he'd seen raped. He'd given her a shirt to wear and helped her get home. He saw her every Wednesday walking down the street, head held high, hips swinging. But he never did anything but watch her. She had been so angry with him that night, hitting him when all he was doing was trying to help her. He didn't even know her name.

And then he began to follow her, and finally one day he spoke. But she is still too angry to let him near her. All she'll do is tell him her name, Ysa.

Will she ever let Thulani show her his love? Will she ever let go of her anger and love him back? Is there a chance for a girl from Haiti and a boy from Jamaica to find love in Brooklyn?

MAJOR THEMES AND IDEAS

- No matter how much you love someone, you can't make them love you back.
- Sex without love is just exercise.
- Mourning a loss or a death takes time.
- No one can take from you what you choose not to give.
- Sometimes you can make your point better if you don't yell.
- Sooner or later you have to find your own way. You can't let family decide your life.
- Love can heal, if you let it.
- Holding onto someone when they want to leave is futile. Let go when it is time to let go.

BOOK REPORT IDEAS

1. Discuss why Ysa first rejected, then accepted Thulani.
2. Describe the metaphor behind Thulani freeing his birds.
3. Color or the absence of it is only one of the books themes. Discuss what color means to Ysa and to Thulani.
4. Speculate on what will happen to Thulani, first in Jamaica and then when he returns to Brooklyn.
5. Shakira finally decides to go against her husband's wishes to get Thulani's money for him. Explain why she did this, based on her previous interactions with Thulani.
6. Show how Thulani and Ysa were able to help each other heal.
7. Explain why Thulani kept his birds and the place they had in his life. What did they symbolize?

BOOKTALK IDEAS

1. Focus your talk on the rape scene and the first part of Thulani's search for Ysa.
2. Use a multicolored piece of cloth like Ysa would have worn as a prop for your talk, or wear a skirt or a scarf similar to one of hers.

RISKS

*   Rape is graphically portrayed.
*   Teen sexuality is included.
*   Language is realistic but includes obscenities.

STRENGTHS

*   Shows process of recovery from two kinds of traumas—unexpected death and rape.
*   Multidimensional characters that grow and gain insight.
*   Unresolved ending leaves room for speculation on an individual and group basis.
*   Powerful love story draws readers in immediately.
*   Multilayered plotline adds complexity to the book.

AWARDS

None

REVIEWS

"Williams-Garcia's writing becomes richer and more realized with each subsequent novel. . . . [her] descriptive prose is elegant, never graphic. This Caribbean love story is a must-have for all public and high school libraries." —*Voice of Youth Advocates*, 6/01, Jennifer Hubert.

"With simplicity and a masterful control of pacing, Williams-Garcia builds a story that aches with the longing of two young lovers in a dance of tentative approach and defensive retreat, and eventual trust and healing." —Amazon, 2001, Patty Campbell.

"[The author] creates characters that are both fierce and gentle. Without graphic language, she portrays violence and anger in contemporary troubled teens who find courage and connection." —*Booklist*, 2001, Hazel Rochman.

⊞⊞⊞

FACING THE MUSIC. Willey, Margaret. Delacorte Press, 1996. $14.95. 184p. ISBN: 0-385-32104-X. Bantam, 1997. $3.99. 192p. ISBN: 0-440-22680-5. Realistic fiction. Reading level: MS. Interest level: MS,YHS. English; Music.

SUBJECT AREAS
music; rites of passage; friendship; family relationships; grief and mourning; self-knowledge; secrets; working; manipulation; lying and deceit.

CHARACTERS
Lisa Franklin: at fifteen, she has an amazing voice and is the singer for her brother's band
Mark Franklin: just out of high school, he wants his freedom, and isn't happy about Lisa singing with his band.
Patti Spinoza: Lisa's one and only girlfriend
Danny Fabiano: the leader of Crawl Space, he persuaded Lisa to sing with them
Ron Howander: Mark's oldest friend and the third member of Crawl Space
Dad: Lisa and Mark's distant, uninvolved father
Elaine Mitchell: she works with and dates Dad

BOOKTALK
It all started because I thought I was home alone, singing while I washed my hair. But when I walked into the living room, there he sat on the couch, Danny Fabiano, my brother Mark's new friend. I stopped singing, of course, but he'd already heard me. Mark, Danny, and Ron, Mark's oldest friend, had started a band and Danny decided I should sing with them. I didn't think I sounded that good, and I knew Mark would never agree—he acted like he hated me. But Danny wore me down and persuaded Mark to give me a chance.

It was wonderful from the very beginning. As soon as I stepped in back of the microphone that first time, I knew it was where I belonged, singing to people, making them feel what I felt in the songs I sang.

It was wonderful, but it didn't last. We weren't a real band any more than Mark and Daddy and I were a real family. In the band, it was truth and trust that were missing. In the family, it was Mom. She'd been gone for three years, and we still didn't talk about her death.

I learned a lot this summer. I learned who I am and even a little about where I'm going. But some of the other lessons were ones I wouldn't wish on my worst enemy, even though they taught me the most important thing: Face the music. Feel the pain. Then figure out how to use it.

MAJOR THEMES AND IDEAS
- Live in the present—you can't change the past.
- Denying something doesn't make it go away.
- Friends don't lie to friends.
- Punishing yourself for something you've done won't make the guilt go away.
- Hiding your emotions from those who love you is never productive.
- Putting off something that needs to be done or said only makes it more difficult to do or say in the end.
- Face the music—don't be afraid to try and fail. Feel the pain, and then figure out how to use it.

BOOK REPORT IDEAS
1. Discuss Danny and Lisa's relationship, including whether or not he ever really cared about her, or was manipulating her from the beginning. Be sure to include not only his actions at the beginning of the book but also at the end.
2. Detail some of the lessons Lisa learned over the summer, and how she was different at the end of the book from what she was at the beginning.
3. There are few details on Danny's childhood and home life. Show how these can be pieced together to explain his actions and attitudes toward women.
4. Show the impact Molly made on Mark and the changes he was able to make because of her.
5. Speculate on the lives and relationships of the main characters when Lisa is Mark's age, eighteen or nineteen.

BOOKTALK IDEAS
1. Format your talk as the book was written, letting first Lisa and then Mark speak.
2. Use a flyer for Crawl Space as a prop for your talk.
3. Focus your talk on the Franklin family and how the events of the summer and the months leading up to it drew them both together and apart.

RISKS
* Language is realistic yet vulgar.
* Lead character is self-involved, deceitful, and manipulative.
* Parents are distant and uninvolved.

STRENGTHS
* Written from two perspectives to give readers a chance to see what each character is feeling.
* Two main characters learn to face their grief, deal with it, and grow to go on.
* Relationships in the Franklin family are realistic and the rifts don't heal easily or quickly.
* Characters are realistic, quirky, and nonstereotypical.

AWARDS
Quick Picks for Young Adults, 1997 (ALA)

REVIEWS
"Paints a picture of a family torn apart by loss, a separation that has inflicted wounds of its own and one that cannot be easily mended." —*Voice of Youth Advocates*, 4/96, Holly M. Ward.

"A powerful novel of adolescent joy and defeat. . . . rendering emotional expression with great care. . . . wonderfully realistic portrayal of the adolescent psyche." —*Booklist*, 1997, Anne O'Malley.

ᙏ ᙏ ᙏ

THE FACTS SPEAK FOR THEMSELVES. Cole, Brock. Front Street Press, 1997. $13.95. 192p. ISBN: 1-886-91014-6. Puffin, 2000. $5.99. 184p. ISBN: 0-141-30696-3. Realistic fiction. Reading level: MS. Interest level: MS, YHS. English, Ethics, Psychology, Sex education.

SUBJECT AREAS
family relationships; abuse, sexual; child abuse; illness, mental; elderly; problem parents; crime and delinquency; sex and sexuality; ethics; lying and deceitfulness; poverty; rites of passage; secrets; self-knowledge.

CHARACTERS
Linda: a thirteen-year-old girl who has had to grow up much too young
Sandra: Linda's irresponsible and immature mother

Stoppard, Tyler: Linda's younger half brothers

Frank Perry: the man with whom Sandra and her children are living when Tyler is born

Jack Green: Sandra's employer, he has an affair with Linda

Sister Mary Joseph: a nun who befriends Linda when she goes to live at the Center

Franny Paschonelle: Linda's social worker

Dr. and Mrs. Hoeksema: Sandra's parents

Peter Hobbs: Stoppard's father who has never acknowledged his son

Glen Rodgers: Tyler's father who was never told about his son

Arthur Bloomberg: an elderly man Sandra and her children live with in Florida

BOOKTALK

How do you know what's right and what's wrong? You learn early in life what gets you punished or rewarded, right? But what if no one ever told you, and you had to figure it out for yourself? What if you had to learn on the streets what your parents didn't teach you at home?

Linda's had to do just that—learn what's right or wrong for herself. Her childish, immature mother certainly couldn't do it. Linda was more Sandra's mother than the other way around. And now Linda's part of a murder investigation, not allowed to live with her mother and the two little brothers she's raised more than her mother has. Linda doesn't think she's done anything wrong and wants to go home. She didn't shoot anyone. She was just standing there talking to Jack when Frank walked up and shot him. She's sure she didn't do anything wrong, but an awful lot of adults are trying to convince her that she did. Sometimes life just doesn't make sense.

MAJOR THEMES AND IDEAS

- The facts don't speak for themselves. It is one's interpretation of those facts that speaks most loudly.
- Children have a right to be taken care of.
- People say you should always do what's right and good, and turn away from what isn't. But what if you can't tell the difference?
- Denying what you don't want to look at doesn't make it go away.
- People judge your actions based on their own view of the world. Therefore, what to you is innocent or acceptable behavior may be defined by someone else as not appropriate or criminal.
- It's up to each of us to define ourselves.
- For better or worse, children do learn from their parents.
- When the chips are down, you do what's necessary to survive and to ensure the survival of those you love.

BOOK REPORT IDEAS

1. Discuss the concept of guilt or blame in the book. Explain who you think was most responsible for what happened to Linda, and most responsible for Jack and Frank's deaths.
2. Examine the concept of right and wrong from Linda's perspective, and show how and why her perspective differs from those of the adults around her.
3. Speculate on what happens to Linda, Sandra, Stoppard, and Tyler after the book ends, and what Linda might be like as an adult, supporting your opinions with quotes from the book.
4. Linda is only thirteen when the book opens, yet she has experienced far more than most girls her age. Discuss whether she was ever allowed to have a childhood, and show how her ideas and decisions were either adult or childlike.
5. Compare this title to others in which a child or teen is sexually abused, such as Cynthia Voight's *When She Hollers*, Erica Tamar's *Fair Game*, Francesca Lia Block's *The Hanged Man*, or Susan Wittlinger's *Fool Reversed*. Show how Linda is similar to and different from the girls in these books.

BOOKTALK IDEAS

1. Write your talk as if you were Linda, letting her tell her own story.
2. Focus your talk on the first chapter of the story, leading up to the scene in which Linda agrees to write her own report of what happened.
3. Have several characters talk about Linda, for example, Sister Mary Joseph, Miss Paschonelle, Sandra, and Frank.
4. Write your talk as if it were a TV human-interest story, focusing on Linda and what she was going through to keep her family intact.

RISKS

- Language is realistic but vulgar.
- Immature and ineffective mother forces her daughter to care for her two younger brothers.
- Mother exhibits many inappropriate and negative behaviors, i.e., casual sex, lack of birth control, self-centeredness, lack of child-rearing skills.
- Depiction of violence—murder and suicide.
- Sexual abuse of a child by an adult.

STRENGTHS

- Clear character's voice and brutal honesty in recounting her experiences makes them come alive.
- Character's strength and survival skills are vividly portrayed.
- Spare plotline has nothing extraneous to distract the reader.
- Raises many discussion questions on sexuality and ethics.

• No graphic sexual scenes are included.

AWARDS
Quick Picks for Reluctant Readers, 1998 (ALA)
Booklist Editors' Choice, 1997

REVIEWS
"This story probably is closer to reality than most fiction. What Cole succeeds in doing with his emotional detachment and open-endedness is inspire all the more outrage and moral indignation from the reader. There is an audience for this profoundly moving story. Many young people have suffered as much as Linda or worse, and those who have not should know, too." —*Voice of Youth Advocates*, 12/97, Edward Sullivan.

"The facts do indeed 'speak for themselves' in the flat, matter-of-fact, but hypnotic voice of a young teen whose dreadful life has taught her to cope with events as they happen without wasting energy on feelings or trying to make sense of things. . . . Its deceptive straightforwardness will certainly be demanding of young adult readers." —*Horn Book*, 11-12/97, Patty Campbell.

"A brilliantly crafted, shocking account. . . . it will slice readers to the bone. . . . raw, powerful character study of someone trying to construct a particular version of reality, and failing, because the 'facts' tell a different story. Cole shows real literary chops in a book whose aesthetic merits outrun, by far, the ethics police." —*Kirkus Reviews*, 1997.

ꜛꜛꜛ

FAIR GAME. Tamar, Erika. Harcourt, 1993. $10.95. 293p. ISBN: 0-152-78537-X. Harcourt, 1993. $3.95. 293p. ISBN: 0-152-27065-5. Realistic fiction. Reading level: YHS. Interest level: YHS, OHS. English, Sex education, P. E., Ethics, Sociology.

SUBJECT AREAS
school; peer pressure; handicaps, mental; rape; sex and sexuality; gossip; sports; prejudice; love; friendship; secrets; manipulation; family relationships; self-knowledge; rites of passage; dating and social life; crime and juvenile delinquency.

CHARACTERS

Laura Jean Kettering: a senior, she's Scott Delaney's girlfriend, and believes in his and the others' innocence

Cara Snowden: she's a freshman, hates being in special education classes, will do anything to be popular, and is very naïve about boys and dating

Scott Delaney, Charlie Goren, Bob Dietrich, John Masci, Mike Clay: seniors and varsity football players, they rule the school, and are the "in crowd"

Joe Lopez: a Hispanic star athlete who hangs out with the other jocks, but who really isn't one of the gang

Dan Gregory: Scott's next-door neighbor, he's into video

Mr. Gilmartin: high school principal

Mrs. Jensen: Cara's track coach

Tony Edison: TV newscaster

Mr. Held: he teaches animal science, tries too hard to be cool, and bends over backwards for the jocks

Ellen Snowden: Cara's mother

BOOKTALK

What those jocks did to Cara may not have been rape, but it wasn't consenting sex, and it sure wasn't making love. Most people thought it was just a bunch of guys getting carried away and going too far. Most people didn't really think they meant to hurt her—she'd been putting out for most of them for ages. She'd do anything for anyone who'd say she was their friend. She didn't object that afternoon when they told her to do a striptease, and she didn't even object to any of the rest of it. But you can't tell your mother things like that, even Cara knew that much. So when her mother asked her what had happened, Cara had to say she'd tried to stop them, she'd said no, she hadn't wanted it to happen. Cara was retarded, but she wasn't *that* dumb!

So now the question is, where's the line between right and wrong? Was what they did wrong? What about the guys who didn't actually do *anything*, who only watched? Watching isn't a crime, is it? Is sex with the school slut a crime? Last year at graduation all the guys in the senior class gave Noreen Malivek a standing ovation, because she'd been with almost every one of them. Should they have all been hauled off to jail?

A lot of people in town don't like what the media's done to the school and the town, and have been saying that it's the *real* crime. It's been a big story from coast to coast—and the folks who know the truth know not much of that story is even *close* to it. All that matters is that it's a good story, and this story's no good unless a crime was committed. So, our boys, sports stars and some of the most popular kids at school, are criminals. At least to the media.

And that's the question everyone has to answer—are they really criminals? Was what they did a crime? Or was it just a big, dumb mistake? Everyone in town has their opinion, and once you know what actually happened that afternoon, you will too.

It all started when the guys on the team had to practice alone because the coach had a meeting to go to. It was hot, too hot to practice, and of course, Cara was hanging around, just like she always was. . . .

MAJOR THEMES AND IDEAS
- It's easy to do evil to someone when you dehumanize them.
- Consent isn't just saying yes, it's also understanding what you're consenting to and why.
- When the crowd goes against something you believe in deeply, it's time to stop fitting in.
- You can only coast on your reputation for so long.
- Teasing, when it goes too far and becomes painful for the target, is cruel and no longer funny.
- Denying reality doesn't change it.
- People will do in a group what they'd never consider doing alone. They can become heroes or criminals.
- Information is leaky—it spreads and so do rumors.
- Watching a crime and not trying to stop it makes you just as much at fault as those that committed it.

BOOK REPORT IDEAS
1. Analyze Scott's character as Laura Jean and Joe saw him before and after the rape, and show how he is one of the major instigators of what happened the day of the rape.
2. Speculate on what will happen to the boys at the grand jury and after.
3. This is a fictional retelling of an actual incident.* Examine the news stories of that event and discuss the similarities and differences between it and the book.
4. Two themes in this book are the aggressiveness of the jock culture in a high school and the dehumanization of someone considered to be outside the group, so that violent and even evil acts can be committed against them without fear of reprisal. Discuss one of these themes in detail, reacting to it on a personal level, and also citing recent current events to support your discussion.
5. Examine the idea of "consent" as expressed by different characters in the book. Show how the jocks, students, student's parents, and community members defined it to mean completely different things. Include in your discussion the comments Cara made on the tape Laura recorded.

*Lefkowitz, Bernard. *Our Guys: The Glen Ridge Rape and the Secret Life of the Perfect Suburb.* University of California Press, 1997. $29.95. Vintage Books, 1998. $15.00 (pb).

BOOKTALK IDEAS

1. Take excerpts from Joe, Laura Jean, and Cara, and let each of them describe the situation from their perspective.
2. Let any of the three characters above tell the story in first person.
3. Talk about this book and *Our Guys* together, and use newspaper clippings and photos as props.
4. Write your talk as if it were a newspaper or TV news story, complete with sound bites or headlines from the book.

RISKS

- A retarded girl is brutally raped by out-of-control high school jocks.
- Shows the excitement present in group violence.
- Teens are portrayed as sexually active.
- High school jock culture is aggressive and tolerated by local adults.
- Racist remarks and concepts are included.
- Characters abuse several substances.
- Girls are seen as objects, not people.

STRENGTHS

- Told from multiple perspectives.
- Powerful portrait of kids with too much power and prestige.
- Graphic depiction of the phenomenon of " groupthink."
- Strong characters grow and gain insight.
- Examines the question of sexuality of the mentally disabled.
- Clear portrayal of the effects of peer pressure.
- Fictional retelling of actual incident makes it more accessible to readers.

AWARDS

Best Books for Young Adults, 1993 (ALA)

REVIEWS

"Written for mature young adults. The author depicts what can happen when one forgets humanity and becomes a savage. It is the story. . . . which will attract readers." —*Voice of Youth Advocates*, 12/93, Lucy Marx.

"In the hands of a weaker writer, this story might have degenerated into sick melodrama. The horror she spins out is riveting. . . . what's described is sex grown out of purposeful misuse of power, a horrifying violation. . . . while her message might have been laid down more subtly, it would certainly not have made as strong an impact." —*Booklist*, 1993, Stephanie Zvirin.

"Characters are carefully individualized, and [Tamar] does a fine job of depicting a community where such a crime could be excused by some parents and teachers; the explicit details here make it absolutely clear how heinous it is. . . . Cara's a real person; legally rape or not, the boys' act was unforgivable. Well wrought and compelling." —*Kirkus Reviews*, 9/15/93.

📖📖📖

FIGHTING RUBEN WOLFE. Zusak, Markus. Scholastic, 2001. $15.95. 219p. ISBN: 0-439-24188-X. Realistic fiction. Reading level: YHS. Interest level: YHS, OHS. P. E., English, Geography.

SUBJECT AREAS
sports; family relationships; working; friendship; secrets; poverty; sex and sexuality; substance abuse; self-knowledge; gossip; rites of passage.

CHARACTERS
Ruben Wolfe: a gutsy fighter, in and out of the ring
Cameron Wolfe: Ruben's younger brother, not as good a fighter as Ruben, but he has lots of heart
Gary, Cassy: police officers who make friends with the Wolfes
Sarah and Steve Wolfe: Ruben and Cameron's older sister and brother
Dad: a plumber who was injured and lost all his jobs
Mum: works two jobs to try and keep things together
Perry Cole: he hires Ruben and Cameron to fight for him

BOOKTALK
You know when you have a line of dominoes, and you knock just one over, and all the others start falling, and there's just no way to stop them? That's pretty much what happened in my family when Dad got hurt and then couldn't find a job after he got well. Mum started working double shifts and looking more and more tired and worn down. Steve and Sarah offered to pitch in with more than their board, but Dad wouldn't stand for it. Steve just got more quiet and more closed off, but Sarah did the opposite. She started drinking more and coming in throwing up drunk at 2 or 3 a.m., then getting up and doing it all over again the next day. Then one day, Ruben, who's just a year older than I am, tells me that there's talk about Sarah at school, about what she's doing besides drinking. He says if anyone dares call her a whore, he'll kill them, he really will. And he nearly did.

That's when the dominoes really started falling faster. Perry, this guy who set up amateur boxing matches, heard about Ruben's fight, and decided he wanted Ruben and me to fight for him. He wanted Ruben 'cause he was a winner, and me 'cause I have heart—I don't give up and just keep coming back for more. Winners got \$50, and even losers got \$20 or so in tips, if they fought a good fight. We needed the money, so we said okay. It was a good deal.

But our lives changed after our first fights, and Ruben started changing too. It seemed like he wasn't just fighting the other guys, he was fighting himself as well. He was winning in the ring, but how could he win against himself?

MAJOR THEMES AND IDEAS
- When a man can't work and has to depend on his wife and kids to bring in the money, he's only half a man.
- No matter what goes on inside the family, we band together to defend each other against outsiders.
- If you fail, you have only yourself to blame.
- Respect comes from the inside.
- A fight's worth nothing if you know from the beginning that you're going to win, because if you don't believe you can win, you won't.

BOOK REPORT IDEAS
1. Discuss the ways Ruben was fighting himself as well as his opponent in the ring.
2. Show how Ruben and Cameron helped bring the family closer together.
3. Compare both Ruben and Cameron at the beginning and the end of the book, showing how they changed and why.
4. Describe the scene you consider to be the most important or pivotal in the book and explain why you chose it.
5. Examine all the fights either Ruben or Cameron fought in the book, both in and out of the ring, decide which one was most important to each of them, and explain why.
6. Speculate on the long-term effects of their boxing career on both brothers, showing how they might be different in five or ten years because of it.

BOOKTALK IDEAS
1. Use a pair of boxing gloves as a prop for your talk.
2. Write your talk in the style of a play-by-play fight announcer.
3. Focus your talk on two scenes, Ruben's fight for his sister's reputation and the boy's first meeting with Perry.
4. Write your talk as if it were one of the late-night conversations between Ruben and Cameron.

RISKS
- Dialogue is realistic and vulgar.
- Characters participate in illegal boxing matches.
- Graphic descriptions of boxing matches and their violence.

STRENGTHS

- Realistic portrait of working-class family.
- Shows strong family values and connections.
- Changes in format give added visual interest—whispered or interior conversations are in a different typeface.
- Australian slang is easily understood and gives a sense of place.
- Gritty, poetic writing style draws the reader into the story quickly.
- Crisp, clipped dialogue conveys much with few words.
- Characters are multidimensional and realistic, giving the reader much to identify with.

AWARDS

None

REVIEWS

"Gritty but poignant story. . . . language is sparse, poetic, and sometimes humorous. . . . vivid imagery [relays] the innermost thoughts of the characters." —*Voice of Youth Advocates*, 4/01, Brenda Moses-Allen.

"Surprisingly complex and touching story that will linger long with readers. The language is hard-hitting, witty and authentic—as are the emotions and action. . . . it's about respect, stubborn pride, and real brotherly love." —Amazon, 2001, Emilie Coulter.

"Tells a dramatic story and effectively bring his characters to full-bodied life. . . . a powerful novel. . . . demanding our attention." —*Booklist*, 2001, Bill Ott.

"Fast-paced narrative captures the physical rigors of the boxing ring as well as the emotional turmoil and ultimate unity of the troubled Wolfe family." —*Horn Book*, 2001.

📖📖📖

THE FOOL REVERSED. Whitcher, Susan. Farrar, Straus & Giroux, 2000. $16.00. 183p. ISBN: 0-374-32446-8. Realistic fiction. Reading level: YHS. Interest level: YHS, OHS. Sex education, English, Creative writing.

SUBJECT AREAS

sex and sexuality; manipulation; friendship; love; dating and social life; problem parents; rites of passage; self-knowledge; abuse, sexual; violence.

CHARACTERS

Anna: at fifteen, she reads tarot cards and dreams of finding her true love
Pauline: two years older than Anna, she's cynical and rebellious
Thorn: a twenty-nine-year-old poet who manipulates Anna to fulfill his own emotional needs
Des: Thorn's editor
Elaine: Thorn's ex-girlfriend
Rennie, Vonda: Anna's older sisters
Dylan: he rescues Anna from a potentially dangerous situation and becomes her friend
Mom: Anna's workaholic mother
Walt: he dates Anna's mother

BOOKTALK

When Thorn looked at Anna for the first time, she fell into his steel-gray eyes as if she were stepping off a cliff, like the fool in the tarot deck she used to tell her future.

Thorn was intrigued the moment he saw Anna. She was so pale, still, serene, perfect. He wanted her immediately.

It was at Café Mezzaluna, a coffee house with an open mike. Pauline and Anna had sneaked in. Anna was fifteen. Thorn was twenty-nine. She dreamed of writing poetry. He was a published poet. She wanted a knight on a white horse. He didn't believe in fairy tales.

When Anna first saw Dylan, she was in love with Thorn, and saw only a guy her own age, tall, bony, hair neither brown nor blond, in baggy clothes. A boy who rescued her from what could have been a dangerous situation, but who didn't really look like Anna's idea of the knight she dreamed of.

Dylan couldn't believe it when he saw Anna for the first time. It was like his whole world changed in that instant. He knew he was in love forever, and one way or another, he was going to make her love him too. And if she didn't love him, all he wanted was to be where he could hear her breathe.

They met in the woods by the river. Anna was fifteen. Dylan was a couple of years older. Anna wanted a friend. Dylan wanted to take care of her, protect her, for the rest of his life.

The Knight of Cups, the Page of Wands, and in between them the Fool, reversed. What will the cards reveal?

MAJOR THEMES AND IDEAS

- A person can go through a whole lifetime with only one or two perfect moments.
- Once you see the real person behind the façade, it's easy to see how you were controlled and manipulated by them.
- When you feel vulnerable, you hide parts of yourself to keep them safe.
- What doesn't kill you makes you stronger, if you let it.

- Sometimes you have to look at people more than once to see who really loves you.
- Lies are not always bad or truth always good.
- Sometimes it's a good thing to take your time and proceed slowly.
- In real life neither love nor white knights look like they do in fairy tales.

BOOK REPORT IDEAS
1. Explain why Anna was so drawn to Thorn, and what parts of her he fulfilled.
2. Compare Dylan and Thorn and how they expressed their love for Anna.
3. Speculate on what will happen to Anna and Dylan in the future. Will they maintain their relationship or go their separate ways?
4. Discuss what you consider the most important idea or concept in the book, and explain why you chose it.
5. Truth versus lies is a major thread in the book. Discuss who lied and who didn't, the reasons why they did or didn't tell the truth, and what they gained or lost as a result.
6. Look at the idea of manipulation—who manipulated whom, when, why, and with what result? (Hint: almost every character is a manipulator at one time or another.)

BOOKTALK IDEAS
1. Use a Rider tarot deck as a prop for your talk, showing several of the cards Anna mentions most frequently.
2. Let the characters in the central triangle introduce each other.
3. Write you talk in first person, as Anna, as she introduces the other main characters.
4. Record parts of Anna's tape diary and play them as part of your talk.

RISKS
- Portrays sex between a teenager and an adult.
- Manipulation of a child by an adult and by an older teen.
- Shows sexual abuse of a minor.
- Language is realistic but vulgar.
- Portrays a suicide attempt.
- Parents are distant and uninvolved.
- Characters abuse a variety of substances.
- Use of tarot cards to tell fortunes.

STRENGTHS
- Multiple story lines give depth and complexity to the book.
- Multidimensional characters readers can easily identify with.

- Characters grow and gain insight and strength from surviving their crises and overcoming the dark parts of their lives.
- Uses symbolism of the tarot deck and card readings to accentuate characters and situations.
- Powerful story connects with readers emotionally and intellectually.
- Sex scenes are handled delicately and nongraphically.
- Story line is to some extent nonsequential.

AWARDS
None

REVIEWS
"This ground-breaking young adult novel tackles a largely unmentioned topic that endangers many vulnerable young girls—exploitation by an older man. . . . readers will respond both emotionally and intellectually to Whitcher's rich language, multilayered style, and characters that leap off the page. . . . Anna. . . . must journey through the darkest of experiences, using her trials to forge growth. Anna emerges knowing how to trust herself instead of blindly following others. . . . This important, highly recommended book should be considered carefully and impartially for mature teen readers in both public and school libraries." —*Voice of Youth Advocates*, 6/00, Joni Richards Bodart.

"Whitcher's writing is cohesive, well constructed and compelling, which makes this disturbing novel all the more bleak. . . . alarming plot, skillfully embedded themes, and clear voice. . . . This disconcerting book demands discussion rather than solitary reading." —*School Library Journal*, 3/00, Francisca Goldsmith.

🕮 🕮 🕮

FORGED BY FIRE. Draper, Sharon M. Atheneum, 1997. $16.00. 156p. ISBN: 0-689-80699-X. Aladdin Paperbacks, 1998. $4.99. 156p. ISBN: 0-689-81851-3. Realistic fiction. Reading level: MS. Interest level: MS, YHS. English, P. E., Sex education.

SUBJECT AREAS
abuse, physical; substance abuse; abuse, sexual; child abuse; stepparents; problem parents; love; family relations; minorities, black; death and dying; secrets; sports; school; friendship; crime and criminals; survival.

CHARACTERS

Gerald Nickleby: a young black boy who has endured years of abuse and disappointment

Angel: Gerald's younger stepsister who has also been abused for years

Aunt Queen: Gerald's aunt who takes him to live with her

Jordan Sparks: Angel's father and Gerald's abusive stepfather, he's married to Monique

Monique: Angel and Gerald's drug-addicted, abusive mother

Rob Washington: a friend of Gerald's

Darryl Washington: Rob's father who helps Angel and Gerald

Andy Jackson: Rob's best friend, he's on the basketball team with Rob and Gerald.

BOOKTALK

Gerald was only three, but he'd already learned not to make mama mad or wake her up, especially if she was in bed with a man, or get near her after she sniffed the white powder, and most important, never play with the hot thing she used to light her cigarettes. But he was only three, so when he found her lighter one day when she was out, he decided to play with it, just a little, and then a little more, and then suddenly, the curtains were on fire!

A neighbor rescued Gerald, his mother went to prison for child abuse, and the six best years of Gerald's life began when he went to live with his Aunt Queen. She gave him the love and caring and attention he'd never gotten from his mother. But on his ninth birthday, when his world fell apart, and he was forced to live with his mother, her abusive husband, and his fragile, battered six-year-old stepsister, his life quickly spun out of control. It would be almost ten years before it became his again. Ten years of dashed hopes, disappointments and frustrations.

Follow Gerald and Angel as they struggle to survive and sometimes find a bit of happiness and joy in the war zone they call their home.

MAJOR THEMES AND IDEAS

- When someone is abused, it's never the victim's fault.
- You can survive almost anything if you work at it hard enough.
- Some people who are abused become very skilled at denial.
- Social class and success in life don't allow you to avoid tragedy.
- Take time for the important things in life: love, laughter, celebrations, and hugs—and the rest will be easier to deal with.
- What doesn't kill you, makes you stronger.
- Sometimes fear is useful, because it keeps you on your toes. Losing your fear may reduce your chances for escape or control.
- Children of ineffective parents frequently lose their childhood, because they must learn to parent themselves and their siblings.

BOOK REPORT IDEAS

1. Fires are featured in the first and last chapters of the book, both of which had a defining impact on Gerald's life. Discuss this impact, and how his life and personality were changed by it.
2. Monique seems to love her children but is unable to care or protect them. Explain why she is not able to play a parental role and why she is unable to separate from Jordan.
3. Aunt Queen played a major role in Gerald's childhood. Discuss what he learned from her, and how he would have been different had he not had her in his life.
4. Gerald and Angel use several things to temporarily escape from the abuse surrounding them. Explain what some of these things were and how they worked.
5. Speculate on what will happen to Gerald, Angel, and Monique after the end of the book. Explain how you think their lives will be different or the same for the next five years.

BOOKTALKS

1. Write a two-part booktalk letting Gerald and Angel each describe their lives.
2. Use the scene in which Gerald first asks Mr. Washington for help as a focus for your talk.
3. Write the talk in first person as Gerald, starting with the first fire and ending with his fear and frustration after he realizes the kind of family his mother and Jordan have formed.

RISKS

- Father/stepfather is both physically and sexually abusive to his children.
- Mother is ineffective as a parent and addicted to drugs and alcohol.
- Language is realistic yet vulgar.
- Violence and sexual abuse are graphically portrayed.
- Characters may be seen as stereotypical.
- Children are forced to bring up themselves.

STRENGTHS

- Multidimensional characters that teens can identify with easily.
- Strong portrayal of characters who survive and succeed in spite of incredible, horrifying life situations.
- Shows the power of strong sibling bonds.
- Characters and plot both inspire hope.
- Several characters who are positive black role models.
- Realistic and accurate portrayal of abuse and addiction.
- Strong message of love and Christian principles woven into story.

- Many opportunities for group discussion.
- Ending is open and leaves the reader an opportunity to speculate on what happens next.

AWARDS
Best Books for Young Adults, 1998 (ALA)
Quick Picks for Reluctant Readers, 1998 (ALA)
Coretta Scott King Award, 1998 (ALA)

REVIEWS
"A grim look at an inner-city home where abuse and addiction are a way of life and the children are the victims. There's no all's-well ending, but readers will have hope for Gerald and Angel, who have survived a number of gut-wrenching ordeals by relying on their constant love and caring for one another." —*School Library Journal*, 3/97, Tom S. Hurlburt.

"With so much tragedy here. . . . there is some danger of overloading the reader. Nevertheless Draper faces some big issues (abuse, death, drugs) and provides concrete options and a positive African American role model in Gerald." —*Booklist*, 2/15/97, Candace Smith.

"Draper creates believable and important heroes for teenage boys—those who are forged from adversity, only to burn more brightly and courageous[ly.]" —Amazon, 1998, Gail Hudson.

📖 SECTION THREE 📖
Give a Boy a Gun to
Nobody Else Has to Know

GIVE A BOY A GUN. Strasser, Todd. Simon and Schuster, 2000. $16.00. 146p. ISBN: 0-689-81112-8. Realistic fiction. Reading level: MS. Interest level: MS, YHS, OHS. Ethics, P. E., English, Creative writing, Drama.

SUBJECT AREAS
bullying; violence; school; manipulation; peer pressure; revenge; anger; rites of passage; fear; death and dying; lying and deceitfulness; intimidation; friendship; stereotypes; secrets; self-knowledge; family relationships; suicide; abuse, physical; computers; crime and delinquency; dysfunctional families; grief and mourning; harassment; prejudice; divorce.

CHARACTERS
Denise Shipley: she is trying to put all the pieces together and answer the question, "Why?"

Gary Searles: bright, sensitive, a computer geek with few friends and many enemies

Brendan Lawlor: an outsider with a strong sense of justice, and a lot of anger to deal with, who became Gary's closest friend

Ryan Clancy: one of Gary and Brendan's closest friends, he's also a geek and an outsider

Allison Findlay: another of Gary and Brendan's friends, and Gary's off-and-on girlfriend, she's also an outsider

Cynthia Searle: Gary's single mother who still feels guilty over her bitter divorce

Kit Connor: a neighbor of the Lawlor's in Springfield, before they moved to Middletown

Dustin Williams: a popular black athlete who is also one of Brendan's neighbors

Emily Kirsch: she used to be one of Brendan's closest friends and still worries about him

Deirdre Bunson: a popular girl who believes high school athletes should be able to do whatever they want to without being punished

Sam Flach: a star football player who enjoys picking on the outsiders at school

Paul Burns: another football player who harasses the outsiders

Beth Bender: the Middletown High School counselor, who saw too little, too late

Douglas Ellin: a biology teacher at MHS

Allen Curry: MHS principal who makes no effort to control the harassment that goes on in the school

Dick Flanagan: English teacher at MHS

Jack Phillips: one of the Lawlor's neighbors

Chelsea Baker: a recent transfer to MHS who is horrified by the cruelty she sees going unpunished and frequently unnoticed

BOOKTALK

It's not easy being different, no matter how old you are. But when you're an "outcast," and catch the eye of a high school football star who's as aggressive off the field as he is on it, life suddenly isn't just difficult, it's hell.

Gary and Brendan were only two of the outcasts Sam harassed and tormented every day at school. Ryan, Allison, Emily, and lots of others were knocked into lockers, pushed and shoved in the halls, laughed at in classes, and jeered at or much, much worse in the restrooms. They all put up with verbal and physical abuse every day, while teachers and classmates looked the other way, or sometimes joined in.

Everyone in school, the students, the teachers, and the administration, all saw what was going on, and no one tried to stop it. There were two sets of rules at Middletown High, one for the popular kids and jocks who ruled the school, and another for everyone else. Jocks, especially football jocks, got away with anything and everything.

Lots of the outcasts talked about retaliation, but Brendan and Gary did more than talk. They planned, they practiced, and they put those plans into violent action. It was time for revenge. Brendan had gotten beaten up once too often, and Gary had gotten farther and farther away from everyone else in his life. Brendan was the only one who knew just how lost he really was. They knew that they couldn't depend on parents, teachers, friends, or anyone else to help them end the torture that their lives had become. They had to do it themselves, with no help from anyone.

And they did end it, with bullets, with blood, with anger, and with desperation. They sent a message to everyone—to the jocks and the popular kids who bullied them, to the teachers who ignored them, to the administration who supported the jocks, and to the parents and the town that encouraged a violent "us/them" mentality in their children and their schools.

When you've been stomped on too many times, when all your options have been taken away, it's easy to believe that violence may be the only voice you have left.

MAJOR THEMES AND IDEAS
- The easier guns are to get, the more people will die from them.
- It's not just the jocks or popular kids who harass the outcasts, it's also the faculty members who look the other way or egg on the harassers.
- Going to high school shouldn't be hell, but for outsiders, that's exactly what it can be.
- Popular kids live the dream. They never have to be afraid of waking up to cold, hard reality, because their reality is warm and cozy.
- There are two sets of rules, one for those who are in favor, another for those who aren't.
- "Sticks and stones will break my bones, but names will never hurt me" is a lie. A bruise stops hurting after a while. Ugly names live on, and are always painful.
- It is all too easy to ignore danger signs from angry, tormented kids who talk or write about violent revenge, and say that they don't really mean it. Sometimes they don't. But sometimes they do.
- There are too many guns. But there are also too many outsiders who are excluded, marginalized, and harassed.
- There's a reason why kids start shooting at school, not at McDonald's or at the mall. It's not random. They're sending a message, and we had better start listening to it.
- When you have no protection, no way of getting away from your tormentors, no way to make your life better, nothing matters any more. Not life. Not death.
- Listen. Pay attention. It's not idle talk. It's not a joke. It's real and it's not going away unless we do something to make things change, and soon.

BOOK REPORT IDEAS
1. Compare and contrast Brendan when he first moved to Middletown and when the shooting took place, citing reasons why he changed and showing what those changes were.
2. Discuss what might have happened had Allison, Ryan, and Emily voiced their concerns to Beth Bender or other school officials. Would it have made a difference in what finally happened? Why or why not?
3. Present your book report as a readers' theater group presentation.
4. There are several antiviolence messages in the book. Choose the one you think is the most important or effective, and explain why.

5. Imagine you are a student at Middletown High, and describe yourself and your experiences at school. Which characters would be your friends? What group would you belong to? How would you relate to Gary and Brendan?

6. Dustin and Emily are characters who seem to straddle the gap between the insiders and the outsiders. Describe what it would be like to be in this position and the pressures that might go with it. Were either of these characters in a place to create a change in the events of the story? If so, what might they have done? If not, why were they unable to act?

7. Examine the pressures on Gary and Brendan both at school and in other settings, and how those pressures brought the boys' breaking point closer and closer.

8. Contrast the attitudes of the various faculty members at MHS and their perspectives on the harassment at school before and after the shooting.

9. There are two main student groups, each stereotypical, the popular/jock crowd and the outcasts. Compare how each group saw the other, and discuss which (if either) viewpoint was the more realistic.

10. Discuss Gary and Brendan's friendship, the effect it had on their response to being harassed, and whether or not you think that they would have been equally violent apart and why. What characteristics did each have that together led to the shooting?

11. Consider the saying by Edwin Markham, "He drew a circle that shut me out, heretic, rebel, a thing to flout. But love and I had the wit to win; we drew a circle that took him in." Which characters might have been able to draw circles that included Brendan and Gary, and what actions might those circles have included?

BOOKTALK IDEAS

1. Write your talk from two contrasting perspectives, one from the popular crowd and one from the outcasts, showing the conflict between them.

2. Write your talk as if it were a television or newspaper story on the shooting.

3. Use the facts in the footnotes as part of your talk.

4. Use the list of school shootings as part of your talk, perhaps to introduce it or to end it.

5. Read the two suicide notes as the body of your talk, using the actual notes printed out as props.

6. Focus on the idea of bullies and what repercussions their harassment can have. You might use a list of the things that were done to the outsiders and how they reacted to them.

RISKS

- It is very reminiscent of the Columbine shootings in Littleton, Colorado.
- Jocks are aggressive, tolerated by school faculty, and allowed to harass other students.
- Teen commits suicide.

- Parents are distant or ineffectual.
- Signs of possible violence in school assignments are ignored.
- Language is realistic and includes some obscenities.
- Teens drink, use drugs, and commit violent acts.
- Didactic anti-handgun, anti-semiautomatic weapons message.
- Details how teens plot a murder-suicide pact.
- Violence is described graphically and in detail.
- Multiple narrators may be difficult for readers to keep track of.
- Violent video games are shown as a possible prelude to real violence.

STRENGTHS

- Multiple perspectives give strikingly different perspectives on characters, and add complexity and depth to the story.
- Different typefaces give added visual interest and differentiate among interviews, factoids, e-mail and chat room messages.
- Strong anti-bullying, anti-teasing, anti-handgun, anti-semiautomatic weapons messages.
- Could be used effectively for readers' theater.
- Realistic characters and actions that teens will immediately identify with.
- Most obscenities are represented by symbols such as #%@*^!&.
- Factoids add a horrifying and realistic counterpart to the fictional story line.
- There is information for teens who choose to become anti-violence, anti-bullying activists.
- Ending is ambiguous, not resolving the characters' or readers' questions about reasons why, allowing for individual speculation and group discussion.
- Makes the enormous negative impact of school cliques and bullying very clear.
- Contrasts two high schools where violence and bullying are and are not tolerated.
- Shows how the administration of a school sets the tone and impacts the culture of the whole school.

AWARDS
Voice of Youth Advocates Top Shelf Fiction for Middle School Readers, 2000

REVIEWS
"An absolute must-read for all who work with middle schoolers. . . . Informative, compelling, and chilling, this book requires thoughtful reading by and responses from administrators, counselors, and teachers. We know that these fictional characters and the issues that make and break them are real."
—*Voice of Youth Advocates*, 2/01, Francisca Goldsmith.

"Vivid, distressing, and all too real. . . . a denunciation of the value system of an entire community that allowed. . . . a select few to rule by bullying. . . . Not written like a traditional novel, [but] a pastiche of various voices. . . . Despite the fact that the cast is large. . . . the multiple points of view create empathy for a wide range of characters and enhance the book's in-your-face reality. Important, insightful, and chilling." —*Kirkus Reviews*, 2000.

"Attempts to give a voice to the countless sides of the school violence issue. . . . An articulate, well-rounded cross section of the many viewpoints on gun control, peer bullying, and the high school social order. . . . will be a useful tool...in exploring this issue and finding some ways of resolving the tragic escalation of teen violence." —Amazon, 2000, Jennifer Hubert.

"Powerful documentary novel. . . . passionate indictment of America's gun culture and the equally pernicious, pervasive caste system that has created a society of disaffected outsiders in America's secondary schools. . . . Includes a contrapuntal collection of quotations, facts, and figures about school and gun violence. . . . Deeply moving and disturbing. . . . Haunting and harrowing, the book deserves a wide readership, discussion and debate." —*Booklist*, 2000, Michael A. Cart.

🕮🕮🕮

HARD LOVE. Wittlinger, Ellen. Simon & Schuster, 1999. $16.95. 224p. ISBN: 0-689-82134-4. Simon & Schuster, 2001. $8.00. 240p. ISBN: 0-689-84154-X. Listening Library Inc., 2001. $25.00. ISBN: 0-807-26192-0. Realistic fiction. Reading level: MS. Interest level: MS, YHS. English, Journalism, Art, Creative writing.

SUBJECT AREAS
writing; love; homosexuality; friendship; lying and deceitfulness; poetry; secrets; divorce; family relations; problem parents; self-knowledge; rites of passage.

CHARACTERS
John Galardi/Giovanni: a writer with his own zine, *Bananafish*
Brian: John's best friend
Anne Van Esterhausen: John's mother who teaches fifth grade
Al: Mom's boyfriend
Marisol Guzman: a lesbian who writes a zine, *Escape Velocity*
John Galardi: John's father who's a publisher
Helen Guzman: Marisol's mother who's a therapist

Emily Prine: a girl Brian is dating
Diana Tree: another writer whose zine is called *No Regrets*

BOOKTALK

Sometimes life is a hard love, a love that hurts instead of heals, a love that takes but can't give back. And that's the kind of love that John and Marisol found—a love that was impossible and painful and futile.

John's into free zines he picks up at Tower Records when he visits his father on weekends. One in particular, *Escape Velocity,* and the girl who writes it fascinate him. Her name is Marisol, and she's a "Puerto Rican Cuban Yankee rich spoiled lesbian gifted-and-talented virgin writer looking for love."

John's a person with almost no connections with anyone. He considers himself and his only friend both losers. His divorced parents don't seem to want him around. His mother won't touch him at all, in fact, she goes out of her way to not even get near him, and his father resents having to give up his weekend social life—John calls it "the bimbo parade"—to spend time with his son.

But Marisol wants to be friends with him, talk to him, listen to him, and before he really realizes what's happening, John has fallen in love with her. It's a hard love, with no hope for the future—or is there?

MAJOR THEMES AND IDEAS

- Each of us needs to escape our parents to find out who we really are.
- It's easier to write about yourself if your audience is unknown and anonymous.
- Sometimes love is hard, painful, and not easy at all.
- Sometimes in a divorce both parents leave.
- Not accepting someone for who they are is painful for both of you.
- There are different ways of telling the truth. It doesn't always have to hurt.
- Lonely, needy people are vulnerable.
- Sometimes you just fall in love with the wrong person.
- Mistakes are not always fatal—you *can* survive them.

BOOK REPORT IDEAS

1. Explain why you think John fell for Marisol even though he knew she was gay.
2. Do your own zine of the book and your reaction to it.
3. Discuss why John's mother refused to touch him, and what affect that had on him.
4. Define your understanding of hard love, in the book, in the song, and in your own life. What is it? Where does it come from and why does it exist?
5. Telling the truth is a major theme in the book. Look at the major characters and discuss how they did and did not tell the truth.

6. Discuss what you think Marisol meant when she said, "There are different ways to tell the [same] truth."

BOOKTALK IDEAS
1. Use a zine as a prop for your talk.
2. Play a tape of the song "Hard Love" as a sound track for your talk.
3. Use John and Marisol's first meeting as the focus of your talk.

RISKS
*   Parents shown as distant and uninvolved.
*   Homosexuality is presented positively.
*   Language is genuine and realistic, but does include some obscenities.

STRENGTHS
*   Format reflects the look of a zine, and typeface changes for different kinds of writing.
*   Homosexuality depicted in a positive way.
*   Realistic characters teens can identify with easily.
*   Shows the pain of first love and of loving wrongly.
*   Demonstrates the importance of having connections with others.

AWARDS
Best Books for Young Adults, 2000 (ALA)
Quick Picks for Reluctant Readers, 2000 (ALA)
Michael L. Printz Award, Honor Book, 2000 (ALA)
School Library Journal Best Books of the Year, 1999
Booklist Editors' Choice, 1999
Lambda Literary Awards, 2000

REVIEWS
"The non-dramatic ending is plausible without insulting teens' intelligence, remembering that adolescence is a trying time filled with questions and feelings . . . an intriguing and absorbing novel for the gay/lesbian and young adult collections of any suburban or rural library." —*Voice of Youth Advocates*, 8/99, Beth Gilbert.

"Tackles the delicate issue of unrequited love between a straight and a gay teen . . . . a thoughtful and on-target addition to the growing canon of gay and lesbian coming-of-age stories." —Amazon, 1999, Jennifer Hubert.

"Changing typefaces, canted blocks of text, and occasional pale background collages give this star-crossed romance a hip look, without compromising legibility. . . . bittersweet portrait of an adolescent writer caught up in a quixotic first love will snare susceptible readers." —*Kirkus Reviews*, 1999.

"Modern tale of unrequited love. . . . Adding a note of realism. . . . are the pages designed to look like authentic zine excerpts, handwritten poems, and letters. . . . Readers. . . . will be pulled along by the story and situations." —*Horn Book*, 1999.

📖📖📖

HATE YOU. McNamee, Graham. Delacorte Press, 1999. $14.95. 119p. ISBN: 0-385-32593-2. Laurel-Leaf Books, 2000. $4.99. 128p. ISBN: 0-440-22762-3. Realistic fiction. Reading level: MS. Interest level: MS, YHS. English, Music, Creative writing, Art.

SUBJECT AREAS
family relationships; abuse, physical; music; problem parents; rites of passage; writing; anger; school; self-knowledge; friendship; love; sex and sexuality.

CHARACTERS
Alice Silvers: her throat damaged by her father's abuse, she writes songs she can never sing
Desiree Silvers: Alice's mother who's an artist and loves reading about murder and mayhem
Raymond Silvers: Alice's father who's dying
Eric: Alice's boyfriend who's a master of insults and cutting remarks, and the love of her life
Janie: Alice's friend since junior high
Rachel Grant: Eric's cousin who can sing like an angel
Andrew Harms: film student who works with Alice's mother
Linda Rosetti: Raymond's girlfriend

BOOKTALK
Alice Silvers is a songwriter who writes songs she can never sing.
"Locked in a cell
with my imaginary friends
in a dungeon
where night never ends . . . .
And it kills me
that I never got a chance
to tell you
how much

I hate you"

Years ago, when Alice told her father to stop choking her mother, he choked her instead. The only voice she's had since then is cracked and broken, a Frankenstein voice, a voice that makes people wince when they hear it, a voice that can never sing.

" My throat turns to stone
and strangles all sound
and I never got a chance
to say how much
I hate you.
And I know you can't hear me
Wherever you are
But I'll scream at you anyway
My face to the bars
I hate you
Hate you"

Alice is seventeen when she picks up the phone and speaks to a woman who changes her life. Her father is dying of cancer in a town only two hours away, and he wants to see her. Alice hasn't seen or talked to him since the day he took her voice away, and she feels like a nightmare has walked into her life. When she tells Eric, her boyfriend and the love of her life, about it, he says, "There are two ways out of a nightmare. You can keep running or you can stand your ground and take your chances."

Listen to Alice's hoarse, rasping, cracked voice as she tells you how she learned to hate—and then to love.

MAJOR THEMES AND IDEAS
- Frequently doing the right thing is neither easy nor fun.
- People have to learn to hate. For some this is easier than it is for others.
- Everyone is responsible for their own life. It's never someone else's fault that you are the person you are.
- Protecting is supposed to be the parent's job, not the kids.
- Don't stay with someone who hurts you, thinking they'll change. They won't.
- You can't sing a song about hate with an angel's voice.
- Hating someone ties you just as close to them as loving them.
- The best way out of a nightmare is to stand your ground and take your chances.

BOOK REPORT IDEAS
1. Alice describes her voice as "broken." Discuss the other ways she and her life are broken.
2. Explore the idea that hatred always ends up hurting the hater most.

3. Examine the three songs in the book, and explain what each says about Alice and how she feels about herself, her father, and her life.
4. Love is expressed in many ways in this book. Show how different characters convey their feelings of love and affection.

BOOKTALK IDEAS
1. Alice compared her voice to Janis Joplin's. Use a tape of a verse or so of one of her songs as a prop for your talk
2. Write your talk in Alice's voice, using brief excerpts from the book to let your audience know how she sounded.
3. Use a cut from the Tom Waits CD, "Small Change" as a sound track for your talk.
4. Focus your talk on two scenes: when Alice's father choked her, and when she gets the call from Linda.

RISKS
- Father is abusive and absent, mother is distant and uninvolved.
- Teens are sexually active.

STRENGTHS
- Nonsequential story line adds complexity.
- Shows the positive results of letting go of hatred/anger.
- Flippant, sarcastic tone will appeal to many teens.
- Safe sex is practiced.
- Characters are able to accept themselves for who they are.
- Distinctive narrator's voice makes it possible to "hear" the story as well as read it.

AWARDS
None

REVIEWS
"The characters are well drawn and easy to empathize with, the story flows with good dialogue, and the lyrics to Alice's three songs are moving. The cover is also attractive. However, I wish (and suspect others will also) that the book had been longer to further the story of these interesting people." —*Voice of Youth Advocates*, 4/99, Susan H. Levine.

"Teens will learn from Alice's struggle that hatred always ends up hurting the hater the most. . . . An engaging read that speaks plainly to teens about forgiveness and acceptance, offering them a gift to take back to their own realities." —Amazon, 1999, Jennifer Hubert.

"While there is no happy reconciliation, Alice takes ownership of her voice, her art, and her life. She is a responsible, monogamous, sexually active teen with successful relationships outside of her family. . . . . reluctant readers will appreciate her haunting lyrics, the short chapters, and the edgy plot." —*School Library Journal*, 3/99, Katie O'Dell Madison.

"This is a powerful first-person narrative about the truth, relationships, and the sadness of a lost childhood." —*Booklist*, 2/99, Karen Simonetti.

ᗕᗕᗕ

HEROES. Cormier, Robert. Delacorte Press, 1999. $21.95. 135p. ISBN: 0-385-32590-8. Laurel-Leaf Books, 2000. $5.50. 135p. ISBN: 0-440-22769-0. Reading level: MS. Interest level: MS, YHS, OHS. English, American history, World history, Ethics, Psychology.

SUBJECT AREAS
self-knowledge; death and dying; revenge; abuse, sexual; friendship; love; war; rites of passage; survival; handicaps, physical; grief and mourning; secrets.

CHARACTERS
Francis Joseph Cassevant: an eighteen-year-old veteran of World War II, he has just returned to his hometown, his face destroyed by a grenade
Larry LaSalle: the recipient of a Silver Star, he is a hero, but he is also the man who destroyed Francis's life
Nicole Renard: the girl Francis fell in love with when he was only fifteen
Mrs. Belander: Francis's landlady
Marie LeCroix: Nicole's best friend who lived in Francis's building
Sister Mathilde: one of the teaching nuns at the Catholic school in Frenchtown
Joey LeBlanc, Louis Arabelle: Francis's childhood friends

BOOKTALK
My name is Francis Cassavant, and I am back in Frenchtown for the first time in three years. After the grenade, I was in the hospital in France, then in one in England, and now they have shipped me home with a Silver Star and no face. I have eyes, because I can see, and eardrums, because I can hear, but no ears to speak of. My nose is gone, with two black holes where it used to be. My teeth are gone as well, but my jaw is intact so I can wear dentures. The grenade also damaged my throat, and I don't even sound like myself any more.

I wear a white silk scarf tied around the bottom part of my face and pull a Red Sox cap low over my forehead, to hide as much of what I look like as I can. Since I'm wearing my old fatigue jacket, everyone knows I'm a veteran. What they don't know, however, is that I am on a mission. I carry a gun in my duffel bag, and I am waiting to use it. I killed in France and Germany; one more death won't make any difference. I am going to do something I should have done three years ago, instead of forging the date on my birth certificate and joining the army when I was only fifteen. In a way I'm glad that no one can recognize me, that my face is gone. It will make it easier to leave when my mission is over. No one will blame Francis—it will be the vet without a face that killed Larry LaSalle.

They say I'm a hero, just like Larry, but it's a lie. I had my chance to be a hero, and I failed. I am determined not to fail again.

MAJOR IDEAS OR THEMES

- Sometimes just surviving is all you need to do to make you a hero.
- The betrayal of a friend can be forgiven, but the friendship may be gone forever.
- Just because someone looks like a hero on the outside, doesn't mean that he really is one.
- There is no way to change the past, no matter how much you wish you could.
- The true heroes of the war are the men who stayed and fought and didn't run away, and who survived, came home, and didn't talk about it.
- Each of us chooses how we will deal with the mistakes in our past, whether to let them make us stronger or destroy us.

BOOK REPORT IDEAS

1. Discuss why Francis didn't rescue Nicole, even though he knew what Larry was doing to her.
2. Show how living in Frenchtown and watching the other veterans changed the way Francis felt about himself and what he had done.
3. Compare the characters in the book described as heroes, showing how they did and did not fit that description. Who was the real hero in the book?
4. Compare Larry and Francis, and show how they were both damaged mentally and physically.
5. Discuss the meeting between Nicole and Francis, and why she won't see him again. Include what you might have done in a similar situation.

BOOKTALK IDEAS

1. Build your talk around the concept of heroism, using quotations about heroes to illustrate your talk.
2. Write a character description talk, letting several characters tell bits of their stories. Be careful not to give too much away.

RISKS
- Rape of a teen by an adult.
- Narrator plots to murder for revenge.
- Character commits suicide violently.

STRENGTHS
- Powerful message presented in a way that is accessible to teens.
- Detailed examination of the nature of heroism.
- Complex, multidimensional characters teens can identify with.
- Story is brief and easy to read, yet presents difficult, complex issues.

AWARDS
Best Books for Young Adults, 1999 (ALA)
Quick Picks for Reluctant Readers, 1999 (ALA)

REVIEWS
"Explores the meaning of heroism and the hidden motivations for what may appear to be heroic acts. The theme of guilt and revenge is also powerful. . . . a suspenseful novel that addresses serious questions of concern to most young adults." —*Voice of Youth Advocates*, 1999, Paula Lacey.

"Emulating the sparse, sturdy prose of Francis' literary idol, Ernest Hemingway, Cormier sketches the dark underbelly of a brief historic time in shadows that will follow the reader long after the story has ended." —*Booklist*, 6/98, Roger Leslie.

"Cormier takes the notion of heroism and deconstructs it. The hero is epitomized by Francis; a white scarf, no more than a veneer, hiding an appalling reality of hypocrisy and betrayal. The thread of Catholicism is woven throughout the narrative. Characters are not absolutes, but capable of great and evil acts. This lean, compelling read. . . . is a powerful and thought-provoking study." —*School Library Journal*, 8/98, Jennifer A. Fakolt.

"A riveting yarn of psychological suspense. . . . Young teens will find it a quick and absorbing read, and older adolescents (and full-fledged adults, too) will relish pondering the many-sided ethical questions Cormier raises about heroism, guilt, and forgiveness." —Amazon, 1999, Patty Campbell.

📖📖📖

HOLES. Sachar, Louis. Farrar, Straus & Giroux, Inc., 1998. $16.00. 233p. ISBN: 0-374-33265-7. Bantam, 2000. $5.99. 240p. ISBN: 0-440-41480-6. Thorndike Press, 1999. $23.95. 286p. ISBN: 0-786-22186-0. (large print) Listening Library Inc., 1999. $23.98. ISBN: 0-807-28071-2. (abridged audiotape) Listening Library Inc., 2001. $33.00. ISBN: 0-807-28611-7. (compact disc) Reading level: MS. Interest level: MS, YHS. English, P. E., American history.

SUBJECT AREAS
family relationships; crime and delinquency; secrets; sports; friendship; rites of passage; mystery and suspense; self-knowledge; survival; revenge; humor; ethnic groups; manipulation; peer pressure.

CHARACTERS
In the present

Stanley Yelnats IV: he just happened to be in the wrong place at the wrong time

Stanley Yelnats III: Stanley's father, an inventor who's smart and has a lot of perseverance, but very little luck

Mr. Sir: he introduces Stanley to Camp Green Lake

Mr. Pendanski: Stanley's counselor

Alan (Squid), Rex (X-Ray), Jose (Magnet), Theodore (Armpit), Ricky (Zigzag), Hector (Zero): Stanley's tent mates

Clyde "Sweet Feet" Livingston: a famous baseball player who donated his sneakers to help raise money for homeless kids

Warden: tall and threatening, she rules the camp, and knows why the boys are digging holes

In the past

Elya Yelnats: Stanley's no good, dirty, rotten, pig stealing, great-great-grandfather

Myra Menke: when she was fourteen, Elya fell in love with her

Madame Zeroni: a friend of Elya's who tells him how to win Myra's hand

Miss Katherine Barlow (Kissing Kate Barlow): she made prizewinning spiced peaches and later was one of the most feared outlaws in the West

Trout Walker: until Kate Barlow turned him down, no one had ever refused him anything

Linda Miller Walker: she married Trout

BOOKTALK
Stanley Yelnats wasn't a bad kid, he just came from a long line of losers. His whole family history was full of folks who were at the wrong place at the wrong time. And now it was Stanley's turn.

Derrick Dunn was a bully and Stanley was his favorite target, in spite of the fact that Stanley was so much bigger than he was. That's why, at about 3:15 on the last day of school, Stanley was fishing his notebook out of one of the toilets in the boy's restroom when his bus left. Missing his bus meant that he had to walk home, which is why a pair of sneakers fell out of the sky and hit him on the head. Stanley was so startled that he just grabbed the shoes and started running, which is why a policeman stopped him to question him, and that's why Stanley was arrested and charged with shoe theft. You see, Stanley didn't have the good luck to be hit by any old pair of sneakers, he had the bad luck to get hit by the pair of sneakers Clyde Livingston, the famous ballplayer, had just donated to charity. They were worth maybe $5,000 at a charity auction, and so in spite of it being Stanley's first offense, the judge gave him not probation, but a choice of jail or Camp Green Lake. Stanley chose Camp Green Lake, only to discover that it wasn't green, there wasn't a lake, it wasn't a camp, and it was the hottest, driest place he'd ever been. And *then* he found out what he was going to do all day, every day.

All the boys at the camp had to go out on the dried lakebed and dig holes. They started at 4:30 in the morning and each boy had to dig until he had a hole five feet in every direction. Then the next morning, they had to get up and do it again.

But they weren't just digging holes; they were also looking for something, something interesting, something that could persuade the Warden to give whoever found it a day off digging.

Is there a reason for Stanley's bad luck? His family's always said it was because of his dirty, rotten, pig stealing, great-great-grandfather, but maybe they're wrong!

MAJOR THEMES AND IDEAS

- Life may not be easy, but that's no reason to quit trying. Many times we learn the most from failure.
- You're responsible for your own life—you can either mess it up or make it work. It's up to you.
- Frequently people get what they deserve, good or bad. What goes around, comes around. Eventually.
- It only takes a moment for your life to change completely.
- Life is full of accidents and coincidences, which may be neither accidental nor coincidental.
- "If only. . . . " accomplishes nothing but keeping you stuck in your mistakes, rather than taking action to correct them.

BOOK REPORT IDEAS

1. The boys dig holes to build character. Explain how this does or does not change them, and discuss which characters in the book show positive or negative traits.

2. The events in the present are interwoven with a description of events from over 100 years ago. Show how they are connected and why the author sequenced the story as he did.
3. "A lot of people don't believe in yellow-spotted lizards either, but if one bites you it doesn't make a difference whether you believe in it or not." Describe what this sentence means to you and how it is significant in furthering the book's plot.
4. There is little predictable in the book, as what seems serious becomes funny, and what is funny becomes serious, and what is serious becomes deadly. Show how this helps highlight the absurdities of the book.
5. Examine the concept of holes, holes in the ground, holes in people's lives, holes in the story, and show which holes have been filled in and which have not, when the book ends.

BOOKTALK IDEAS
1. Write a character description talk focusing on the boys in tent D and how they relate to each other. Include information on their status, ethnicity, and how they cope with being at the camp.
2. Focus your talk on Camp Green Lake itself, describing what it was like, and contrast that to how it is now. Build up to Mr. Sir's description of what Stanley will be doing every day and how impossible it is to escape.
3. Use the family history information as part of your talk, telling how it is still affecting the current Stanley Yelnats.

RISKS
- Vicious, uncaring adult characters abuse their charges.
- Peer manipulation/harassment pits the characters against each other.
- Humor is dark and satirical, as are many of the characters.

STRENGTHS
- Quirky, appealing characters teens can easily identify with.
- The good are rewarded; the bad are punished.
- Challenges the reader, who must "fill in holes" that the author left empty.
- Multiple story lines are interwoven, adding complexity to the plot.
- Can be read on several different levels.
- Ambiguous ending leaves room for speculation.

AWARDS
Best Books for Young Adults, 1999 (ALA)
Quick Picks for Reluctant Readers, 1999 (ALA)
Selected Audiobooks for Young Adults, 2000 (ALA)
Newbery Award, 1999 (ALA)
Children's Notables, 1999 (ALA)

National Book Awards, 1998
100 Best Books for Teens, 2000 (ALA)

REVIEWS

"This delightfully clever story is well-crafted and thought-provoking, with a bit of folklore thrown in for good measure." —*Voice of Youth Advocates*, 12/98, Mary Ann Capan.

"Sachar's novel mixes comedy, hard-hitting realistic drama, and outrageous fable in a combination that is, at best, unsettling. The comic elements . . . work well, and the adventure story . . . provides both high drama and moving human emotions." —*Booklist*, 6/98, Bill Ott.

"Each of the boys is painted as a distinct individual through Sachar's deftly chosen words. The author's ability to knit [the] compelling story in and out of a history of intriguing ancestors is captivating . . . skillful braiding of ethnic folklore, American legend, and contemporary issues is a brilliant achievement." —*S chool Library Journal*, 9/98, Alison Follos.

"An exceptionally funny, and heart-rending, shaggy dog story . . . filled with twists in the lane, moments when the action is happily going along only to turn toward somewhere else that you gradually, eventually . . . realize was the truest destination all along. . . . We haven't seen a book with this much plot, so suspensefully and expertly deployed, in too long a time." —*Horn Book*, 9-10/98, R.S.

📖📖📖

HONOR BRIGHT. Platt, Randall Beth. Delacorte Press, 1997. $14.95. 229p. ISBN: 0-385-32216-X. Laurel-Leaf Books, 1998. $4.50. 240p. ISBN: 0-440-21987-6. Realistic fiction. Reading level: MS. Interest level: MS, YHS. English, Ethics, American history.

SUBJECT AREAS

family relationships; lying and deceitfulness; stepparents; elderly; self-knowledge; anger; revenge; secrets; war; writing; music; poverty; substance abuse; death and dying; grief and mourning; problem parents; rites of passage; friendship.

CHARACTERS

Theodora/Teddy Ramsey: fourteen years old, she's cocky, angry, and proud

Howard/Howie Ramsey: Teddy's twin brother who dislikes her as much as she dislikes him
Dee Dee Ramsey: the twin's beautiful, perfect mother
Grandma Rose: Dee Dee's mother, with whom the twins will spend the summer, she looks just like her daughter
Steve Maloney: a local boy who makes friends with the twins
Sid Spirk: Dee Dee's new husband

BOOKTALK

Teddy and Howie couldn't have been more alike—they were twins. They also couldn't have been more different. And while some twins are also the best of friends, they were not—they were bitter enemies. It was the summer of 1944, and their mother had left them with her mother so she could work two shifts at the plant. They hadn't seen their grandmother for years, not since the fire ten years ago when they were only four, the fire that killed their father and baby sister and left Teddy's hands horribly scarred.

There are secrets in their family, secrets about the fire, secrets between mother and grandmother, between mother and daughter. And when Teddy begins exploring her grandmother's attic, those secrets begin to come out of the dark places where they've hidden all these years.

Fire almost destroyed this family once. Will secrets revealed make it happen again?

MAJOR THEMES AND IDEAS

- Some secrets may be better kept.
- Sometimes sharing pain or sorrow can reduce their impact.
- When we make assumptions about why people do what they do, based on incomplete information, those assumptions are almost always incorrect.
- Anger can make it easier to keep the truth from someone.
- If you cannot forgive, you will be stuck in your anger forever, unable to grow or go on with your life.
- Alcohol can dull your pain for a while, but sooner or later you have to face pain head-on, and go through it to find the peace on the other side.

BOOK REPORT IDEAS

1. Discuss why Teddy is so determined to prevent Howie from learning her secret. Explain what this says about both her and Howie and the impact it has had on their relationship and the anger between the two of them. What do you think might happen if/when Howie learns the truth?
2. Forgiveness is a major theme of this book. Explore who is able to forgive whom, why, and with what results.
3. Speculate on what you think happens to the six main characters after the book is over. What will they be like in five years? In ten years?

4.   Compare the relationships between Rose and Dee Dee, and between Dee Dee and Teddy, showing how they are both similar and different.
5.   There are many secrets being kept in this family. Discuss these secrets, who is keeping them, from whom, and why.

BOOKTALK IDEAS
1.   Focus your talk on Teddy and on the secret of her burned hands.
2.   Write your talk as a dialogue between Teddy and Howie, letting them introduce the situation and hint at some of the secrets in the family.
3.   Use the chapter of the book when Teddy and Howie meet Rose, ending up with Rose taking off shoes, wig, and makeup to become a different person, and how that change will make their summer far different from what they'd expected.

RISKS
- Portrays a dysfunctional family with many secrets.
- Language is realistic but vulgar.
- Teens drink and smoke.
- Shows weak maternal role model.

STRENGTHS
- Strong multidimensional characters that grow and gain insight.
- Ending doesn't provide all the answers, allowing the reader to speculate.
- Detailed, layered, suspenseful plot.
- Shows the effects of war on several different groups and individuals.

AWARDS
None

REVIEWS
"Ultimately, revelation and openness leave us with a family whose members have grown in self-knowledge and forgiveness. . . . Teddy is a well-crafted character whose development is satisfying to watch." —*Voice of Youth Advocates*, 4/97, Nancy Gregg.

"Platt's prose is as forceful as her main character, realistically conveying the torments of true mother-daughter conflict while sustaining a plot that develops and surprises to the ending." —*Booklist*, 4/1/97, Susan Dove Lempke.

"Although sometimes disturbing and overdone, the frequent ugly spats, profanity and heavy teen drinking are startling but effective ways of getting beneath each character's surface. A tour de force with a tough, unforgettable protagonist." —*Kirkus Reviews*, 1/1/97.

ᛥᛥᛥ

IRONMAN. Crutcher, Chris. Greenwillow, 1995. $16.00. 181p. ISBN: 0-688-13503-X. Laurel-Leaf Books, 1996. $4.99. 228p. ISBN: 0-440-21971-X. Realistic fiction. Reading level: YHS. Interest level: YHS, OHS. Creative writing, Sex education, P. E., English, Ethics, Psychology, Vocational education.

SUBJECT AREAS
problem parents; divorce and separation; self-knowledge; rites of passage; dysfunctional families; abuse, sexual; abuse, physical; dating and social life; secrets; homosexuality; school sports; child abuse; therapy; death and dying; ethics; friendship; grief and mourning; lying and deceitfulness; peer pressure; manipulation; family relationships; poverty; prejudice; racism; survival; violence; working; writing; crime and delinquency.

CHARACTERS
Beauregard/Bo Brewster: a seventeen-year-old high school senior and Ironman triathlete
Keith Redmond: English teacher and head football coach
Lionel/Lion Serbousek: Journalism teacher and one of Bo's supporters
Dr. Stevens: High school principal
Mr. Noboru Nakatani/Mr. Nak: he teaches an anger management class at the high school—the Nak Pak
Jordan Brewster: Bo's little brother who is difficult to say the least
Mom: Bo and Jordan's mother who is acrimoniously divorced from their father
Lucas Brewster: Bo and Jordan's dad, with whom Bo has been terminally angry ever since he can remember
Don Sheridan: head janitor at the high school for fifteen years
Shelly, Shuja, Elvis, Hudgie, Joey: other members of the Nak Pak
Ian Wyrak: a university swim team member who hates Bo because he can't beat him

BOOKTALK
Bo Brewster is the Ironman. He pushes his body to the ultimate every day. He swims, bikes, and runs marathons, and he loves it. It's the way he deals with the anger that's about to take over his life, anger at the two men in his life who try to control him, his father and his former football coach.

He's much better at dealing with his dad—there's not much of an audience. But when Redmond, who's an English teacher as well as coach, humiliates him in class again, Bo loses it and calls him an "asshole." It's only October and it's his third suspension. He has a choice—go to anger-management class or be tutored at home by the worst teacher in school. It's a no-brainer. He reschedules his swim practice to before dawn, and joins the Nak Pak, Mr. Nakatani's group of thugs, losers, and assorted weirdos.

From the start he doesn't think he fits in—all he needs to do is just chill out, keep quiet, and do his time. But Mr. Nak doesn't run his group this way, and gradually Bo's drawn into the stories the others tell, and begins to share his own. Like how when he was nine his father banished him from the family for nine months, September to Easter. He stayed in his room the whole time, except when he was in school. He had his meals in his room, and without a TV, stereo, computer, or phone, all he did was homework, eat, sleep, and remember how angry he was at his father. He's a senior now, and his folks are divorced, so he doesn't have to see his dad as often, but the anger and the power struggle still continue.

Then there's Elvis, who's trying to take care of his little brother and sister alone, after their abusive father ran off. Shelly, whose uncle abused his daughter until Shelly told on him. It made her dad so mad, he kicked *her* out of the family. Plus, she's had run-ins with Redmond, too, and agrees with Bo's assessment of him. There's Hudgie, who's been abused so much he's just outta touch with reality a lot of the time—reality is simply too frightening to deal with. And guiding them and the others, is Mr. Nak, industrial arts teacher and Japanese cowboy, who is also fighting his own ghosts.

So come join the circle, listen to what these kids have to say. Some of their stories may have something in common with yours.

MAJOR THEMES AND IDEAS
- Your feelings are real and you are the only one who can identify them. Don't let anyone else tell you how you feel.
- When the chips are down, you have to live with yourself and with how you respond to the people in your life.
- Own what you do in a way you can be proud of. If you make a mistake, stand up and say so.
- Fighting and name-calling are one way to hide your fear. The more fear, the more anger it takes to cover it up.
- Denial is dangerous. So is letting someone else control you and not standing up for what you know is right. Both damage everyone involved.
- We are each responsible for what we allow in our lives.
- There is no act of heroism that doesn't include standing up for yourself.
- To see how something works, look at it broken.
- In a good tribe, every adult is a parent to every child.
- Mercy allows for all things—it excuses nothing, but it allows everything. It is the medicine for our anger, our hurt, and our desperation.
- Life has good people and evil ones. They both have their place, whether you understand it or not.

- We can learn from the most horrible of experiences, but only if we choose to see them as blessings or lessons.

BOOK REPORT IDEAS

1. Examine one of the Nak Pak's sessions and show how Mr. Nak is able to share some of his wisdom.
2. The last Nak Pak session ends with a discussion of mercy and how it allows all things. Explain what that means to you and why you think it is or is not true.
3. There are several fathers who play major roles, Bo's, Shelly's, Elvis's, and Hudgie's. Compare these men and discuss how they impacted the lives of their children in similar ways.
4. Most of the book is written letters to Larry King. Discuss why the author chose to structure the novel this way and why he chose Larry King.
5. Discuss the character of Lion Serbousek and how and why he was willing to go out on a limb to help Bo.
6. Analyze Bo's reaction to learning that Mr. Serbousek is gay, and why that reaction is so intense and so negative.

BOOKTALK IDEAS

1. Create you talk from excerpts of Bo's letters.
2. Focus your talk on the relationship between Bo and his father, and how Bo's anger got him into the Nak Pak.
3. Focus your talk on Mr. Nak and the members of the Nak Pak and their problems. Be careful not to tell too much of the story.

RISKS

- Language is realistic yet vulgar.
- Homosexual teacher is portrayed positively.
- Parents are portrayed as abusive and enablers.
- Sexual and physical abuse of children is discussed openly.
- Parents lie and manipulate their children in the name of love.
- Angry, manipulative teacher deals negatively with everyone and refuses to confront his anger.

STRENGTHS

- Intense writing style engages readers immediately.
- Multidimensional characters who are able to gain insight and grow.
- Many characters with different problems that teens can identify with.
- Strong, realistic scenes of group therapy give readers a chance to discover new options as characters do.
- Gay teacher is strong, positive gay role model, deeply supportive of his students.

- Characters show both their strengths and their weaknesses.
- Doesn't offer easy or quick fix solutions to problems.
- Ending does not resolve all problems or give absolute answers.

AWARDS
Best Books for Young Adults, 1995 (ALA)
Quick Picks for Reluctant Readers, 1996 (ALA)
School Library Journal Best Books of the Year, 1995
Popular Paperbacks for Young Adults/Good Sports, 1999 (ALA)
100 Best Books for Teens, 2000 (ALA)

REVIEWS
"Ironman Bo's memorable and honorable fight for his own identity will leave your heart in shreds." —*Voice of Youth Advocates*, 6/95, Mary K. Chelton.

"Through Crutcher's masterful character development, readers will believe in Bo, empathize with the other members of the anger-management group, absorb the wisdom of Mr. Nak, and despise, yet at times pity, the boy's father. . . . *Ironman* is one of [Crutcher's] strongest works yet." —*School Library Journal*, 3/95, Tom S. Hurlburt.

"Crutcher again demonstrates his genius for tackling big issues and thought-provoking philosophies in an accessible and entertaining way. . . . a novel that doesn't strive for easy answers, but does ask many intriguing questions of both its characters and its readers." —*Horn Book*, 9-10/95, Peter D. Sieruta.

"With its highly charged intensity channeled into riveting prose, an array of eccentric and strong characterizations, and dramatic plot climax. . . . *Ironman* is a combination of the psychological and the sports novels at their best." —*Booklist*, 1995.

📖📖📖

JUMPING THE NAIL. Bunting, Eve. Harcourt, 1991. $15.95. 148p. ISBN: 0-152-41357-X. Harcourt, 1993. $6.00. ISBN: 0-152-41358-8. Realistic fiction. Reading level: MS. Interest level: MS, YHS. English, Ethics, Psychology.

SUBJECT AREAS
death and dying; crime and delinquency; illness, mental; problem parents; peer pressure; dating and social life; love; suicide; self-knowledge; rites of passage; family relationships; ethics; friendship; secrets; lying and deceitfulness.

CHARACTERS
Dru Driscoll: a senior in high school
Mike Moriarty: Dru's friend
Scooter Navarro: the first person in ten years to jump the Nail
Elisa Fratello: Dru's friend who's dating Scooter
Sam Moriarity: Mike's father who used to date Dru's mother and is now a
    wealthy contractor
Andy and Connie Driscoll: Dru's parents
Virginia: a homeless woman who sleeps under a beachfront restaurant
*Tweeney Chalmers, Betsy Patterson, Lizzie, Diane Skoval, Fred Gowland/Hopi,
    Tom and Grant McInerney, Jeremy Poulson, Jill Elesco*: La Paloma High
    School students who go to watch Scooter and Elisa at the Nail

BOOKTALK
It was called the Nail, ninety feet from the top to the rocks below. The water
beneath was supposed to be bottomless and lined with caves. Everyone said
there was a car, with two teens still trapped inside, down there somewhere. But
jumping the Nail was still the way to show your virility, commitment, or
whatever else you had to prove to the world. Only a handful had gone over in all
those years, their names emblazoned on a board at the top. It had been over ten
years since anyone had even tried—not since the last person had misjudged the
bump in the cliff and ended up in a wheelchair, permanently.

Today, though, Scooter and his girlfriend Elisa were going to take the
plunge. Knowing Elisa's shaky state of mind, Dru was terrified for her friend
and what might happen to her. Elisa survives physically, but is mentally and
emotionally shattered, and leans on Scooter even more than before, rejecting
Dru's attempts to help her. That first jump sets off a dangerous game of one-
upmanship in Dru's crowd. Scooter's threatening to take Elisa over with him
again, and some of the other boys start boasting about their own plans for
making the leap. Dru knows that a greater tragedy will occur if something isn't
done to stop them—but what can she do?

MAJOR THEMES AND IDEAS
- A person who asks you to prove your love doesn't really love you at all.
- You don't have to prove anything to anyone.
- Sometimes it's necessary to go against the crowd when someone's life is in
  danger.
- Don't let anyone talk you out of your dreams.
- There are risks in every relationship, and trying to avoid them won't make
  them go away.

BOOK REPORT IDEAS
1. Discuss what Mike and Dru might have done to prevent Elisa's death.

2. Manipulation is a theme in the book, with many characters forcing others to do something they don't want to do. Analyze what these characters did and what their motivation was.
3. Peer pressure is a powerful force. Discuss how characters in the book were controlled by it.
4. Speculate on what happens after the book ends, first to Dru and Mike, and then to the other teens who went to the Nail that summer.

BOOKTALK IDEAS

1. "Jumping the Nail" is a secret that teenagers kept from adults. Focus your talk on the Nail itself, gradually leading up to Scooter and Elisa's jump. Be sure to include the legend of the two kids in the car.
2. Write your talk in first person as Dru.
3. Focus your talk on Scooter and his need to show off, leading up to his and Elisa's jump, but ending before they actually jump.

RISKS

-   Peer pressure pushes both boys and girls to do foolish, dangerous things to impress someone they like.
-   Girl commits suicide as a result of peer pressure.
-   Characters keep secrets to go along with the crowd.

STRENGTHS

-   Powerful picture of what failing to be responsible can do.
-   Realistic fast-moving plot draws in readers.
-   Several themes woven together add complexity to this brief novel.
-   Unresolved, ambiguous ending good for discussions.

AWARDS

Best Books for Young Adults, 1993 (ALA)

REVIEWS

"Without didacticism, the author shows the result of following the crowd in times of bad judgment, as well as the insensitivity sometimes exhibited when ego needs prevent people from responding to, and understanding, others." —*Voice of Youth Advocates*, 6/92, Barbara Flottmeier.

"Skillfully, Bunting homes in on the dynamics of daredevil behavior. . . . Satisfying suspense that unobtrusively incorporates wholesome values while drawing a credible picture of ordinary teens enthralled by their own escalating frenzy." —*Kirkus Reviews*, 10/15/91.

⊞⊞⊞

THE KILLER'S COUSIN. Werlin, Nancy. Bantam Doubleday Dell, 1998. $15.95. 240p. ISBN: 0-385-32560-6. Dell, 2000. $4.99. 240p. ISBN: 0-440-22751-8. Thorndike Press, 1999. $22.95. 277p. ISBN: 0-786-22188-7. (large print) Realistic fiction. Reading level: MS. Interest level: MS, YHS, OHS. English, Ethics.

SUBJECT AREAS
crime and delinquency; death and dying; secrets; family relationships; school; sports; occult and supernatural; anger; violence; friendship; rites of passage; self-knowledge; problem parents; revenge; lying and deceitfulness; dysfunctional families; fear.

CHARACTERS
David Bernard Yaffe: after being tried for murder, he is repeating his senior year of high school in another state
Vic and Julia Shaughnessy: David's uncle and aunt who let David live with them in Cambridge.
Lily Shaughnessy: David's cousin who's eleven
Stuart and Eileen Yaffe: David's parents
Dr. Edythe Walpole: headmistress at St. Joan's where David will repeat his senior year
Raina Doumeng: an artist who lives in the first floor apartment of the Shaughnessy's house
Greg: Emily's brother and David's friend who lied at the trial
Frank Delgado: a senior at St. Joan's and a skinhead, there's much more to him than his appearance

BOOKTALK
There's a before, and an after, and once you have crossed the line between them, you can never go back, no matter how much you'd like to. David crossed that line when he killed Emily. It didn't matter that he hadn't meant to do it or that he was acquitted. All that mattered was that Emily was gone, and he knew he was the one responsible for it.

His parents didn't understand that. They wanted to pretend that things could go back to the way they were before, and just go on with their lives. But that wasn't going to happen. You can't ever go back, you could only go forward. And that's what David had to do.

He couldn't live in Baltimore any longer, and had to repeat his senior year, so his parents sent him to live with his aunt and uncle and cousin in Massachusetts. He didn't know them; his mother and aunt had been feuding for years. The last time he saw them had been four years ago, when Kathy, their older daughter, had committed suicide. But they had room for David and a private prep school in Cambridge had accepted him. So he went.

There was no way he could have known what he was getting into, what was going on in that house, or in the upstairs apartment they gave him. But it didn't take long to find out. That first day he realized that neither his eleven-year-old cousin Lily nor her mother wanted him there. And that wasn't all—the apartment had strange shadows, and humming, buzzing noises that he couldn't identify.

Something was wrong, very wrong—and David knew it was up to him to figure out what.

MAJOR THEMES AND IDEAS
- Life's crises change you and once they have, you can't ever go back to who you were before.
- It's always better to face your demons than run from them. Running just makes them look larger and more frightening.
- Sometimes it's most important that the people you love believe you *before* you tell them the truth.
- Your own intuition can sometimes tell you what your intellect cannot.
- You have to live with what you've done and how your actions have changed you and your life. You can't go back to who you were before.
- Those who share similar burdens can help each other learn how to survive.
- Anyone can have the power of life or death over anyone else.

BOOK REPORT IDEAS
1. Discuss how David and Lily are alike and how they are different.
2. There are several supernatural elements in the story. Explain whether you think they add or detract from it and why.
3. Lily is a very complex character. Explain her actions toward David and the motivation behind those actions.
4. Discuss David's concept of the Abyss, and the idea that killing someone, whether deliberately or accidentally, changes you forever.
5. Explore the idea that once a crisis or a milestone in life has occurred, you cannot ever go back to being the person you were before.
6. Examine Raina's part in the plot, and how she helped further David's healing.
7. Speculate on what David and Lily will be like as adults. Will they still define themselves as killers and if not, what other terms or characteristics will they use?

BOOKTALK IDEAS
1. Write a mood based talk, focusing on the supernatural manifestations in the story.

2. Write your talk in first person as David.
3. Focus your talk on the first three chapters in the book, ending with Lily's question to David, "How did you feel?"

RISKS

- Child portrayed as killer.
- Supernatural elements, the ghost of a dead girl.
- Substance abuse by teens.
- Negative portrayal of a dysfunctional family.

STRENGTHS

- Multidimensional characters that grow and gain insight.
- Suspenseful style encourages reader to keep going.
- Somewhat unresolved ending leaves room for speculation.
- Unique narrator—the voice and perspective of an accidental killer.

AWARDS

Best Books for Young Adults, 1999 (ALA)
Quick Picks for Reluctant Readers, 1999 (ALA)
Booklist Editors' Choice, 1999
Bulletin for the Center for Children's Books, Blue Ribbon Book, 1999
Edgar Allen Poe Award for Best Young Adult Novel, 1999

REVIEWS

"Once they get started, readers will be hard pressed to put this book down."
—*Voice of Youth Advocates*, 1998, Melissa Thacker.

"A blazing climax. . . . resolves this subtle psychological thriller." —Amazon, 1998, Patty Campbell.

"Utterly terrifying psychodrama. . . . Positioning her characters in an intricate, shadowy web of secrets, deception, bad choices, family feuds, and ghostly warning, Werlin winds the tension to an excruciating point, then releases it in a fiery climax. . . . tautly plotted thriller, rich in complex, finely drawn characters." —*Booklist*, 9/1/98, John Peters.

"The thriller unfolds tantalizingly slowly. . . . young adults will eat this one up."
—*Horn Book*, 1999.

KISSING DOORKNOBS. Hesser, Terry. Delacorte Press, 1998. $15.95.
176p. ISBN: 0-385-32329-8. Bantam, 1999. $4.99. 160p. ISBN: 0-440-41314-1.
Thorndike Press, 2000. $21.95. 213p. ISBN: 0-786-22190-9. (large print)
Reading level: MS. Interest level: MS, YHS, OHS. English, Psychology.

SUBJECT AREAS

Illness, mental; family relationships; self-knowledge; friendship; school;
religion; love; problem parents; anger; therapy; unwed mothers; secrets;
prejudice; violence; dysfunctional families.

CHARACTERS

Tara Sullivan: a teenager struggling with OCD/Obsessive Compulsive Disorder
Mom and Dad: Tara's parents who try to understand Tara's behavior
Keesha, Kristin, Anna: Tara's best friends
Greta: Tara's younger sister
Donna DeLuca: a tough, cool girl who makes friends with Tara
Mr. Jacobson: an old friend of her father's who finally figures out why Tara is
    acting so strangely
Sam: a boy with OCD who explains it to Tara
Susan Leonardi: Sam and Tara's therapist

BOOKTALK

Tara Sullivan's life changed when she was ten years old and heard the rhyme,
"Step on a crack and break your mother's back." It didn't leave her head; she
just kept hearing it in her mind. "Step-on-a-crack-and-break-your-mother's-
back. Step-on-a-crack-and-break-your-mother's-back. Step-on-a-crack-and-
break-your-mother's-back." She couldn't make it quit. It was as if a whole army
of dictators had snuck into her brain and made her a slave to their demands.
Soon she wasn't just avoiding the cracks to keep her mother safe, she had to
count them as well. She couldn't walk to school with her friends any more—she
couldn't be distracted from counting. If she was interrupted, she had to go back
to the beginning and start over.

The demons in her head forced her to do other strange things—cross herself
and pray constantly, arrange the food just so on her plate, and of course, keep
counting. It was the only way she could get any peace. Sometimes it was better,
sometimes it was worse. Her parents took her to one doctor after another, but
nothing worked.

Tara's life was in chaos. Her friends finally drifted away, unable to put up
with her strange behavior. Her parents fought constantly about her. Her mother
slapped her over and over, trying to make Tara stop.

And then one day in January, on her way out the front door of her house,
the voices in Tara's head gave her a new ritual, one more strange and
frightening than any of the others—kissing doorknobs.

MAJOR THEMES AND IDEAS

- It's better to live one day as a lion than a hundred days as a lamb. The trick is to find out what you think a lion acts like.
- Facing your fears and doubts can frequently make them go away. A coward dies many times; a brave man dies but once.
- No matter what you do, people are going to think whatever they want about you.
- Sometimes you can't control your actions, no matter how hard you try.
- To understand someone's actions, look at the person, not the behavior. Acting crazy does not necessarily mean that you *are* crazy.
- When you don't understand why someone acts or looks a particular way, you begin to fear them, their actions, and their appearance.
- Change is almost always uncomfortable, because it forces you to deal with situations in a new way.
- Sometimes the positive new action is more frightening than the old, familiar, negative one.

BOOK REPORT IDEAS

1. Imagine you are Keesha or Anna and describe how you feel as Tara's illness gets worse and worse. Explain how you would deal with embarrassment, fear, anger, love, or other emotions you might feel toward Tara.
2. Trace the path of Tara's illness from its earliest symptoms to the end of the book.
3. Discuss how her disease changed the lives of Tara's family and friends.
4. The therapy used with Sam and Tara was aversion or exposure/response prevention therapy. Based on the book, explain what it is and why it is or isn't effective.
5. Tara's OCD escalates and recedes several times. Explain your understanding of why these ebbs and flows occurred.

BOOKTALK IDEAS

1. Have several characters describe Tara and her behaviors from their point of view. For instance, Tara's mother, Keesha, Greta and one of the doctors who misdiagnosed Tara.
2. Focus your talk on the year when Tara's behavior suddenly focused on counting. In first person, show her confusion and fear as her life is taken over by her disease.
3. Make Tara's behaviors the focus of your talk, showing how they got more and more bizarre. You might even demonstrate some of them as part of your talk.
4. Use a crystal doorknob as a prop for your talk.

Note: Because Tara's final compulsion about doorknobs comes so late in the book, you may choose to tell more of this book than the usual 25 percent. However, you must be careful not to give away any more of the story, i.e., anything about how she learned the name of what she had and began therapy for it. Do not reveal the story after chapter 15; keep your audience in suspense!

RISKS

- Parents are mentally and physically angry, abusive, distant.
- Portrait of mental illness is unflinching.
- Language is realistic yet vulgar.
- Portrayals of substance abuse, teen sex and pregnancy.

STRENGTHS

- Character with OCD portrayed realistically, so teen readers can identify with her.
- Shows impact of mental illness on friends and family.
- Shows positive effect of friendship—acceptance, loyalty, regardless of strange behaviors.
- Lets teens know there is a reason for OCD and also help—they are no longer alone or at the mercy of their disease.
- Offers an accurate description of several possible therapies for OCD.
- Ambiguous ending leaves room for individual and group reflection and consideration.

AWARDS

Best Books for Young Adults, 1999 (ALA)
Quick Picks for Reluctant Readers, 1999 (ALA)
100 Best Books for Teens, 2000 (ALA)

REVIEWS

"This book has the elements of a horror story as the reader watches Tara's family being tormented by unseen demons. A few outdated terms from the 1970s are used but the grace and power of this novel flows like a classic ballet." —*Voice of Youth Advocates*, 12/98, Nancy Thackaberry.

"Perfect blend of farce and sorrow. . . . what saves this from heavy case history is Tara's funny, desperate, first-person account of her rituals and their effect on her family and friends. The dialogue is fresh and contemporary, the characters close to all of us. Like Tara, fellow-suffers will be thrilled to discover that they are not alone or crazy." —*Booklist*, 6/98, Hazel Rochman.

LEARNING TO SWIM. Turner, Ann. Scholastic, 2000. $14.95. 128p. ISBN: 0-439-15309-3. Verse novel, Realistic fiction. Reading level: MS. Interest level: MS, YHS, OHS. English, Sex education, Psychology,Creative writing, Poetry.

SUBJECT AREAS
abuse, sexual; family relationships; friendship; self-knowledge; secrets; love.

CHARACTERS
Annie: a young girl who likes to play with her brothers and whose father is teaching her to swim.
Nicky, Peter: Annie's brothers
Mother and Daddy: Annie's parents
Grandma and Grandpa: Annie's grandparents
Kevin, Lonny, Angie: kids down the street who play with Annie and her brothers.

BOOKTALK
"Listen, I am trying
to remember everything
because it keeps coming back
like a skunk dog
on the porch
whining to get in,
and I'm afraid
if I don't let it in
it will never
go away.
This is what I remember:
that hot room,
your strange body,
your hands hurting,
and harsh words in my ears
telling me terrible things
would happen
if I ever
told.
But now you can't
find me or reach me
or hurt me ever
again
and once I tell the words
I am going to kick
you off my porch
and learn to breathe
again."

It was summer and hot and sticky. We packed to go to the summerhouse. Mother, Daddy, Grandma, Grandpa, Nicky, Peter, and me. I'm Annie. Nicky, Peter, and I play hide-and-seek and run races with the kids who live down the street, Kevin and Lonny and Angie. It seems like I am always it, hiding in the dark, away from the hands that reach to grab me.

Daddy and I go down to Dresser's Pond where I am learning to swim. I miss my pink plastic ring that holds the water back, but I churn my arms and kick my feet, and for just a moment rise above the dead leaves that float on the water. "You'll make a fine swimmer," Daddy says.

But one day all that changes. "I'll read you a book in your room," you say to me. Then when the door closes, the book falls to the floor and I feel your hands inside my clothes hurting me, and your voice telling me I can never tell. Your clenched fist floats in front of my face, warning me.

I never knew I could say no. The secret is locked inside me. Even your shadow makes me cringe. And still you take my hand and pull me into the hot yellow room, shut the door, and hurt me, again and again.

I can't swim. All I can see is myself sinking among the leaves. I wonder if anyone would notice if I did disappear. If I went somewhere far away, where you couldn't chase me and grab me, and pull me up the stairs into my room. When I look at the blue willowware plates on the table, I wish I could live in that safe blue world forever.

I tell no one what happens to me in that room. Only my dolls and baby Peter who can't talk know what you do to me. I hide from other people, drawing away from them when they try to touch me or hold me. But no one notices that I am going away, disappearing into the blue willowware world.

Then one day Mother says, "What book do you read upstairs in your room?" and the splintered words stuck in my throat begin to come out.

MAJOR THEMES AND IDEAS
- Some secrets must be told, no matter how painful the telling.
- If someone hurts you or does things to you that you don't like, you have the right to tell someone about it.
- Sexual abuse touches every part of your life and changes how you relate to others around you.
- Sometimes an innocent comment or question can release the floodgates and let out a long-held secret or shame, and allow you to begin to heal and grow.
- Those who love you will not reject you, no matter what happens to you.

BOOK REPORT IDEAS
1. Discuss the metaphor of swimming and how it reflects what is happening in Annie's life.

2. Give examples of the ways Annie changes in attitude, in actions, and in her responses to others after the abuse begins.
3. Explain why you think Annie didn't tell her parents immediately what was going on and why she was finally able to do so. What had to happen to allow her to tell her mother?
4. Explain how you think the summer's events will shape Annie's life in the future. Discuss what things might help her recover and what might cause her to stay trapped.

BOOKTALK IDEAS
1. Use the first poem in the book as part of your talk.
2. Weave bits and pieces of several poems into a whole, to tell the story up to when or just after the abuse begins.
3. Include the author's comments as part of your talk.

RISKS
• Sexual abuse of a very young girl by a young boy.

STRENGTHS
• Powerful images of a young girl trapped in and then freed from sexual abuse.
• Verse novel shows reader brief, lyrical, haunting images.
• Demonstrates the healing power of sharing shameful secrets.
• Offers hope to those who have been in similar situations.

AWARDS
Best Books for Young Adults, 2001 (ALA)

REVIEWS
"A moving and powerful memoir." —*School Library Journal*, 2000, Sharon Korbeck.

"Language is regular and prose-like, and though no one poem stands on its own, the entire narrative works together as one. . . . Teen readers will appreciate this work not just for its story, but for its illustrations of the writing process and the power one can wield with words." —*Kirkus Reviews*, 2000.

"In searingly simple language, Turner walks us through the little girl's forever-altered world, past the place where the truth comes out and healing can begin." —Amazon, 2000, Karin Snelson.

LIFE IN THE FAT LANE. Bennett, Sheri. Delacorte Press, 1997. $15.95. 320p. ISBN: 0-385-32274-7. Dell, 1999. $4.99. 260p. ISBN: 0-440-22029-7. Realistic fiction. Reading level: MS. Interest level: MS, YHS, OHS. P. E., English, Psychology, Sociology.

SUBJECT AREAS

prejudice; dating and social life; self-knowledge; gossip; rites of passage; stereotypes; eating disorders; bullying; family relationships; problem parents; divorce; friendship; school; love; illness, physical; secrets; peer pressure.

CHARACTERS

In Tennessee

Lara Lyn Ardeche: tall, slender, beautiful, she has just been elected Homecoming Queen when she starts to gain weight uncontrollably

Molly Sheridan: Lara's best friend since third grade, she's always been plump and outspoken

Carol Ardeche: Lara's mother who diets and works out regularly, believing that staying thin and attractive is essential to a happy marriage

James/Jimbo Ardeche: Lara's father, he is tall, handsome, and travels constantly on business

Scott Ardeche: Lara's fourteen-year-old little brother who knows more of the family secrets than anyone suspects

Jett Anston: Lara's boyfriend, he's tall, dark, and thin, a talented artist who refuses to follow the crowd

Amber Bevins, Lisa James: pretty and popular, they are Lara's friends only when she is thin

Blake Poole: Amber's boyfriend, he has a cruel streak and makes fun of kids who are different or unpopular

Dr. Fabrio, Dr. Laverly, Karen DeBarge: Lara's allergist, endocrinologist, and therapist

Dr. Bernard Axell, Dr. Maxwell Crowne: endocrinologists who have postulated the existence of Axell-Crowne Syndrome, which explains why some teens, like Lara, gain large amounts of weight, even while dieting and exercising strenuously

In Michigan

Perry Jameson: a fat sax player, he wants to date Lara

Suzanne Silver: Lara's piano teacher who is even fatter than Lara, and who helps her begin to accept herself

Tristan McCoy: a guitar player, he's Suzanne's gorgeous boyfriend

Devon: Tristan's student, he's blind, a college freshman, and likes Lara

Captain Bizarro: chef, musician, owner of the jazz club Lara starts going to

Cleo: she teaches Lara that you can choose "fat and fine" not "fat and ugly"

BOOKTALK

Lara had the perfect life. She was tall, thin, beautiful, and popular. Her parents were gorgeous and in love. She was going with the boy of her dreams, and was about to be elected Homecoming Queen, even though she was just a junior in high school.

But then one morning, her size 6 clothes were tight—really tight—and in just a month or so, she couldn't get into them anymore. Everyone said she should just quit eating so much and exercise more. They didn't know that Lara worked out every day till she was exhausted, and ate only a few bites of food a day. There was no way she could be gaining all this weight. Something was wrong with her! But all the tests came back negative—nothing abnormal at all. But the weight gain continued, pound after pound, forcing her to buy clothes in bigger and bigger sizes. Soon she was even bigger than the fattest girl in school, someone Lara used to make fun of.

Lara's life wasn't so perfect anymore. Kids at school laughed at her, and her thin friends deserted her. Then she found out that her family wasn't perfect either. In fact, it was falling apart. Her perfect, gorgeous parents had kept their secrets for years, but now they were out in the open, and they were ugly.

Will Lara ever get her perfect body and her perfect life back, or will she be serving out a life sentence in a size 24 body?

MAJOR THEMES AND IDEAS

- Who you are is more important than what you look like. You are far more than just a body.
- If you focus too much on someone else, you lose track of who *you* are.
- Friends are those who stick by you no matter what you do or say.
- Many times people say rude or cruel things to hide their own insecurities and fears.
- You can choose what you see when you look in the mirror, and decide to see yourself as "fat and ugly," or "fat and fine."
- Those who base their opinion of others on their appearances are as shallow as the beauty they so admire.
- Being thin, beautiful, and popular doesn't make you or your life perfect.
- Surface appearances are frequently false. A beautiful exterior can hide the flaws and problems inside for only so long. Sooner or later, everyone shows their true colors.
- It's our flaws that make us individual and interesting.

BOOK REPORT IDEAS

1. Compare Lara as who she was when the book opens and who she was at the end of it. How had she changed?
2. Set your book report at Lara's twentieth high school reunion in Tennessee. Speculate about what kind of a person she might be. You could also

compare who she might have been at that point had she never gotten fat, or describe some of the other people in her life who might attend the reunion, like Molly, Jett, Patty, Amber, Lisa, Jennie, or Sarah.

3. Include information in your report about the obsession with thinness that exists in the United States today, and how body image has changed over the last fifty or so years.

BOOKTALK IDEAS

1. Write your booktalk with Molly as the narrator, explaining what happened to Lara, and how she reacted to it, as Molly tried to keep on being her friend.

2. Illustrate your talk by using as props the tiny amounts of food that Lara eats as she tries to lose weight. On page 70 of the paperback edition, Lara's dinner is a slice of bread, some fresh veggies, 1/2 cup of cottage cheese, a small orange, and a glass of water. If you don't want to deal with the real thing, a picture of such a meal might also work.

3. Focus your talk on the way kids in Tennessee and Michigan talked about Lara when she was fat. Use excerpts to make it seem like a gossip session, talking about how awful she looks, and then bringing in the idea of Axcell-Crowne Syndrome, and how silly that was. Then stop your talk, and end it with one or two sentences about the very real problems Lara was facing, and whether she'd ever be thin again.

RISKS

• Portrays a dysfunctional family, including an adulterous father/husband and a self-absorbed, narcissistic mother/wife.

• Graphic picture of how fat people are treated cruelly in this society.

• Parent attempts suicide and abuses drugs.

STRENGTHS

• Powerful statement that an individual's appearance is not a reflection of that person's personality, worth, or soul.

• Realistic portrayal of the effects of peer pressure and persecution on the self-esteem of teens who are perceived by their peers as "different" and "not acceptable."

• Strong, clear contrast between characters who judge people by their appearance and those who see beyond that to who they are as individuals.

• Main character's growth as she moves from a preoccupation with her looks to acceptance of herself as a person, aside from her looks.

• Depiction of an overweight girl as something other than self-indulgent and out of control.

• Positive adult women role models who demonstrate that women are more than just their bodies.

- Unresolved and ambiguous ending, which allows readers to find a level of resolution without a "happily ever after ending."

AWARDS
Best Books for Young Adults, 1999 (ALA)
Selected Audiobooks for Young Adults, 2000 (ALA)

REVIEWS
"At times almost too painful to read, [this book] accomplishes two important goals: it cautions image-conscious adolescents to build a base of meaningful values, and it reassures overweight teens that the world is full of wonderful people who see right past the flesh and into the beauty of each person's essence. . . . offers a full measure of wisdom and hope." —*Voice of Youth Advocates*, 8/98, Beth E. Andersen.

"All these characters and situations are skillfully drawn, resulting in a compelling story. Bennett captures the voices of teenagers well and offers insight into what it's like to be overweight in a society that is so caught up in appearances." —*School Library Journal*, 3/98, Dina Sherman.

"Author lays out the issues with unusual clarity, sharp insight, and cutting irony." —*Kirkus Reviews*, 1998.

📖📖📖

LIFE IS FUNNY. Frank, Lucy. DK Publishing, Inc., 2000. $17.95. 272p. ISBN: 0-789-42634-X. Short story collection, Realistic fiction. Reading level: YHS. Interest level: YHS, OHS. English, Sex education, Creative writing.

SUBJECT AREAS
abuse, sexual; abuse, physical; self-knowledge; family relationships; problem parents; suicide; substance abuse; friendship, survival; rites of passage; sex and sexuality; illness, mental; working; violence; love; dysfunctional family; unwed mothers; secrets; poverty; ethnic groups; dating and social life.

CHARACTERS
China, Ebony: best friends who are black
Grace: she's beautiful, and friends with China and Ebony, but her mother doesn't like them because they're not white
Eric: he looks mad-scary and doesn't love anyone but his little brother Mickey
Keisha: she's forgotten how to laugh until she meets Gingerbread

Sonia: it's difficult to be a good Muslim girl in a Brooklyn school, but she knows she has to be perfect

Drew: having money and possessions doesn't stop his dad from beating his mother

Sam: he's half Puerto Rican, very handsome, and works after school in his father's garage

Monique: her abusive ex-boyfriend got her pregnant, and she's terminally angry at the world

Hector: he works at the prenatal clinic Monique goes to

Gingerbread: son of a crack addict, he's hyperactive, but he loves life

Marge and Tom: Sam's aunt and uncle who ask Keisha to stay with them during the summer

Linnette: Eric and Mickey come to live with her and her parents after her older brother dies

BOOKTALK

"Life is funny," Gingerbread says, and if *he* can say it, and mean it, than perhaps it's really true. Gingerbread is hyperactive, and can't be still for more than minutes at a time, a legacy from his crack-addicted mother. Keisha, who thinks life has very little to smile about, falls in love with him and begins to believe he just may be right about life.

But Eric sees life as a struggle to survive, and to protect his little brother Mickey, the only person he allows himself to love.

Sonia puts her family first, and tries to be a perfect Pakistani girl in a crowded Brooklyn school.

Grace and Sam are the two most beautiful people at school, yet both are haunted by their mothers' problems. Beauty doesn't buy happiness.

Drew has everything money can buy, but nothing he does can make his dad quit beating up on his mom, or make his mom leave.

And Monique and Ebony are angry, so angry that's its taken over their lives. Monique is angry with her abusive ex-boyfriend who got her pregnant, and Ebony's anger at her absent father makes her cut herself to escape the pain.

They're just a few of the kids who tell their stories here, all students in the same Brooklyn school for seven years. They share their lives with you, their friendships, their problems, their hopes, and their pain. Listen to their voices, because they speak the naked truth without any attempt to cover it up or make it look pretty. Let them challenge you, let them touch you, and even let them change you.

MAJOR THEMES AND IDEAS
- Your life changes based on who you meet and how you interact with them. Friends change your life, but so do enemies.
- It's not required that children follow in their parents' footsteps and patterns. It's worth the effort to make your own way.

- You *can* succeed against high odds, but it takes hard work, determination, and persistence.
- Some situations have to be endured until they can be escaped.
- You are responsible *only* for your own behavior, no one else's. When someone blames you for what they did, they're lying.
- If you have someone to love you, care about you, and stand with you, you can almost do anything.
- Drugs not only harm the addict, but also that person's friends, family, and children.
- Skin color is irrelevant, or should be. Choose your friends based on who they are on the inside, not how they look.
- When you're beautiful, it's sometimes hard to know if someone is reacting to your appearance or your self.
- We have no idea how many lives we change, unaware of the effects of our actions.
- The person who was never shown genuine love as a child will find it hard to recognize, give, or accept love as a teen and as an adult.
- If you shut yourself off from everything, you exclude the good as well as the bad. Love is worth the risk of being vulnerable.

BOOK REPORT IDEAS

1. All kinds of families are included in this book. Compare the two that you consider to be the most and least dysfunctional and explain why you chose them.
2. Discuss the three or four characters that you see as most and least successful at the end of the book and explain your choices.
3. Many kinds of love are shown in this book. Discuss several of them, and tell how and why the characters acted in loving ways.
4. Many of the parents in this book are involved in some kind of negative behavior—drug abuse, mental illness, physical abuse, desertion. Explain how the actions affected their children in physical, mental, and emotional ways.
5. There are many turning points in life that we can look back on later and say, "What if that hadn't happened?" "What if I'd made a different decision?" "What if I'd never met that person?" Look at some of these turning points in the book and speculate on what might have happened had things gone differently, playing out one of the "What if" scenarios above.
6. Discuss what character was the most important to you and explain why.
7. There are several sets of siblings in the book. Discuss the differences in the ways they related with each other and explain the reasons for those differences.

8. The teens in this book cover a variety of ethnic groups and cultures. Discuss whether, in your opinion, their interactions, because of these differences, were or were not realistic.

BOOKTALK IDEAS
1. Write a character description talk, with one-sentence descriptions of each of the eleven major characters.
2. Choose one character and narrate the booktalk from that person's perspective.
3. Focus on one scene in which several characters interact, showing their relationships.
4. Pretend you are a student at the school in the book, and describe what life is like for the students there, using several of the characters as examples.

RISKS
- Includes families that are dysfunctional in various ways.
- Teens are sexually active.
- Both teens and their parents abuse a variety of substances.
- Language is realistic but vulgar.
- Frank discussions of sexual activity, incest, physical and sexual abuse are included.
- Portrays interracial couples.
- Teen girl gets pregnant.

STRENGTHS
- Realistic language sounds like teens speak today.
- Multicultural characters so realistic teens can see themselves and their friends in them.
- Characters' voices are distinct and lyrical.
- Powerful, intense story lines draw in the reader immediately.
- Shows the power of love and friendship.
- Many diverse issues for teens to grapple with and discuss.
- Ambiguous ending leaves room for individual and group reflection and speculation.
- Multiple perspectives and story lines all woven together create a layered, complex plot.
- Characters are able to succeed in spite of adversity.
- Strong message of love, hope, and survival.
- Takes a gritty, complex look at real life.

AWARDS
Quick Picks for Reluctant Readers, 2001 (ALA)
Booklist Editors' Choice, 2000

REVIEWS
"This book belongs in the hands of mature readers who enjoy realistic stories and like to share the emotional highs and lows of the characters within." —*Voice of Youth Advocates*, 2000, Kevin Beach.

"Frank is a gifted writer whose talents give the gritty stories an almost lyrical quality. [It] is appropriate for bibliotherapy, especially for those professionals who help teenagers in a clinical setting." —*ALAN Review*, 2000.

"Frank has penned a high-intensity, multicultural, multidimensional teen reading experience that will challenge and change those who open it. These are real teens in real time. Be prepared for them to rock your world." —Amazon, 2000, Jennifer Hubert.

"Realistic language, rough and profane, fierce situations that are nearly too much to bear, and a savagely honest portrayal of the nature of the interconnectedness of life make this not a novel for the faint of heart or timid reader. But those who [read it] will come away rewarded and inspired by the strength and fortitude of its characters." —*Kirkus Reviews*, 2000.

"Succeeds most of all in showing how lives are shaped over years, for better or worse, by the people kids run into, away from and with." —*Horn Book*, 2000.

ロロロ

LIKE SISTERS ON THE HOMEFRONT. Williams-Garcia, Rita. Dutton, 1995. $15.99. 165p. ISBN: 0-525-67465-9. Penguin, 1998. $5.99. 176p. ISBN: 0-140-38561-4. Realistic fiction. Reading level: MS. Interest level: MS, YHS. English, Sex education, American history.

SUBJECT AREAS
family relationships; unwed mothers; minorities, black; sex and sexuality; self-knowledge; elderly; religion; dating and social life; friendship; rites of passage; poverty; prejudice; racism.

CHARACTERS
Gayle Ann Whitaker: streetwise and trash talking, she's a fourteen-year-old single mother
Ruth Ann Whitaker: Gayle's mother who sends her to live with her older brother's family
José/Emmanuel Whitaker: Gayle's seven-month-old son

Reverend Luther Gates: Gayle's rigid, conservative uncle
Virginia Gates: Gayle's determinedly cheerful aunt
Constance/Cookie Gates: Gayle's pious, virtuous sixteen-year-old cousin
Great: Gayle's great-great-grandmother who's about to die
 Stacy Alexander: a college freshman Cookie has a crush on

BOOKTALK
Gayle is a streetwise, trash-talking fourteen-year-old with a seven-month-old son when she gets pregnant *again*. As soon as Mama finds out, she marches Gayle off to an abortion clinic and then ships her down south to live with her aunt and uncle.

Suddenly Gayle feels like she's been dropped into a foreign country. Her man and her homegirls are gone and surrounding her are tall, loud, and sanctimonious family members who disapprove of her illegitimate son and her trashy mouth. Uncle Luther, the last in a long line of fiery, soul-searing preachers, won't even talk to her. Miss Auntie is sugar-sweet when she lists all the chores Gayle will have to do to keep busy so she'll stay out of trouble. Cookie, Gayle's sixteen-year-old cousin, is almost too good to be real, quoting the Bible and talking about getting saved. Gayle thinks she should just get real and get a *life*!

Great is the only person Gayle connects with, 'cause Great doesn't preach to her or try to change her. Incredibly old, Great is Gayle's great-great-grandmother, who never leaves her bed and is expected to die at any minute. But Great still has a bit of the devil in her, and sees Gayle as a kindred spirit. She knows the whole family's history, including all the scandals, and shows Gayle a side of her mother she's never seen.

But when Gayle shows Cookie how to catch the guy she's got a crush on and a few other choice tidbits she picked up on the street, things get out of control real fast. Will she ever fit in with these strangers who are also her family, and more important, does she even want to try?

MAJOR THEMES AND IDEAS
- Family are the people who always take you in.
- Sex is more than just a physical act and if you limit it to just that, you're missing out.
- People change. Finding out who someone was can help you understand who they are now.
- Age doesn't necessarily always bring wisdom and perspective, but when it does, make sure you listen closely.
- Important lessons in life are more frequently learned through adversity.
- In getting to know your family's history, you can also learn about yourself.
- Religion can either free someone or bind them.
- Having a baby doesn't make you a woman or a mother.

- Not crying about anything doesn't indicate either bravery or strength.

BOOK REPORT IDEAS
1. Compare and contrast Gayle's life in South Jamaica and Cookie's life in Georgia. Show the economic and class differences between them, which explain why Gayle feels so out of place in Georgia.
2. Discuss the Telling, its importance, and whether Great was aware of what she was doing and who she was talking to.
3. Explain the meaning of the title, and who Gayle's sisters turned out to be.
4. Gayle hides a large part of herself. Explain why this is necessary and how and why she changes.
5. Discuss the importance of family and family history in the book, including its influence on Gayle and her other family members.

BOOKTALK IDEAS
1. Write your talk from Great's perspective, in first person, as she introduces herself, Gayle, and other family members.
2. Using first person, let Gayle tell her own story in her own words.

RISKS
- Teen sexuality is discussed frankly.
- Language is realistic yet vulgar.
- Central character is unwed teen mother.
- Fundamentalist religion shown to be constricting.

STRENGTHS
- Shows the power and strength of family ties.
- Presents a wonderful portrait of feisty old woman determined to die in her own way.
- Religion is seen as a strength and a comfort.
- Portrays a deep friendship between a teen and a very elderly woman.
- Realistic, multidimensional characters grow and gain insight.
- Situations, characters, language teens can identify with.
- Gritty, readable, street talk written with style and flair.

AWARDS
Best Books for Young Adults, 1996 (ALA)
Quick Picks for Reluctant Readers, 1996 (ALA)
Coretta Scott King Award, Honor Book, 1996 (ALA)
Booklist Editors' Choice, 1995
YALSA Popular Paperbacks/Different Drummers, 1999 (ALA)

REVIEWS

"Should be a 'must read' for both young adults and adults. . . . well written book puts into action tough love that is used to help an irresponsible youth to become responsible through strong family ties, not outside social services. . . . " —*Voice of Youth Advocates*, 4/96, Hazel Moore.

"She has surpassed herself. . . . [in] the manner in which she has set these fictional characters along a historical continuum that roots them firmly in the real world while still allowing them the lightness of spirit to rise from the pages and into the reader's hearts." —*Horn Book*, 11-12/95, N.V.

"Beautifully written, the text captures the cadence and rhythm of New York street talk and the dilemma of being poor, black, and uneducated. This is a gritty, realistic, well-told story that will make an excellent addition to YA fiction collections." —*School Library Journal*, 1995, Carol Jones Collins.

"Williams-Garcia breathes life into what could have been a stereotypical portrait of a trash-talking, streetwise city teen, and while its scales are tipped in favor of responsible life, the book is honest enough to acknowledge the pleasures of the other kind." —*Bulletin of the Center for Children's Books*, 1995, Deborah Stevenson.

📖📖📖

MAKE LEMONADE. Wolff, Virginia Euer. Henry Holt & Company, 1993. $15.95. 208p. ISBN: 0-805-02228-7. Scholastic, 1994. $4.99. 200p. ISBN: 0-590-48141-X. Verse novel, Realistic fiction. Reading level: MS. Interest level: MS, YHS, OHS. English, Creative writing, Sex education.

SUBJECT AREAS

family relationships; unwed mothers; poverty; working; friendship; love; gangs; death and dying; fear; self-knowledge; school; survival; rites of passage.

CHARACTERS

LaVaughn: a fourteen-year-old who needs a job
Jolly: a seventeen-year-old unwed mother who needs a baby-sitter for her two kids
Jeremy, Jilly: Jolly's children
Mom: LaVaughn's mother who works hard to get the best she can for her daughter
Myrtle, Annie: LaVaughn's friends

Barbara: she helps Jolly to get back in school

BOOKTALK

Jolly's seventeen, she has two children from two different, long-gone fathers, and a dead-end job she's going to lose if she doesn't find a baby-sitter fast.

LaVaughn is fourteen, lives with her mother, and is determined to be the first one in her family or her apartment building to go to college. She works after school and answers Jolly's ad—"Baby-sitter needed bad!" LaVaughn and her mother live in public housing, but their apartment is clean and neat, and her mother heads up a tenant association that keeps drugs and gangs out.

Jolly lives in a tiny, smelly, filthy apartment, in an equally dirty and run-down building. Both of her kids are in diapers, every surface is caked with dirt and grime, and roaches roam everywhere unafraid.

The two teenagers couldn't be more different, but they have one thing in common. They both want out—somehow.

LaVaughn knows she'll make it someday and takes steps toward that day. Jolly doesn't see how things could ever change, and blames everyone else for her problems. Will LaVaughn be able to show her how to make lemonade from all the lemons life has handed her?

MAJOR THEMES AND IDEAS

- Stop and think before you hit a kid; stop and think until you know you won't do it after all.
- You can either pull yourself up or let yourself down. It's your choice.
- There's a thin line between doing someone a favor and letting them take advantage of you. Be sure you don't cross it.
- When you decide to get your life together, you have to do it your own way, not someone else's.
- When life gives you lemons, make lemonade.
- You do what you have to do to survive.

BOOK REPORT IDEAS

1. LaVaughn and Jolly are very different and yet alike in some ways. Explain how and why they are different and alike.
2. LaVaughn puzzles about how she might be taking advantage of Jolly, and Jolly might be taking advantage of her at the same time. (chapter 45) Explain how and why you agree or disagree with her.
3. This novel in written in blank verse, in a very spare style. Explain why this style has more impact than regular prose might, giving examples of descriptions you found particularly vivid.
4. Discuss the steps Jolly took to break the downward cycle she was trapped in and turn her life around.

BOOKTALK IDEAS

1. Write your talk from both LaVaughn and Jolly's perspectives, alternating between them as they describe their lives.
2. Use brief excerpts from several chapters as the main part of your talk.
3. Focus your talk on the chapters describing how LaVaughn got her job.

RISKS

- Unwed teen mother is unable to take care of herself, her children, or her home.

STRENGTHS

- Novel in blank verse gives characters and situations depth and immediacy.
- Language is gritty and realistic.
- Frank and vivid portrait of inner-city poverty.
- Characters teens can identify with easily.
- Shows how cycle of poverty can be broken.
- Strong, spare style brings characters and setting to life.
- Characters grow and gain self-esteem and insight.
- Gives strong message of hope and survival.

AWARDS

Best Books for Young Adults, 1994 (ALA)
Quick Picks for Reluctant Readers, 1994 (ALA)
100 Best Books for Teens, 2000 (ALA)

REVIEWS

"A wonderful story of two girls living very different lives. . . . Young girls will enjoy this story." —*Voice of Youth Advocates*, 10/93, Karen Hartman.

"Spare, beautifully crafted. . . . La Vaughn's narrative—brief, sometimes ungrammatical sentences in uneven lines, like verse—is in a credible teenage voice suited to readers like Jolly herself; yet it has the economy and subtlety of poetry. . . . the setting is deliberately vague; but their troubles—explored in exquisite specificity—are universal." —*Kirkus Reviews*, 1993.

"Sixty-six brief chapters, with words arranged on the page like poetry perfectly echo the patterns of teenage speech." —*Horn Book*, 1993.

"Rooted. . . . in the community of poverty, the story offers a penetrating view of the conditions that foster our ignorance, destroy our self-esteem, and challenge our strength. That education is the bridge to a better life is the unapologetic, unmistakable theme." —*Booklist*, 1993, Stephanie Zvrin.

⊞⊞⊞

MONSTER. Meyers, Walter Dean. HarperCollins, 1999. $15.95. 281p. ISBN: 0-060-28077-8. HarperCollins, 2001. $5.95. 281p. ISBN: 0-064-40731-4. Realistic fiction. Reading level: YHS. Interest level: YHS, OHS. English, Ethics, Psychology, Filmmaking, Drama.

SUBJECT AREAS
crime and delinquency; minorities, black; minorities, hispanic; ethics; writing; secrets; abuse, sexual; violence; lying and deceitfulness; manipulation; justice; ethnic groups; legal system.

CHARACTERS
Steve Harmon: sixteen years old and on trial for murder
Sandra Petrocelli: prosecuting attorney and assistant DA who labels Steve a "monster"
Kathy O'Brien: Steve's defense attorney
James King: also on trial for murder for the same incident
Richard Evans/Bobo: he and King committed the crime
Osvaldo Cruz: fourteen years old, he participated in the crime and turned in the others to keep out of jail
Jose Delgado: drugstore employee, he found the body
Asa Briggs: King's lead attorney
Salvatore Zinzi, Wendall Bolden: convicts who turned in King and Evans for a deal with the DA
Detective Karyl, Detective Williams: policemen who investigated the murder scene

BOOKTALK
Sixteen-year-old Steve Harmon is on trial for felony murder. He could get twenty-five to life without parole if he's found guilty. But Steve's not your average criminal or even juvenile delinquent. He's kind of quiet, a loner. He's in Mr. Savicki's film club, and the films he makes are about his Harlem neighborhood and what goes on there.

But the film he's making now isn't for class, it's only for him, and he's scripting and filming it only in his head. It's called "Monster," and it's the story of his trial. Why "Monster"? Because it's what the prosecuting attorney called him during her opening statement—a monster, someone willing to kill and steal with complete disregard for the rights of others.

But is he a monster? Maybe he's just someone in the wrong place at the wrong time. He says he didn't do anything. Can *not* doing something be just as much a crime as taking action?

Steve didn't rob a store or shoot the owner or split the profits. He did nothing. Does that make him guilty or innocent?

MAJOR THEMES AND IDEAS
- The truth looks different from different points of view.
- A crime, or a lie, can be one of omission as well as one of commission.
- Life isn't predictable.
- When people look at you, very often they don't see *you*, they see the person they want you or need you to be.
- Once someone's faith and trust in you has been destroyed, it is very hard to rebuild it.
- You are most comfortable with what you have the most experience, what you see as normal. So for some people, violence is normal.
- Whatever situation you're in, do what's necessary to survive, even if that means doing something that might be wrong in another situation.
- Think of all the tomorrows of your life before you decide what to do today.

BOOK REPORT IDEAS
1. Discuss Steve's involvement in the robbery. Explain why you think he did or did not commit a crime.
2. Discuss the different concepts of truth in the book. On pages 221 and 222, Steve says, "It's what you know is real," and another inmate says, "Truth is something you gave up when you were out there on the street. Now you're talking survival." Decide which view of truth Steve told on the witness stand, and explain and justify your decision.
3. Examine the character of Kathy O'Brien, and discuss whether or not she believed in Steve's innocence. Explain how her understanding of him did and did not change during the course of the trial, and what her last look to him meant.
4. Explain what you see as the purpose of the movie script and how it affected Steve's behavior during the trial.
5. On pages 220-221, there are two questions written in the margin of the pages. Discuss their significance and why they are there.
6. Discuss the different formats the author used to tell his story and the impact they had on the story and on the reader.

BOOKTALK IDEAS
1. Introduce Steve by having several characters describe him in varying ways. Use quotes from the book or make up lines that characters might have said.
2. Have Steve introduce himself and talk about why he is writing a movie.
3. Write your talk as if it were excerpts from news stories—the crime, the arrests, and the beginning of the trial. Be sure to create doubt in your

audience's mind about Steve's guilt or innocence by including quotes from people who cared about him as well as those convinced of his guilt.

RISKS

- Gangs, drugs, and violence involving young teens are depicted frankly.
- Jail inmate violence is depicted graphically, and includes fights and homosexual rape.
- Portrayal of justice system can be seen as either realistic or negative and corrupt.
- Language is realistic but vulgar.

STRENGTHS

- Gives brutal, yet realistic, view of street life in Harlem.
- Ending gives readers a chance to speculate on what *really* happened.
- Gives accurate picture of a criminal trial.
- Shows reprisals for criminal behavior.
- Varied visual format appeals to today's teens.
- Ending is ambiguous, and not-guilty verdict does not assure Steve's innocence.

AWARDS

Michael L. Printz Award, 2000 (ALA)
Coretta Scott King Award, Honor Book, 2000 (ALA)
Best Books for Young Adults, 2000 (ALA)
Quick Picks for Reluctant Readers, 2000 (ALA)
Selected Audiobooks for Young Adults, 2001 (ALA)
Booklist Editors' Choice, 1999

REVIEWS

"The journal and script techniques, distinguished by two reader-friendly typefaces, move the story along quickly. This pace, along with the casual type, courtroom drama, gritty jail descriptions, and the fate of the protagonist will make teen readers whiz through the book. Myers says a lot about circumstances, prejudices, justice, and the thin line many young men walk." —*Voice of Youth Advocates*, 8/99, Avis D. Matthews.

"Expertly presents the many facets of [the] protagonist's character and readers will. . . . feel. . . . both sympathy and repugnance for him. . . . will challenge readers with difficult questions to which there are no definitive answers. . . . an emotionally charged story. . . . compelling and disturbing." Edward Sullivan, —*School Library Journal*, 7/99

"Myers adeptly allows each character to speak for him or herself, leaving readers to judge for themselves the truthfulness of the defendants, witnesses, lawyers, and most compellingly, Steve himself...Tailor-made for readers' theater, this book is a natural to get teens reading—and talking." —*Horn Book*, 5-6/99, R.S.

"Innovative format, complex moral issues, and an intriguingly sympathetic but flawed protagonist. . . . the thorny moral questions raised in Steve's journal. . . . will endure in readers' memories. Although descriptions of the robbery and prison life are realistic and not overly graphic, the subject matter is more appropriate for high school-age." —*Booklist*, 5/1/99, Debbie Carton.

📖📖📖

THE MUSIC OF DOLPHINS. Hesse, Karen. Scholastic, 1996. $14.95. 181p. ISBN: 0-590-89797-7. Scholastic, 1998. $4.99. 192p. ISBN: 0-590-89798-5. Realistic fiction. Reading level: MS. Interest level: MA, YHS. Science, English, Psychology, Ethics.

SUBJECT AREAS
self-knowledge; animals; friendship; orphans; ethics; survival; science; homeless; manipulation; intimidation; rites of passage; grief and mourning.

CHARACTERS
Mila: a girl who grew up in a pod of dolphins, and is rescued when she is a teenager
Dr. Elizabeth Beck: a research professor at Boston University, she had a facility designed to stimulate a human response from wild children, and took Mila there
Shay: a wild girl discovered in the mountains of Idaho shortly before Mila was found, who was also at Dr. Beck's facility
Sandy: one of Dr. Beck's assistants
Dr. Troy: one of the doctors at the facility who worked with Shay
Justin: Dr. Beck's son who made friends with Mila
Dr. Peach: one of the doctors at the facility
Mr. Aradondo: a janitor at the facility who was afraid of Mila at first

BOOKTALK
She looked like a mermaid, hair wrapped around her body, acting more like an animal than a human. But she was a girl, a girl who'd lived with the dolphins for years. Could she ever learn to be a human girl, instead of a dolphin girl?

They found her on an island off the coast of Cuba. Her hair hung down to her feet, and she was covered with seaweed. Her height and body development were of a human girl between eleven and sixteen years old. Her skin was streaked with salt, and she had barnacles and strange circular scars all over her body. She was unable to speak; instead she made a high-pitched crying noise like a seagull. The Coast Guard crew that rescued her called her Mila. They later discovered that she had been living with the dolphins since she was three, thirteen years ago.

But now Mila must go from the world of the dolphins to the world of humans; from a world of togetherness to a world of separateness; from a world with no boundaries, to a world with walls and locked doors. Her body is human, but her mind, her thoughts, her ideas, are those of the dolphins. Will she ever be able to knit the two halves of herself together in a seamless whole?

MAJOR THEMES AND IDEAS
- First, do no harm.
- There are many ways of being human, and all of them should be respected.
- Forcing an individual to conform to the mold that someone else thinks they should fit into is cruel and unnecessary.
- Animals and humans can work together in ways most people have never even considered. Humans are not the only creatures with families to love, protect, and provide for. Nor are they the only creatures who have emotions.
- A human child who has been brought up by animals may never be able to fully adjust to his or her humanity. However, the easier that process is, the kinder and more "humane" it is, the greater its chances of success.
- Your family is who you trust and choose to live with, no matter whether they are human or animal.
- Not everyone will have the same solution to their problems.
- If your actions and your choices make sense and are logical to you, it doesn't matter if others don't understand them. No one has an infallible knowledge of what is best for someone else.
- People fear what they do not understand, and frequently express that fear in inappropriate ways.

BOOK REPORT IDEAS
1. The author used different typefaces and sizes to show the changes in Mila's thinking. Trace those changes, and discuss how the differences in formatting made them easier or more difficult to understand.
2. Explore the idea of individual freedom, showing how and why Mila's freedom was restricted in many ways.
3. Discuss the concept of personal and professional ethics, and how each of the major characters demonstrated their ethical beliefs concerning Mila.

4. Compare the concept of humanness and that of animalness. What separates humans from animals? What doesn't? Can a child reared as an animal, by animals, ever become truly human?
5. Speculate on what Dr. Beck might have done differently to help Mila adjust more easily and completely to the human world. Include in your discussion what the doctor did that interfered with Mila's adjustment process and discuss how she did and didn't genuinely understand Mila.
6. Compare Shay and Mila, explaining why you think they were so different, and what the causes for that difference were.

BOOKTALK IDEAS
1. Tell the story as if you were Mila, changing your way of speaking just as she did.
2. Do a character description talk, having the main characters describe Mila from their own points of view.
3. Format your talk as if it were a series of newspaper stories similar to the one at the beginning of the story.

RISKS
*   Feral children are treated as if they were lab rats rather than human beings.
*   Several adults are portrayed as cold, unfeeling, and distant.
*   Children are controlled and manipulated by adults "for their own good" without consideration of their needs and wants.

STRENGTHS
*   Visual elements in text will appeal to readers as Mila's growth and changes in thinking patterns are graphically represented in font type and size.
*   Powerful portrayal of dolphins as intelligent and nurturing creatures.
*   Mila is allowed to spend her life as she chooses to.
*   "Good" conquers "evil."
*   Characters gain insight and wisdom during the story.
*   Raises the questions, "What is humanity?" and "How are animals and humans different and the same?"

AWARDS
Best Books for Young Adults, 1997 (ALA)

REVIEWS
"A profound study of being human and ways in which communication unites and separates living beings, Hesse's prose poem combines an intriguing format and typeface. . . . the seeming simplicity of the story line belies the complex technique." —*Voice of Youth Advocates*, 6/97, Mary Arnold.

"The book works largely because of Mila's sharp observations, the stranger-in-a-strange-land scenario, and the incredible notion of the dolphin family."
—*Booklist*, 1996, Anne O'Malley.

"Changes in type size and style signal Mila's inner shifts as she turns toward humanity, then away, finding in the dolphins a wiser, more comfortable society. A probing look at what makes us human, with an unforgettable protagonist."
—*Kirkus Reviews*, 9/15/96.

"A reminder that the link between humankind and nature is mysterious and ignored at our peril. This powerful exploration of how we become human and how the soul endures is a song of beauty and sorrow, haunting and unforgettable." *School Library Journal*, 11/96, Kate McClelland.

📖📖📖

NOBODY ELSE HAS TO KNOW. Tomey, Ingrid. Delacorte Press, 1999. $15.95. 231p. ISBN: 0-385-32624-6. Bantam, 2000. $4.99. 240p. ISBN: 0-440-22782-8. Realistic fiction. Reading level: MS. Interest level: MS, YHS. English, Ethics, Driver's education, Psychology.

SUBJECT AREAS
family relationships; self-knowledge; lying and deceitfulness; crime and delinquency; secrets; elderly; grief and mourning; love; illness, physical; rites of passage; manipulation; friendship; school.

CHARACTERS
Webber Freegy: a fifteen-year-old runner with a secret no one should have to keep
Grampa Freegy: he will do anything to protect the grandson he loves
Chessie Freegy: Webb's widowed mother who owns a sewing shop
Dr. Rosenberg: Webb's doctor
Mike Clark: a police officer investigating the accident, and Dylis's father
Maxie Gallagher: a cheerleader Webb has a crush on
Peter Pocknis: a fellow runner and the guy Webb's always wanted to beat
Dylis Clark: she was a friend of Taffy's and has known Webb for years
Ken Olivetti: Webb's physical therapist

BOOKTALK
It was the dreams that began to make him wonder what had really happened that afternoon when he and Grandpa had the wreck. The dreams that dangled pieces

of memory just out of reach, making Webber begin to wonder where the truth was, in those dreams, or in the story his grandfather told him. He'd been running home from school when Grandpa picked him up. The next thing he remembered was waking up in the hospital with his right leg in a cast and his head wrapped up in bandages. Grandpa said he'd had a wreck and hit a ten-year-old little girl, riding her bike on the shoulder of the road. Webber had a concussion and a broken leg, Grandpa had broken ribs, but the little girl, Taffy, was still in a coma. She might never wake up.

Webber didn't think his grandfather would lie, but the differences between what he said had happened, and what Webber's bits of returning memory told him got larger and larger. Finally, Webber began to wonder if there was a reason for the differences. Could his grandfather be lying to protect someone? To protect *him*?

MAJOR THEMES AND IDEAS
- Denials and lies don't change the truth.
- Protecting someone isn't always the best way to help them.
- "If only. . . . " changes nothing. You can't undo what has already happened.
- Guilt can sometimes explode into anger and denial.
- The more times you tell a lie, the bigger it gets, and if you hear a lie often enough, you start to believe it.
- When you are consumed by guilt about lies you've told, telling the truth brings you peace.
- Sometimes people do the wrong thing even with the best intentions.
- Being a hero isn't only about doing great things or saving lives, it's also about being there everyday, strong, loving, and dependable.

BOOK REPORT IDEAS
1. Webb felt so guilty about the lies he was telling that it took over his entire life. Discuss his final downward spiral, detailing when it started and why, what happened on the way down, and how he finally resolved it before he went to the Clarks' house.
2. Compare and contrast Webb's father and grandfather, and show how that contrast set the stage for Grampa's lies.
3. Speculate about how the kids at school will treat Webb when they find out the truth, and what his life will be like at school for the next three years.
4. Grampa told a lie for his own sake, and Webb told the truth for the same reason. Discuss the effect of the lie on Webb and the effect of the truth on Grampa.
5. Compare and contrast the varying portrayals of heroism in this book with the way it is portrayed in Robert Cormier's *Heroes*.

BOOKTALK IDEAS

1. Focus your talk on Webb's dreams and flashbacks before he regains his memory. First describe the accident briefly, as Grampa told it, then bring in the dreams and bits of memory that make Webb realize that there's something about it he isn't remembering. Stop either before or just when he remembers.

2. Center your talk around the fact that life can change completely in only a moment, and how once that change has happened, you can never go back. "Something as small as letting a car drift just a foot or two in the wrong direction can change lives forever."

RISKS

- Grandfather lies to protect grandson.
- Teen accepts grandfather's taking the blame for his actions.
- Police officer condones and supports the lies.
- Language is realistic but contains occasional obscenities.

STRENGTHS

- Shows the effect of long-term lying on an individual's sense of self and honor.
- Presents several varying portrayals of heroism.
- Main character is able to overcome the manipulation of adults to be true to himself.
- It's a quick read, easily accessible to younger readers.
- Ambiguous ending allows for individual speculation and class discussion.

AWARDS

Best Books for Young Adults, 2000 (ALA)
Quick Picks for Reluctant Readers, 2000 (ALA)

REVIEWS

"Tomey's coming of age story involves more issues than a boy facing the consequences of his actions. This title dealing with guilt, death and dying, and values is a nice tie-in with Caroline B. Cooney's *Driver's Ed.* . . . Paul Fleischmann's *Whirligig.* . . . and Eve Bunting's *Blackwater.*" —*Voice of Youth Advocates*, 4/00, Cheryl Karp Ward.

"Most of the central characters in this story are well developed, and readers are drawn into the teen's struggle as he slowly comes apart under the weight of what happened. However, the ending. . . . may be too abrupt for some readers, who will want to know what happens after he confesses." —*School Library Journal*, 1999, Karen Hoth.

"This compelling, well-written novel looks at the process of sorting right from wrong, and insightfully portrays how tragedy impacts many lives in varying ways. Characters are realistic and dimensional. . . . truth leads to healing, reconciliation, and even redemption." —*Booklist*, 12/15/99, Shelle Rosefeld.

"Tomey suggests that age doesn't always bring wisdom in this emotionally turbulent tale of a teenager contending with a grandfather blinded by love and guilt...It's an unusually engrossing inner journey of discovery, with a protagonist who really earns the maturity he achieves." *Kirkus Reviews*, 6/1/99.

📖📖📖

📖 SECTION FOUR 📖
On the Fringe to *Swallowing Stones*

ON THE FRINGE. Gallo, Donald R., editor. Dial, 2001. $17.99. 225p. ISBN: 0-803-72656-2. Short story collection, Realistic fiction. Reading level: MS. Interest level: MS, YHS, OHS. English, Ethics, P. E.

SUBJECT AREAS
violence; peer pressure; self-knowledge; family relationships; problem parents; anger; school; revenge; secrets; harassment; abuse, physical; fear; death and dying; manipulation; bullying; suicide; sex and sexuality; friendship; love; rites of passage.

CHARACTERS
"Geeks Bearing Gifts" by Ron Koertge
Renee: she's writing an article on kids who are outsiders
Bobby: Renee's boyfriend who's a football player and into control

"Great Expectations" by M.E. Kerr
Brian/Mousey: a wimpy kid who pretends to be a convict's son
Onondaga John: he's serving a fifty year sentence for bank robbery

"Shortcut" by Nancy Werlin
Lacey: she's determined to warn Catrine about the school bully
Catrine: she's always been an outsider

"Through a Window" by Angela Johnson
Nia: after her best friend commits suicide, she tries to cope with the loss

"Muzak for Prozac" by Jack Gantos
Narrator: he desperately wants to ease his guilt over what he did

"Standing on the Roof Naked" by Francess Lantz
Jeannie: she's a tomboy who's harassed by the jocks at school
Reilly: an outsider who is also a DJ

"Mrs. Noonan" by Graham Slaisbury
Billy: he dreams of revenge and spies on his chemistry teacher's wife
Nitt, Johnson: they love to pick on Billy

"WWJD" by Will Weaver
Suzanne: a transfer student who's mocked by other students
Eddie: Suzanne's main tormentor

"Satyagraha" by Alden R. Carter
Ramdas: he's from India, is a trainer for the football team, and a pacifist
Kenneth: a football player who decides to put Ramdas' theories to the test

"A Letter from the Fringe" Joan Bauer
Dana: she writes a letter to the in-crowd from the fringe

"Guns for Geeks" by Chris Crutcher
Sam: he learns more about himself and guns than he ever wanted to know
Gene: abused and harassed all his life, he finally decides to fight back

BOOKTALK

Hi, my name's Sam, and I want to tell you about Gene Taylor and what he did. Gene's been just about everyone's whipping boy his entire life, getting the worst of it from his folks, kids at school, even from some of the teachers. I wonder what all those folks think now, and if they could go back and change what they did, would they. Especially now that they know how Gene got his revenge, or at least part of it.

And those kids who laughed at him and hassled him, how would they feel if they were suddenly standing in his shoes? Maybe you're like them, cool, attractive, popular, a cheerleader or a jock. Maybe you'd have joined the chorus of jeers. If you had, you might have been one of his targets. But this is just a story, right? Geeks don't get guns and come to school shooting, the way Gene did. Sure they do, all too often, and people die, just like they did in Mr. Beeler's government classroom, while we all watched and waited to see which one of us would be the next victim.

What's it like to be like Gene, to be someone everyone treats like dirt? Let him tell you, and then listen to what Dana and Suzanne and Brian and Jeannie and Billy and Marco and Arnie have to say.

What's it like to be an outsider? They know, and they'll tell you all about it, in "Guns for Geeks," by Chris Crutcher.

MAJOR THEMES AND IDEAS

- Someone who ridicules another person in order to feel powerful is far smaller than the person being laughed at.
- Some things you don't understand till you look back in hindsight. Others you never understand at all.
- You can know some people for their whole lives and still not know who they really are.
- You don't need a gun to blow someone away—words can work even better, and they're legal.
- You can turn the other cheek only so many times. After that you fight back, one way or another.
- Don't ask someone you've hurt for help—it's not likely you'll get it.
- Don't think of yourself as a victim—it makes you vulnerable to attack.
- Meanness comes back on you, and frequently returns more intensely than it was sent.
- "No one can make you feel inferior without your consent."—Eleanor Roosevelt
- Why do some people think they have the right to decide for everyone else who's best, who's acceptable, and who's not?
- Why do some people choose to make the world a worse place by hating people who aren't just like them?
- Other people's actions are never your fault. Each person is responsible only for his own actions.
- Kids who use violent means to take revenge on their tormentors are punished *before* they take action. They've been punished for years before they do anything. Inclusion, not exclusion, is the answer.

BOOK REPORT IDEAS

1. Choose the story that affected you the most deeply and discuss it, explaining why you chose it.
2. In "WWJD," Suzanne changes her behavior at the end of the story. Discuss why you think she did what she did, and speculate on what might have happened if the story had continued.
3. Discuss the concept of nonviolent resistance, and the role that it can play in a harassing situation.
4. Respond to the question in "A Letter from the Fringe": Why have some people chosen to make the world a worse place by hurting those who are different from them?
5. In "Guns for Geeks," Mr. Waller says, "Guys like Gene Taylor are punished *before* they do their deed." Explain whether or not you agree, and why.
6. Looking at the book as a whole, explain what characteristics do all or most of the outsiders have, and what different and similar characteristics do the insiders have.

7. Explain what you think might have happened if Dana had sent her "Letter from the Fringe." How might the ICIs have responded?
8. Discuss what you think some solutions to harassment might be. Include in your discussion the solutions from the stories and any you have thought of yourself.
9. Explain how "groupthink" is a part of almost all harassment, and how it is depicted in several stories.

BOOKTALK IDEAS
1. Choose the story you liked best and tell it as your talk.
2. Use information from the introduction as part of your talk.
3. Combine snippets from the harassing scenes in several stories to introduce the topic of harassment.
4. Use the tag lines at the beginning of each of the stories to help you introduce them.
5. Become one of the characters you most identified with, and let him or her introduce themselves and several of the stories.

RISKS
- Jocks and the in-crowd are portrayed as violent and harassing.
- Shows graphic violence.
- Language is realistic and occasionally vulgar.

STRENGTHS
- Unflinching, hard-edged portrait of how outsiders are treated by their peers and sometimes by adults as well.
- Shows a variety of ways to respond to harassment.
- Painfully realistic characters teens will identify with.
- Demonstrates the necessity for teaching tolerance and inclusion.
- Some stories are told nonsequentially, making them more complex and challenging to the reader.
- Topic is timely and needs to be openly discussed and explored.
- Has many topics for group discussion and individual reflection.
- Most stories rise from authors' adolescence, giving them additional credibility.
- These stories are absolutely essential for all teens, insiders and outsiders alike, to read.

AWARDS
None

REVIEWS
"The stories come complete with moral underpinnings. They are, however, sufficiently different to keep interest high, and, as usual, they have been written by a talented bunch of YA authors already familiar to many teen readers...may make them think about who's 'in' and who's 'out,' and why. —*Booklist*, 2001, Stephanie Zvirin.

"Geeks, unathletic, poor, emotionally fragile, loners, or unattractive [teens]. . . . form the heart of [these] exceptional stories. . . . authors pondered what sorts of heartbreak could cause teens to react so powerfully and violently, and how being isolated and shut out of. . . . groups could tear down the fragile walls of self-esteem, making vulnerable individuals snap and cause massive destruction." —*School Library Journal*, 2001, Susan Riley.

⊞⊞⊞

ORDINARY MIRACLES. Tolan, Stephanie S. Morrow, 1999. $16.00. 221p. ISBN: 0-688-16269-X. Avon, 2001. $4.95. 221p. ISBN: 0-380-73322-6. Realistic fiction. Reading level: MS. Interest level: MS. English, Ethics, Science.

SUBJECT AREAS
family relationships; science; religion; self-knowledge; school; animals; friendship; death and dying; grief and mourning.

CHARACTERS
Mark and Matthew Filkins: twin fifteen-year-olds from a fundamentalist family that plans for them to become preachers
Dr. Colin Hendrick: a Nobel Prize winning geneticist who opens Mark's eyes to new ideas about science and about God
Johanna, Luke: Mark and Matthew's little sister and brother
Reverend Filkins: pastor of the Rock of Ages Community Church and a conservative fundamentalist
Mrs. Filkins: She plays the piano at church and believes in her family
Mrs. Gerston: the twin's science teacher who invited Colin to teach with her
Dr. Robert Hendrick: Colin's father

BOOKTALK
I know I won't ever forget Colin. Among the other things he taught me was how to be an individual, not half of a set of identical twins. How to be "Mark" and not "Matthew and Mark." He made me think about things I'd always taken for

granted, to ask questions and look for answers. He was a teacher and a friend, and for a little while, I was like a son to him.

But the most important things he taught me were about the wonderful complexities of the world, and about how God always answers prayers, even when we don't like or want to accept the answers we get. I'll never forget Colin, because he changed my life forever.

But I didn't know that the first time I saw him. Matthew and I were supposed to preach our first sermon in our dad's church that night, and I was scared. So instead of going to soccer practice with Matt, I went to the park. That's when I saw Lydia, an incredible dog who could dive just like the ducks in the pond, and her owner, Colin. That was the afternoon I made friends with a scientist and my life began to change, and change, and change.

MAJOR THEMES AND IDEAS

- Sooner or later we each have to recognize that we are unique and individual. Not even identical twins are truly identical.
- We each define God and religion for ourselves, and discounting someone else's definitions, no matter how much they disagree with our own, is inappropriate.
- This astonishing universe, with all its complexities, eccentricities, and patterns, could not possibly be an accident.
- The world is full of ordinary miracles; we just need to know where to look to see them.
- Every experience changes us, and once changed, we cannot go back to who we were before.
- Real teachers are those who make their students care about what they learn, not what grade they will get.
- The web of life, and the miracle of it, doesn't work without death.
- Grief is like a broken leg. It hurts like crazy and takes a long time to heal, but eventually we can walk again.

BOOK REPORT IDEAS

1. Compare Mark at the beginning and end of the book, discussing how he has changed, what he has gained and what he has lost.
2. Discuss the concept of prayer in the book, and the idea that one only has to ask for something to have it granted. Explain how this does or does not fit in with your own beliefs.
3. A major theme in the book is the complexity and connectedness of life. Examine your own concept of life and the connections and complexity you see in it.
4. Speculate on what Mark and Matthew will be like in the future, in ten or twenty years, and show how you think Colin's influence will resonate in their lives and their beliefs.

BOOKTALK IDEAS

1. Focus your talk on the conflict between religion and science, which causes a similar conflict between the twins.
2. Concentrate on the first four chapters of the book and how Mark feels like Matthew's shadow until he meets Colin.
3. Let Mark introduce the story in first person, as he does in the book, ending with his and Colin's first meeting.

RISKS

- Deals straightforwardly with the conflicts between fundamentalist religion and science.

STRENGTHS

- Portrays strong family values in an intact nuclear family.
- Ending is realistic yet poignant.
- Shows the complexity and interconnectedness of life as a powerful reason to believe in a Supreme Being.
- Portrays the individuation between identical twins and the importance of creating your own identity.

AWARDS

None

REVIEWS

"Tolan does not flinch from setting up a truly difficult dilemma for her character, and she realistically portrays the confused feelings of an adolescent attempting to individuate, and of a young Christian trying to figure out whom to believe. . . . Such well-written fiction exploring Christian themes is rare, and many libraries will want to snap this up." —*Booklist*, 10/1/99, Susan Dove Lempke.

"Attempts to reconcile the strict beliefs of the fundamentalist family. . . . with the modern world. . . . Readers will identify with this down-to-earth teenager as he struggles to find his own identity, understand the values of his parents, and come to his own conclusions about the merits of faith and science." —*Kirkus Reviews*, 1999.

"A novel that addresses conflicts between science and faith. . . . presents an even-handed and thoughtful examination of a complex issue." —*Horn Book*, 1999.

"Very satisfying to see religion treated as an important and integral part of people's lives, without either negative stereotyping or heavy-handed preaching."
—*School Library Journal*, 10/99, Elaine Fort Weischedel.

📖📖📖

OUT OF THE DUST. Hesse, Karen. Scholastic, 1997. $15.95. 227p. ISBN: 0-590-36080-9. Scholastic, 1999. $4.99. 227p. ISBN: 0-590-37125-8. Listening Library Inc., 1998. $18.00. ISBN: 0-807-28050-X. (unabridged audiotape) Verse novel, Historical fiction. Reading level: MS. Interest level: MS, YHS, OHS. Creative writing, English, American history.

SUBJECT AREAS
poverty; family relationships; death and dying; music; self-knowledge; rites of passage; handicaps, physical; working; school; illness, physical; friendship.

CHARACTERS
Billie Jo: a long-legged, redheaded girl who loves to play wild piano
Daddy: a farmer whose roots are sunk deep into his land
Ma: a farmer's wife who loves music and her apple trees
Miss Freeland: Billie Jo's teacher
Arley Wanderdale: leader of the band called Black Mesa Boys, he teaches music at Billie's school
Mad Dog Craddock: a plowboy with a smooth singing voice, who sings with the Black Mesa Boys
Joe De La Flor: a neighbor of Billie Jo and her family
Louise: a woman who knows how to come in a house without stepping on a ghost's toes

BOOKTALK
I don't really remember how it was before the dust, when the land was green with grass, and the air was clean and the sky blue. I was born in August 1920, when the winter wheat was ripe. Daddy'd always wanted a boy, but he got me instead, a red-headed, long-legged girl with long hands and a hunger to play wild piano. He named me Billie Jo. By the time I was nine, he'd given up on having a boy and tried to make do with me. But in January 1934, when I was fourteen, Ma told us she was expecting again.

Daddy won't ever leave this farm. He's like the ground itself, solid, rooted. Ma and I aren't like that. The dust could blow us away, and I wouldn't mind. I'd like to get out of the dust, away from the grit that gets into everything. It sifts through the walls, under the doors, and past the windows. At night I sleep with a damp cloth over my face so I don't breathe in the dust.

Ma had her own way of coping with the dust. She was particular about how the table should be set. Plates upside down, glasses upside down, napkins folded around knives and forks. Food went on the table last, when we sat down. Then we'd shake the dust out of our napkins, and turn over our plates and glasses, leaving clean round circles in the dust on the table. Her trees are another way she fights the dust, apple trees she planted when she and Daddy came to the farm. She carries water out to them, and every year they're covered with blossoms, all pink and white, and then with apples that grow round and red. And we make apple pie, apple butter, canned apples, and apples piled in a bowl on Ma's piano.

That piano is the way I cope with the dust. When my fingers point at the keys, the music just flows out of them. I'm whole when I play, there is no dust, only me and the music. Ma doesn't like my music, she'd prefer me to play the sweet melodies that she does. Daddy got her the piano for a wedding present, and she draws him to her when she plays. Even after the last milking, when he's so tired he can't think of anything but the mattress under his bones, he'll come into the parlor and listen to Ma play. And it's beautiful music, but it's not my music. My music is wild and free and loud. And when I play, people stop and listen, and forget the dust, just the way I do.

But all that's over now, the music, Ma, my little brother. The fire changed all that. And there are things I can't forgive. I can't forgive Daddy for leaving the pail of kerosene by the stove. I can't forgive myself for what I did with that pail. And I can't forgive Ma for not being here now when I need her so much. We were a family, just three, almost four of us, and there was laughter, and love, and music to keep the dust at bay. Now there are only two of us left, me and Daddy, and we sit and stare at each other in silence, unforgiving, each alone. I don't know if we can ever be a family again.

And still the dust comes, howling across the empty fields, seeping into the houses, stealing hope just as it steals the wheat out of the fields. Sometimes the rain follows, but never the kind our farm needs, soft and plentiful. It's just enough to keep our last bit of hope alive for one more day or month or year. Daddy will never leave this land. Maybe I will. I don't know if it's my home any longer. I want out, out of the despair, out of the loneliness, out of the poverty, out of the dust. But can I ever really leave?

MAJOR THEMES AND IDEAS

- Hard times come when dreams dry up and blow away.
- You have to forgive yourself before you can forgive anyone else.
- Tragedies happen, but so does survival, if you choose it.
- Dreams don't stay alive without attention and effort. But if you nourish them, they can not only stay alive, they can also grow into reality.
- When you run away, you don't leave your problems behind, you carry them with you.

- When the chips are down, you do what you have to do to survive, even if it isn't what you want to do.

BOOK REPORT IDEAS

1. Compare the person Billie Jo is when the book opens, and the one she has become when it closes. Discuss how the dust has changed her and her life.
2. Consider the meaning of the title. Explain whether or not Billie Jo ever gets "out of the dust."
3. This novel is written in verse. Speculate on why the author chose that format, and how it might be a different story if written in prose. How does the format determine the impact of the story?
4. Speculate on what you think might happen to Billie Jo after the book is over. Show how this year has changed her life in a variety of ways.

BOOKTALK IDEAS

1. Use excerpts from several poems as the body of your booktalk.
2. Use pictures from the Depression and the Dust Bowl to illustrate your talk.
3. Have several other characters (Mad Dog, Arley, Miss Freeland) talk about Billie Jo and her life. Be sure not to give away too much of the plot, including Billie Jo's part in her mother's death.

RISKS

- Format may be off-putting to some readers.

STRENGTHS

- Verse novel format brings the time period with its problems and tragedies to vivid life.
- Characters are multidimensional and completely realistic.
- Format allows readers to make their own interpretations of events and feelings.
- Clear voice of narrator draws reader into novel immediately.
- Excellent for readers' theater or drama productions.
- Powerful depiction of the Depression and the effects that it had on ordinary people.

AWARDS

Newbery Award, 1998 (ALA)
Children's Notables, 1998 (ALA)
Best Books for Young Adults, 1998 (ALA)
Selected Audiobooks for Young Adults, 1999 (ALA)
Booklist Editors' Choice, 1997

REVIEWS

"This novel celebrates the tenacity of the human spirit. . . . could be used as a complement to a social studies unit about the Depression or read aloud before a study of Steinbeck's *The Grapes of Wrath*, or used as a model for a poetry writing unit." —*Voice of Youth Advocates*, 4/98, Sarah K. Herz.

"Fourteen-year-old narrator Billie Jo writes in sparse, free-floating verse. . . . in this compelling, immediate journal. . . . there are no tight, sentimental endings here—just a steady ember of hope that brightens Karen Hesse's exquisitely written and mournful tale. . . . Elegantly crafted, gut-wrenching novel." —Amazon, 1998.

"Told in free-verse poetry. . . . this is an unremittingly bleak portrait of one corner of Depression-era life. . . . presents a hale and determined heroine who confronts unrelenting misery and begins to transcend it." —*Kirkus Reviews*, 1997.

"Language, imagery, and rhythms are so immediate that after only a few pages it will seem natural to have the story related in verse. . . . a wonderful choice for classrooms involved in journal-writing assignments, since the poems often read like diary entries. It could also be performed effectively as readers' theater." —*School Library Journal*, 9/97, Carrie Schadle.

OVER THE WALL. Ritter, John. Philomel, 2000. $17.99. 312p. ISBN: 0-399-23489-6. Recorded Books, 2001. ISBN: 0-788-74570-0. (unabridged audiotape) Realistic fiction. Reading level: MS. Interest level: MS. English, Ethics, P. E., American history, World history, Government.

SUBJECT AREAS

sports; anger; ethics; war; grief and mourning; friendship; self-knowledge; rites of passage; death and dying; peer pressure; family relationships; bullying.

CHARACTERS

Tyler Waltern: thirteen years old, baseball is the most important thing in his life
Lyle Waltern: Tyler's father, still grieving over a nine-year-old accident
Mom: Tyler's mother, who makes excuses for his father
Aunt Chrissy and Uncle Phil: they invite Tyler to spend the summer in New York playing ball

Coach Trioli: a Vietnam vet and Little League coach who knows a lot about anger

Louie: Tyler's fourteen-year-old cousin who plays on the same team

Breena: Louie's thirteen-year-old sister who is pretty and nice, and hates fighting

Carmine DeLucca: a good ball player, the enemy, but still a person

BOOKTALK

Tyler was good at baseball, and a shoo-in for shortstop in the all-stars. He was short, only five feet, but he was a five tool player—strong arm, good speed, good fielding, hits for average, and hits for power. He had only one thing against him, but it was a killer. He had a hair trigger temper, and when he got angry, people got hurt. Trash talking is part of baseball, but Tyler couldn't just let it roll off him anymore than he could a miscalled play against him.

But Coach Trioli is a Vietnam vet, and he knows a lot about anger and how to deal with it. And when Tyler gets kicked off the team, coach goes to bat for him and gives him one more chance. But Tyler has to meet his conditions—no unsportsmanlike conduct, stay in control, no slip-ups, not even one, and demonstrate that he has the maturity and control it takes to play ball at the all-star level. He didn't care how Tyler showed that maturity, but if he didn't, he'd have no chance of being and all-star shortstop.

Will thirty bats, sixteen porcelain birds, four war memorials and an eye-opening soccer game get Tyler into the all-stars? Go *Over the Wall* and find out.

MAIN THEMES AND IDEAS

- It takes more courage to step back from a fight than it does to step into one.
- It takes only a moment for life to go from a dream to a nightmare.
- Anger can be a cover-up for fear—fear of looking foolish, fear of failure, fear of caring too much.
- Anger's easy, but holding onto your temper is smart, because when you lose your temper, you hurt yourself first.
- Sitting on your anger, stuffing it, won't make it go away, it'll just make the final explosion bigger and more destructive.
- To really get rid of anger, you have to look for its source, its root, and deal with that.
- The people on the other side of any conflict are no different from you. They're just people, too.

BOOK REPORT IDEAS

1. Compare Tyler at the beginning and end of the novel, and show how he changed over the summer.
2. Discuss your reaction to Tyler's monument and the reason he created it. Explain whether you agree with him and why.

3. There are two sets of parents in the book. Show how they are alike and different in how they interact with each other and their kids.
4. Examine the idea that many people use anger to hide their fear, and explain whether or not you agree, based on examples from your own life and from the book.

BOOK TALK IDEAS

1. Write your talk in first person as Tyler, letting him tell his own story.
2. Focus on one of the games when Tyler loses his temper, and show how that can keep him out of the league.
3. Tell the story from Breena's pacifist point of view.

RISKS

- Parents are portrayed as distant and unavailable.
- Scenes of fighting and violence by several characters.

STRENGTHS

- There is a strong anti-war, anti-violence message.
- Factual information on the Vietnam War is woven into the story.
- Includes information about the importance of controlling or channeling anger appropriately.
- Exciting sports story that will appeal to boys.
- A powerful portrayal of healing the scars left by tragedy and anger.

AWARDS

None

REVIEWS

"Most of the book's focus lies in its treatment of the ways the Vietnam War affected and continues to affect those involved in it on both sides." —*Voice of Youth Advocates*, 2000, Karen Herc.

"A fully fleshed-out story about compassion and absolution." —*Booklist*, 2000, Roger Leslie.

"A complex novel, with the events of the past haunting the lives of several of the major characters. . . . Sports are just a part of this ambitious work that presents a compelling, multilayered story." —*School Library Journal,* 2000, Todd Morning.

"A poignant and accessible coming-of-age-story for young readers. . . . particularly appealing to middle school boys." —*ALAN Reviews*, 2000.

ロ ロ ロ

PAPER TRAIL. Gilbert, Barbara Snow. Front Street Press, 2000. $16.95. 161p. ISBN: 1-886-91044-8 . Realistic fiction. Reading level: MS. Interest level: MS, YHS. English, Ethics, Government.

SUBJECT AREAS
secrets; war; activism; crime and delinquency; fear; death and dying; violence; friendship; rites of passage; manipulation; politics; self-knowledge.

CHARACTERS
Walker Morgan: at fifteen, he has seen his mother shot, and he and his father stalked by killers
David Morgan: the boy's father who infiltrates the Soldiers of God
Sean Talliferrs, Davis Johns, Jim Redhawk, Ronald and Johnny Murray, Cherry Martindale, Roy Royl, Vince and Shelly Williams, Scotty Thomas, Jake and Ricardo Lucero, Wolfman: members of the Soldiers of God
Reverend General: leader of the Soldiers of God
Tony Rossetti: Jim Redhawk's grandson and the boy's friend and a Soldier of God member
Roxanne McReynolds: owner of the diner
Sky McReynolds: Roxanne's daughter and the boy's friend

BOOKTALK
The fifteen-year-old boy wiggled into the hollow log, his goal a knothole that would provide both light and air. Someone was calling his name. His mother— but she was supposed to be running away in the other direction, away from the Soldiers of God. He heard the distinctive crack of a sniper's rifle, once, then twice. The leaves next to the log crackled and crunched as something fell into them. The boy squeezed his eyes shut for a long time, then opened to see his mother's face with bits of crushed leaves sticking to it. A thread of spit hung from her lips, and as the boy watched, a fat red ant started to climb it.

Then the boy heard men walking toward his log, and one man walked up to the log and stopped. The boy could see the red and black militia patch on the outside of his boot, two M-16's crossed over the Christian sign of the fish. The insignia of the Soldiers of God, a symbol he'd seen all of his life, but now the sign of his mother's murderers. The sign of the men who were still searching for him and his father, so they could kill both of them as well. An FBI man and his family who had infiltrated the Soldiers of God and didn't deserve to live.

MAJOR THEMES AND IDEAS
- If you want to survive badly enough, you will figure out how to do it.

- Sometimes the cause you are fighting for is important enough to place your own life and the lives of your family members in danger.
- When the truth is too horrible to accept or understand, your mind finds a way to cover it up.
- One parent is barely enough.
- A scar is a sign of healing.

BOOK REPORT IDEAS
1. Walker's name is not revealed until the end of the book. Discuss the reason for this anonymity.
2. Explain the significance of the material in the "Scraps" section and how it related to the story.
3. Explain what happened to Blanche Morgan, in Walker's mind and in reality. Why didn't she obey her husband's orders?
4. Speculate on what will happen to Walker and his father after the story ends. What will they be like in five years? In ten?
5. Discuss the significance of Walker's scrapbook. What did it represent to him?

BOOKTALK IDEAS
1. Use excerpts from the "Scraps" section to lead into your booktalk.
2. Write your talk in first person, as Walker.

RISKS
- Depicts violence and murder in a paramilitary organization.

STRENGTHS
- Frightening picture of paramilitary militia organizations.
- Ambiguous ending leaves room for individual speculation and group discussion.
- Story partially told from excerpts from a variety of actual documents and books.
- Nonsequential story line adds complexity to plot.
- Plot and characters are realistic, giving teens much to identify with.

AWARDS
None

REVIEWS
"The core escape story and the persistent theme of identity keep the book from becoming a tract, and while regular insertions of real news reports and government documents about the militia movement do edge into didacticism,

they are also scary and provide abbreviated context for the first-person events."
—*Horn Book*, 2000.

"Individual chapters are. . . . exciting, written with a vividness that has the potential to keep young adventure fans on the edge of their seats." —*School Library Journal*, 2000, Todd Morning.

⊞⊞⊞

THE PERKS OF BEING A WALLFLOWER. Chbosky, Stephen. Simon and Schuster, 1999. $12.00. 213p. ISBN: 0-671-02734-4. Books on Tape, Inc., 2000. $25.95. ISBN: 0-736-64936-0. (unabridged audiotape) Realistic fiction. Reading level: MS. Interest level: MS, YHS. English, Drama, Filmmaking, Creative writing.

SUBJECT AREAS
self-knowledge; dating and social life; school; family relationships; friendship; sports; sex and sexuality; grief and mourning; homosexuality; illness, mental; substance abuse; rites of passage; art.

CHARACTERS
Charlie: a fifteen-year-old writing letters about himself to someone he trusts
Susan: a friend of Charlie's who was Michael's best friend
Charlie's older brother: he plays football for Penn State and taught Charlie how to fight
Charlie's older sister: she is very pretty and mean to boys who like her
Patrick: a senior in Charlie's shop class
Sam: Patrick's stepsister
Mom and Dad: Charlie's parents
Bill: Charlie's advanced English teacher
Bob: a friend of Patrick's
Brad: high school football quarterback
Mary Elizabeth: a girl who's into Zen Buddhism and the *Rocky Horror Picture Show*

BOOKTALK
Hello. My name's Charlie, and I want to tell you about my freshman year in high school. I've always been more of a watcher than a doer, and most people think because I'm small, I'm a wimp. But that's not true. My older brother plays football at Penn State and wants to go pro when he graduates. He taught me how to fight, and when it's necessary, I can. I don't do it that often though, so it

always surprises people. Sean was surprised when he started hitting on me the first week of school and I did what my brother taught me to do—go for the knees, throat, and eyes. He really got hurt and I would've been in trouble, except there was a kid who saw the whole thing and told the principal it had been self-defense.

It was about a month later I went to a high school football game and saw this guy I remembered from my shop class. He did a really funny impersonation of the teacher one day and I've never laughed so hard in my life. Even the teacher laughed 'cause he wasn't being mean or anything, just funny. Because of that he seemed like someone I could walk up to and say hi, even if he was a senior and with a girl. So I did, and he said his name was Patrick and the girl, who was very pretty, was Sam. Then we watched the game and listened to Patrick's play-by-play analysis, and I realized that Patrick really knew a lot about football. After the game we went to the Big Boy and talked and talked.

I had no idea that night that it would change my life forever, and within a year I'd be a completely different person. It was a very educational year. I got drunk, got stoned, and started smoking. I had my first girlfriend and fell in love. I read a lot of books my advanced English teacher gave me, and started going to the *Rocky Horror Picture Show*. I got my driver's license and listened to a lot of family fights.

And I wrote all of that down, plus a lot more, 'cause all that stuff I just said barely scratches the surface of that year! So sit back and listen while I tell you what it's like to be a wallflower.

MAJOR THEMES AND IDEAS
- It's better to stand up to bullies than to run away from them.
- If you're small and too emotional, it's smart to know how to fight.
- We accept only the love we think we deserve.
- Sometimes in families everyone really loves each other but no one actually *likes* anyone else.
- When you feel happy for someone else, it makes you happy too.
- People who are into control are afraid that if they don't control everything, they'll control nothing.
- If you aren't honest with your friends then you aren't really being their friend.
- We are who we are for a lot of reasons, some of them we know about, but others we may never discover.
- Even if we don't have the power to choose where we came from, we *can* choose where we go on from here.
- Each of us controls our own life, and we are the only ones who can change it.

BOOK REPORT IDEAS

1. Charlie changed a lot during his freshman year. Discuss two or three of the changes he made that you consider most significant, and explain why you chose them.
2. Discuss Charlie's shyness and watching other people rather than participating, and explain what perks he got because he was an onlooker instead of a participant.
3. Speculate what Charlie will be like as a high school senior and as an adult.
4. Explore who the friend Charlie writes to might be, and share how you would have responded to his letters, letters remember, which you couldn't answer because he concealed his identity.
5. Discuss what Patrick and Sam see in Charlie that makes them befriend him. These are going to be things that Charlie may not, or does not, know about himself.

BOOKTALK IDEAS

1. Write your talk as if it was one of Charlie's letters.
2. Use one of the songs Charlie likes as a sound track for your talk.
3. Include the poem Charlie gave Patrick in your talk.

RISKS

- Includes frank discussion of several difficult topics centering around teen sexuality: masturbation, sexual abuse, teen pregnancy, sexually active teens.
- Language is explicit and realistic.
- Young boy witnesses a rape.
- Teens drink and smoke.

STRENGTHS

- Narrator's voice is strong and realistic.
- Language is realistic yet vulgar.
- Deals nonjudgmentally with many issues teens today have to face.
- Sees the humorous as well as the painful or complex side of growing up.
- Characters survive and resolve a variety of crises and traumas, giving readers examples of how they can also survive and go on.
- Sense of innocence changes into self-knowledge and then hope and confidence.
- Format of letters allows the reader to immediately get into the mind of the narrator.
- Plot and characters reflect the realities of teen life today.

AWARDS

Best Books for Young Adults, 2000 (ALA)
Quick Picks for Reluctant Readers, 2000 (ALA)

REVIEWS

"Chbosky never falters, always maintaining Charlie's perspective perfectly. . . . novel has the disjointed and almost dreamlike quality of a music video. Designation of this title as an "MTV Book" should ensure wide readership. —*Voice of Youth Advocates*, 12/99, Jamie S. Hansen.

"[Characters] are palpably real. This report on [Charlie's] life will engage teen readers for years to come." —*School Library Journal*, 6/99, Francisca Goldsmith.

"What is most notable about this funny, touching, memorable first novel. . . . is the resounding accuracy with which the author captures the voice of a boy teetering on the brink of adulthood. . . . We learn about Charlie through the letters he writes. . . . a stylistic technique that adds to the heart-wrenching earnestness saturating this teen's story." —Amazon, 1999, Brangien Davis.

"Aspiring filmmaker/first-novelist Chbosky adds an upbeat ending to a tale of teenaged angst. . . . right combination of realism and uplift to allow it on high school reading lists, though some might object to the sexuality, drinking, and dope-smoking." —*Kirkus Reviews*, 1/15/99.

📖📖📖

PLAGUE YEAR. Tolan, Stephanie S. Beech Tree Books, 1999. $5.95. 208p. ISBN: 0-688-16125-1. Fawcett Books, 1991. $5.99. 185p. ISBN: 0-449-70403-3. Realistic fiction. Reading level: MS. Interest level: MS, YHS, OHS. English, Ethics, Government, P. E.

SUBJECT AREAS

secrets; crime and delinquency; death and dying; gossip; prejudice; school; self-knowledge; bullying; friendship; problem parents; family relationships; child abuse; rites of passage.

CHARACTERS

David Watson: a runner and loner who tries to befriend Bran
Molly Pepper: she has been David's best friend for years, and knows Bran better than anyone else
Bran Slocum: a newcomer who stands out because of his ponytail, gold earring, and wild eye
Nick Bruno: a loud, obnoxious bully who is determined to get a reaction from Bran

Matt Singleton, Jerry Ritoni, and Gordon Krosky: Nick's friends who join him in tormenting Bran

Kristin Mattis: the cheerleader whom David is dating

James Watson: David's father, a woodcarver

Mr. Byrd: the contemporary social issues teacher who defends Bran before the whole town

Mr. and Mrs. Ridley: Bran's uncle and aunt

Angela Ridley: Bran's cousin and the twins' mother

Kipp and Keith Ridley: Bran's twin nephews for whom he baby-sits after school

Zach Lewis: a reporter on the school newspaper who tries to interview Bran, and a friend of David's

Jeremy Collier: Bran's father, a convicted serial killer

BOOKTALK

Molly called what happened that October a plague, but I'm not all that sure she was right. A plague comes from outside and infects people. What happened here wasn't something from outside; it was something that was inside the people here, or most of them. It was surely inside Molly and me.

It all started the day Bran Slocum came to town. He looked different, with his ponytail and gold earring, and he acted different, never reacting to any of the taunts or tricks Nick and his gang played on him, always quiet and always alone. Then the reporter came to town with a story about the son of a serial killer going to our school, and the description fit Bran like a glove. It was all over town right away, and the ugly side of people I'd known all my life began to show. They said he was a bad seed, that he'd start killing kids like his father did. That wasn't true. Molly and I were the only ones who really knew him. We knew how gentle he was, how great he was with his twin nephews, and how much he loved them.

Maybe if I'd done something more it would've made a difference, or maybe Molly was right and nothing could have changed anything. This plague didn't have a cure. All I know now is that I don't like this town as much as I used to, now that I've seen what lies behind those smiles and kind words. It's changed, and it'll never be the same—and neither will I.

MAJOR THEMES AND IDEAS

- Sometimes it's best to let people keep their secrets.
- Standing out in a crowd can be dangerous.
- Standing up for the underdog may mean that you will also be persecuted.
- Groupthink is always too easy to get caught up in. People in a group will do things they would never consider doing alone.
- Bullies come in all shapes and sizes, and their actions usually say more about themselves than the people they persecute.
- You can survive in hostile territory as long as you don't confront the natives head on.

- There are bad things in the world you can't fix, no matter how much you hate them, or how much you want to.
- Children do not always follow in their parent's patterns.
- Swords cut both ways. If you restrict someone else's rights, you may later find your own restricted as well.

BOOK REPORT IDEAS

1. There are a number of killers in this book other than Joseph Collier and they, like him, seemed normal most of the time. Identify these people and explain why you selected them.
2. There are several instances of irony in this book, one of which is the fact that Bran chose to look so different because his father looked so conventional. Discuss some of the other instances of irony you found.
3. Molly said what happened to the town when Bran arrived was like a plague and that nothing could have stopped it. Take a stand and agree or disagree with that view, citing incidents from the book to support your argument.
4. Bran was quiet and didn't respond violently to anything anyone did to him. Discuss how that was or was not a result of his father's actions and what he might have been like before his father was arrested.
5. Discuss the final scene at the quarry and the actions of each person involved. For instance, why did Bran show himself and take on Nick and his gang when he had not responded violently before?
6. Explain what this book says to you and what you felt the most powerful or memorable part of it was for you. What will you take away with you from this book, and what do you think you will not be able to forget about it?

BOOKTALK IDEAS

1. Use the idea of the plague in your talk and how anger and hatred spread from Nick and his gang to the whole town.
2. Make Bran the focus of your talk using a character description technique.
3. Use the idea of secrets in your talk, the one that Bran had, the secret darker side of the town, and hinting at the one that Molly and David share at the end of the book.

RISKS

- Includes a variety of homophobic slurs and actions.
- Persecution of someone who looks different.
- Townspeople react violently when they learn Bran's identity, adopting a KKK-like mentality.
- Ending raises many questions.
- Portrayal of jocks as violent, intolerant, in control of the school to some extent, and feared by the students.

STRENGTHS

- Multidimensional characters grow and gain insight.
- Strong portrayal of friendship.
- Raises many questions about the nature of prejudice, our judicial system, and the concept of equal rights for all.
- Ending provides for both group discussion and individual speculation.

AWARDS

None

REVIEWS

"The story is a riveting one. The characters and their struggles are complex and beautifully handled. Finally, the reader simply cannot put the book down, and the ending is chilling. The questions raised by this book are haunting and timely. No one who begins this book will put it aside." —*Voice of Youth Advocates*, 6/90, Shirley Carmony.

"Good suspense, well executed." —*Kirkus Reviews*, 1990.

"A contemporary morality play that offers ample opportunity for discussion of ethical behavior." —*Horn Book*, 1990.

📖📖📖

PLAYING SOLITAIRE. Antle, Nancy. Dial, 2000. $16.00. 103p. ISBN: 0-803-72406-3. Realistic fiction. Reading level: MS. Interest level: MS, YHS. English, Psychology, Sociology, Ethics.

SUBJECT AREAS

problem parents; abuse, physical; substance abuse; dysfunctional family; divorce; friendship; handicaps, physical; ethics; self-knowledge; violence; illness, mental; elderly.

CHARACTERS

Ellie: she's about to enter ninth grade and is worried about other students staring at her mutilated hand.

Grandpa/Tom Whiteday: Ellie's mother's father with whom Ellie lives

Grandma/Marie Whiteday: Ellie's grandmother who lives in a nursing home because of a brain injury she had in a car wreck

Joy Collins: Grandpa's next-door neighbor, and a good friend to both him and Ellie

Daddy/Vince McCoy: Ellie's drunk and abusive father who is on the run from the police

Dex Hill: a cute guy who lives near Ellie

Mr. Hill: the local sheriff and Dex's dad

Dwayne: the sheriff's deputy and cousin

Mr. Chitwood: he lives in the same nursing home as Ellie's grandmother

BOOKTALK

Ellie was afraid. Ever since Daddy had hurt her, he'd been on the run from the police, and she'd been living with Grandpa. She just knew Daddy was going to come back and maybe hurt her some more. But she had no place else to go. Her mother was dead, and Grandpa was her closest relative.

But she wasn't just afraid of her father, she was also afraid about starting high school in the fall, just four weeks away. She knew kids would stare at her hand, and ask questions about it. She didn't want to answer any questions. She didn't want to remember what Daddy had done to her.

So she kept her hand in her pocket most of the time. It was easier that way. But all that changed when she made friends with Dex, who lived just down the street from her and was also going into ninth grade. He liked playing solitaire, and so did Ellie. But she was careful about how she held her cards, and when it was her turn to shuffle, she did it in her lap. Until the day she and Dex were playing Hell, a kind of double solitaire, and she accidentally used her left hand to slap the final card down on the table. The hand she's always kept hidden, ever since that last solitaire game with Daddy when he was so drunk and so angry.

MAJOR THEMES AND IDEAS

- Some things are too awful for an apology to fix.
- Sooner or later you have to quit running and face your fears.
- You are not responsible for your parent's negative habits or behaviors.
- If you choose to, you can survive even the worst of occurrences.
- Friends don't base their opinion of you on how you look, but on who you are on the inside.
- Don't hold your fear inside. Share it with someone who can help you.
- If you need help, ask for it. Needing help is nothing to be ashamed of.
- When someone says or does something mean to you, it says that they are unlovable, not that you are.

BOOK REPORT IDEAS

1. Discuss why Dex was able to accept Ellie's injury so easily.
2. Explain why Ellie was safer from her father in a small town than she would have been in a large city.
3. What do you think might have happened if Ellie had not refused to play cards with her father when he was drunk and angry?

4. Discuss why Ellie didn't go to her grandfather before her father hurt her.
5. What characters and incidents in the story helped Ellie find the strength she needed to cope with her situation?
6. Ellie's father hurt her physically, but he also hurt her emotionally and psychologically. Show how she expressed that hurt.

BOOKTALK IDEAS
1. Write your talk as Ellie, in first person.
2. Tell the story from Dex's perspective.
3. Ellie's story made the front page of newspapers. Write your talk as if it were a newspaper story. Be careful not to give away too much about her injury—let the reader find it out on his own.

RISKS
*   Includes spousal and child abuse and violent behavior.
*   Scenes about Ellie's mutilation are shockingly graphic.
*   Ellie plots to murder her father.

STRENGTHS
*   Terse, first-person narrative allows reader to identify with character immediately.
*   Ellie grows and survives her nightmare.
*   Shows the trauma that can occur when alcoholic behavior is not controlled.
*   Strong portrayal of acceptance and friendship.
*   Strong, nurturing, functional adults are present to care for Ellie and as role models.

AWARDS
None

REVIEWS
"A well-paced novel. . . . no teen will be able to put the book down. . . . This recommended slim volume is an excellent booktalking candidate." —*Voice of Youth Advocates*, 2000, Jennifer Hubert.

"In straightforward, simple prose, the first-person narrative relates one teen's devastating response to emotional and physical abuse. . . . Ellie's experiences and emotions. . . . illustrate how fear and hatred can lead to desperate, extreme actions, and show the importance of getting outside help, no matter how difficult the circumstances." —*Booklist*, 3/1/00, Shelle Rosenfeld.

"A somber story. . . . trim, direct, first-person narrative. . . . the terse storyline is black-and-white." —*Kirkus Review*, 2000.

⊞⊞⊞

RATS SAW GOD. Thomas, Rob. Simon and Schuster, 1996. $17.00. 224p. ISBN: 0-689-80207-2. Simon and Schuster, 1996. $4.50. 202p. ISBN: 0-689-80777-5. Realistic fiction. Reading level: MS. Interest level: YHS, OHS. English, Shop, Art, Creative writing.

SUBJECT AREAS
school; philosophy; friendship; dating and social life; divorce; sex and sexuality; substance abuse; problem parents; working; art; writing; activism; rites of passage.

CHARACTERS
Steve York: an eighteen-year-old misfit writing the story of his life so he can graduate from high school
Alan York: Steve's father who's been a football star and an astronaut
Jeff DeMony: senior counselor at Wakefield High School
Sarah York: Steve's sister who is brilliant and an activist
Luke "Sky" Walker: creative writing teacher at Grace High School in Houston
Wanda "Dub" Varner: another misfit, Steve's best friend and more
Doug Chappell: president and founder of Skate or Die and the Grace Order of Dadaists (GOD), both clubs at Grace High
Allison Kimble: a National Merit finalist at Wakefield High
Bill and Matt Whiteside, Beverly Shoaf, Rhonda Smith, Missy Carmichael, Zipper, Virginia Cole, Holly Cooper, Samantha Ellis, Lynette Sirls, Ben Kemper/Veg, Trey Collier: other members of GOD
Cindy and Chuck: Steve and Sarah's mother and stepfather who are embarrassingly in love

BOOKTALK
"What happened to you?" DeMony, the senior guidance counselor, asked. "For five semesters of high school you have a 4.0 grade average and perfect attendance. Then the last semester of your junior year it all falls apart, and you flunk English and move to San Diego. What happened in Texas that turned you into a school-hating pothead?"

Steve didn't answer him—he couldn't. There's no way he could explain that would make sense. It was like he was a different person now.

Then DeMony reminded him that he was still a credit short in English and wouldn't be able to graduate. "But I think we can work something out. I want you to write a paper, one hundred typewritten pages. Turn them in to me five to ten pages at a time. Pick any topic you want, fiction or nonfiction, though it's going to be easier if you choose something you know about."

Steve would do anything, even eat ground glass, to keep from going to summer school, so he agreed. And since he had a hundred pages to do it in, Steve decided to answer DeMony's questions and tell him what happened. That meant opening wounds that had never really healed. So, a few pages at a time, DeMony found out about Steve, and Doug, and Dub, and Sky, and the Grace Order of Dadaists, and just exactly how a National Merit finalist can turn into a school-skipping pothead in just a few months. Listen up, and he'll tell you too.

MAJOR THEMES AND IDEAS

- One of the lessons that parents should learn early, but frequently don't, is that you can't make your kids into carbon copies of yourself and you can't live your life through theirs.
- You can let tragedy consume your life, or you can put it behind you and go on.
- Being in love is sometimes neither easy nor fun.
- Hard times are best endured with friends.
- Losing your virginity in real life is not anything like it is in books, movies, or TV.
- Sex changes relationships.
- Even misfits want to fit in with someone.
- In school, a freewheeling class discussion can usually teach you more than a teacher's lecture can by really making you think about your and other's opinions.

BOOK REPORT IDEAS

1. Discuss GOD and what the club did for its members.
2. Discuss the changes in Steve's attitude toward his father, showing how and why it changed.
3. Compare Steve's relationships with Dub and Allison, showing how they were different and similar.
4. Read the two story lines sequentially, first Steve' life in Houston, and then his senior year in San Diego. How does this change your perception and understanding of him and how he changed?
5. Decide what you think is the most important lesson Steve learned and explain why you chose it.

BOOKTALK IDEAS

1. Focus your talk on the paper he wrote about why he changed so much.
2. Write your talk as Steve, in first person.
3. Write a character description talk describing Steve as he was when he began each of his high school years, end your talk with a comment about how he could change so much in one year.
4. Center your talk on the GOD group and some of the things they did.

RISKS
- Depicts sexually active teens.
- Includes teen smoking and using dope.
- Language is realistic but vulgar.

STRENGTHS
- Format—different typefaces make text more visual.
- Realistic teen characters readers can identify with.
- Realistic language sounds like teens talk today.
- Teens practice planned, safe sex.
- Multiple story lines add complexity to the story.
- Shows the humorous side of being a teen.
- Characters grow, change, and gain insight over the four years of high school.
- Moving portrayal of first love, its betrayal, and recovery from it.
- Told from the perspective of an anti-hero.

AWARDS
Best Books for Young Adults, 1997 (ALA)
Quick Picks for Reluctant Readers, 1997 (ALA)

REVIEWS
"Steve goes from not even being able to talk to girls, to his first kiss, eventually followed by his first sexual experience. Please note this is not casual sex. Steve is in love. . . . aware of safe sex. . . . A good book with a positive realistic message—teenagers are just like everyone else in this screwy world only with less power. . . . These kids sound right—they are the ones that come in your libraries." —*Voice of Youth Advocates*, 6/96, Julie Hudson.

"Dead-on description of life as a bright underachiever makes the gradually converging stories, past and present, a delightful, challenging read...layers of cynical wit and careful character development accumulate achingly in this beautifully crafted, emotionally charged story." —*School Library Journal*, 6/96, Joel Shoemaker.

"Thomas proves his thorough grasp of young adult issues and emotions. Teens will appreciate the author's empathy and humor, and teachers and parents will examine his work for clues to the mystery of adolescence." —Amazon, 1997, Jennifer Hubert.

"Off-beat tale brings a fresh new voice to YA literature." —*Kirkus Reviews*, 1997.

📖📖📖

ROMIETTE AND JULIO. Draper, Sharon M. Simon and Schuster, 1999. $16.00. 240p. ISBN: 0-689-82180-8. Aladdin Paperbacks, 2001. $4.99. 240p. ISBN: 0-689-84209-0. Realistic fiction. Reading level: MS. Interest level: MS, YHS. English, Drama, Creative writing, Ethics.

SUBJECT AREAS
minorities, black; minorities, hispanic; love; dating and social life; family relationships; prejudice; violence; gossip; crime and juvenile delinquency; friendship; self-knowledge; rites of passage; survival; school; racism; peer pressure; secrets; ethnic groups; gangs.

CHARACTERS
Romiette Capelle: a black junior in high school who dreams of a boy she can talk to and be herself with
Julio Montague: a junior in high school, he's just moved to Cincinnati from Texas and hates it there
Destiny Dodson: Romi's best friend who believes in astrology
Ben Olsen: tall, skinny, with hair that's a different color every day, he's the first friend Julio makes
Cornell Capelle: Romi's father, a TV newscaster
Lady Capelle: Romi's mother who owns an African boutique
Luis Montague: Julio's father who moved his family from Corpus Christie to Cincinnati when he lost his job
Maria Montague: Julio's mother and a peacemaker
Terrell: one of the leaders of the Devildogs, a black gang
Malaka: she used to be a friend of Romi's before she started dating Terrell and became a member of the Devildogs
Captain Escaluski: he led the search for Romi and Julio

BOOKTALK
Have you ever dreamed of meeting your soulmate? The one person who is the other half of you? Your perfect mate? Romiette and Destiny have those dreams too, and decided to order the Scientific Soul Mate System to find the two boys who are perfect for them.

But fate steps in before it arrives. Romi, aka Afroqueen, and Julio, aka Spanishlover, met in an internet chat room and immediately hit it off. Julio's just moved to Cincinnati from Texas, and it's not long before they discover they go to the same high school. The day they met for the first time to have lunch in the school cafeteria, it was love at first sight. They both knew they'd found their soulmates, and they laughed about the fact their names, Romiette Capelle and Julio Montague, were so close to Romeo and Juliet. They knew their love story would have a happy ending! Or would it? The Devildogs, a violent black gang at school, didn't like the idea of a sister dating someone who wasn't black, and they were willing to go further than threats to separate Romi and Julio.

Will their story have a happy ending or will it, like Shakespeare's play, end with too many senseless deaths?

MAJOR THEMES AND IDEAS

- Don't let past experiences color your world or your opinions today.
- Look at the content of someone's heart, not their appearance or the color of their skin.
- The speed with which love develops has little to do with its validity. Love at first or second sight is possible.
- A wise parent will negotiate with a teenage child rather than setting absolute and arbitrary limits.
- Chat rooms can be fun places to meet people, but they can also be dangerous, because you have no way of knowing who's lying and who isn't.
- It's easier to dislike or be prejudiced against a stranger than someone you know and have something in common with.
- Friends are the people who take you as you are, don't ask you to change, value you as a person, and stand by you in good and bad times, willing to face danger or take chances for your sake.

BOOK REPORT IDEAS

1. Friendship is a major theme in the book. Compare and discuss the friendships between Julio and Ben and Destiny and Romi, showing what characteristics in each of them contributed to the strong connections between them.
2. Compare the book to *Romeo and Juliet* and *West Side Story*, showing the similarities and the differences.
3. Prejudice and racism feature prominently in this book. Discuss some of the positive and negative messages it has for both teens and their parents.
4. Explain the significance of Romi's dream, including what it meant and why she had it over and over.
5. Ben and Destiny are each unique, and both try not to fit in with the crowd. Discuss what each gains from their individualized appearances and behaviors.

BOOKTALK IDEAS

1. Use excerpts from E-mail, chat room conversations, and Romi's diary to tell the story of how Romi and Julio met.

2. Introduce the four main characters by letting them introduce each other. For instance, Destiny could introduce Romi, Ben could introduce Julio, and Julio and Romi could talk about each other.
3. Compare Romi and Julio to Romeo and Juliet—"You've all heard of Romeo and Juliet, their feuding families and their tragic deaths. But this is a new version of that story, with several major changes. . . ." Be sure not to tell too much, ending your talk when Romi and Julio realize the danger in the Devildog's threats.

RISKS
*   Includes interracial couples.
*   Shows gang violence.
*   Teens and parents show prejudice and racism.
*   Teens take on a gang alone rather than going to the police.

STRENGTHS
*   Typefaces change to indicate different kinds of situations, making the book more visually accessible to teens.
*   Strong portrayal of friendships.
*   Teens reject the prejudices of peers and parents.
*   Builds on familiar theme of forbidden love.
*   Provides many opportunities for group discussion.
*   Powerful depiction of the value of judging others by who they are, apart and aside from their race.
*   Strong family values are shown.

AWARDS
None

REVIEWS
"Draper has captured the voices of teens; the dialogue and the students' attitudes about the gang situation are believable. The convincing exchanges between the characters and the descriptions move the plot, while the action keeps the reader in suspense." —*Voice of Youth Advocates*, 12/99, Deborah L. Dubois.

"Draper has created Julio's parents and Romiette's mother with sensitivity and has given readers a pair of intriguing, unusual protagonists with the sort of real thoughts and feelings that will make this interracial story satisfying." —*Booklist*, 9/15/99, Holly Koelling.

"A realistic portrayal of the interactions among high school students as well as their relationships with their parents . . . also examines how gangs can gain power and take control. All of the characters have unique voices and the writing style shifts according to the action." —*School Library Journal*, September, 1999, Jane Halsall.

📖📖📖

RULES OF THE ROAD. Bauer, Joan. Putnam, 1998. $16.00. 201p. ISBN: 0-399-23140-4. Puffin, 2000. $4.99. 201p. ISBN: 0-698-11828-6. Realistic fiction. Reading level: MS, YHS. Interest level: YHS. English, Psychology, Geography, Sociology, Vocational education.

SUBJECT AREAS
travel; elderly; substance abuse; self-knowledge; rites of passage; working; family relationships; problem parents; lying and deceitfulness; divorce.

CHARACTERS
Jenna Boller: the best salesperson at Goldstone's Shoes of Chicago, at sixteen, she is a shoe professional
Murry Castlebaum: Jenna's boss, the store manager
Dad/Mr. Boller: Jenna's divorced, alcoholic father
Mrs. Madeline Gladstone: the owner of Gladstone Shoes, 176 outlets in 37 states with corporate offices in Dallas, Texas
Elden Gladstone: Mrs. Gladstone's slimy son who will take over the business when she retires
Faith Boller: Jenna's fourteen-year-old sister, she is blonde, beautiful, and misses her father
Mom: Jenna and Faith's mother who works as a night-shift emergency room nurse
Grandma: Jenna and Faith's grandmother who has Alzheimer's and lives in a nursing home
Opal Kincaid: Jenna's best friend

BOOKTALK
"I leaped onto the sliding ladder in the back room of Gladstone's Shoe Store of Chicago, gave it a shove, and glided fast toward the end of the floor to ceiling shelves of shoeboxes. My keen retailer's eye found the chocolate loafer, size 13, I slid the ladder to the Nikes, grabbed two boxes of easy walkers, beige and white, in size 4½ narrow, pushed again to women's saddles, found the waxhides, size 7, and rode the ladder to the door one-handed. Children, do not try this at home. I am a shoe professional."

I can sell shoes to anyone. I started at Gladstone's last year, when I was a sophomore and my life fell apart. I gained almost twenty pounds, dropped to second string on the basketball team because I couldn't jump, and got a C- in history, which knocked me off the honor roll. I staggered through the whole year wondering why God had invented adolescence. Gladstone's saved me. When I was there, I was somebody. I didn't feel big, awkward, or lost. I was successful. I helped people. And I loved it.

Selling shoes is how I ended up driving Mrs. Gladstone to Texas. She was in the store the night that Dad came in and demanded to see me. He was, as usual, messy, drunk, and loud. I hadn't seen him for two years, and I wasn't happy to see him now. Last time he'd spent the whole summer hanging around, drinking, not drinking, making promises and breaking them. It had been awful. I took him outside and poured him into a cab, then went back in to apologize to Mrs. Gladstone for the scene he'd made. Luckily, she didn't blame me for his problem, and I went back to selling shoes. And although I didn't realize it at the time, Mrs. Gladstone went back to watching me.

I couldn't have been more surprised to hear her voice on the phone later that night, telling me she wanted me to be her driver. "Pick me up at seven tomorrow morning and drive me downtown. Then we'll see." Her car was a huge old Cadillac, and I'd never been in one, much less driven one. I much preferred selling shoes. But Mrs. Gladstone was nothing if not determined, so just a few days later, I found myself driving out of Chicago in a blinding rainstorm, heading for Gladstone's Shoe Stores of Peoria, Springfield, St. Louis, Kansas City, Little Rock, Shreveport, and Dallas. Mrs. G and I were on a road trip to end all road trips. So come along with us, and find out what road trips—and selling shoes—are all about.

MAJOR THEMES AND IDEAS
- It's the difficult parts of life that make us strong.
- Confronting what you are afraid of or controlled by takes away its power over you.
- Unhappiness makes you look and feel worse both mentally and physically. When you feel good about yourself, you also look good.
- Be sure you care more about the person you're selling to than the product you are selling them.
- What doesn't kill you makes you stronger. Even the most difficult situation has something to teach you, if you choose to learn it.
- Love the person, hate the action.
- Everyone does something well. All you have to do is figure out what it is for you.
- If you don't like yourself or your life, you have the power to change yourself or your view of life to one you like better. Just remember, you can't make anyone else change. You have to do the changing.

BOOK REPORT IDEAS

1. Illustrate your talk with a map of the route Jenna and Mrs. Gladstone traveled.
2. Jenna learned a lot of lessons on the road. Discuss which one you think was the most important, explain why it was important, and show how Jenna changed after she learned it.
3. Several of the characters used platitudes or sayings to convey ideas. Select several of these and discuss them, pointing out how they were helpful to those who used them and why.
4. Discuss why it was important for Jenna to know her enemy and how that impacted the resolution of the story.
5. Quality vs. profits was a recurring theme throughout the book. Discuss examples of this theme other than the conflict between Mrs. Gladstone and her son.
6. Have your perceptions of the elderly changed because you read this book? Explain how and why they have either changed or not changed. What do you think you will be like when you are Mrs. Gladstone's age?
7. Having an alcoholic father controlled Jenna's life for many years. Trace the changes she made in her relationship with him, in person and in her mind, that allowed her to finally confront him.
8. Project the story five years into the future. What will the characters be doing, and who will they have changed? Support your ideas with quotations from the book.

BOOKTALK IDEAS

1. Write the talk from several different points of view, letting Mrs. Gladstone, Jenna, Faith, Alice, and others tell their parts of the story.
2. Illustrate your talk with pictures of some of the shoes that Jenna sells.
3. Write your talk as if you were a shoe salesman, selling the book as you would the shoes.
4. Jenna uses brief headline-like phrases throughout the book to comment on what is happening. Work several of these into your talk.

RISKS

- Shows alcoholic and abusive parent.

STRENGTHS

- Several story lines are woven together to create complexity in the story.
- Characters are realistic and multidimensional and teens can identify with them easily.
- Narrator grows and gains insight, and learns to take control of herself and her decisions.
- Ending does not tie up all the loose ends.

- Narrator seeks out, evaluates, and acts upon advice from adults.
- Characters act as positive role models, both in their actions and in their relationships with others.

AWARDS
Best Books for Young Adults, 1999 (ALA)
Quick Picks for Reluctant Readers, 1999 (ALA)
Children's Notables, 1999 (ALA)
Popular Paperbacks for Young Adults/Humor, 2001 (ALA)
100 Best Books for Teens, 2000 (ALA)

REVIEWS
"Here is the book that has everything; good writing, humor, moral enlightenment . . . a remarkable book, presenting lessons of respect for others, courtesy, and honesty gently but persistently. Its messages about values and self-esteem bring laughter and tears." —*Voice of Youth Advocates*, 6/98, Candace Deisley.

"A protagonist who is smart, moral, funny, confident (mostly), and open-minded about grown-ups . . . sad moments . . . show the long-term damage alcoholism has on families and individuals . . . also a warm, funny, insightful story about ordinary people who look beyond age to the things they have in common and the wisdom they can share." —*Booklist*, 2/1/98, Stephanie Zvirin.

"Bauer's juxtapositions are inviting—young and age, wealth and work-a-day struggle, big-city loneliness and big-state caring, practicing alcoholism and big-hearted sobriety, stockroom wisdom and boardroom chicanery . . . fabulous and sometimes flamboyant characters, witty dialogue, and memorable scenes." —*School Library Journal*, 3/98, Cindy Darling Codell.

       🕮 🕮 🕮

RUNDOWN. Cadnum, Michael. Viking, 1999. $15.99. 168p. ISBN: 0-670-88377-8. Puffin, 2001. $5.99. 176p. ISBN: 0-141-31087-1. Realistic fiction. Reading level: MS. Interest level: MS, YHS, OHS. English, P. E., Ethics.

SUBJECT AREAS
sports; legal system; lying and deceitfulness; family relationships; cooking; friendship; dysfunctional family; revenge; crime and delinquency; ethics; secrets; suicide.

CHARACTERS

Jennifer Thayer: to get attention, she said she was raped when she wasn't

Cassandra Thayer: Jennifer's sister whose wedding is only a month away

Bernice Heath: the Thayers' housekeeper

Terry Thayer: Jennifer's father who is a chef and has a line of gourmet salad dressings

Elizabeth Thayer: Jennifer's mother an industrial psychologist

Detective Margate, Detective Ronert: Berkeley police officers who were the first to question Jennifer

Marta Emmit: Jennifer's best friend

Mr. DaGame: Jennifer's boss at Animal Heaven

Tommy Dixon: he owns Sandalwood Ranch where Jennifer's horse is stabled

Quinn McGowan: Jennifer's ex-boyfriend who now lives in Reno, Nevada

BOOKTALK

One month before her sister's wedding, Jennifer did something terrible. It wasn't just an impulse—she planned it carefully—where, when, how, why, and even planned which police department she'd report it to.

She chose Strawberry Canyon where she loved to run, just at dusk, when there was a long summer twilight. She made sure she had the scratches and bruises to prove her story, and no witnesses who could tell the truth about what she did.

It was all planned carefully and precisely, including what she'd say to the first police officer she met. But when she gasped out my story to him, she didn't realize she couldn't plan what would happen after she said, "He tried to rape me!" nor what all the consequences of that statement would involve.

MAJOR THEMES AND IDEAS

- The longer a lie goes on, the more difficult it is to continue concealing it, and in the end, giving up your lie can be a relief.
- Watch and listen. Liars usually give themselves away if they don't know how to conceal their lies.
- In conversations, even silence talks.
- Lies can give people power and attention they might not otherwise have.
- Rape, even attempted rape, is a subject that makes people uncomfortable and to which they react strongly.

BOOK REPORT IDEAS

1. Jennifer's mother had unknowingly taught her how to lie. Decide if you think Jennifer could have carried off her lie without that knowledge, and explain why.
2. Discuss whether or not Jennifer's suicide attempt was part of her original plan and why. If it wasn't part of her plan, explain why you think she did it.

3. People had different reactions to Jennifer's story. Select two or three characters and explain why they acted the way they did.

4. Speculate on what happened after the book ended, and explain how Jennifer, her family, Marta, and Quinn were affected.

5. Jennifer talks a lot about her sister. Analyze Cass's character, explaining her actions and reactions as much as possible, including her relationship to Jennifer.

6. Cass's statement to Jennifer seems to have been the motivation behind Jennifer's lie. Decide whether or not Cass was lying by looking at the characteristics and personalities of the four people involved: Terry, Elizabeth, Cass, and Jennifer.

7. Jennifer says she lied to attract attention. Is this the whole truth, or did other factors also enter in?

BOOKTALK IDEAS

1. Write your talk as if it were a newspaper story. You can use as a prop a story clipped out of a newspaper.

2. Use the comments from Jennifer's family and friends as they react to the news of her "attack" as the body of your talk, ending with Jennifer's own story.

3. Focus your talk on the idea of lying and how Jennifer's mother taught her how to lie.

RISKS

• Teen lies to get attention.

• Several characters are unsympathetic.

• Dysfunctional family system contributes to teen's problems.

STRENGTHS

• Abrupt ending challenges readers and leaves room for speculation.

• Examines the psychology of lying from several perspectives.

• Realistic portrayal of police work.

• Nonstereotypical characters that teens will be able to identify with.

• Multilayered plot, with some layers only hinted at, or subtlety alluded to, challenges the reader.

AWARDS

Quick Picks for Reluctant Readers, 2000 (ALA)

REVIEWS

"Emotionally distant characters, dysfunctional families, and fascinating plot lines . . . classic Cadnum . . . neither easy nor fun to read. Teens will probably avoid it, but encourage them to read it . . . will make them look at themselves and their families in a whole new way . . . a dark, enigmatic book . . . the reader is ultimately engaged by Jennifer's process of self-discovery and self-destruction." —*Voice of Youth Advocates*, 10/99, Sara Thorsen.

"Deft characterization and adroit descriptions of setting and motivation raise Cadnum's writing above the commonplace. Readers may not always like the people who populate this book, but they will believe they are real." —*School Library Journal*, 9/99, Miriam Lang Budin.

"A novel about voices, about family silences and failures of communication, about what is said and what is too often left unsaid . . . an atmosphere of foreboding and exploring subtle nuances of character." —*Booklist*, 6/99, Michael Cart.

📖📖📖

THE SACRIFICE. Matchek, Diane. Farrar, Straus, and Giroux, Inc., 1998. $16.00. 198p. ISBN: 0-374-36378-1. Puffin, 1999. $4.99. 198p. ISBN: 0-141-30640-8. Historical fiction. Reading level: MS, YHS. Interest level: YHS, OHS. American history, Geography, Sociology.

SUBJECT AREAS
survival; travel; self-knowledge; family relationships; love; ethics; animals; minorities, Native American; religion; rites of passage; friendship; death and dying; war; prejudice; secrets.

CHARACTERS
The Apsaalooka Tribe

Weak-one-who-will-not-last or *Danger-with-snarled-hair*: a fifteen-year-old girl who is kidnapped by a Pawnee tribe while trying to prove her worthiness to her own people

Born-great: Weak-one's twin brother who died when he was four years old

Chews-the-bear: Weak-one's father, once one of the tribe's leaders, but shamed by the tribe after the death of his son

Grasshopper: a childhood friend of Weak-one, he has a crippled arm and cannot be a warrior

Broken Bough: the tribe's medicine man and the father of Grasshopper and Lies-down-in-water

Lies-down-in-water: Broken Bough's oldest son, he vows to avenge Chews-the-bear's death

The Pawnee Tribe
Wolfstar: as keeper of the Wolf Star bundle, it is his job to care for Weak-one
Two-voices: Wolfstar's adopted father
Her-corn-says-so: Wolfstar's adopted mother
Dreamer: the tribe's medicine man
Hummingbird-in-her-hair: Dreamer's wife, and the girl Wolfstar loved

BOOKTALK

"When the time is right," her father had said. "When the time is right." But Weak-one wasn't willing to wait any longer to prove to the warriors of her tribe that she was worthy to be one of them. "The time is now," she said to herself, and began to make plans to avenge her father's death. It was unusual among the Crow Indian tribes for a woman to be a warrior, but it was not forbidden.

Weak-one was an outsider in the tribe, and many thought she was crazy. At fifteen, she was skinny, long-limbed, with black hair that snarled in a grimy mess down her back. Her face, with its high cheekbones and straight nose, might have been beautiful, but it was a hard mask, filled with determination, her mouth a taut, straight line. She wore crudely sewn boy's clothing, and her eyes smoldered from deep within, like a wildcat's eyes at night from inside its den.

She waited until the war party had been selected and then stood and faced the warriors. "I, too, wish to go with the war party. My father was killed by a Headcutter, and as my father's only kin, I have the right to settle this matter by slaying a Headcutter warrior." But they laughed at her, and refused to let her go with them. When she realized she could not join them openly, she decided to follow them and join them later, when it was too far to send her back. After the battle, when they returned to the village, everyone would finally recognize her as the Great One, the most powerful warrior in her tribe, just as her father's dream had predicted so many years ago.

But nothing went according to her plan, for the gods had their own plans for the girl called Weak-one, who called herself Great One. She knew that in order to have a real name, she must earn it. Yet that night as she crept away from the only home she had ever known, the girl had no idea how many hardships waited for her in the months ahead. Would she have the courage, the determination, the knowledge to survive months alone in the wilderness, and even more months as a prisoner of a Pawnee tribe that was unwilling to reveal why they had captured her? Would she be able to prove to herself and everyone else that she did not deserve the name Weak-one-who-will-not-last-long?

MAJOR THEMES AND IDEAS

- Courage does not mean that one is without fear, but that one endures and overcomes it with action.
- Each of us creates ourselves by the way we chose to live and to confront the events of our lives.

- Sometimes believing in ourselves means ignoring and rejecting the things others say about us.
- Total focus on your goal and hardheadedness can be very useful tools sometimes, ones that can help you survive when others might not.
- Look inside your own heart for your definition of right and wrong, and not to anyone else, no matter what their stature might be.
- If you do not believe in yourself, no one else will either.
- When we have a choice between what we want and what is honorable, frequently, doing the honorable thing will give us more satisfaction and self-esteem in the end. Knowing we did what was right can be better than getting what we want.

BOOK REPORT IDEAS

1. Discuss the idea that we each create our own self, based on how we respond to people and events in our lives. Include examples of how the girl changed who she was during the course of the book by her thoughts and her actions.
2. There are many sacrifices in the book. Explain how each of them moves the story along to its final resolution.
3. Speculate about what will happen when the girl returns to her own tribe with her dramatically changed physical appearance and mental strength. Will the warriors believe her story of killing the grizzly or not?
4. Two different Native American religions clash in this book. Explore the idea of how what is right and ethical can be decided in such a situation. Is there ever an absolute right? Support your view with examples from the book
5. Speculate what might have happened in the Pawnee tribe after Danger and Wolfstar left.

BOOKTALK IDEAS

1. Present the talk from Wolfstar's point of view, showing his conflict about making friends with the girl when he knows what will happen to her. Be careful you do not reveal too much, leaving some mystery about why he is being kind to her.
2. Do the talk in first person, as the girl, showing her anger and determination to be the person she wants to be rather than who those around her want her to be.
3. Use one of the scenes from the Land of Boiling Water as an anecdote, with just a few sentences leading up to it to set the stage. Do not use the fight with the grizzly if you use this technique, since it gives away too much of the plot.

RISKS

- Several scenes contain graphic violence.

- A religious ceremony includes human sacrifice.

STRENGTHS
- Well-researched portrayal of two Native American tribes.
- Stunning depiction of Yellowstone National Park in the 1800s.
- Strong, independent female character teen girls can identify with.
- Realistic portrayal of an individual surviving the wilderness alone.
- Strong, fast-moving plot involves reader immediately.

AWARDS
Best Books for Young Adults, 1999 (ALA)

REVIEWS
"Plot is the driving force behind the book . . . good characterization coupled with a tight plot and authentic setting make this book a good choice not only for readers interested in early Native American life but also for readers looking for a good coming-of-age or adventure story." —*Voice of Youth Advocates*, 2/99, Melissa Thacker.

"Stunning first novel fuses breathless adventure, a bittersweet love story, and an intriguing role reversal—all played out in an unusual (and thoroughly researched) Native American setting . . . the breathtaking conclusion will have young adults closing the book with tremulous but satisfied sighs." —Amazon, 1999, Patty Campbell.

"Matcheck makes a stunning debut in a survival story that reveals not only the dangers of the wilderness but the risks to the human heart." —*Booklist*, 6/98.

📖📖📖

SAYING IT OUT LOUD. Abelove, Joan. DK Publishing, Inc., 1999. $15.95. 136p. ISBN: 0-789-42609-9. Puffin, 2001. $7.99. 240p. ISBN: 0-141-31227-0. Realistic fiction. Reading level: MS. Interest level: MS, YHS. English, Psychology, Ethics.

SUBJECT AREAS
death and dying; family relationships; grief and mourning; friendship; problem parents; minorities, Jewish; love; self-knowledge.

CHARACTERS
Mindy: a sixteen-year-old girl whose mother is dying

Gail: Mindy's best friend
Mindy's father:, he is strict, rigid, and proudly Jewish
Mindy's mother: an at-home mom who has taken good care of her family
Bobby: a new boy in Mindy's class who's tall, skinny, and Italian
Gert: Mindy's next-door neighbor

BOOKTALK

My mother is dying and no one will even talk to me about it! First she was sick and sometimes acted strange, then after the operation, she just went away. Her body is there, but she is gone. My father spends all his time at the hospital and won't talk to me at all. It's almost like when mother vanished, I did too.

And I need someone to talk to, someone to listen to all these thoughts inside my head. My father sees me as a little girl, pats me on the head, and says, "You'll be fine." But I'm not fine and maybe I'll never be fine again.

My mother is dying! Why am I the only one who can say that horrible truth out loud?

MAJOR THEMES AND IDEAS

- You never really believe someone's going to die until they do.
- Sometimes speaking the truth makes it less painful.
- We can't go back and change the past, no matter how much we want to.
- It is unfortunate that sometimes we don't see the value of another person until they are gone.
- No one ever dies until your memories of them die also.
- Sometimes friends understand you far better than parents or other adults.

BOOK REPORT IDEAS

1. Examine the character of Mindy's father, and explain how he shows his love for Mindy and her mother, both before and during her illness.
2. Gail and Bobby were Mindy's closest friends. Show what they gave her that no one else did.
3. Speculate on the relationship between Mindy and her father in the future, both on how it changed and how it stayed the same.
4. Discuss how this book might have been different had Mindy's family not been Jewish, and show how their ethnicity did or didn't impact the story.

BOOKTALK IDEAS

1. Tell the story from Gail's perspective.
2. Write your talk as if it were Mindy's journal.

RISKS

- Distant father withdraws from his daughter after his wife dies.
- Includes prejudice against non-Jews.

STRENGTHS

- Powerful portrayal of friendship.
- Realistic, evocative depiction of a teen's response to the death of a parent and the stages of grief.

AWARDS

Best Books for Young Adults, 2000 (ALA)

REVIEWS

"A very quiet book that effectively illustrates the loss of a loved parent and the estrangement of a child from a father. . . . A sad yet hopeful story." —*Voice of Youth Advocates*, 10/99, Judy Sasges.

"A beautifully written and tender portrayal of one young woman coming to grips with loss." —*School Library Journal*, 9/99, Barbara Auerbach.

📖📖📖

SHADE'S CHILDREN. Nix, Garth. HarperCollins, 1997. $16.95. 310p. ISBN: 0-060-27324-0. HarperCollins, 1998. $5.95. 345p. ISBN: 0-064-47196-9. Science fiction. Reading level: YHS. Interest level: YHS, OHS. English, Sociology.

SUBJECT AREAS

ethics; adventure; death and dying; friendship; computers; fear; manipulation; revenge; self-knowledge; war; survival; secrets; betrayal; cultural identity; rites of passage.

CHARACTERS

Gold-Eye: he has the intermittent ability to see into his immediate future, and is in his middle teens

Drum: he has telekinetic abilities, and is unusually big and strong for a teenager

Ella: she's nineteen, has been out of the Dorms since she was eleven, and has the ability to create objects with her mind

Ninde: she's Gold-Eye's age and is a telepathic

Shade: the computer-generated adult who helps the children, and a sworn enemy of the Overlords

Sim: he looks after the new arrivals on Shade's sub, plus many other things

BOOKTALK

"I am Shade. I am the protector of the human race . . . but I send children out to die. . . . I must protect humanity from the Overlords. . . . .but more must die. . . . I must protect . . . death, death, too much death."

When the change occurred and the Overlords took over Earth, everyone over the age of fourteen vanished, and the rest, or most of them, were herded into dormitories and kept captive until they were fourteen, and then taken to the Meat Factory, where their brains and muscles were harvested to help create the hideous creatures the Overlords used to fight their battles.

Few children escape the dorms, and the Trackers, Ferrets, and Myrmidons are designed to hunt them down. But in an old submarine, wedged under an abandoned wharf, a computer-generated adult has created an army of children to fight the Overlords. They are trained and equipped and sent out on missions to get information about the Overlords that will lead to their destruction.

Ella leads the top team, four children with special powers they gained as a result of the change. Ella is able to create objects with her mind. Drum is huge and muscular, and has the ability to manipulate objects with his mind. Ninde is telepathic, and can hear the thoughts of the Overlords' creatures. Gold-Eye is the newest member of the team, and his talent is intermittent and uncontrolled, but allows him to see a few minutes into the future.

Their mission, to get into an old university laboratory and bring back computer disks and equipment for their leader, the only adult on the planet, the person they all trust and admire—the hologram who calls himself Shade.

But is he as benevolent as he appears to be, or does he have his own agenda that he's unwilling to reveal?

MAJOR THEMES AND IDEAS

- In a war, death is a necessary evil.
- Sometimes there are no happy endings, just endings.
- Machines are not human beings, even if they look like they are.
- You don't leave your friends in danger; you go after them.
- Don't be deflected from your goal.
- The needs of the many outweigh the needs of the few.
- Wars are not won without sacrifice, but they *are* won.
- A selfish person will sacrifice anyone and anything to get what he wants.

BOOK REPORT IDEAS

1. Shade and his children are at war with aliens and their machines. Compare their battles with actual historical battles, showing both differences and similarities.
2. Describe what happened to Shade and why. Was his disintegration due to mental illness, mechanical failure, or some other force?
3. Describe the Overlords and what their occupation of Earth meant to them.

4. Discuss the effect of the content of the excerpts from the archives on the program of the story, and how they changed your perception of Shade.

5. The change occurred many years ago. Discuss how the Overlords were able to ensure a reliable supply of children.

BOOKTALK IDEAS

1. Build your talk around the idea of war and Shade's children as warriors.
2. Write a character description talk as Ella, letting her introduce the four other main characters.
3. Use the first few chapters in your talk, as Gold-Eye is rescued and joins Shade's children.

RISKS

- Children are used as soldiers.
- Teens are sexually active.
- Shows graphic violence.
- Language is realistic but includes obscenities.

STRENGTHS

- Story line is seen from multiple perspectives adding complexity.
- Gradual sense of encroaching evil, impending doom, creates suspense.
- Format uses different typefaces to create visual interest.
- Multidimensional characters teens can sympathize with.

AWARDS

Best Books for Young Adults, 1998 (ALA)

REVIEWS

"Through a fast-paced combination of narrative, transcripts, chilling statistical reports, and shifting points of view, Nix depicts a chilling future . . . the characters are compelling, their frailties emphasizing their humanity in sharp contrast to the Overlords . . . grim vision of the future is laced with hope . . . and it is this hope that sustains the reader through the nail-biting plot to the satisfying conclusion." —*Voice of Youth Advocates*, 6/98, Donna L. Scanlon.

"Although this is a fast-paced, exciting and often graphic story, it is pretty serious science fiction. . . . A well-written and engaging book." —*School Library Journal*, 8/97, Carrie Schadle.

"Thoughtful explorations of the nature of fear, bravery, and violence—natural conversations during wartime add depth and balance to the edge-of-the-seat action and intense first-person narration." *Horn Book*, 9-10/97, J.M.B.

〔🕮🕮🕮〕

SILENT TO THE BONE.

SILENT TO THE BONE. Konisberg, E. L. Atheneum, 2000. $16.00. 261p. ISBN: 0-689-83601-5. Realistic fiction. Reading level: MS. Interest level: MS, YHS. English, Sex education, Ethics, Communication, Psychology.

SUBJECT AREAS
abuse, physical; abuse, sexual; child abuse; sex and sexuality; family relationships; manipulation; illness, physical; divorce and separation; self-knowledge; friendship; ethics; love; lying and deceitfulness; mystery and suspense; rites of passage; secrets; stepparents.

CHARACTERS
Branwell Zamborska: when he calls 911 to save his sister's life, he is suddenly unable to speak
Connor Kane: Branwell's best friend who figures out how to communicate with him
Dr. Zamborska: Branwell and Nikki's father, and a research scientist at the university
Dr. Tina Nguyen Zamborska: Branwell's stepmother and Nikki's mother, she is also a researcher at the university
Nikki Zamborska: Branwell's baby sister
Vivian Shawcurt: the Zamborska's English au pair
Margret Kane: Connor's older stepsister
Mr. and Mrs. Branwell/The Ancestors: Branwell's maternal grandparents
Roderick Kane: Connor and Margaret's father and the Registrar at the university
Morris Ditmer: a pizza delivery boy who has an affair with Vivian
Yolanda: a housekeeper who works for the Zamborskas and several other families on the same block

BOOKTALK
It's easy to pinpoint the minute when Branwell began his silence. It was Wednesday, November 25, 2:43 p.m., Eastern Standard Time. It was there—or not there—on the tape of the 911 call. It was Vivian who finally told the dispatcher that something was wrong with Nikki, Branwell's baby sister. And she also said that it was Branwell who had hurt her. Bran still said nothing. He was still saying nothing when later that day a police car took him to the Clarion County Juvenile Behavioral Center.

Connor's known Bran all his life and they've always been best friends. Connor had no way of knowing what had happened in that house, but he was certain that Bran would never, ever have hurt Nikki. He simply wasn't capable of it. It was because of that long friendship that Bran's dad, Dr. Zamborska, asked Connor if he'd go to the center and see if he could persuade Bran to talk.

Connor agreed to go, even though he didn't think it could make a difference. What Dr. Zamborska didn't know was that they weren't friends the way they always had been. They still caught the bus to school together, and talked, and from the outside, to someone else, it probably looked like nothing had changed. But something had. Ever since Columbus Day, six weeks before, Branwell had been different. He seemed to have less time for Connor, less to say to him, and Connor was sure that there something that Bran was keeping from him, keeping hidden. But as soon as Connor saw Bran, he knew that he would have to forget the distance that had grown between them, and be the old friend he always had been, if he was ever going to get Bran to speak to him.

And, with the help of a set of homemade flash cards, he did. Connor was the first one he spoke to, because Bran knew that even before Connor learned all the details, he knew Bran could not have hurt the baby. Let Connor tell you what those first words were, and what came before them, and all the things he heard in Bran's silences.

MAJOR THEMES AND IDEAS
- Your friend is someone you can trust with your life, in the most literal sense.
- Embarrassment comes from outside; shame is something you do to yourself. Embarrassment makes you blush, but shame makes you angry.
- Shame is what you feel when you lose respect, self-respect or the respect of others.
- Sometimes silence is a weapon, not a retreat.
- There are layers to secrets, which have to be removed one at a time, before the inner core can be revealed.
- Don't assume people know what you need or want—tell them. If you don't, you have only yourself to blame when those needs and wants are ignored.
- Listening is just as important as speaking. If you don't listen to what someone is saying, and discern what they are trying to communicate, it is as if they did not speak.
- Manipulation of any kind is about the power one person needs to have over another. It is totally selfish and predatory.

BOOK REPORT IDEAS
1. Bran is not the only person in the book who used silence to communicate something. Discuss how other characters do the same thing.
2. Connor put a variety of words on the cards he used with Bran. Explain why you think he chose the words he did, and list some other words he might have chosen, and why he might have chosen them.
3. Consider the Drs. Zaborskas as parents. Explain in what ways were they good parents to both their children and in what ways were they not.

4. Bran and Connor's friendship is central to the book. Discuss why you think they were such good friends and what each gained from the relationship.
5. Speculate on how the Zaborska and Kane families might change after the ending of the book.

BOOKTALK IDEAS
1. Make your own pack of cards and use them as a prop for your talk.
2. Get into Bran's head and tell the story from his perspective.
3. Write your talk as a newspaper story.
4. Make a tape of the 911 phone call and use it to begin your talk.

RISKS
- Child abuse and mistreatment are not punished by any legal proceedings.
- Busy, working parents are distant from their children.
- Seduction of a minor boy by a woman several years older in a straightforward but not graphic scene.
- Sexual manipulation of a minor.

STRENGTHS
- Realistic, fast-moving, complex, multilayered plot draws in readers immediately.
- Multidimensional characters who grow and gain insight during book.
- Powerful portrayal of friendship.
- Shows family healing after difficult divorce.

AWARDS
Best Books for Young Adults, 2001 (ALA)

REVIEWS
"Takes the themes of friendship, family, loyalty, trust, communication, and growing up, and merges them into a tightly woven take that explores human relationships at their deepest levels. At first, some readers might be put off by the brilliant characters' sophisticated banter, but the pace will quickly grab readers' attention." —*Voice of Youth Advocates,* 12/00, Denise Beasley.

"Konigsburg gets behind today's tabloid headlines with a compelling mystery that is also a moving story of family, friendship, and seduction . . . the mutism is an eloquent part of the narrative. Like his silent friend, Connor comes to know the power of keeping quiet, that "the cruelest lies are often told in silence." —*Booklist,* 2000, Hazel Rochman.

"Achieves the right blend of quasi-adult sophistication and adolescent embarrassment . . . edgy, thought-provoking novel . . . written with

Konigsburg's characteristic wit and perspicuity—an incisive understanding of psychology that cuts to the bone and an awareness of human emotion that pierces the heart." —*Horn Book*, 2000.

"A complex, multilayered tale of human desires, adolescent confusion and a touch of menace. . . . This beautifully written story is darker than some of her others, with a remarkably true glimpse into a young man's inner world." —Amazon, 2000, Emilie Coulter.

"Every decade or so a book comes along that both encapsulates a genre and sends it on a new course." —*Horn Book*, 11-12/99, Patty Campbell.

📖📖📖

SLOT MACHINE. Lynch, Chris. HarperCollins, 1995. $14.95. 241p. ISBN: 0-060-23584-5. HarperTrophy, 1996. $5.95. 256p. ISBN: 0-064-47140-3. Realistic fiction. Reading level: MS. Interest level: MS, YHS. Art, P. E., English, Ethics, Writing.

SUBJECT AREAS
prejudice; peer pressure; sports; friendship; self-knowledge; abuse, physical; crime and delinquency; manipulation; intimidation; stereotypes; bullying; ethics; lying and deceitfulness; rites of passage; secrets.

CHARACTERS
Elvin Bishop: a fat freshman with two friends
Mikie: Elvin's number one friend who always knows what to do
Frankie: Elvin's number one-A friend who's too handsome and manly for his own good
Brother Jackson: Dean of Men at Christian Brothers Academy
Mr. Buonfiglio, Mr. Roarke, Coach Wolfe: respectively, the football, track and field, and wrestling coaches at CBA
Thor: Elvin and Frankie's Cluster Leader
Paul Burman: a tall, skinny kid who's forced to play basketball, even though he hates it
Eugene, Bellows, Lummox, Axe, Victor, Lute, the Dwarf: other members of the wrestling slot
Obie, Odie, Okie/"the O's": senior football players in the golf/tennis slot with Frankie who seem to befriend him
Oskar: a second-year freshman who knows the ropes

BOOKTALK

Would it be three weeks of summer camp for incoming freshmen or twenty-one days of nightmares?

Elvin, Mikie, and Frankie are best friends and incoming freshmen at the Catholic Brothers Academy in the fall, which means that they have to go to summer camp to meet their classmates and faculty members, and to have FUN, whether they want to or not. But when they arrive, they discover that it's not just a summer camp, it's a *sports camp*, and that FUN means playing and playing and playing that sport, day after day after day. That's not really a problem for Mikie, who's good at basketball, or Frankie, who's cool, tall, handsome, and knows how to play golf and tennis, but it's a nightmare for Elvin. El's your classic uncoordinated fat kid who hates sports. When his Cluster Leader asks him what sport he likes best, he says "None." Frankie, who's also in his cluster, is appalled to hear El acting like such a geek.

But El has to go somewhere—everyone has to have a slot, a pigeonhole to fit into, so they send him to football, where he becomes intimately acquainted with what it feels like to have several real football types jump on top of him all at once. To say the least, it isn't pleasant. When the coach kicks him out, he goes to baseball, but only lasts one day. Finally he ends up in wrestling—with lots of other fat kids. Maybe he can make a go of this—if he could only figure out the rules.

Meanwhile, Mikie's fitting in, coasting the way he usually does, but Frankie is having some problems. The seniors from the football team, who are in the golf/tennis slot and also the school leaders, are grooming Frankie to take their place after they graduate, and some of the things they want him to do aren't fun at all, and others just seem cruel. But he wants to fit in, to find his slot, more than anything else, so he goes along with it, while Mikie and Elvin wonder if he'll survive.

It may be only three weeks, but those twenty-one days change Mikie, Frankie, and Elvin in ways they never expected. They knew who they were when they were fed into the slot machine, but who were they when they were spit back out?

MAJOR THEMES AND IDEAS

- Sometimes the price you have to pay to fit in is too high.
- Friends are the people who are honest with you and stick by you, no matter what.
- If you have to change yourself too much to fit in with a group, it may be more productive to find another group.
- It's more important to be an individual than to fit into a group.
- Being a hero on the playing field doesn't automatically make you one off the field as well.
- People aren't what they look like, but who they are inside.

- Being handsome doesn't hide the ugliness and unhappiness that people have inside.
- "To thine own self be true, and thou canst not then be false to any man."—William Shakespeare

BOOK REPORT IDEAS

1. Discuss the idea of slotting and how well it did or didn't work. Examine the effects it had on several of the boys at camp.
2. Examine the conflict between the O's and the Art Sector. Discuss how realistic you think it was, and how often you've seen similar conflicts occur. Be sure to include in your comments how both faculty and students responded on each side, and what that says about the culture of this school.
3. Look at Frankie's experiences with the O's, and speculate on their personalities and why they treated Frankie as they did. Then look at Frankie's personality and speculate why he responded as he did, and how this will affect his behavior in the future.
4. Elvin's last letter to his mother says he, Mikie, and Frankie have changed. Explain how and why you think those changes have taken place, and how they are different from the people they were when they got to the camp.

BOOKTALK IDEAS

1. Use Elvin's letters to his mother as the focus of your talk.
2. Write your talk in first person, as Elvin.
3. Have the three main characters introduce themselves and share a little of their first reactions to camp during the first week. It might be interesting to include their opinions of each other as well.

RISKS

- Language is realistic but vulgar.
- Scenes of nudity and sexual posturing.
- Hazing of younger campers by older ones, including alcohol, property destruction, physical abuse, pornographic films, and deliberate cruelty.
- Campers who don't fit in are ridiculed by staff and other campers.
- "Us-them" mentality encouraged by camp staff, especially pertaining to jocks and nonjocks.
- Portrayal of artists as homosexuals who are harassed by the jocks.

STRENGTHS

- Realistic portrayal of early teenage males.
- Strong friendships were not damaged by outside input.
- Characters increased in insight and self-knowledge during book.
- Portrayal of rites of passage.
- Characters are nonstereotypical and quirky.

- Author uses dry wit and humor.
- Lively writing style engages the reader.

AWARDS
Best Books for Young Adults, 1996 (ALA)
Quick Picks for Reluctant Readers, 1996 (ALA)
Booklist Editors' Choice, 1995

REVIEWS
"Lynch's craftsmanship becomes apparent as the reader starts peeling away the layers of the story. . . . Lynch really is condemning the pernicious effect organized sports can exercise on society . . . tells the story . . . [in] a style that is crisp, humorous, sarcastic, sad, sensitive, realistic, and sometimes raunchy, but never dull." —*Voice of Youth Advocates*, 12/95, William R. Mollineaux.

"Lynch has a knack for writing in a style (and in the raunchy vernacular) that rings true with Yas . . . filled with drama, humor, and pathos." —*School Library Journal*, 10/95, Tom S. Hurlburt.

"Lynch writes a damning commentary on the costs of conformity and the power gained by standing up for oneself in his biting, sometimes hilarious novel. . . . realistic look at growing up male in a society that values athleticism and charisma at all costs." —*Horn Book*, 11-12/95, M.V.K.

🕮🕮🕮

SMACK. Burgess, Melvin. Henry Holt and Company, Inc., 1998. $16.95. 327p. ISBN: 0-805-05801-X. William Morrow and Co., 1999. $6.99. 293p. ISBN: 0-380-73223-8. Realistic fiction. Reading level: MS. Interest level: YHS, OHS. English, World history, Art.

SUBJECT AREAS
substance abuse; friendship; family relationships; unwed mothers; survival; crime and delinquency; runaways; poverty; problem parents; homeless; abuse, physical; self-knowledge; ethics; manipulation.

CHARACTERS
David/Tar: at fourteen, he runs away to the city to avoid being abused by his father
Gemma: Tar's girlfriend who joins him after a fight with her parents
Skolly/Joe Scholl: he runs a tobacco shop and helps Tar find a squat
Richard: a friend of Skolly's who sets up squats for kids to live in

Vonny: in her early twenties, she tries to mother Tar and Gemma
Jerry: Vonny's boyfriend who spends most of his time stoned
Andrew and Emily Brogan: Gemma's parents
Charles and Jane Lawson: Tar's parents
Oona: Tar and Gemma's daughter
Lily: she ran away from home when she was twelve and is very wild
Rob: Lily's boyfriend who looks scary but is actually very gentle and polite
Sunny: Rob and Lily's son
Dev: a drug dealer
Sal/Sally: she's tight with Lily and Gemma and lives with them, Rob, and Tar

BOOKTALK

There were turning points in Tar's life—times when things changed drastically and were never the same again. The first was when he ran away because he didn't want to be his father's punching bag. The next was when he met Richard, Vonny, and Jerry, who offered him a place to stay, so he wasn't homeless any more. Then Gemma, the girl he loved, moved in, and Tar was sure he had it made.

And maybe it would've worked out okay, if Gemma and Vonny had gotten along. But Gemma had run away to get away from her controlling parents, and she didn't like Vonny telling her what to do.

And if Richard hadn't invited Lily and Rob to their housewarming party, Gemma wouldn't have met them. When Gemma saw Lily, she could see Lily's confidence, her magic, and she wanted to have them too. She just didn't realize that they didn't come from inside Lily, but from the heroin she was addicted to.

Things changed again for Tar and Gemma when they decided to try Lily's magic. It wasn't dangerous—it was fun! It was a way to let go of all the problems and hassles.

They had no idea how quickly their lives would go from heroin heaven to heroin hell.

MAJOR THEMES AND IDEAS

- You are never responsible for someone else's pain. If someone lets themselves be abused, it's their responsibility.
- Sometimes the best thing you can do in an abusive situation is leave, any way you can.
- Promises and confessions made under pressure don't count.
- Running away because your parents are too strict is not a solution. It's compounding the problem.
- You can be anybody you want to be. Be true to who you are.
- Carry your own baggage but don't take on anyone else's.
- Even when you think you're stronger than the drug you're taking, you are in its power.

- Addicts are weak, not strong, and they drag each other down. Misery loves company.
- Abusive behavior goes from one generation to another.
- Once an addict always an addict.
- To love another person, you have to feel safe with them and with yourself.
- When you're depressed or your self-esteem is at a low ebb, it's easy to give into your craving.
- When you feel bad *about* yourself, it's easier to do something bad *to* yourself.

BOOK REPORT IDEAS

1. Discuss why there's no note from Gemma at the end, and what she might have said if she'd written a last note.
2. Show the insight the note from Tar's father provides.
3. Discuss whether or not you think Tar and Gemma will stay clean and why.
4. Speculate on where Tar, Gemma, Lily, Rob, and Sally will be in five years and why.
5. Discuss whether or not this book is a love story and why.
6. Explain how this book makes you feel about doing drugs.
7. Decide which person you identify with most and explain why you chose that person.
8. Discuss whether or not Tar and Gemma will ever get back together.
9. At one point Lily says that everything is free—you can have anything you want. Show how Lily actually paid a high price for "free" things.

BOOKTALK IDEAS

1. Use a picture of a dandelion as a prop.
2. Use Tar's statement, "It was a love story, me, Gemma, and smack," as the focus of your talk.
3. Focus your talk on two scenes: the first when the squatters see drugs as under their control, and the second whey they realize that smack controls them. End with a question about whether they will ever get off them.

RISKS

- Parents portrayed negatively: physically abusive father and sexually manipulative mother.
- Graphic scenes of drug use/addiction/dealing.
- Portrays teen sexuality/pregnancy.
- Language is realistic but includes obscenities.
- British slang may be difficult for some readers.
- Shows prostitution, crime, and delinquency.

- Length of book—readers may put it down when drugs are still seen as glamorous and controllable, and not see the true horror and degradation that comes later.

STRENGTHS

- Powerful statement on the dangers of drugs.
- Multidimensional characters that teens can identify with.
- Horrifying look at what heroin does to people's lives.
- Realistic, gritty picture of the life of a junkie and the difficulty of getting off drugs.
- Clear message: drugs addict, drugs kill, they are not fun!
- Realistic language and situations teens can identify with.
- Multiple perspectives and points of view add complexity and depth to the novel.

AWARDS

Best Books for Young Adults, 1999 (ALA)
Carnegie Medal, 1998
Guardian Prize for Children's Fiction, 1998

REVIEWS

"The perfect young adult novel because it delivers what it advertises. . . . It tells the truth. It doesn't preach. It makes you think. . . . It has no answers. It offers no vacuous hope that everything will turn out fine. Instead it shows, horrifyingly and heartbreakingly, that if one is swayed by friends or lovers or the need to belong, without cultivating one's inner strength, one is unlikely to make it. And even if one is strong, other forces can be stronger. . . . the censors' radar will be out for this one. It contains every youth crime in the book . . . and will be interpreted as undermining . . . family values because it insists that young readers judge those values for themselves. . . . . No adult who works with youth can afford to ignore it. No teenager can afford to be without it. *Smack* is the YA novel of the decade." *—Voice of Youth Advocates*, 6/90, Cathi Dunn MacRae.

"Present[s] a chilling reality. . . . the results of unleashed adolescent experimentation . . . powerful and calculated, intent on affecting readers and shattering pat illusions . . . not a lecture to be yawned through . . . [but] a slap in the face, and vicariously, a hard-core dose of the consequences of saying 'yes.'" *—School Library Journal*, 5/98, Alison Follos.

"Neither romanticizes nor preaches the dangers of heroin use, but . . . clearly shows both the allure of the drug and the often inevitable addiction it creates . . . an honest, unpatronizing, unvarnished account of teen life on the skids." *—Booklist*, 4/15/98, Debbie Catron.

ⅉⅉⅉ

SPEAK. Anderson, Laurie Halse. Farrar, Straus, and Giroux, Inc., 1999. $16.00. 198p. ISBN: 0-374-37152-0. Puffin, 2001. $7.99. 198p. ISBN: 0-141-31088-X. Thorndike Press, 2000. $20.95. 276p. ISBN: 0-786-22525-4. (large print) Listening Library Inc., 2000. $22.00. ISBN: 0-807-28264-2. (unabridged audiotape) Realistic fiction. Reading level: MS. Interest level: YHS, OHS. Psychology, Sociology, English, Ethics, Sex education.

SUBJECT AREAS
abuse, sexual; crime and delinquency; bullying; dating and social life; ethics; family relationships; lying and deceitfulness; peer pressure; gossip; secrets; sex and sexuality.

CHARACTERS
Melinda Sordino: she is being shunned by everyone at school for calling the cops to an end-of-summer party
Mom and Dad: Melinda's parents who communicate with her mostly through notes on the refrigerator
Rachel, Ivy, Nicole: Melinda's ex-friends
Heather: a new girl who doesn't know what Melinda did, and wants to be friends with her
Mr. Freeman, Mr. Neck, Hairwoman, Mr. Stetman, Ms. Keene: high school faculty members
David Petrakis: Melinda's lab partner, one of the Cyber-genius clan
IT/Andy Evans: Melinda's nightmare, and the reason she called the cops

BOOKTALK
Melinda is an Outcast. She called the cops to an end-of-summer party, and a bunch of kids got arrested. But no one has asked her why she called them, they just believe she's a traitor. So she walks down the halls at school alone, and speaks to no one. If she tries to talk to teachers, her voice just seems to freeze up. She chews at her lips till they're raw and ugly, and bites her nails till they bleed. There's a beast inside of her eating her up. When she tries to tell someone what is happening to her, her throat strangles all the words. Not even her parents know what happened to her at that party. The only time they talk to her is to yell at her about grades. The rest of the time they all leave notes for each other on the refrigerator.

And the secret Melinda is holding back continues to pull her down. The only place she feels free or at peace is in art class, where she is drawing a tree over and over and over. Can her art help her break her silence? Can anything? Will she ever be able to share her secret and rejoin her world?

MAJOR THEMES AND IDEAS

- You have to tell someone what is hurting you in order to get help. Keeping quiet only makes it hurt worse.
- No one can know your thoughts. To communicate, you must share them.
- Showing your fear to a bully only makes him even meaner. Standing up to him and showing your anger is a better choice.
- What you do is far more important than how you look.
- Our bodies frequently reflect what is going on in our minds.
- Life is about making mistakes and then learning from them. Always look for the lesson.
- When people don't express themselves and their feelings, they die inside, a little at a time.
- The flaws, the uniqueness of things and people are what make them interesting and individual.
- You can always survive, if you choose to do so. But it will not always be easy or quick.

BOOK REPORT IDEAS

1. Melinda doesn't like having to look for the symbolism in Hawthorne, but her writing and her life are full of symbols. Discuss them and their meaning.
2. Examine the different ways Melinda draws her trees, and how they reflect her inner state and her turmoil.
3. Compare and contrast the reputation Andy had as a popular senior with what was written about him on the walls of the girls' restroom. Why didn't anyone expose him sooner?
4. Discuss what you think Melinda's sophomore year will be like, based on what was happening at the end of the book.
5. Discuss the concept of friendship in the book and the various ways it was expressed by different characters at different times. Be sure to include the way Melinda was perceived both before and after she and Andy were found in the closet.
6. The book is written in sections corresponding to the grading periods. Examine Melinda's grades for each of the periods, comparing what she got in each area with what was going on in her life at that time.
7. Compare this title with others about teens who won't reveal what has happened to them, for instance, John Marsden's *Letters from the Inside*.
8. Examine the cliques Melinda mentions and discuss how realistic they are, and how they change the ways students interacted with her and with each other. Compare this to your own situation in your school. How realistically is her high school portrayed?

BOOKTALK IDEAS

1. Using first person, let Melinda tell her own story.

2. Write your booktalk from different points of view, letting several characters describe Melinda in their own voices, then let her speak a few sentences about herself. But be careful not to give away what has happened to her, other than letting your audience know it was the most horrible thing that could ever have happened.
3. Heather was Melinda's closest friend during the year. Describe Melinda, her appearance, and her actions, from Heather's point of view, using first person and expressing Heather's confusion about Melinda's actions and appearance.

RISKS
- While the scene is not written explicitly, Melinda is raped by an older boy with a reputation among his peers for brutality.
- Parents are more involved in their own lives than with their daughter's problems, even when those problems are pointed out to them.
- Teachers are portrayed as stereotypes, to their detriment.
- Peer pressure used to punish teen who broke "the code."

STRENGTHS
- Rape scenes are not portrayed graphically.
- Complex characters teens can easily identify with, and who grow and gain strength and insight.
- Ambiguous, somewhat unfinished ending leaves room for speculation.
- Speaks directly to teens who might find themselves in similar situations.
- Shows the wisdom and the need for telling the truth no matter what happens.

AWARDS
Best Books for Young Adults, 2000 (ALA)
Quick Picks for Reluctant Readers, 2000 (ALA)
Michael L. Printz Award Honor Book, 2000 (ALA)
Selected Audiobooks for Young Adults, 2001 (ALA)
Booklist Editors' Choice, 1999
School Library Journal Best Books of the Year, 1999

REVIEWS
"Portrays a large suburban high school with a fresh and authentic eye—all the cliques are there, from the jocks, to the Goths, to the "Marthas." . . . This extremely well-written book has current slang, and accurate portrayal of high school life, and engaging characters . . . powerful story has an important lesson: never be afraid to speak up for yourself." —*Voice of Youth Advocates*, 12/99, Rebecca Vnuk.

"Anderson expresses the emotions and the struggle of teenagers perfectly. Melinda's pain is palpable, and readers will totally empathize with her." —*School Library Journal*, 10/99, Dina Sherman.

"Melinda's voice is distinct, unusual, and very real as she recounts her past and present experiences in bitterly ironic, occasionally even amusing vignettes. . . . perfectly captures the harsh conformity of high-school cliques and one teen's struggle to find acceptance from her peers." —*Booklist*, 9/15/99, Debbie Carton.

"The wonderfully descriptive language, along with the suspense, capture and propel the reader through this tale." —*ALAN Review*, Winter 2000, Katherine Barr.

🕮🕮🕮

STAYING FAT FOR SARAH BYRNES. Crutcher, Chris. Greenwillow, 1993. $16.95. 216p. ISBN: 0-688-11552-7. Laureleaf Books, 1995. $5.50. 216p. ISBN: 0-440-21906-X. Realistic fiction. Reading level: MS. Interest level: MS, YHS, OHS. English, P. E., Sex education, Psychology, Ethics.

SUBJECT AREAS
sports; secrets; friendship; self-knowledge; child abuse; rites of passage; school; survival; lying and deceit; religion; sex and sexuality; activism; dating and social life; problem parents; dysfunctional families; ethics; manipulation; love; peer pressure; prejudice; violence.

CHARACTERS
Eric Calhoune/Moby: a smart, fat, eighteen-year-old whose dad split before he was born
Sarah Byrnes: her hands and face were burned when she was three and her dad won't let her have reconstructive surgery
Mrs. Lemky: Eric's English teacher and swim coach
Laurel: Sarah's counselor
Mr. Mantz: Eric and Sarah's junior high school principal and high school vice principal
Steve Ellerby: Eric's good friend who drives the Christian Cruiser, and a preacher's kid who has a lot of opinions about religion
Dale Thornton: in the eighth grade, even though he's sixteen, he's a bully who hides his secrets
Mark Brittain: a swim team member and a Christian who objects to Ellerby's car and to his sacrilegious antics
Mr. Patterson: the high school principal

Jody Mueller: the best looking girl in school and Mark's girlfriend, who hides a terrible secret

Virgil Byrnes: Sarah's smart, mean, and abusive father

Reverend Ellerby: a liberal Episcopalian priest and Steve's father

Sandy Calhoun: Eric's mother and a newspaper columnist

Carver Middleton: Sandy's boyfriend and an accountant with unplumbed depths

BOOKTALK

Hi, my name is Eric Calhoun, but you can call me Moby, everyone does. I've always been a fat kid and now I'm a swimmer, so naming me after a whale didn't take a lot of imagination.

This story I'm about to tell you is about me and Sarah Byrnes and what happened our senior year in high school. We'd been best friends for our whole lives, at first because we both had the "terminal uglies." I was the fattest kid in school, and she was the ugliest. When she was three, Sarah Byrnes tipped a pot of boiling spaghetti over herself, and her dad didn't let her have any plastic surgery. Her face and hands were horribly scarred—she is truly one of the ugliest human beings around. He said he did it to teach her a lesson. Until I met him, it was hard to imagine a man that evil.

Sarah Byrnes and I reacted to being picked on and hassled in different ways. I got scared; she got mad. At least I was scared 'til she taught me how to fight back, if not with fists, then with words and actions. But no matter what, Sarah Byrnes was there for me, and I was there for her. I even stayed fat for a year after I joined the high school swim team, because I was afraid things would change between us if I wasn't fat any more. I mean, there was nothing she could do about how she looked.

That's why when she just stopped talking a little while ago, and went into an all but catatonic state, I knew I couldn't desert her. Every day, I went to the psychiatric hospital where they'd taken her, trying to get her to tell me what was wrong, and how I could help. But no matter what I did, she just sat there staring at nothing. It was frustrating, 'cause I had other stuff going on in my life. I was training hard for the state swimming meet, my mother was dating a total dweeb, and we were getting into some seriously heavy discussions on religion and abortion in one of my classes that just happens to be taught by my swim coach.

But if Sarah Byrnes wasn't going to talk I was gonna have to do some explaining on my own. So I did, and things got real complex, real fast.

MAJOR THEMES AND IDEAS

- Trusting adults to help when things get too hard can be a good thing.
- Best friends are there for you—all the time.
- The more times you outsmart a bully, the smarter you get. It's a matter of survival.
- When you want information always go to the expert.

- If you have a secret to share, the person you go to is probably someone who can say, "been there, done that."
- Sadly, looks do count all too much of the time.
- Some families that look good from the outside can be very messed up when seen from the inside.
- Anything that's known can't be unknown.
- Our beliefs color what we see and help us create our own realities.
- People frequently aren't who they appear to be.
- When a fool and a wise man argue, sometimes it's hard for observers to tell the difference.
- No one is responsible for your actions and decisions except you. Period.
- Feeling guilty about someone else's actions or decisions is not only wrong, it is hurtful to you.

BOOK REPORT IDEAS

1. Choose one of the CAT class discussions, analyze it, and explain your own beliefs on the subject and why you have them.
2. Eric stayed fat for a year after he started swimming to protect his friendship with Sarah Byrnes. Even though he didn't continue to do that, he found other ways to "stay fat." Show what some of these ways were.
3. There is a saying that, "What doesn't kill you makes you stronger." Discuss the truth or falsity of that saying in terms of the characters in this book.
4. Analyze the character of Mark Brittain showing his strengths, weaknesses, and the reasoning behind his actions.
5. Compare the relationships between Steve and his father, and between Mark and his father. Speculate on how these two relationships might change in the future.
6. Discuss whether or not you think Sarah should have plastic surgery.

BOOKTALK IDEAS

1. Focus your talk on Sarah Byrnes and the scene in which Eric first learns she is listening to everything he says, and he decides to go find Dale.
2. Focus your talk on the idea of friendship and why Eric and Sarah Byrnes were friends, leading up to his first attempt to persuade her to talk.

RISKS

- Shows the weaknesses of rigid, conservative Christianity.
- Portrays evil and abusive father and weak, distant mother.
- Shows physical and mental child abuse.
- Language is realistic yet vulgar.
- Peer manipulation and harassment of teens perceived as "different."

STRENGTHS

- Strong, appealing characters teens can identify with, and who struggle to survive and succeed
- Pro/con class discussions on several controversial topics, especially abortion and religion.
- Moving portrayals of several strong friendships.
- Adults seen as positive role models in a variety of settings.
- Several story lines skillfully woven together make the plot more complex and interesting.
- Many messages about thinking for yourself and learning from experiences, both good and bad.

AWARDS

Best Books for Young Adults, 1994 (ALA)
Margaret A. Edwards Award, 2000 (ALA)
Popular Paperbacks for Young Adults/Good Sports, 1999 (ALA)
100 Best Books for Teens, 2000 (ALA)

REVIEWS

"More tightly plotted than his earlier YA novels. . . . full, complete character development of the teen protagonists in related subplots. . . . Crutcher's darkest and most riveting work to date, almost entirely unrelieved by any humor. Older YAs are likely to read this in one sitting, and then will be left thinking about it for weeks afterward." —*Voice of Youth Advocates*, 8/93, Susan R. Farber.

"Once again, Crutcher assembles a crew of misfits to tackle the Big Issues . . . language, characters, and situations are vivid and often hilarious. . . . Pulse-pounding, on both visceral and intellectual levels—a wild, brutal ride." —*Kirkus Reviews*, 3/15/93.

"Strong on relationships, long on plot, and has enough humor and suspense to make it an easy booktalk with appeal across gender lines." —*Booklist*, 1993, Janice Del Negro.

ᗕᗕᗕ

STONES IN WATER. Napoli, Donna Jo. Penguin, 1997. $15.99. 209p. ISBN: 0-525-45842-5. Penguin, 1999. $5.99. 224p. ISBN: 0-141-30600-9. Reading level: MS. Interest level: MS, YHS. English, American history, World history.

SUBJECT AREAS
friendship; survival; prejudice; war; minorities, Jewish; racism; rites of passage; death and dying; secrets; grief and mourning; animals; travel; poverty; self-knowledge.

CHARACTERS
Roberto: a Venetian boy who's caught by Germans and sent to a labor camp in
    Germany
Samuele/Enzo: Roberto's best friend who is Jewish
Sergio: Roberto's older brother
Wasser, Arbeiter: German guards
Ragazzo: a mute boy Roberto finds after his village has been destroyed
Dr. Maurizio: an Italian soldier who helps Roberto

BOOKTALK
Their lives changed forever because they wanted to see an American western movie. American movies didn't come to Venice very much any more because of the war. But tonight Memo had money to pay for Roberto, Samuele, and Sergio. Suddenly, just after the newsreels were over and the movie started, the lights came on, and German soldiers began forcing the crowd out of the theater, down the street, and onto a train. They were prisoners.

Germans needed someone to build highways and airfields, and kidnapping boys and young men from their allies was one way to get the slave labor they needed.

Sergio, Roberto's older brother, was put on board a different train from the three boys, and it's not long before Memo is put in a different group and Roberto and Samuele, now called Enzo to hide his Jewishness from the guards, are alone in a crowd of strangers.

Feel the cold and the brutality of the labor camps, as the boys fight to survive, not only the weather and the backbreaking work, but also starvation, and clothes and shoes that fall apart, worn completely to shreds. And always, daily, there is the danger that someone will discover that Enzo is a Jew.

What do you do when you think you can't go on? You lean on your friend, and take another step, another breath, and another, and another.

MAJOR THEMES AND IDEAS
- In war there are no laws.
- You can survive almost anything with the love and support of a good friend.
- It is almost always true that if you look you can find someone who is worse off than you.
- Happiness can come to us even in the most miserable of situations if we allow it to.

- Fight those who want to control you. Even if you can't fight physically, fight mentally. Keep your mind strong and remember who you are.
- Ensure your own survival, and when you can, do what is possible to help others survive also.
- Sometimes a bold action is less noticeable than a furtive one.
- In a situation where all struggle to survive, those who hesitate may be lost.
- You can always do something to fight back against your oppressors, even if it is only a small thing, the effect of many small things combined together can be very large indeed.

BOOK REPORT IDEAS

1. Discuss the idea of friendship as it is seen in the book, and the different kinds of friendships Roberto experiences.
2. In the labor camps, the boys fought and stole from each other instead of working together against the Germans. Explain your understanding of why that happened, both because of things the Germans did and things the boys themselves did.
3. Both Samuele and Roberto could be called survivors. Show what mental and physical characteristics helped them live when so many died.
4. Compare Roberto at the beginning and end of the book, and show how he changed. Then predict what you think his life will be like after the book is over.
5. Use a map of Europe during the war to trace the boys' travels.

BOOKTALK IDEAS

1. Write a character description talk letting Roberto tell the story of the boys' capture.
2. Use photographs from World War II to illustrate your talk.
3. Choose one chapter to focus on—for instance, Roberto and Enzo's interaction with the Polish girl and her sister.

RISKS

- Clear portrayal of man's inhumanity to man, whether it was Germans' actions toward Jews and their prisoners, or the boys fighting for food and clothing.
- Grim picture of the effects of war.

STRENGTHS

- Shows the power of love and friendship to triumph over evil and despair.
- Chilling portrait of a little-known part of World War II.
- Characters who refuse to give up or give in to their captors, and eventually triumph over them.

AWARDS
Best Books for Young Adults, 1998 (ALA)
Children's Notables, 1998 (ALA)

REVIEWS
"Based on the real experiences of a Venetian youth. . . . harrowing tale of inhumanity, strength and friendship. . . . it stays with you, haunts you, and makes you wish that people were not really like this, when in reality you know that war is hell and people can be savage. . . . a good choice for novels about World War II, survival, or overcoming odds." —*Voice of Youth Advocates*, 2/98, Janet Mura.

"Roberto . . . is a displaced gondolier trying to navigate his boat on a modern Styx, a hellish river journey with slim chances for survival. . . . An intense, gripping tale." —*School Library Journal*, 11/97, Marilyn Payne Phillips.

"Looking at World War II from a unique perspective, this is an affecting coming-of-age novel with a vivid and undeniable message about the human costs of war." —*Horn Book*, January-February, 1998, Kitty Flynn.

"A powerful novel set in a vividly realized wartime milieu. . . . riveting." —*Kirkus*, 1997.

📖📖📖

STOP PRETENDING: WHAT HAPPENED WHEN MY BIG SISTER WENT CRAZY. Sones, Sonya. HarperCollins, 1999. $14.95. 160p. ISBN: 0-060-28387-4. HarperCollins, 2001. $6.95. 160p. ISBN: 0-064-46218-8. Verse novel, Realistic fiction. Reading level: MS. Interest level: MS, YHS, OHS. English, Creative writing, Psychology.

SUBJECT AREAS
illness, mental; family relationships; self-knowledge; school; friendship; rites of passage; art; love; gossip; dysfunctional families; secrets; therapy; writing.

CHARACTERS
Cookie: the narrator, who mourns the loss of her older sister
Sister: she has a nervous breakdown and has to be hospitalized
Mom and Dad: parents who try to cope with the sudden changes in their family
Molly, Kate, Sarah, Liz, Beth, Ariel: Cookie's friends
Dr Saunders: Cookie's therapist

John: Cookie's boyfriend
Mrs. Zolli: Cookie's teacher

BOOKTALK

It happened so suddenly. One day everything was fine. The next day my sister went crazy. There was no warning, no time to prepare. My sister was gone, leaving a strange, angry person in her body.

Sunday is visiting day. My parents usually chat with Sister before they go down the hall for their therapy session. Then Sister and I talk. Sometimes I have too much homework and stay home. Sometimes I just say I have too much homework.

I want my sister back again, not crazy, not psycho. I want my parents back again, not fighting, not worrying if I'm going crazy, not wondering if my friends would laugh at me if they knew.

In *A Wrinkle in Time*, Meg cures her little brother by telling him she loves him. Why won't that work for me?

What's it like when your big sister goes crazy? Let Cookie tell you what it was like for her.

MAJOR THEMES AND IDEAS

* When one family member is seriously ill, the whole family is affected.
* People sometimes laugh at what they fear or don't understand.
* Friends are those who accept you completely. Those who don't, you probably don't need anyway.

BOOK REPORT IDEAS

1. Cookie goes through a variety of emotions while learning how to deal with her sister's illness. Show the sequence of these emotions and how she shifts from one to another.
2. Cookie's friends turn away from her when they find out about her sister. Explain how she feels about this, and what she does as a result.
3. Sister's illness has several turning points. Discuss them and show their effects on her and on her family.
4. Show how Cookie and her parents cope with Sister's illness in both positive and negative ways.
5. The author's note specifies Sister's illness as manic-depression. Give several examples of how she acted in both states of mind.
6. Suppose one of your family members went crazy. Explain how you might respond, comparing that response to the ways Cookie responded.
7. Several times Cookie asks Sister to remember something from the past. Discuss how this might or might not help Sister.

BOOKTALK IDEAS

1. Include excerpts from several poems in your booktalk.
2. Write your booktalk in first person as Cookie.
3. Write your talk as a dialogue between Cookie and Sister, showing their struggle to reconnect with each other.

RISKS

- Portrait of a dysfunctional family.
- Gives a negative portrayal of mentally ill.

STRENGTHS

- Powerful poems convey emotions clearly.
- Easy to read while examining complex concepts.
- Shows impact of severe illness on the structure of a family.
- Extremely honest and straightforward, making it very accessible to teens.

AWARDS

Best Books for Young Adults, 2000 (ALA)
Quick Picks for Reluctant Readers, 2000 (ALA)
Christopher Book Awards, 2000

REVIEWS

"Blank verse is perfect for a story with such heightened emotion, and is a format that has been used with great success in other fine novels for teens." —Amazon, 2000, Patty Campbell.

"Individually, the poems appear simple and unremarkable. . . . collected, they take on life and movement, individual frames of a movie that in the unspooling become animated, telling a compelling tale and presenting a painful passage through young adolescence. The form . . . fits the story remarkably well." —*Kirkus Reviews*, 1999.

"An unpretentious, accessible book that could provide entry points for a discussion about mental illness—its stigma, its realities, and its affect on family members. . . . simply crafted but deeply felt poems." —*School Library Journal*, 10/99, Sharon Korbeck.

ᚙᚙᚙ

STUCK IN NEUTRAL. Trueman, Terry. HarperCollins, 2000. $14.95. 114p.
ISBN: 0-060-28519-2. Realistic fiction. Reading level: MS. Interest level: MS,
YHS, OHS. English, Ethics, Creative writing, Psychology.

SUBJECT AREAS
Illness, physical; self-knowledge; family relationships; divorce and separation;
ethics; love.

CHARACTERS
Shawn McDaniel: a fourteen-year-old who lives entirely in his own mind
    because he has cerebral palsy, and no way to communicate with the world
    around him
Cindy, Paul McDaniel: Shawn's older brother and sister who love him dearly
Lindy McDaniel: Shawn's mother who still sees him as a baby
Sydney McDaniel: a Pulitzer prizewinner for a poem about his son, he's never
    been able to deal with his son's condition
Mrs. Hare: Shawn's teacher at Shoreline High School
William, Becky: Shawn's teacher's assistants

BOOKTALK
My life is kind of a good news/bad news thing. But let's do the good part first.
I'm almost fifteen, live in Seattle with my Mom and Cindy and Paul, my older
brother and sister. And I have this weird and wonderful gift—I can remember
everything I've seen or heard. It started when I was four or so, and since about a
year after that I can remember everything! It's really incredible—conversations
on the street, TV shows, bulletin boards, lines from TV or movies—it's all there,
ready for me to pull out and play any time I want to. Only lately, there have
been some things I don't want to remember, things about Dad and me. You see,
when I was four years old, my dad split. My being born changed everything in
our family, and he couldn't handle it. He didn't divorce mom or Cindy or Paul,
not really. He divorced me!

   And that brings me to the bad part of my life. I have CP, cerebral palsy.
When I was born, a blood vessel burst in my brain, and as a result, I have no
muscle control. Zero, zip, zilch. I can't even do the, "Blink once if you
understand" bit—my eyes blink the way the rest of my muscles function—when
they want to—not when I want them to. So no one has any idea that I exist
inside this useless body—and not only exist, but like my life. I mean, it's not the
way I'd choose to live if I had a choice, but since I don't, I focus on the good
stuff.

   But now my dad's started acting really strange, and based on some things
he's said and done, I think he's gonna kill me. Kill me because he loves me, and
he thinks I'm in pain. Kill me to put him out of his suffering, and there's nothing
I can do! No way I can tell him that even if he thinks my life isn't much, it's
important to me. I want to live!

MAJOR THEMES AND IDEAS
- Just because someone can't communicate doesn't mean he's not a person.
- It's unwise to make assumptions about how happy or unhappy someone else's life is.
- No one has the right to kill someone else, not even for the best and most humane of reasons.
- A handicapped child puts a major strain on a family. The worse the handicap, and the less able family members are to accept it, the more intense the strain.
- Memory is all we have—it's what makes us each a unique individual. And we live on, in the memories of those we love, who loved us.

BOOK REPORT IDEAS
1. Discuss the ethics of taking someone's life without their consent.
2. If you were Shawn, discuss whether you would choose life or death and why.
3. Speculate on what happened after the end of the book, and the effect on the other characters in the book.
4. Discuss the way Shawn and other handicapped kids are treated by outsiders.

BOOKTALK IDEAS
1. Write your talk as a dialogue between Shawn and his father, in which neither can hear the other.
2. Have Shawn's family each describe him, and then have Shawn describe himself.

RISKS
- Father plans to kill his son.
- Language is graphic and occasionally vulgar.

STRENGTHS
- Narrator who draws reader into story and into his world immediately.
- Unresolved ending allows for group discussion and individual speculation.
- Powerful portrait of the handicapped as individual, unique people.

AWARDS
Best Books for Young Adults, 2001 (ALA)
Quick Picks for Reluctant Readers, 2001 (ALA)
Michael L. Printz Award Honor Book, 2001 (ALA)
Booklist Editors' Choice, 2000

REVIEWS
"Presents readers with thought-provoking issues. The character of Shawn, compassionately drawn, will challenge them to look beyond people's surfaces. His struggle to be known, and ultimately loved, is vividly captured, and the issue of euthanasia is handled boldly but sensitively." —*School Library Journal*, 2000, Tim Rausch.

"Tthe abrupt, ambiguous ending . . . transmits his inner debate to readers. Shawn will stay with readers, not for what he does, but for what he is and has made of himself." —*Kirkus Reviews*, 2000.

"A truly unique journey into the mind of a truly unique character. . . . will serve as a powerful metaphor for teens who feel cornered by circumstances or their own physical shortcomings...an original and moving debut." —Amazon, 2000, Jennifer Hubert.

📖📖📖

SWALLOWING STONES. McDonald, Joyce. Delacorte Press, 1997. $15.95. 256p. ISBN: 0-385-32309-3. Laurel-Leaf Books, 1999. $4.99. 256p. ISBN: 0-440-22672-4. Realistic fiction. Reading level: MS. Interest level: MS, YHS, OHS. English, Ethics.

SUBJECT AREAS
lying and deceitfulness; secrets; death and dying; grief and mourning; self-knowledge; love; family relationships; guilt; friendship; working; rites of passage; peer pressure.

CHARACTERS
Michael MacKenzie: on his seventeenth birthday, he fires his new rifle into the air and kills a man
Jenna Ward: she sees her father die
Joe Sandowski: Michael's best friend who persuades him to keep silent about what he did
Darcy Kelly: Michael's girlfriend
Dave Zelenski: Briarwood chief of police
Meridith Ward: Jenna's mother
Josh MacKenzie: Michael's thirteen-year-old brother
Simon Goldfarb: Michael's boss at the Briarwood Community Pool
Amy Ruggerio: she has a reputation for being "easy"
Toni and Karen MacKenzie: Michael's parents
Andrea Sloan: Jenna's best friend

Jason Friedman: Jenna's boyfriend
Annie Rico: she works at her husband's pharmacy and knows all the gossip in town
Poppy: Amy's grandfather and her only family

BOOKTALK

The bullet travels over a mile, missing trees, houses, and unsuspecting birds, finally falling out of the sky, a fatal homing pigeon.

Jenna Ward watches her father fixing the roof, staple gun in hand. She looks up at him, shielding her eyes. He lifts his hand to wave, but it flaps suddenly, as his eyes widen like dark coals and his mouth falls open, a silent black zero. Slowly his body folds over and plunges to the porch roof below, rolling like a heavy log over the side, and coming to rest by Jenna's bare feet.

On the other side of town, in the woods behind his house, Michael MacKenzie gently strokes the silky stock of his .45-70 Winchester rifle while he holds it out for Joe Sandowski's admiration. Because he could not wait to feel the smooth curve of the trigger beneath his finger, he has just fired one shot into the air. It's the Fourth of July, his seventeenth birthday, and the rifle was a present from his grandfather. His parents are throwing an all-day pool and barbecue to celebrate. Before the sun sets Michael will eat six hot dogs, four hamburgers and a half a pound of potato salad. He will sneak into the garage with Amy Ruggerio—even though Darcy, his girlfriend, is at the party—because Amy is a "babe" and wants him, and he will drive the neighbors crazy with the heavy metal blasting from his stereo. He will, in fact, think that this is the best day in his life, because he doesn't know that he has accidentally killed a man.

MAJOR THEMES AND IDEAS

- No matter how much you may want to, you can't forget what you've done, and how your actions changed others' lives.
- Sometimes tragedy dulls our emotions, making it impossible to feel anything.
- A friend is someone who'll stand by you no matter what.
- Frequently bad reputations are based on gossip rather than reality.
- You aren't the same person after a tragedy that you were before.
- The longer a lie goes on, the more convoluted and difficult to conceal it becomes.
- The only way to begin to heal is to face up to what's happened, confront it, and go through it.

BOOK REPORT IDEAS

1. Discuss what you think will happen at Michael's trial and what might have happened had he confessed immediately to the shooting.

2. Michael and Jenna begin having similar dreams after her father's death. Discuss the meaning of these dreams and give reasons for their similarity.
3. When he and Michael first hear the story of the shooting, Joe is very insistent that Michael not turn himself in. Explain why he feels hiding the evidence is the right thing to do, and how is he affected by the resulting stress.
4. Both Michael and Jenna say they aren't the same person as they were before the shooting. Show how each of them changed and why.
5. Discuss the meaning of the title, and who has stones that they must swallow.

BOOKTALK IDEAS
1. Write your talk as the book is written, letting Michael and Jenna speak for themselves.
2. Use newspaper clippings of a shooting to illustrate your talk.
3. Write your talk as if it were one of the newspaper stories Michael reads.
4. Focus your talk on the scene in Joe's car when he and Michael first hear the newscaster on the radio.

RISKS
- Teens drink and smoke.
- Character refuses to admit to a crime and lies to escape the consequences of an action.

STRENGTHS
- Accurate portrayal of family's reaction to tragedy.
- Multidimensional characters that change and gain insight.
- Ambiguous ending leaves room for individual consideration and group discussion.
- Clearly shows how a lie can become convoluted and difficult to control.
- Dual perspective of story line gives reader added insight into the main characters.

AWARDS
Best Books for Young Adults, 1998 (ALA)
100 Best Books for Teens, 2000 (ALA)

REVIEWS
"This well-written novel . . . explores 'a world where things you never thought could happen to you did'. . . . will appeal to a broad audience, and it is a great vehicle for discussions about guns, violence, and responsibility. A good companion read for even more discussion is *One-eyed Cat* by Paula Fox."
—*Voice of Youth Advocates,* 12/97, Joyce Sparrow Bukowski.

"Mesmerizing story largely derives its power from the respect McDonald demonstrates for these teens and their emotions, and her unwavering focus on their changing relationships in response to the tragedy. . . . The almost magically surreal ending will leave many readers turning the page to find out what happens next." —*School Library Journal*, 9/97, Joel Shoemaker.

"Three-dimensional characterizations with sound psychological underpinnings lend distinction to the somber novel." —*Horn Book*, 1998.

ⅢⅢⅢ

📖 SECTION FIVE 📖
The Taking of Room 114 to *Wringer*

THE TAKING OF ROOM 114: A HOSTAGE DRAMA IN POEMS.
Glenn, Mel. Dutton, 1997. $16.99. 182 p. ISBN: 0-525-67548-5. Verse novel,
Realistic fiction. Reading level: MS. Interest level: MS, YHS, OHS. English,
Creative writing, Ethics, Drama, Psychology, History.

SUBJECT AREAS
school; secrets; grief and mourning; death and dying; unwed mothers;
minorities, black, minorities, hispanic, minorities, Asian, minorities, Russian;
friendship; self-knowledge; peer pressure; anger; gossip; problem parents;
poetry; family relationships; crime and delinquency; dating and social life.

CHARACTERS
Joseph Wiedermeyer: a high school history teacher with over twenty years of
    experience
Douglas Atherton, Derek Bain, Patti Bennett, Omar Clarkson, Andrew Curran,
    Cory Deshayes, Devonne Elliot, Rhonda Ellis, Kathleen Gennaro, Alissa
    Hayley, Dwight Henderson, Eddie Kellerman, Lynette Kincaid, Holly
    Lester, Brad McCall, Morton Potter, Renata Reznitskaya, Justin
    Singleberry, Denise Slattery, Esther Torres, Franklin Waters, Wing Li Wu:
    Mr. Wiedermeyer's senior history class
Sherwood Cowley: principal
Roger Dunlop: assistant principal
Harry Balinger: police captain
James Sanchez: police officer
Frank Picardi: emergency unit member
Barbara Gilchrist, Gloria Messinger, Aaron Washington Jr.: faculty members
Vinnie Delvecchio, Sandi Wilmat, Cosmo Gennaro: parents
Shawn Ferguson, Bruno Willis, Thomas Findlay: spectators

Cherise Graham, David Rush: TV anchor and reporter
Jessica Ruiz, Erik Semler: students

BOOKTALK

"Hey, what's goin' on? How come we're gettin' outta school?"

"Something's up in room 114—you know, Wiedermeyer's room."

"I heard one of the cops say somebody's got a gun, holding the class for ransom."

"Chill out man, who's gonna pay a ransom for a bunch of high school kids?"

"Did you hear that? That guy just said they think it's Mr. W. himself with the gun!"

"No way, he's cool. He'd never do that."

"Yes, way! I betcha he's finally just flipped out!"

What is going on in room 114? The students inside had expected a history test. What they got instead was a test of a whole different kind.

MAJOR THEMES AND IDEAS

- Grief and depression can sometimes make us do strange things.
- To see the whole picture, you have to look at it from many differing perspectives.
- Everyone has their own agenda, their own plan for their life. When you understand what that agenda is, their actions make more sense.
- Change may seem sudden or dramatic, but when you look back at what came before, it is easier to see that it is a gradual process, with most of it hidden or ignored until the final explosion.
- Your life can change in major ways because of a small, quickly made, seemingly inconsequential decision.
- It's impossible to know what traumas another person may be going through until that person decides to reveal them.

BOOK REPORT IDEAS

1. Contrast the ways several students felt before, during, and after class.
2. Examine the teacher's notes, and explain what they show about his state of mind.
3. Several students were not in class on June sixteenth. Speculate on what they might say about what happened, and whether or not they are glad they were not there.
4. Discuss what will happen to Mr. Weidermeyer, and what kind of punishment would be most appropriate for him.
5. Explain which students will be most and least affected by what happened, and why.

BOOKTALK IDEAS

1. Use brief phrases from different poems to set up the scenario, being careful not to reveal too much.
2. Write your talk as if it were a news bulletin or an interview with one of the students outside the school.
3. Write your talk from the perspective of one of the students in room 114. Again, be careful not to reveal too much.

RISKS

*   Severely depressed teacher holds class hostage.
*   Several sets of parents are completely out of touch with their children.

STRENGTHS

*   Verse format is appealing to teens.
*   Language is accessible to teens.
*   Suspenseful plot keeps readers hooked.
*   Ending leaves room for speculation and discussion.
*   Could easily be used as readers' theater.
*   Characters are individual and clearly delineated.

AWARDS

Quick Picks for Reluctant Readers, 1998 (ALA)

REVIEWS

"Free verse by an accomplished poet is used to provide a vivid picture of high school life. . . . format is appealing, with a lot of white space that would make it a terrific read for reluctant readers. . . . this is an interesting premise in which nicely crafted poems are tied together neatly in the end. . . . a page-turner that is a dissection of high school life, with a dollop of terror thrown in." —*Voice of Youth Advocates*, 2/98, Bonnie Kunzel.

"Uses first-person narrative poems to relate an ongoing story. . . . The topic and the format are fresh and unusual, and Glenn branches out in the poems themselves, employing interesting typographical devices such as shaped poems. . . . The tense plot and clever format will hold readers." —*Booklist*, 3/1/97, Debbie Carton.

"The many points of view expressed, the typographical versatility, and the creative use of white space all add interest to the unfolding story of the tragedy of a teacher's life and the vivid stories of his students. . . . YAs will find their interest piqued and reluctant readers particularly will be drawn to the excitement of design and content." —*School Library Journal*, 4/97, Marjorie Lewis.

📖📖📖

TANGERINE. Bloor, Edward. Harcourt, 1997. $17.00. 304p. ISBN: 0-152-01246-X. Scholastic, Inc., 1998. $4.99. 294p. ISBN: 0-590-43277-X. Realistic fiction. Reading level: MS. Interest level: MS, YHS. English, P. E., Ethics.

SUBJECT AREAS
sports; lying and deceitfulness; family relationships; self-knowledge; problem parents; environmental issues; ethics; school; friendship; violence; abuse, physical; rites of passage; revenge; bullying; secrets; justice.

CHARACTERS
In Lake Windsor
Paul Fisher: legally blind, but a great soccer goalie
Erik Fisher: Paul's big brother, a football star, and their parents' favorite
Mr. and Mrs. Fisher: Paul and Erik's parents who have a terrible secret
Joey Costello: a soccer player and Paul's best friend who has a cocky, smart-ass attitude
Coach Warner: high school football coach
Arthur Bauer: a third-string football player who's Erik's best friend
Paige Bauer, Tina Turrenton: cheerleaders who are Erik and Arthur's girlfriends
Grandmom and Grandpop: Mrs. Fisher's parents
Charley Burns: Mr. Fisher's boss and a football fan
Mr. Costello: president of the Lake Windsor Homeowners Association
Mike Costello: a football player and Joey's big brother
Mrs. Gates: middle school principal
Mr. Murrow: middle school guidance counselor
Mr. Walski: middle school soccer coach
Mr. Bridges: high school principal
Bill and Terry Donnelly: their Lake Windsor house has been struck by lightning three times
Cara Clifton: a girl Joey likes
Kerri Gardner: a girl Paul likes

In Tangerine
Theresa Cruz: Paul's guide at the middle school
Tino Cruz: Theresa's twin and a soccer star
Hernando: a soccer player
Maya Pandhi: she learned to play soccer in England
Shandra Thomas: middle school soccer goalie
Nitak Shirali: Maya's cousin and a good soccer player
Dolly Elias: a team member and Theresa's best friend
Henry Dilkes: a soccer player

Ms. Bright: middle school soccer coach
Luis Cruz: Theresa and Tino's older brother who's developed a new variety of
    tangerine

BOOKTALK

The weirdness had always been there for Paul, but it took Tangerine to help him
put it all together. Paul has been legally blind since he was five, and has to wear
thick, ugly glasses so he can see. But even though his brother and parents have
told him it's because he stared at an eclipse too long, he doesn't remember doing
that and can't believe he'd ever be that dumb, anyway. And he does remember
some things, bits and pieces that don't fit together, until his family moves to
Tangerine County, Florida.

Tangerine is almost like another planet. Hundreds of acres of citrus trees
have been burned down to make room for huge, ostentatious housing
developments. Strange fires smolder under the earth and can't be put out;
lightning strikes at the same time every day. An enormous sinkhole swallows
the whole middle school. And in Tangerine, like many other places, football
players are worshipped and exceptions made for them.

Paul's older brother is a football star—a place kicker who can kick the ball
fifty yards and make sure that his team always wins. His parents dote on him
and make sure he gets whatever he wants.

But Paul, who's a soccer player, an unbeatable goalie, can see that there's
something strange and wrong about the way his parents defer to Erik and ignore
him. He also knows that he's afraid of Erik because of something he can't quite
remember. Maybe Tangerine is the place that can help him fit those bits and
pieces of memory back together and show him the reason he's afraid of his big
brother.

MAJOR THEMES AND IDEAS

- Humiliating a star almost always means revenge. Somebody has to pay.
- Ignoring environmental needs and characteristics can be dangerous, with
  lasting consequences.
- Pretending someone's negative side doesn't exist can have difficult and
  dangerous consequences.
- Believing in yourself and your abilities works.
- There's always a reason why you're afraid of someone, even if you don't
  know what it is.
- Many people see only what they want to see.
- Fear can defeat you before you even start to play the game. Your opponents
  win on the strength of your fear, not their ability.
- Actions echo down the years. You have no way of knowing what
  consequences await you in the future for your past actions.

BOOK REPORT IDEAS

1. Many characters make ethical decisions in the book. Select several of these decisions you agree with and others that you do not, and compare and contrast them, explaining why the characters made their decisions, and why you do or don't agree with them.
2. Explain why Paul was able to succeed at Tangerine Middle School when Joey couldn't, showing what characteristics they did and didn't have in common.
3. Several different kinds of families are portrayed in Lake Windsor and Tangerine. Discuss how and why they are different.
4. Paul was visually handicapped. Discuss how other characters were "handicapped" in other ways.
5. Speculate on what will happen in Paul's family after the book ends, showing how you think family members will relate to each other in different and/or similar ways.
6. This is a story of sports. Discuss which characters are true athletes and which are not.
7. Discuss how the Fishers "protection" of Erik injured both their sons in various ways.

BOOKTALK IDEAS

1. Focus your talk on the environmental oddities in Tangerine, ending with the idea that Paul's memory is hiding an even more menacing secret.
2. Center your talk around a description of the "Erik Fisher Football Dream" and end with Paul's description of why he isn't part of it, and is deeply afraid of his brother.
3. Use Paul's description of his returning memories as a major part of your talk.
4. Use a prop in your talk—a soccer ball, a tangerine, or something else mentioned in the book.

RISKS

- High school jocks idolized for their athletic ability and unpunished for their violent acts.
- Parents favor one child and ignore the other.
- Parents allow favored son to physically and mentally abuse sibling.

STRENGTHS

- Anti-hero/underdog survives and succeeds on many levels.
- Smart, tongue-in-cheek portrayal of the consequences of irresponsible urban development.
- Comparison of honorable vs. dishonorable school athletic programs.
- Strong, clever plot weaves together multiple subplots effectively.

- Smart and savvy main character teens can identify with.
- Contrast of genuine and superficial ethical and value systems.

AWARDS
Best Books for Young Adults, 1998 (ALA)
Popular Paperbacks for Young Adults/Good Sports, 1999 (ALA)
Bulletin for the Center of Children's Books Blue Ribbon Book, 1998
Junior Library Guild Selection, 1998
100 Best Books for Teens, 2000 (ALA)

REVIEWS
"An exciting, suspenseful, and thought-provoking book." —*Voice of Youth Advocates,* 8/97.

"Equally clear is the class consciousness and racism that have built fences through which Paul chooses to blast holes. . . . Mix a sensitive male protagonist. . . . ratchet the soccer scenes. . . . several degrees of intensity, and enjoy this family healing/coming-of-age struggle in which everyone takes some licks, but Paul keeps on kicking." —*School Library Journal,* 4/97, Joel Shoemaker.

"So much happens so quickly that you are pulled right along in the story, and the engaging sports scenes highlight the personalities of the players as well as the action on the field. . . . Paul Fisher is an immensely likable character—a bright, funny, straight-talking, stand-up kid—and it's a real pleasure to watch him grow." —*Horn Book,* 9-10/97, L. A.

"Sparkles with wit, authenticity, unexpected plot twists, and heart. The writing is so fine, the story so triumphant, that you might just stand up and shout when to you get to the end." —Amazon, 1997.

"A memorable protagonist in a cast of vividly drawn characters; multiple yet taut plotlines lead to a series of gripping climaxes and revelations." —*Kirkus Reviews,* 1997.

ᚷᚷᚷ

TENDERNESS. Cormier, Robert. Delacorte Press, 1997. $16.95. 240p. ISBN: 0-385-32286-0. Laurel-Leaf Books, 1998. $5.50. 240p. ISBN: 0-440-22034-3. Realistic fiction. Reading level: MS. Interest level: YHS, OHS. English, Psychology, Ethics.

SUBJECT AREAS

crime and delinquency; secrets; revenge; abuse, sexual; death and dying; family relationships; love; problem parents; runaways; self-knowledge; music; legal system; justice; illness, mental; unwed mothers.

CHARACTERS

Eric Poole: eighteen years old, and about to be released from a juvenile detention facility, he is a calculating murderer

Lieutenant Jake Proctor: one of the officers who arrested Eric for killing his parents, he believes Eric is a psychopath, a monster who will kill again just as soon as he can

Eric's mother: she loved him and read to him when he was a little boy, but he believed she betrayed him when she married Dexter

Dexter: Eric's stepfather, they detest each other

Aunt Phoebe: his mother's sister who takes him in when he is released

Lori Cranston: a runaway who remembers Eric being kind to her years before when she was only twelve, she wants to stay near him

Lori's mother: she loves her daughter but sometimes ignores her, and has very bad taste in men

Gary: Lori's mother's latest boyfriend

Throb: lead singer in a heavy metal band, on whom Lori is fixated before her involvement with Eric

Senorita/Maria Valdez: a beautiful girl in the detention facility who fascinates Eric

Sonny Boy: a bully in the detention facility

Sweet Lefty Stanton: one of Sonny's victims, he repaid Eric's favor with two of his own

Phyllis Kentall: head of Harmony House, a home for unwed mothers

Ross Packer: a newspaper reporter, his story on Lori draws her to Eric's attention

BOOKTALK

Tenderness. Eric has looked for it his entire life, finding only glimpses of it now and again. But now, after three years in a juvenile detention facility, he is free, free to go looking once again for the fleeting emotion he's felt so infrequently.

Lori is looking for tenderness also, someone to love her and be gentle with her. When she sees Eric's face on a television news program the day of his release, she knows that she has found the boy who was so tender and caring to her three years ago.

Jake Proctor has never had much tenderness in his life, preferring to live alone and avoid the possibility of pain. He's a cop with over twenty years of experience, and he's certain Eric is a serial killer, responsible for the deaths of two teenage girls in addition to those of his parents. Jake calls Eric a psychopath and a monster, and when Eric is released, stalks him, waiting for him to make a mistake.

Who is Eric? The gentle boy who protected Lori from a motorcycle gang when she was only twelve? The cold, calculating murderer Jake believes him to be? Or is he someone else entirely, someone known only to himself, and to those who gave him their tenderness and their lives?

MAJOR THEMES AND IDEAS
- Even criminals can have a sense of honor.
- Unconditional love can change both the giver and the receiver.
- People can always choose to change.
- In many ways we are the products of our own childhoods. Until we truly realize this, we cannot hope to change that.
- Sometimes innocence can overcome evil.
- "No man chooses evil because it is evil, he only mistakes it for happiness, the good he seeks."—Mary Shelley

BOOK REPORT IDEAS
1. Discuss the different meanings of tenderness in the book, and how each of the characters related to it.
2. Examine the concept of the truth in the novel. Who told the truth and who didn't? What were the results?
3. Show what might have happened to Eric and Lori if she hadn't drowned. Could Eric have changed or would he have been unable to?
4. Eric is seen in the book as a monster, a victim, and a hero. Discuss which of these views are most accurate, and show why.
5. Discuss the ending of the book, and how it did or didn't show justice.
6. Compare and contrast Lori's and Jake's views of Eric, and discuss which, if either, was more accurate.

BOOKTALK IDEAS
1. Write your talk in first person, as Eric, or as Lori.
2. Write your talk as if it were a newspaper or television news story.

RISKS
- A serial killer is released from prison in spite of the fact that he is guilty.
- Sexual abuse of a child by an adult.
- Running away shown as a way to solve problems.
- Has negative portrayals of adults.
- Shows dysfunctional families and their impact on the children in them.
- Naïve character becomes involved with sociopath.

STRENGTHS

* Author's reputation.
* Multi-dimensional characters teens can identify with.
* Thought-provoking ending, brings up more questions than it answers.
* Lack of absolute answers allows reader to speculate on what those answers might be.

AWARDS

Popular Paperbacks for Young Adults/Different Drummers, 1999

REVIEWS

"Vivid characterizations highlight this book in which action is secondary. . . . Cormier performs literary magic by making us empathize with these two teenagers who live at society's far edges. He gets inside the heads of a precocious runaway and a psychopath. . . . and reveals both Eric's and Lori's great need for love. . . . Both characters are desperately seeking tenderness, and in a way they end up providing it for one another." —*Voice of Youth Advocates*, 4/97, Florence M. Munat.

"Cormier is in top form in this chilling portrait of a serial murderer. . . . The ugliness of the story contrasts with the beauty of the language. Perfectly titled with characteristic irony, a sense of "tenderness" pervades this gripping tale. . . . Cormier is the model of decorum. No overt blood and gore are needed for this author to terrify his readers. . . . A meaty horror study." —*School Library Journal*, 3/97, Marilyn Payne Phillips.

"In juxtaposing a sexually precocious, obsessive runaway and a psychopathic murderer, each seeking a kind of tenderness, Cormier creates a lurid, violent, grating world not fit for the tender-hearted. . . . The style is vintage Cormier, short pithy sentences and bends in the text that take the reader along startling paths." —*Horn Book*, 3-4/97, Barbara Harrison.

ᙏᙏᙏ

THE TERRORIST. Cooney, Caroline B. Scholastic, 1997. $15.95. 208p. ISBN: 0-590-22853-6. Scholastic, 1999. $4.50. 198p. ISBN: 0-590-22854-4. Realistic fiction, Mystery/suspense. Reading level: MS. Interest level: MS, YHS. English, Geography, Psychology, Sociology, Ethics.

SUBJECT AREAS

death and dying; family relationships; rites of passage; self-knowledge; ethics; violence; grief and mourning; prejudice; religion; other countries; mystery and suspense; minorities; revenge; travel; friendship; secrets.

CHARACTERS

Laura Williams: sixteen years old, she lives in London with her family, while her father travels for his company

Billy Williams: Laura's eleven-year-old little brother who loves to collect things, keep lists, make money, and be his own inimitable self

Thomas and Nicole Williams: Laura and Billy's parents

Robbie, Chris, Georgie: Billy's friends from school

Eddie, Jehran, Consuela, Andrew, Mohammed, Samira, Jimmy, Bethany, Tiffany: Laura's friends from school

Mr. Evans: Laura's bodyguard

Mr. Hollobar, Mr. Frankel: two of the faculty members at LIA

BOOKTALK

Have you ever wondered about the signs in airports, "Do Not Accept Packages From Strangers. Never Leave Your Luggage Unattended." If someone asked you to keep an eye on their suitcase while they went to the restroom or to get something to eat or drink, would you do it? It seems easy to trust the other people in the departure lounge—because they look perfectly normal, right? None of them might be carrying a bomb, right? No one would have a package that might have something dangerous or illegal in it, right? Wrong! Terrorists don't always look like Ted Kazinksky, with strange eyes and wild hair—sometimes they can look like normal people. Sometimes they can even look like your best friend.

Eleven-year-old Billy Williams was on his way to school, the London International Academy, running up the subway steps, when a guy stopped him and said, "Your friend dropped this," and handed him a package wrapped in plain brown paper. He took it, even though he didn't remember either of his friends carrying a package, just their bookbags. He looked at it and its plain brown paper wrapper, and suddenly the signs and warnings at Heathrow Airport flashed into his mind, and he remembered the fire drills at school that the older kids called bomb drills.

Suddenly he knew what was in the package—but there was nothing to do, no place to go. He couldn't just put it down on the crowded steps and run. He couldn't throw it into the crowd. The man who gave it to him was gone—he couldn't give it back. In front of him was a sleeping baby in a stroller. Billy looked at it in horror and turned away, wrapping himself around the package. And just as he did, the package exploded.

What does a terrorist look like? Not what you'd expect one to look like. Follow Billy's sister as she searches for her brother's killer.

MAJOR THEMES AND IDEAS

- Violence is not always random, even when it seems like it is.
- When someone you love is killed, the most important thing is not revenge, but learning to go on.
- Evil is not always punished.
- Innocence and naiveté are not always rewarded.
- As long as you can remember someone you love who has died, he or she is not really dead for you.
- Very often revenge does not relieve the pain of losing a friend or family member.
- Friends are those who love you and stand up for you, even when you have not acted as their friend.
- Sometimes people are nice to you not because they like you, but because you are in a position to do something for them.
- Some secrets are meant to be kept—but some are not.
- When you are in pain, it is not wise to withdraw from your family and friends, even if you think it will be easier for you to do so. They may be the best sources of support and comfort that you have.

BOOK REPORT IDEAS

1. Laura is very naïve about dealing with people from other countries. Discuss how the novel might have been different if she had been more aware of international conflicts and agendas, and how they affected the other LIA students she knew.
2. Now that you have read the entire novel and know what the terrorist's plans were, speculate on what the Williams family might have done to save Billy's life, and how he and Laura might have responded to these new rules.
3. Examine the idea of ethics in the book, from the perspectives of the Williams family, the LIA students, and the terrorist. Discuss your views of morality, right and wrong, as presented in the book.
4. Speculate on how the events in the book will change the lives of students at LIA, and what the school might or might not do to protect them. Take into consideration the perspectives and ideas of the faculty.

BOOKTALK IDEAS

1. Write the talk in first person, as narrated by Laura.
2. Let several of the main characters describe Billy, but don't give away the fact that he is already dead.
3. Base your talk on the first chapter of the book, writing in first person as Billy.
4. Use a brown paper-wrapped box as a prop. Drop it on the floor just as you say, "And the bomb exploded."

RISKS

- Shows graphic depiction of senseless violence.
- Perpetrator, who is a minor, is not punished and shows no genuine regret for her actions.

STRENGTHS

- Gives extremely realistic view of terrorism.
- Ambiguous ending allows readers to speculate on their own.
- Strong characters who are forced to deal with tragedy, violence, and the lack of absolute answers.

AWARDS

Quick Picks for Reluctant Readers, 1998 (ALA)

REVIEWS

"Characterizations are well done, the terrorist bombing is taken from today's headlines, and the setting is exotic enough to add to the mystery, but familiar enough to seem real to the reader. The fact that a youngster dies and his family is left to handle their grief with no real answers is tragic and ambiguous yet realistic—there are few definite answers in acts of terrorism." —*Voice of Youth Advocates*, 10/97, Rosemary Moran.

"While this book is not as gut-wrenching terrifying as Robert Cormier's *After the First Death*, Cooney's fans will find it more accessible and even harder to put down." —*School Library Journal*, 9/97, Marilyn Payne Phillips.

"Does a fine job of conveying the ambiguity and void facing a family looking for answers from the dark underground of terrorism." —Amazon, 1997, Anne O'Malley.

"Bullet-train pacing and entertaining prose. . . . exciting, compulsive reading." —*Kirkus Reviews*, 1997.

TOMORROW, WHEN THE WAR BEGAN. Marsden, John. Houghton Mifflin Co., 1995. $16.00. 288p. ISBN: 0-395-70673-4. Laurel-Leaf Books, 1996. $4.99. 286p. ISBN: 0-440-21985-X. Science fiction. Reading level: MS. Interest level: MS, YHS, OHS. English, Geography, Ethics.

SEQUELS: *Dead of Night*, 1997; *A Killing Frost*, 1998; *Darkness Be My Friend*, 1999; *Burning for Revenge*, 2000; *Night Is for Hunting*, 2001; *Other Side of Dawn*, 2002.

SUBJECT AREAS

war; violence; death and dying; self-knowledge; friendship; family relationships; grief and mourning; love; survival; crime and delinquency; revenge; secrets; justice; ethics; adventure.

CHARACTERS

Ellie: she and Corrie proposed the trip to Hell and everyone decided she should tell the story of what happened

Robyn: she's quiet and serious, but very determined, dependable, and likes to win

Chris: he wanted to go on the trip, but his father made him stay home and take care of the farm

Homer: he's wild, outrageous, and always seems to be in trouble, and is one of the biggest guys in school

Corrie: she's Ellie's best friend, who has camped out with her for years and is very determined

Lee: Thai and Vietnamese, he's a townie, good at most things, but sulks and won't talk to anyone when things don't go his way

Fiona: small, delicate, she lives in town and looks like she's never worked a day in her life

Kevin: he dates Corrie, is very self-confident and likes to take credit for things

Mr. Clement: the dentist who avoided being taken prisoner and hid his family

Mr. and Mrs. Lang: Chris's parents who were overseas when the invasion happened

Mr. and Mrs. Mathers: Robyn's parents

Mr. and Mrs. Yannos: Homer's parents

Mr. and Mrs. McKenzie: Corrie's parents

BOOKTALK

It happened in Australia, in what might be the near future. The seven of them were camping in a wilderness called Hell when the black jets flew over late at night, flying low, without lights. It seemed like there were hundreds of them, and it took all night for them to pass. But the next morning when Lee said maybe it was World War III, and they'd been invaded, no one took it seriously.

It wasn't until days later, when they walked out of Hell to discover deserted homes, corpses of livestock and pets, empty streets patrolled by armed soldiers speaking a foreign language, and their friends and families held prisoner by more armed guards, that they realized Lee's passing comments about World War III had been true. While the seven of them had been camping, Australia had been invaded. Their small rural town, with its nearby deep harbor, was one of the first places to be captured. If they'd stayed in town, they would be prisoners, or they'd be dead. There were no alternatives.

But they hadn't been there, and now they were free, as long as none of the enemy discovered them. What could they do now? They were only seven, against thousands of armed and vicious invaders. Only one thing was clear. Hell was not the isolated wilderness where they'd felt so safe. Hell was what they found waiting for them when they left that wilderness to go home, only to find that home no longer existed.

MAJOR THEMES AND IDEAS

- Hell doesn't have to do with places but with people.
- Once you label something, you cease to see it as anything but its label.
- When you'd most like to get hysterical it's most necessary to stay calm and look for a solution.
- Killing someone, even when it's the right thing to do, changes you.
- During a war normal rules don't apply.
- It only takes an instant for your life to change forever.
- There doesn't have to be a right or a wrong. Both sides can be right or both sides can be wrong.
- It's up to each of us to find our own meaning in life. Live life with your heart as well as your head.
- Trust yourself, your instinct, to tell you what is right or good or moral. Let your inner self decide the morality of your actions.
- Don't worry when you question yourself and your decisions. Many evil or cruel people have an absolute faith that they are right and everyone else is wrong.
- Evil doesn't exist in nature—it's a human invention.
- When in danger, it is frequently necessary to sacrifice what is comfortable for what is right.

BOOK REPORT IDEAS

1. Compare the reactions of Ellie and her friends on learning they were at war, and explain why they all reacted differently.
2. Some of the characters changed greatly after they realized they were on their own. Choose the one you think changed the most and explain why and in what ways that person changed.
3. Discuss the realism of the book, and whether or not it is an accurate portrayal of an invasion and the citizens' reaction to it.
4. Discuss Ellie's idea that hell isn't about a place, but about people, and each of us carries hell with us. Explain whether you agree or disagree and why.
5. Explore the idea of moral and ethical laws during peacetime and during a war. How does the situation change how those laws are interpreted?

BOOKTALK IDEAS

1. Focus your talk on the idea that hell is not about places, but people.
2. Write your talk as Ellie, in first person.
3. Build your talk around one scene in which all seven of the campers are discussing something important, such as the morning after the jets flew over, or when they finally realized they were at war.
4. Have Ellie introduce all of the eight campers in a series of minicharacter descriptions.
5. In the book, the campers make do with what they can find. Build your talk around several of these improvisations, for instance, their alternative uses for a riding mower, earthmover, and a Mercedes; as a bomb, a rescue vehicle, and an ambulance.

RISKS

- Shows the violence of war as the teens fight against enemy soldiers.
- Characters break laws and destroy property as part of their guerrilla tactics.
- Teens are sexually active.

STRENGTHS

- Shows how and why people change in the face of danger.
- Unflinching look at war and its horrors.
- Tense, exciting writing style draws reader in immediately.
- Contains many philosophical ideas for group discussions or individual contemplation.
- Examines the ethics of war and peace.
- Abrupt ending persuades readers to continue reading sequels.
- Realistic characters teens can identify with easily.

AWARDS

Best Books for Young Adults, 1996 (ALA)
Popular Paperbacks for Young Adults/Facing Nature Head-on, 1998 (ALA)
Selected Audiotapes for Young Adults, 2000 (ALA)
100 Best Books for Teens, 2000 (ALA)

REVIEWS

"Tense survival story. . . . a riveting adventure through which Marsden explores the capacity for evil and the necessity of working together to oppose it." —*Horn Book*, 7-8/95, M.V.K.

"Fast-paced and provocative, it's a natural for booktalking." —*School Library Journal*, 6/1/95, Jack Forman.

"This suspenseful adventure story has something for everyone and just enough insight into what makes us tick in times of stress." —*Booklist*, 4/15/95, Jeanne Triner.

⊔⊔⊔

TUNES FOR BEARS TO DANCE TO. Cormier, Robert. Holt, 1992. $15.00. 108p. ISBN: 0-385-30818-3. Laurel-Leaf Books, 1994. $4.99. 108p. ISBN: 0-440-21903-5. Historical fiction. Reading level: MS. Interest level: MS, YHS. English, American history, World history, Sociology, Ethics, Psychology.

SUBJECT AREAS
friendship; racism; prejudice; minorities, Jewish; crime and delinquency; intimidation; family relationships; survival; working; grief and mourning; art; death and dying; war; aging; rites of passage.

CHARACTERS
Henry Cassavant: he's eleven years old, new in town, and works for Mr. Hairston after school and on Saturdays
Mrs. Cassavant: Henry's mother who works as a waitress at the diner
Mr. Cassavant: Henry's father who has not worked since his son's death, and seldom leaves the tenement
Mr. Hairston: owner of the Corner Market, he always seems angry at someone or something
Doris Hairston: Mr. Hairston's daughter who's twelve, Henry thinks her eyes look haunted and afraid, but he has never spoken to her
Jackie Antonelli: a friend of Henry's, he likes to fight
George Graham: a gentle giant of a man, he runs the city's arts and crafts centers
Jacob Levine: a elderly Holocaust survivor, he lives at the mental institution next door to Henry's tenement, and spends his days at the arts and crafts center

BOOKTALK
Prejudice. Racism. Hatred. Revenge. Control. Power. Evil. They're hard words, words that can hurt and tear, and destroy you from the inside out. I know all about it—some of those same words are destroying me. And yet I never meant to hurt anyone—especially not my friend Mr. Levine, who'd already been hurt so much, too much. I never meant to let someone else control what I did, what I thought—especially not my boss, Mr. Hairston, who was as mean a man as you could imagine. But I did it. I betrayed my friend because an evil man asked me to do it. And I did.

Now I don't like myself so much. I don't like living with the person I've become—the person who destroyed an old man's dream, an old man who never did anything to harm me, who offered me friendship and asked nothing in return. How could I have done it? How could I have turned my back on all I thought was valuable and important? I'm sure I had a good reason at the time, but somehow I can't recall it anymore. All I can remember is what I did, what I destroyed, and how I destroyed myself as well.

MAJOR THEMES AND IDEAS
- Anger destroys everything it touches.
- It is always necessary to resist evil, no matter what form it appears in.
- Prejudice and anger go hand in hand.
- When you decide to hurt a friend, you hurt yourself as well. We always have a choice when faced with the decision to do right or wrong.
- You will always have to live with the results of your decisions, whether they were good or bad choices.
- Creating beauty can help heal old wounds.
- Sadness or depression can become a disease that takes over your life completely.
- If someone orders you to commit a crime, you cannot use that as an excuse, either in your own mind or if you are caught. Following orders does not absolve you of guilt. Doing the wrong thing for a good reason doesn't make it right.

BOOK REPORT IDEAS
1. Discuss Mr. Hairston's bargain with Henry, and his insistence that Henry accept the rewards for his actions. Why did he tell Henry that accepting the rewards was necessary to validate the smashing?
2. What does the book say about evil and its effect on people?
3. Show the steps Mr. Hairston went through to manipulate Henry, and the effects that each step had on him.
4. Compare the ways that Eddie's father and Mr. Levine coped with pain and loss.

BOOKTALK IDEAS
1. Write the talk as if you were Mr. Hairston. Lead up to the point at which he begins to plan the destruction of the village, using your words and voice to convince your audience of his evilness. Be sure not to give away his actual plans, but just hint at the horrible deed Henry will have to do.
2. Focus your talk on Henry's dilemma and the guilt he feels afterward, but don't explain exactly what he has done.
3. Let each of the main characters speak for himself or herself, in a series of mini first-person paragraphs. Show the contrasts between the characters and

their beliefs and actions. For example, contrasting Mr. Hairston's hatred, Mr. Levine's love, Mr. Cassavant's sadness, and Doris's fear, showing how those emotions controlled their lives.

RISKS

- Graphic portrayal of racism, prejudice, and manipulation of a child by an adult.
- Sexual abuse of a child by an adult.
- Fathers portrayed as abusive or ineffectual and depressed.
- Evil character plots to destroy good solely for the sake of destruction.

STRENGTHS

- Reputation of author.
- Shows the powerful contrast between good and evil.
- Characters refuse to be overcome by evil.
- Characters learn to survive their tragedies and grow as a result of them.
- Spare, concise writing style draws reader in immediately.
- Reads fast, but many issues encourage more thoughtful attention.
- Appropriate for many age levels.

AWARDS

Best Books for Young Adults, 1993
Quick Picks for Reluctant Readers, 1993

REVIEWS

"Brief, compelling book conveys the devastating effects of evil, whether its form is as huge and incomprehensible as the Holocaust, or as small and personal as another human being. . . . more a parable than a fully realized novel, [it] is sharp, short, and to the point." —*School Library Journal*, 1993, Lucinda Snyder Whitehurst.

"Explores a child's confrontation with the evil side of humanity. . . . the portrait of evil may inspire discussion." —*Horn Book*, 3/1/93, A.E.D.

"Characters have a vigor and authenticity surpassing creations of less accomplished authors. . . . The conclusion is unexpected, with surprise grounded less in the events than in the characters' moral readings of them. Briefer, more easily read, and ultimately less grim than much of Cormier's fiction, a thought-provoking story." —*Kirkus Reviews*, 10/1/92.

📖📖📖

TWELVE SHOTS: OUTSTANDING SHORT STORIES ABOUT GUNS. Mazer, Harry, Editor. Laurel-Leaf Books, 1998. $5.50. 229p. ISBN: 0-440-22002-5. Realistic fiction, Short stories. Reading level: MS. Interest level: MS, YHS, OHS. English, Ethics, Government, Sociology, Psychology.

SUBJECT AREAS
violence; death and dying; self-knowledge; crime and delinquency; intimidation; friendship; animals; bullying; manipulation; peer pressure; war; grief and mourning; rites of passage; poverty; elderly.

CHARACTERS
"Briefcase" by Walter Dean Myers
Narrator: a bike messenger
Little Jimmy: he works in a barbershop
Pookie: a good kid that got beat up, then figured out how to get a gun and use it.

"Cocked & Locked" by Chris Lynch
Oakley: a good kid whose best friend is Pauly
Pauly: folks expect only the worst from him
Lilly: Pauly's girlfriend

"Hunting Bear" Kevin McColley
Jack Taylor: he wants to shoot a bear
Gerry Lind: he's a hunting guide

"God's Plan for Wolfie and X-Ray" by David Rice
Wolfie, X-Ray: best friends who decide robbing a store would be easy
Senor Vasquez: an old man who works nights in a small store
Renee: Wolfie's cousin
Jesus: a bad shot who knows God has a plan for everyone

"War Games" by Nancy Werlin
Jo: she hides her fascination with Tallyrand to look like a normal kid
Lyle: Jo is his only friend, but he doesn't know enough to hide his feelings to protect himself from other kids

"Custody" by Frederick Busch
Pete: the unhappy victim of a custody battle
Pop: a retired New York cop, who took his son away with him in the middle of the night.
Miz Bean: school psychiatrist who's dating Pete's dad
Mom: his father told Pete she'd run away with a man and left him behind

"Shotgun Cheatham's Last Night above Ground" by Richard Peck
Joey, Mary Alice: every summer they went to visit their grandmother in the
    country
Grandma Dowdel: definitely *not* your average grandmother
Effie Wilcox: she loves to gossip

"War Chest" by Rob Thomas
Lester Conradt: an irascible old veteran who lives in a nursing home
Jeff: a basketball player doing his community service hours visiting Mr. Conradt
Jenny Robinson: the girl Jeff likes
Charlie Roberts: another war veteran, and Lester's friend

"Eat Your Enemy" by Nancy Springer
Cassidy: her father insists she learn to handle a gun
Dad: a gunsmith and single father who wants the best for his daughter

"Until the Day He Died" by Harry Mazer
Mike: a gunner on a B-17 during World War II

"Fresh Meat" by Ron Koertge
Narrator: he got his first rifle when he was ten
J.J., Pam: his best friends
Mom, Dad: his parents

"Chalkman" Rita Williams-Garcia
Eamon: the chalkman
Nkese, Nijri, Jimmy, Cherise: his friends

BOOKTALK

Guns are everywhere in our society. The right to own and use them is protected
by our Constitution. They are a part of our lives and unlikely to disappear. But
can we live with them? Bullets are cheap; life is not. Guns have one purpose:
putting holes in another living being. Sometimes those holes kill, sometimes
they don't. Guns can be used "for" something or "against" something. They put
meat on our tables and defend us in wars.

But what happens when teens and guns are brought together? Here are
twelve answers.

In "War Games" we discover the danger of letting your fear show,
especially when you're an individual facing a group.

"Eat Your Enemy" looks at the way knowing how to use a gun allows a girl
to do the right thing in a difficult situation.

"Hunting Bear" is about the power of money and the arrogance of those
who think they can buy happiness.

In "Cocked & Locked" a gun is a symbol of power, intimidation, and manipulation.

Guns are always involved in war, and the gunner in "Until the Day He Died" loved his job, until it was too late.

His father's antique guns were toys to Jeff, but to the veteran who owned "The War Chest," it was a weapon he knew exactly how to use.

And for people who believe robbing a convenience store is really as easy as it looks on TV, "God's Plan for Wolfie and X-Ray" will give you a more realistic perspective.

Take a look at what these and other people gain or lose when they pick up a gun.

MAJOR THEMES AND IDEAS

- There is no way to know how a casual remark you make to a stranger will reverberate and cause actions you never intended.
- Showing people too much of who you are inside can make them uncomfortable. Don't wear your inside on your outside. As a kid if you want to survive, you have to blend in.
- Money is power. Enough money means you can control people, but there's no way any amount of money by itself can bring happiness.
- Real life isn't as easy as a movie or a TV show—you can't reshoot the scene if you make a mistake.
- It's dangerous to show your fear—it marks you as a victim.
- Sooner or later, in times of stress and despair, if a gun is available, it will be used.
- If you want folks to leave you alone, it is best to enhance your reputation every so often.
- Those who shared the same kind of hellish experience may also share a special bond or friendship as a result.
- Eat your enemy. Take the good and the strength of him and leave the poison behind.
- Knowing how to use a gun doesn't mean you will use it to harm others. You may use it to give you some control in a difficult or dangerous situation.
- War ceases to be an exciting game when it becomes your daily reality. Wars kill.
- Guns do one thing: they kill. Owning and using them is a huge responsibility.
- Kids who live with violence every day become used to and casual about it.

BOOK REPORT IDEAS

1. Select the story that had the most impact on you and explain why.
2. Compare the views of guns in " God's Plan for Wolfie and X-Ray" and "Fresh Meat."

3. Explain how and why Jeff and Lester Conradt saw guns differently.
4. In "War Games," Jo says she's the best friend Lyle ever had. Explain what you think she meant, and whether or not you agree with her.
5. Explain Pauly's actions in the story "Cocked & Locked," and show the reasons behind those actions.
6. Speculate on what might happen after the ending of "Custody." How will that last night change the relationship between Pete and his father?

BOOKTALK IDEAS
1. Select your favorite story and tell it.
2. Do mini plot summaries on several stories.
3. Include some of the statistics about guns in your talk.

RISKS
- Gritty, often horrifying scenes of violence.
- Language is realistic and gritty.
- Guns are used irresponsibly.

STRENGTHS
- Varying perspectives on owning and using guns.
- Realistic situations and characters teens can identify with.
- No pat responses to questions about guns.
- Presents both positive and negative views of guns.
- Many opportunities for individual and group reflection/discussion.

AWARDS
Quick Picks for Reluctant Readers, 1998
Popular Paperbacks for Young Adults/Short Takes, 2000

REVIEWS
"Some of our best young adult authors contribute to this superb collection of stories about guns. . . . There is enough variety in this collection to satisfy any reader. . . . A book no library should be without." —*Voice of Youth Advocates*, 8/97, Edward Sullivan.

"Quality selections about a growing social concern make it a book worthy of consideration by all libraries." —*School Library Journal*, 9/97, Tom S. Hurlburt.

"Not only timely and thought provoking but also an excellent springboard for discussion." —*Booklist*, 1997, Helen Rosenberg.

"Searing tales. . . . mercifully offset with lighter entries." —*Kirkus Reviews*, 7/1/97.

📖📖📖

VANISHING. Brooks, Bruce. HarperCollins, 1999. $14.95. 160p. ISBN: 0-060-28236-3. Avon, 2000. $6.95. 112p. ISBN: 0-064-47234-5. Realistic fiction. Reading level: MS. Interest level: MS, YHS. English.

SUBJECT AREAS
death and dying; illness, physical; stepparents; problem parents; substance abuse; family relationships; eating disorders; friendship; self-knowledge.

CHARACTERS
Alice: she doesn't want to leave the hospital so she goes on a hunger strike
Rex: Alice's friend, who is dying
Alice's mother: she drinks too much and feels guilty
Nat: Alice's stepfather who is cold, rigid and religious
Alice's father: he's always been close to his daughter, but living with her and his mother is difficult
Nana: Alice's paternal grandmother, a rather cold woman
Dr Jonathan: Alice's psychiatrist

BOOKTALK
It's all a matter of control—who's in charge of your life, you or someone else? It seemed to Alice that her family was a lot more in charge than she was. She bounced from one to another, never quite belonging anywhere.

This time her father had shipped her back to her mother so fast he didn't realize how sick she was, which is why she'd ended up in the hospital, where she met Rex, who showed her a way to turn her life around. In other words, if you didn't want to go home and start imitating a Ping-Pong ball again, find a reason to stay in the hospital like Rex. But he had a terminal disease, which was in remission for who knew how long. Alice didn't and couldn't fake it. There was nothing she could do, but there was something she could not do. She put down her fork, looked at Rex, smiled, and pushed her food tray away. She could not eat.

MAJOR THEMES AND IDEAS
- Ultimately, you are the only person in control of your life. But you can't control anyone but yourself.
- Very few things are worth dying for.

- Live every day as well and as fully as you can.
- A friend is someone whose needs you place before your own.
- If you have only a limited time to live and refuse to live it with whatever zest and energy you have, you are already dead.
- Sometimes it takes time for big changes to sink in.
- Just because a doctor says you're going to die, it doesn't mean you have to live like you believe it.

BOOK REPORT IDEAS
1. Controlling your own life is a major theme in the book. Discuss how both Rex and Alice control their lives in different ways and also how they influence others' lives.
2. Describe how and why Alice is in control at the end of the book and speculate on how she will maintain her control in the future.
3. Rex has decided to take advantage of his remission. Describe how he does that and how his attitudes and actions differ from those of his parents'.

BOOKTALK IDEAS
1. Focus your talk on why Alice is in the hospital and her first conversation with Rex, ending with her decision not to eat.
2. Write your talk in first person from Rex's point of view as he introduces himself and Alice.

RISKS
- Alcoholic mother is always drunk.
- Ineffectual father fails to protect his daughter.
- Harsh, rigid, stepfather who dislikes his stepdaughter intensely.
- All families depicted are dysfunctional in some way and all adults are shown in a negative light.
- Child tries to starve herself to gain control of her life.

STRENGTHS
- Beautifully written with lyrical passages.
- Strong pro-living/pro-life message.
- Shows the positive and negative sides of control.
- Powerful portrayal of friendship.
- Gives a realistic picture of dysfunctional families.
- Powerful, realistic final scenes.

AWARDS
None

REVIEWS

"A powerful novel that addresses several themes, including the concerns faced by children of divorce. . . . impact of not feeling loved or valued is overwhelming. . . . reader is reminded that there is always someone who cares." —*Voice of Youth Advocates*, 10/99, Cheryl Karp Ward.

"The author presents these bleak events with style and a considerable amount of dramatic tension and offers a resolution that holds at least a small measure of hope. . . . A deeply felt, unusual, and absorbing story. It's not for every reader, but kids with a melodramatic turn of mind may love it." —*School Library Journal*, 6/99, Lauralyn Persson.

"Dialogue is so inventive and witty that it achieves a kind of hyper-reality, catching perfectly the way that seemingly offhand banter can conceal—and reveal—truths too cruel to express more directly. . . . A trenchant and powerful fable." —*Horn Book*, 5-6/99, J.R.L.

"A very powerful story [told] very simply. . . . Brooks does not shy away from describing the sense of control over her destiny that Alice feels with every mouthful she doesn't eat, and he describes in eerily perfect detail the light-filled hallucinations that can come with starvation." —*Booklist*, 5/15/99, GraceAnne A DeCandido.

VIRTUAL WAR. Skurzynski, Gloria. Simon and Schuster, 1997. $16.00. 152p. ISBN: 0-689-81374-0. Simon and Schuster, 1999. $4.50. 160p. ISBN: 0-689-82425-4. Science fiction. Reading level: MS. Interest level: MS, YHS. English, Ethics, Government, American history, Psychology.

SUBJECT AREAS

war; manipulation; friendship; bullying; computers; violence; anger; self-knowledge; secrets; rites of passage; psychology; lying and deceitfulness; ethics.

CHARACTERS

Corgen: fourteen years old, he's a genetically engineered perfect soldier who always plays by the rules

Sharla: also fourteen, she is a cryptanalyst, bred to be an expert code breaker who also knows how to break the rules

Brig: ten years old, he's a brilliant strategist and a mutant, a genetic experiment gone partially wrong

Mendor: Corgen's computerized teacher and source of rewards and punishments
Supreme Council: six people who control everything in the Western Hemisphere
    Federation
Jake: a friend of Sharla's who works as a hover car mechanic

BOOKTALK

Corgan is the perfect soldier, genetically engineered to have the fastest reflexes possible. In 2080, he's fourteen, and the War is only eighteen days away. He lives in a Box, a small room with walls made of aerogel, which can put him into any virtual setting he needs or wants to be in. He has never been with another real human being, only virtual images. He has never been outside in real time, even though in virtual reality, he's been all over the world. He does what he's supposed to, doesn't ask a lot of questions, believes what he's told, and follows the rules.

All that changes when he meets Sharla, one of his two teammates in the War. She is also fourteen and genetically designed to break any code in nanoseconds. She also loves to break the rules and laughs at punishments, because she knows they need her to win the war. She's been going all over the city since she was eight, and has been around lots of people. But she's the first actual person Corgan has ever seen or touched.

Brig is the second person. He's the third member of their team. But his genetic engineering didn't turn out as well as Corgan's or Sharla's. He's only about half as tall as a normal ten-year-old, with a huge head and spindly, weak arms and legs. He spent the first six years in the Mutant Pen before the caretakers discovered he was a double genius and began training him. But in spite of his brain, he can be a real pain in the neck, and has a smart mouth besides.

Three genetic experiments, three children designed to win a virtual war with the two other federations on Earth. The Prize? The Isles of Hiva, one of the last uncontaminated places on Earth, a real paradise, not a virtual one. But are Corgan, Sharla, and Brig being told the truth, or is the Supreme Council hiding things from them? Corgan discovers that some things don't add up the way they're supposed to, and Sharla begins to ask more questions, including the most important one, the one no one wants to ask or answer—what happens to us if we lose?

MAIN THEMES AND IDEAS

- People are more than their appearances.
- Follow your instinct—if something feels wrong, it may be wrong.
- Manipulating someone else for your own benefit is wrong.
- Reality is better than living virtually, even though it's more difficult.
- Which is better, cheat to win or lose with honor? Each of us must make our own individual decision.
- War is hell, even virtual war.

- The good of the few is sacrificed for the good of the many.
- A society that throws away its mistakes and makes heroes only of its successes cannot be said to be truly honorable.
- Knowing someone you love believes in you is a potent motivating force.
- Virtual violence can impact an individual just as much as actual violence can.

BOOK REPORT IDEAS

1. Discuss the concept of honor as it is seen in the book, including how characters and society in general were and were not honorable.
2. Compare Sharla's cynicism and Corgan's innocence and how their lives were affected by the amount of information they were able to access.
3. Explain the ending of the book, what Sharla's final comment to Corgan meant, and why she waited until she was leaving to tell him.
4. Discuss the effects of the virtual war on the team members and compare it to the impact of today's violent computer games.

BOOKTALK IDEAS

1. Let one of the main characters introduce him or herself and then describe the other two.
2. Let each team member introduce themselves.
3. Focus on the society, rather than the team members, describing how Earth was contaminated and devastated and why virtual war was decided on, ending with the idea that this war will be fought by three genetically engineered children, two successes and one failure.
4. Use the quote on the back of the hardback dust jacket as part of you talk, focusing on how the violence gradually got more and more violent as the day of the war got closer and closer.

RISKS

- Heartless society sees individuals only as pawns in a game.
- Humans who are not genetically perfect are discarded.
- Children are manipulated for the good of society.
- Graphic depiction of war's violence.
- Lying and deceitfulness are justified.

STRENGTHS

- Strong anti war message.
- Shows the impact of virtual violence on individuals.
- Individuals defy society and win.
- Realistic characters and dialogue teens can identify with.
- A fast read that teens will get into easily.
- Many opportunities for group discussion and individual reflection.

AWARDS
Best Books for Young Adults, 1998
Quick Picks for Reluctant Readers, 1998

REVIEWS
"This relatively short book is a quick read and holds the reader's interest to the very last page. As with many futuristic books, the world portrayed is a bleak place to live for most people, unless you've got special talents valued by the leaders of society. . . . Teens who enjoy science fiction or imagine what life might be like in the future should really enjoy this book." —*Voice of Youth Advocates*, 8/97, Linda Roberts.

"The story builds to a searing conclusion as Corgan must confront the gruesome spectacle of war, which Skurzynski makes vividly real, and as he faces questions of honor, duty, and purpose." —*Booklist*, 8/97, Susan Dove Lempke.

"A timely and familiar tale of adolescent rebellion set on an intriguing future Earth. Corgan, the ethical, honorable hero; Sharla, the intelligent, cynical rebel; and Brig, the bitter dwarf with a heart of gold, are stereotypical but still empathetic characters, and many readers will enjoy this fast-moving, easy read about a possible future where the best video-game player is the ultimate hero." —*School Library Journal*, 7/97, Susan L. Rogers.

ᗊᗊᗊ

WHALE TALK. Crutcher, Chris. HarperCollins, 2001. $15.95. 224p. ISBN: 0-688-18019-1. Realistic fiction. Reading level: MS. Interest level: MS, YHS, OHS. English, P. E., Ethics.

SUBJECT AREAS
ethnic groups; love; adoption; sports; violence; peer pressure; family relationships; anger; friendship; revenge; school; self-knowledge; rites of passage; death and dying; therapy; grief and mourning; abuse, physical; bullying; problem parents; dysfunctional families.

CHARACTERS
The Tao Jones/T.J.: a black/Japanese/white senior in high school who's a great athlete but hates organized school sports
Abby Jones/Mom: T.J.'s adoptive mother who's a white upwardly mobile lawyer
John Paul Jones/Dad: T.J.'s adoptive father who's a white motorcycle enthusiast and TV buff

Mr. Simet: T.J.'s English teacher and journalism teacher and swimming coach
Coach Benson: football coach
Mr. Morgan: high school principal
Coach Murphy: wrestling coach
Mike Barbour: linebacker who objects to someone wearing a letter jacket he hasn't earned
Rich Marshall: a sports fan, head of Marshall Logging, and one really mean guy who hates T.J.
Georgia Brown: T.J.'s former therapist and current friend who's also mixed race
Carly Hudson: an athlete, beautiful, and the girl T.J. is head over heels in love with
Alicia Marshall: Rich's wife and Heidi's mother
Heidi Marshall: Rich's stepdaughter, her father was black

Swim Team Members
Chris Coughlin: permanently brain damaged, he likes to wear his dead brother's letter jacket
Dan Hole: a swimmer who never uses one syllable words when a bigger one is available
Jackie Craig: a nondescript kid who was cut from Junior Varsity football
Tay-Roy Kibble: a musician and body builder who's decided he'd rather swim
Simon Delong: he's 5'7" and weighs 300 pounds
Andy Mott: a surly bodybuilder who volunteers for the team
Oliver Van Zant: he lives at the health club and is the unofficial team coach

BOOKTALK

What a concept! Losers in letter jackets! I could show those small town jocks, those crown princes of athletics, just how much those jackets *really* meant!

Hi. I'm T.J. Jones, and while I love to play sports, I hate being told what to do, and that's what high school coaches do. I'd decided four years ago to go all the way through high school without one semester on any team, and I almost made it. What happened? Mr. Simet happened. He was my English teacher, one of the few folks on the faculty that I had any real respect for. In September of my senior year, he asked me for a favor. He didn't want to coach wrestling, and he'd have to unless he and I could come up with a swim team.

It sounded crazy—a swim team in a town that had only one pool, at the twenty-four-hour health club, which wasn't even close to meeting the rules for a regulation pool, so we'd never have a home swim meet—we'd be on the road one hundred percent of the time. I was going to turn him down—I mean, he's a great teacher and a great human being, but this was a *BIG* favor, when I saw something that gave me the *perfect* motivation.

Two of the bigger, meaner football players were hassling Chris for wearing his dead brother's letter jacket. Chris was brain damaged, and everyone knew it, including these two lamebrains. Wearing Brian's jacket was the only way Chris could feel close to his brother. I chased them off, and then later that day, when I went by the health club and saw Chris swim with his beautiful, natural stroke, my plan burst into my head, fully formed and ready to put into play.

I'd create a swim team of the very guys the jocks hated, the ones they saw as losers, and then watch how those jocks felt when guys they'd spit on wore the same letter jackets they did! *Yes!*

So who made the team? Chris, of course; Dan, the original multisyllabic genius geek; Tay Roy, a bodybuilder who decided he'd rather swim; Jackie, who's so average that he's nearly invisible; Simon, who's 5'7" and almost 300 pounds; and Andy, who's terminally angry, has major bad attitude, and walks with a limp that he's never explained. In other words, the team consisted of one real swimmer of color (I'm a mix, white/black/Japanese), two representatives from the top and bottom of the IQ curve, a muscle man, a giant, a chameleon, and a psycho. Would we succeed in yanking the chains of every jock and ex-jock in town, or go under for the last time?

Come to practice, take a ride on our team bus, and find out for yourself. We just might manage to surprise you—more than once!

MAJOR THEMES AND IDEAS

- The color of a person's skin has to do only with where his ancestors came from.
- There are no coincidences, and when two seemingly related events occur, they *are* related and should be treated that way.
- The better you know yourself, the better chance you have of steering clear of trouble.
- When an activity has outlived its usefulness in this country, we keep it alive as a sport.
- When sports are too big a deal in a high school, the jocks get too much, and that doesn't leave enough for the rest of us.
- Healthy people want to solve their own problems, not let someone else do it for them.
- The Universe offers up whatever we need, whenever we need it.
- All-out, go-for-it exercise is a good way to work off rage.
- Racist thought and action say much more about the person they're coming from than the person they're aimed at.
- The Universe doesn't make allowances for mental lapses or ignorance—you have to pay the price.
- Being a good, successful human being isn't easy. It's risky and dangerous, but worth it.
- You don't respond to what's good for you, you respond to what is familiar and therefore more comfortable.
- Not one moment for revenge. Don't live a life of what might have been.

BOOK REPORT IDEAS

1. Discuss the different kinds of families portrayed in the book, comparing those who were and were not dysfunctional.
2. Analyze the character of T.J.'s father, showing how he became the man, husband, and father he was.
3. Anger and revenge are two themes in the book. Compare how different people handled these two things.
4. Examine the jock culture as it is portrayed in the book, and explain how realistic you feel that portrayal is.
5. Spousal, date, and child abuse are another theme in this book. Examine the ways abuse occurs and the steps that are taken to prevent it, giving your emotional and intellectual response to those situations.
6. Analyze T.J.'s parents' and Grace's responses to T.J.'s attempts to beat up Mike Barbour. Explain how they do or do not make sense to you and how you would have reacted in T.J.'s place.
7. Describe the person and/or the scene/situation in the book that was most important or significant to you and explain why.

BOOKTALK IDEAS

1. Let T.J. tell the story in his own voice, focusing on how forming the swim team was his way of getting back at the jocks.
2. Use a letter jacket as a prop.
3. Focus your talk on two areas—the swim team and abusive athletes.
4. Describe the different team members and their coaches. (Be careful not to give too much away—don't tell the secret of Matt's limp.)

RISKS

- Narrator is a multiracial character.
- Retarded teen is hazed by violent jocks.
- Language is realistic and includes obscenities.

STRENGTHS

- Strong statement against school violence.
- Realistic multidimensional characters teens can identify with.
- Realistic language reflects the way teens speak today.
- Positive adult characters play role models and mentors.
- Shows the power of team spirit and friendship.
- Depiction of positive, supportive nuclear family.
- Points out what's right and what's wrong subtly, without beating the reader over the head.
- Strong, clear, individual narrator's voice shows he doesn't take himself as seriously as he does other things.

- Multiple story lines seamlessly woven together add to the story's complexity.

AWARDS
None

REVIEWS
"Cartoon character Pogo's words "We have met the enemy and he is us" chillingly describe Crutcher's latest book in which hatred simmers, boils, and burns its characters. . . . Although the ending is foreshadowed, it is shocking and horrifying, yet sadly realistic. . . . Crutcher is at his darkest but also his funniest here, and the book conveys his most timely message—forgiveness, not revenge." —*Voice of Youth Advocates*, 6/01, Lisa A Spiegel.

"In the hands of a lesser storyteller, the tale would fall apart under its own weight, but Crutcher juggles the disparate elements of his plot with characteristic energy, crafting a compulsively readable story that rings true." —*Kirkus Reviews*, 2001.

"Another wise and compassionate story full of the intensity of athletic competition and hair-raising incidents of child abuse." —Amazon, 2001, Patty Campbell.

"[Crutcher] uses well-constructed characters and quick pacing to examine how the sometimes cruel and abusive circumstances of life affect every link in the human chain, and a heartwrenching series of plot twists leads to an end in which goodness at least partially prevails." —*Booklist*, 2001, Kelly Halls.

📖📖📖

WHAT JAMIE SAW. Coman, Carolyn. Front Street, Inc., 1995. $13.95. 126p. ISBN: 1-886-91002-2. Viking Penguin, 1997. $4.99. 127p. ISBN: 0-140-38335-2. Listening Library Inc., 2000. $18.00. ISBN: 0-807-26157-2 (unabridged audiotape) Reading level: MS. Interest level: MS. English, Ethics, Psychology.

SUBJECT AREAS
child abuse; stepparents; problem parents; family relationships; secrets; friendship; anger; school; survival; fear.

CHARACTERS

Jamie: a third-grader who has seen terrible things
Nin: Jamie's baby sister
Patty: Jamie and Nin's mother
Van: the man Patty used to live with and Nin's father
Earl: Patty's best friend
Agnes: Van's mother who baby-sits Nin sometimes
Mrs. Desrochers: Jamie's teacher

BOOKTALK

Jamie woke up just in time to see Van throw Nin, his baby sister, across the room as straight and fast as a bullet fired from a gun. Before he could even understand what he'd seen, his mother stepped into the room and caught Nin, plucked her out of the air, and she was safe.

But was Jamie safe? Van just stood by the crib, head and shoulders drooping, he didn't look dangerous anymore, but Jamie couldn't take a chance. His mother had to call him four times before he could make his frozen body move. And then he's there, clutching his mother around the waist, safe.

What's it like for a third-grader who sees his sister just seconds away from death, who suddenly learns that a man he'd trusted is now a danger to himself and his sister, someone all three of them must run and hide from? Let Jamie tell you about child abuse, and about what he saw.

MAJOR THEMES AND IDEAS

- Don't stay with people who hurt you.
- Mothers can't always protect their children.
- Sometimes fear can eat you up inside and make you angry. Other times it can make you strong.
- Saying you're sorry isn't always enough.
- Some things are too awful to be forgiven.
- Do all you can to protect the ones you love.

BOOK REPORT IDEAS

1. Fear is a major theme in this book. Discuss how it impacts the lives and actions of the major characters.
2. The first sentence of the books starts in the middle of a crisis. Write what you think came before the book began—a day, a week, a month before.
3. Explain why Jamie's teacher came to visit him and his mother, and what she said to Patty when Jamie was outside.
4. Discuss the significance of Jamie's magic book and show why it is so important to him, his most-loved possession.

BOOKTALK IDEAS
1. Have Jamie tell his own story. Be sure to use the thoughts and feelings of a young child, not a teen.
2. Write your talk from Patty's perspective, showing her fear for her children.
3. Write a first-person talk, as Jamie looks back on this time in his life from the perspective of ten years in the future.

RISKS
- Unflinching portrait of child abuse and violence.

STRENGTHS
- Mother does what's necessary to protect her children.
- Powerful narrator's voice draws readers into the story.
- Ambiguous ending without unrealistic answers.
- Gripping depiction of the power of fear.
- Characters hold onto their hope despite overwhelming odds.

AWARDS
Newbery Award Honor Book, 1996
Booklist Editors' Choice, 1995
Children's Notables, 1996

REVIEWS
"Wrenching simplicity and mesmerizing imagery . . . revealed through the boy's clear, unprejudiced eye, characters, though rough and uneducated, are not stereotyped. . . . Shocking in its simple narration and child's-eye view . . . a bittersweet miracle in understated language and forthright hopefulness." —*School Library Journal*, 12/95, Alice Casey Smith.

"This brief novel explodes into the reader's consciousness from the very first page. . . . Coman's poetic prose is unsentimental and concise. The elements of plot and characterization meld into a finely balanced blend. This is a powerful story that proves with painful insistence the insidious nature of fear and its consequences." —*Horn Book*, 3-496, N.V.

WHAT'S IN A NAME? Wittlinger, Ellen. Simon and Schuster, 2000. $16.00. 146p. ISBN: 0-689-82551-X. Short story collection, Realistic fiction. Reading level: MS. Interest level: MS, YHS. English, Sex education, Government, P. E., Drama, Creative writing.

SUBJECT AREAS

school; homosexuality; ethics; poetry; friendship; dating and social life; self-knowledge; family relationships; sex and sexuality; working; politics; problem parents; sex education; stereotypes; poverty; activism.

CHARACTERS

Georgie: she lives with her mother live above a dog grooming parlor

Mary Linn: owner of The Pampered Pooch, and Georgie's boss

Mrs. Carstenson: a local clubwoman who wants to change the town's name from Scrub Harbor to Folly Bay

Gretchen Carstenson: an officer in every school club, she's also Quincy's girlfriend

O'Niell: Quincy's younger brother, smarter than most, and a poet

Quincy: a star football player who's embarrassed by his younger brother and dates Gretchen

Mr. Thompkins: he's an English teacher, gay, and sponsors the Gay/Straight Alliance

Christine: coeditor of the literary magazine, she is interested in O'Neill, and is Georgie's best friend

Ricardo: an exchange student from Brazil who lives with Christine's family

Nadia: a Russian immigrant who has a crush on Nelson

Nelson: son of an insurance executive and a doctor, he plans to go to an Ivy League college

Shaquanda: bused into Scrub Harbor with other black kids, she's learned to succeed in spite of the poverty of her life

Adam: a senior who has just moved to Scrub Harbor and doesn't fit in anywhere

BOOKTALK

It's a rich white suburb of Boston. Only ten percent of its residents don't own their own homes. Specially selected kids from urban neighborhoods are bused to the high school to take advantage of the better educational opportunities Scrub Harbor offers. It's the kind of place where everyone has a label and a role. But what happens when those labels get pushed aside? Whose faces and whose secrets will be revealed?

O'Neill is just the quiet, smart, younger brother of the star football player until a teacher challenges him to tell the truth about himself, and he posts that truth on the school bulletin board.

Nelson is one of the few blacks in school, second in the class, slated for Harvard, but according to Shaquanda, who lives in an inner-city ghetto, he doesn't know the first thing about being black. The only thing they have in common is the color of their skin—the colors of their lives are very different.

Adam's just been in town for ten weeks. In his old school, he was at the top of the popular crowd. Here, he's a zero who doesn't fit in, and wonders which person is the "real" Adam.

Gretchen is on every committee, in every club, and always has something to do. Can it be she's keeping busy to keep from having to look at questions she'd rather not answer?

And they aren't the only ones who have questions without answers. Christine, Georgie, Ricardo, Quincy, and Nadia are struggling too, to find out who and what they are.

What's in a name? A label? A stereotype? A person? Join the students at Scrub Harbor High School and find out.

MAJOR THEMES AND IDEAS

- Just when you think you know someone, they surprise you.
- Sometimes if you need the money enough, you have to forget where it comes from.
- Starting a new school, where no one knows you, is like figuring out who you are all over again.
- If a lie separates you from other people, maybe it's time to tell the truth, no matter how difficult that is.
- People are far more than the roles they play or the stereotypes they seem to be. But to find that out, you have to get to know them.
- Some roles are hard to escape from, no matter how much you'd like to.
- If you're going to survive, you have to keep your eyes on your goal and not sweat the small stuff.
- You can choose to define yourself rather than let others do it for you.

BOOK REPORT IDEAS

1. Each of the ten main characters in the book are defined or described both by themselves and by their peers. Choose two or three of these characters and compare how they see themselves to how others see them.
2. The Scrubs and the Follys are only two of the subgroups the high school is divided into. Describe and define the other divisions in the school.
3. Several characters mention meeting at their twenty-fifth high school reunion. Describe who the main characters might have become, and why, and whether any of the connections within the groups have lasted over the years.
4. Secrets kept and secrets told are major themes in the book. Discuss who had secrets and how keeping or telling them impacted their lives.

BOOKTALK IDEAS

1. Describe Scrub Harbor High School briefly, then introduce each of the main characters with a one-sentence profile.
2. Focus your talk on the idea of stereotypes—football jock, prom queen, new kid in town, etc.—and hint at what those stereotypes hide and the secrets those kids have to keep.

RISKS
- Gay character comes out of the closet.
- Openly gay teacher.
- Inner-city family supported by drug dealer who's part of the family.

STRENGTHS
- Several story lines woven together add complexity and depth to the plot.
- Shows the falseness of stereotypes.
- The interactions/connections/dialogues among the characters are realistic.
- Presents each main character from several points of view.
- Characters mature and gain insight.
- Brief, easy read, not intimidating to poor or nonreaders.
- Individual chapters could be adapted to reader's theater.

AWARDS
Best Books for Young Adults, 2000 (ALA)
Bulletin for the Center for Children's Books Blue Ribbon Book, 2000

REVIEWS
"Dramatize[s] . . . identity issues in a sharp, funny, touching contemporary narrative . . . show[s] you the stereotypes from the outside . . . and then take[s] you up close as the characters tell their own stories and reveal their yearning and difficulties." —*Booklist*, 1/00/00, Hazel Rochman.

"A subtle and completely realistic novel told in multiple voices. . . . these teens are all struggling to find out who they are, and. . . . constantly in flux, becomes the main theme that links all of these seemingly unconnected narrative threads together. The teenagers are compelling, and there's more depth to them and the story than readers might expect from the simplistic title." —*School Library Journal*, 2/00, Linda Bindner.

"Although it's low on surprises, this gallery of clean-cut high schoolers does offer a hopeful view of youth on the way to adulthood." —*Kirkus Reviews*, 12/15/99.

"Thoughtfully structured novel. . . . characters struggle with who they are— discovering (or guessing) how others see them while figuring out how they see themselves. In the process, they reveal their feelings about change in circumstances and in their identities. . . . intriguing, complex, and believable . . . will keep readers engrossed." —*Horn Book*, 2000.

WHEN KAMBIA ELAINE FLEW IN FROM NEPTUNE. Williams, Lori Aurelia. Simon and Schuster, 2000. $17.00. 246p. ISBN: 0-689-82468-8. Listening Library, Inc., 2001. $40.00. ISBN: 0-807-28850-0. (unabridged audiotape) Realistic fiction. Reading level: MS. Interest level: MS, YHS. English, Ethics, Sex education, Art, Creative writing.

SUBJECT AREAS
child abuse; abuse, sexual; abuse, physical; friendship; sex and sexuality; fear; secrets; family relationships; art; love; rites of passage; minorities, black; poverty; lying and deceitfulness; problem parents; anger; elderly; prejudice; runaways; writing; religion; eating disorders.

CHARACTERS
Shayla DuBois: at twelve, she's an observer of life, a reader and a writer, but not much of a talker

Tia Maria DuBois: Shayla's pretty fourteen-year-old sister who's kicked out of the house for fooling around with an older man

Vera DuBois/Mama: Shayla and Tia's mother who loves hard and doesn't forget easily

Grandma Augustine: Shayla and Tia's maternal grandmother, a wise and perceptive woman

Kambia Elaine Joiner: she sees wolves with claws in the wallpaper and other strange and fantastic things

Miss Earlene Jackson/Frog: Doo-Witty's mother who isn't fond of the DuBois family, and sometimes talks with her hands instead of her mouth

Doo-Witty/Donald Dwight Jackson: Frog's son who is considered stupid by everyone in the neighborhood, and who has been going out with Tia

Maxi: Tia's best friend

Mr. Anderson Fox: Shayla's father who rarely visits his daughter

Jasmine Joiner: Kambia's mother who has lots of boyfriends

Miss Marshall: she's in charge of the writing contest Shayla enters

Sister Ashada: a minister at the Tabernacle of the Blessed Redeemer

BOOKTALK
There was no doubt of it—Shayla's life was falling apart just as fast as water dripped out of a leaky bucket. First the family piece came leaking out. It began the day Mama found the box of condoms in her sister Tia's drawer. Mama had gotten pregnant with Tia when she was only fifteen, and she wanted something more for her daughter! But Tia was stubborn and in love with Doo-Witty, who was twenty-three and not all that bright. She and Mama fought again and again, until finally Mama gave Tia an ultimatum, "Get rid of Doo-Witty or don't come home!" And Tia didn't.

Then the friendship piece got all muddy and started flowing away. Shayla knew there was something wrong with her best friend and next-door neighbor,

Kambia Elaine. Kambia was little and skinny, and only had one tattered dress. She told Shayla incredible stories about the Memory beetles and the Lizard People, she pretended to be a flower or a pecan tree or a piece of driftwood. Shayla knew there was something wrong when she saw the ugly red and purple bruises on her thigh, but Kambia made her swear not to tell anyone. The Wolves in the Wallpaper had done it with their claws and if Shayla told, what they did to her would get worse.

Shayla's life is dripping away as she watches her mother sit for hours regretting what she said and hoping her daughter will come home. As she watches her best friend grow thinner and paler, trying to avoid the Wolves.

Shayla says she's a watcher and a writer, not a talker, but has the time finally come when keeping quiet is no longer an option?

MAJOR THEMES AND IDEAS

- Some secrets need to be told. Going back on your word isn't always bad.
- Just about everyone is smart in one way or another.
- Love makes you see people differently.
- People do all kinds of strange things to hide their pain.
- Don't judge someone's actions before you know the reasons for them.
- Don't let anyone tell you how to think or to express yourself.
- "Some things have to boil to the top before they can cook down nice and smooth" (pg. 53).
- Once you say something, you can't take it back, no matter how much you want to.
- "Sometimes you have to go down the wrong path to get to the right place" (pg. 81).
- Others have found their way out of trouble and pain. Look at their example and you can too.
- You can't fight wrong with wrong.
- Focus on the good things in your life instead of the bad.
- Sometimes it's okay to change the rules if it makes things better instead of worse.

BOOK REPORT IDEAS

1. Several characters in this book are caught in moral, ethical dilemmas they can find no way out of. Discuss these dilemmas and the solutions the characters find to resolve them without violating their own moral code.
2. There are four mothers in this book. Compare them, showing the different ways they mother their children, and the effects of those different styles on their children.
3. Examine two significant scenes in the book when Shayla entered her story in the writing contest and when she signed up to take a poetry class.

Examine the messages those scenes gave Shayla about herself and her neighborhood.

4. Kambia told lots of stories about many things. Discuss why they were so important to her and what each of them represented to her.

5. Explain your understanding of what Grandma meant when she told Shayla at the hospital, "It's OK to do the wrong thing for the right reasons, if the results are good, not bad."

BOOKTALK IDEAS

1. Have Shayla introduce herself, her family, and Kambia in first person.
2. Focus your talk on the idea of secrets and friendship, and how some secrets have to be told.
3. Write your talk in first person, as Tia defending herself, as Kambia telling one of her stories, or as Shayla caught between them, unable to really help either.

RISKS

- Depicts child abuse and sexual abuse.
- Language is vulgar yet realistic.
- Sexually active teens.
- Teens defy parental authority.
- Stereotyping of a slow or retarded boy.
- Father shown as promiscuous, often absent.

STRENGTHS

- Strong female characters believe in their families and work to make them successful.
- Powerful message about not keeping secrets involving child abuse of any kind.
- Lyrical writing style is in sharp contrast to the darkness of the characters' problems.
- Characters don't get easy answers but powerful lessons and messages.
- Author pulls no punches, asking as much of her readers as she does of her characters.

AWARDS

Best Books for Young Adults, 2001 (ALA)

REVIEWS

"Readers will realize early on that Kambia's fantasies hide the horrifying facts of her sexual abuse. In contrast, the revelations about Doo-Witty are astonishingly upbeat. In a beautiful take on the Cinderella story, he's the dummy who turns out to be a prince." —*Booklist*, 2/15/00, Hazel Rochman.

"First-time author Lori Aurelia Williams has written a novel that eloquently ties together the importance of family, the power of imagination, and the simple strength of innocence." —Amazon, 2001, Jennifer Hubert.

"Searing . . . debut. . . . the suffering hard-loving, strong minded women in the cast will carry readers over any soft spots in the story's logic." —*Kirkus Reviews*, 2000

"A voice as fresh and original as the novel's title. . . . cast of original characters living on the edge. . . . Inventively voiced if sprawling, and not always convincing in its narrative particulars, this first novel serves notice of a writer to watch." —*Horn Book*, 4-5/00, S.P.B.

📖📖📖

WHEN SHE HOLLERS. Voigt, Cynthia. Scholastic, 1994. $13.95. 177p. ISBN: 0-590-46714-X. Realistic fiction. Reading level: MS. Interest level: MS, YHS. Ethics, English, Sex education; Psychology.

SUBJECT AREAS
abuse, sexual; problem parents; rites of passage; school; survival; self-knowledge; family relationships; fear; anger; bullying; legal system; stepparents.

CHARACTERS
Tish: a teen who is sexually abused by her stepfather
Tonnie: Tish's manipulative stepfather
Barbie: Tish's mother who pretends not to know what is going on
Brad, Luley: Tonnie's children and Tish's stepsiblings
Mrs. Wyse: Tish's teacher
Kipper: Tish's boyfriend
Chrissie: one of Tish's friends
Mr. Battle: a lawyer and Chrissie's friend

BOOKTALK
Tish has been pushed far enough. She has suffered, she has endured, she has survived. Now it is enough. Now is the time to fight back. No one has protected her—now it is time to protect herself.

　　She put the knife down on the kitchen table, the point aimed at her tormentor, her stepfather Tonnie. "From now on," she said, "I'll have the knife. Always. In the bathroom. In my bedroom. If you ever come in there again, I'll— I'll cut your hands off, I'll cut your eyes out. I'll cut your heart out. You'd better believe me. . . . "

But it's hard to protect yourself with a stepfather as clever and cruel as Tonnie, and a mother who chooses to be deaf to all of Tish's pleas, believing her husband instead of her daughter. Tish is desperate, but she doesn't know where to turn. Who should she trust? What should she do? She knows she must do something soon—if she doesn't, she may not be able to go on. She may end up like Miranda, hanging herself from the tree in her front yard, death the only exit available. But Tish isn't quite that desperate yet—she has her knife, and she's safe as long as she's at school, especially now, with the knife hidden in the boot, always available, even in gym class, even when she's sent to the principal's office. She has to have the knife—it's her only protection.

Parents are supposed to protect their children, and keep them safe. Sometimes when they don't, when they are the source of the fear and the pain, not the solution to them, sometimes children have to protect themselves any way they can. Tish's first way is the knife, and then the letter.

MAJOR THEMES AND IDEAS
- You have to decide to save yourself—no one else will do it for you.
- When the pain and shame grow too large, you must fight back with whatever weapons you can find.
- If reality is too frightening people can refuse to see it, no matter how awful it is.
- Actions and appearances can be deceiving. It's said that the devil is beautiful and charming, as well as the essence of evil.
- Confronting bullies instead of giving in to them frequently makes them back down.
- Words can sometimes be as potent a weapon as a knife.
- Suicide is the ultimate expression of the lack of hope and of giving in to the problem, the evil. It solves nothing and lets the one who stole that hope go free to steal it from someone else.

BOOK REPORT IDEAS
1. The adults surrounding Tish react to her in varying ways. Compare how Mrs. Wyse, Coach Marchon, Mr. Sutterfield, Mr. Battle, and her mother respond to Tish and to her anger.
2. Discuss whether or not Tonnie will now let Tish alone. Speculate about the confrontation scene between them, what it will look like, how it will sound, and why the author did not include it in the book.
3. Tish is a loner, hiding her secret shame from everyone. Discuss whether or not Kipper and Chrissie realize what is happening to Tish when they talk to her after the scene in the gym.
4. The scene with Mr. Battle is one of the most powerful in the whole book. Explain how and why you think he decided to protect Tish, and how and why she was able to begin to protect herself.

BOOKTALK IDEAS
1. Focus your talk on the knife and on why Tish needed it.
2. Have Tish tell her own story in first person.

RISKS
- Sexual abuse of a child by a parent.
- Mother denies and enables the continuing sexual abuse of her daughter.
- Teacher denies student's hints of sexual abuse.
- Graphic portrayal of extreme anger and violence.
- Suicide of a teen girl.

STRENGTHS
- Realistic description of how to combat sexual abuse.
- Intense emotions, graphically and realistically portrayed.
- Portrait of a victim of sexual abuse from within her own mind.
- Ambiguous ending allows reader to speculate on what happens.
- Powerful subject, realistically portrayed, pulls no punches.

AWARDS
Best Books for Young Adults, 1994 (ALA)

REVIEWS
"Raw pain is etched into every page of this novel. Tish's feelings of isolation, entrapment, and ambivalence are real. Voigt's style is extremely effective. Tight, short sentences clearly convey Tish's anguish and confusion. . . . the reader is part of Tish's limited world. Brief dialogue moves the plot and language is appropriate for the situation." —*Voice of Youth Advocates*, 12/94, Judy Sasges.

"An intense, powerful novel. . . . relentless. Voigt tells her story with short sentences and thought fragments, mirroring Tish's emotional disintegration...not an easy book to read nor an easy one to recommend to an adolescent. There is no happy ending. . . . May give some readers hope and may help others to understand why a victim of abuse might turn to violence." —*Horn Book*, 1-2/95 M.V.K.

"Searing portrait of a teenage incest victim. . . . At the novel's end she faces not only her stepfather, but also the consequences of telling the truth, thus transforming herself from victim to survivor. . . . unsparing in depicting the ruination of a teenage girl's life. . . . told in strong language from the victim's point of view. Its resulting immediacy is harrowing." —*Booklist*, 1994, Merri Monks.

⊞⊞⊞

WHEN SHE WAS GOOD. Mazer, Norma Fox. Scholastic, Inc., 1997. $16.95. 220p. ISBN: 0-590-13506-6. Scholastic, Inc., 1999. $4.99. 240p. ISBN: 0-590-31990-6. Realistic fiction. Reading level: YHS. Interest level: YHS, OHS. English, Psychology.

SUBJECT AREAS
abuse, physical; anger; bullying; death and dying; dysfunctional families; fear; illness, mental; intimidation; manipulation; poverty; family relationships; working; secrets; homeless.

CHARACTERS
Em Thurkill: after years of emotional and physical abuse from her older sister, she is finally on her own
Pamela Thurkill: dead of a stroke, her voice lives on inside Em's head
Ray Thurkill: Em's father
Sally Pearson: Ray's second wife
Mr. Elias: social worker from the homeless shelter
Mr. Bielic: the maintenance man at Em's apartment building
William: a retarded man who lives in Em's building
Louise D'Angelo: she lives in Em's building
Mr. Becker: he gives Em a job
Warren Weir: a man Em meets in a drugstore just after Pamela's death

BOOKTALK
I didn't believe Pamela would ever die. She was too big, too mad, too furious for anything so shabby or easy as death. At first I thought it was just one of her jokes, that any minute she would spring up, seize me by the hair, and drag me around the room. But she didn't. She just lay there on the floor in front of her chair, watching me with one angry eye, until gradually I realized that she was dead. It was over at last, and I didn't really know what to do. There would be no more beatings, or slaps, or angry words. Pamela, my angry, abusive, older sister, was gone.

But she wasn't really gone—she was still there in my head, shouting at me in her ugly, destructive voice, still telling me all the things she'd been screaming at me ever since I could remember. I'm bad, ugly, stupid, crazy. And I think that if I cannot get her voice to shut up, perhaps I will go crazy.

And there are other things I have to think about. Pamela's disability check no longer comes, the rent isn't paid, and there's no money for food. I look for a job every day, and every day they all say, no, nothing, come back next month. I try to look normal, but somehow it's like the store managers can see inside my head, see Pamela screaming at me, see that I'm not nice and normal, and jobs are only for nice, normal people.

But I don't blame them. I have had to live so carefully with Pamela, controlling my voice and my expression and my words, that I no longer know how to talk to someone, how to make friends, how to hold a conversation. All I can hear is Pamela's harsh, angry, critical voice, so loud I'm surprised everyone else can't hear it too. I thought it would end when she died, but it didn't. The beatings stopped, but her voice is growing louder and louder inside of me. Even though I beg her to stop, over and over again, her words spill into my mind, blocking out everything else.

I can't go on like this! She's dead, she's gone, and she can't hurt me anymore. Somehow, I need to find a way to survive, to work, pay the rent, buy food. Before Mother died, I was happy, I knew how to live. It hasn't been that long, only four years. Surely I can learn to live again, learn to ignore her, learn to do and say the things that will make that voice begin to fade, and let me be a part of the world around me. If she will not leave me, I will leave her. I'm only eighteen, and I want my life back. I want to be happy. I want to be normal. And I will be. Soon.

MAJOR THEMES AND IDEAS
- If you're told you're no good often enough, you'll begin to believe it.
- If you are good enough, patient enough, for long enough, your reward will come.
- Sometimes you have to fall to the bottom of the barrel before you can climb back out.
- It's up to you to see that you don't fall through the cracks.
- Learning how to survive alone may be difficult, but it's possible.
- Taking abuse can become a habit, one that isn't easy to break.
- When the person who has been abusing you is gone, you are free to find yourself again.

BOOK REPORT IDEAS
1. Compare and contrast Em at the beginning and end of the book, showing how she changed and what some of the milestones in that change were.
2. Discuss the idea that abuse is a generational disease, and show how seeing their father abuse their mother, and her passive, enabling response affected both Pamela and Em.
3. Speculate on what Em's life will be like from now on, and whether she will ever completely heal and be "normal."
4. Em tries desperately to get a job, but is unable to. Describe what the people she talks to see in her that makes them immediately turn her down, and what Mr. Becker sees that makes him offer a job immediately.

BOOKTALK IDEAS

1. Write your talk as a dialogue between Em and Pamela, revealing only at the end that Pamela's voice is only in Em's head.
2. Focus your talk on the descriptions of Pamela's death, gradually revealing that her abuse has left Em unable to cope with daily living.
3. Write your talk in Em's voice, showing her confusion and despair at her inability to cope with life.

RISKS

- Descriptions of physical and emotional abuse are vivid and graphic.

STRENGTHS

- Main character grows and gains insight about herself and her life, and how she can heal both.
- Frightening portrait of mental illness and its effect on all members of a family.
- Shows how one person decides to survive, and learns what she needs to do it.
- Multiple story lines add depth and complexity.

AWARDS

Best Books for Young Adults, 1998 (ALA)
Booklist Editors' Choice, 1997

REVIEWS

"This is a powerful and moving story that belongs in all YA collections." —*Voice of Youth Advocates*, 10/97, Victoria Yablonsky.

"A stunning piece of young adult fiction for readers mature enough to understand all of its psychological complexities. No typical tale of teen angst. . . . . Readers will share her pain, her few joys, and her ultimate will to survive. Mazer at her very, very best." —*School Library Journal*, 9/97, Dina Sherman.

"Told by Em, the story delineates her pain with careful spareness. . . . at its best when showing Em's tentative grasping for a new life of her own after Pamela's death, when her dignity, and hope begin to assert themselves and our feelings change from pity to respect." —*Horn Book*, 11/12/97, R.S.

📖📖📖

WHIRLIGIG. Fleischman, Paul. Holt, 1998. $16.95. 133p. ISBN: 0-805-05582-7. Laurel-Leaf Books, 1999. $4.99. 133p. ISBN: 0-440-22835-2. Realistic fiction. Reading level: MS. Interest level: MS, YHS, OHS. English, Ethics, Shop, Creative writing, Art.

SUBJECT IDEAS
suicide; family relationships; friendship; war; substance abuse; legal system; peer pressure; justice; death and dying; grief and mourning; travel; self-knowledge; rites of passage; ethics; art.

CHARACTERS
Brent Bishop: a junior who's moved four times in seven years, he always feels like the new kid, not fitting in.
Chaz: he hosted the party with a black and white theme
Jonathan: he invited Brent to the party, but forgot to tell him the dress code
Brianna: the girl Brent has a crush on
Lea Zamora: a high school senior who died in a wreck with Brent on his way home from the party
Mrs. Zamora: Lea's mother who asked Brent to make whirligigs as his reparation for Lea's death
Tony: seeing Brent's first whirligig in Washington changed his summer
Jenny and Grandma: seeing Brent's second whirligig gives a new way to look at life
Flaco: finding Brent's third whirligig helps him see his family in a new light
The painter: she helps Brent finish his quest and find healing
Alexandra, Stephanie: eighth graders in Maine who find Brent's last whirligig

BOOKTALK
It only took a moment. Brent closed his eyes and took his hands off the wheel. He didn't remember the actual impact, just the police and ambulance lights flashing, and a policeman who told him he'd escaped with only a minor head injury. He'd failed. He'd have to go back to the kids at school who'd laugh and jeer at him, to knowing he'd never fit in no matter how hard he'd tried, to knowing there would be no end of everything for him. But then he was told everything had ended for Lea Zamora, the eighteen-year-old high school senior who'd been driving the car he hit when his car went out of control. She was dead.

Brent went numb. He was a murderer. Instead of killing himself, he'd killed a pretty, popular girl who made people happy just by being around her. He was alive. Lea was not. And there was nothing he could do that would ever bring her back or take away his guilt. He was charged with drunk driving and manslaughter and was placed on probation.

But it didn't end there. Brent met with Lea's mother, who told him her daughter had spread joy her entire life, from when she was a baby, and her favorite toy was a whirligig. Lea's mother wanted Brent to make whirligigs in Lea's memory, so her spirit of joy could live on. He was to go to the four corners of the United States and build whirligigs, take pictures of them and bring them back to her.

And so Brent's second life began. His first had ended with the crash. His second began with he stepped onto the first of many buses that would take him all over the country.

No one lives alone, and there are no accidents. Our lives touch others in ways we cannot anticipate and we may never even know about. Go with Brent on his journey and discover how the whirligigs changed not only his life, but also many others.

MAIN THEMES AND IDEAS
- "No man is an island"—the events of our own lives resonate in the lives of others, just as they do in our own.
- Everything happens for a reason. Life is not a series of accidents.
- Look for the lesson, the meaning, in the chaos or the tragedy, to help you see its value, its purpose.
- Retribution, atoning for your acts, is a healing process.
- Sometimes it's important to live in the nonhuman world of nature for a while. It gives you a chance to discover a new perspective on your own life.
- Much of the time we have no idea how our own actions affect the lives of other people we may never have met, in hurtful or in positive ways.
- Survival means concentrating on the good memories, not the bad ones.
- Sometimes disappointments can turn into our best experiences.
- People don't live alone but in groups. That means that sometimes they get along, and sometimes they don't. And that's OK.

BOOK REPORT IDEAS
1. The stories, or chapters, in this book swirl about each other just as the parts of a whirligig do. Explain why you think the author sequenced them in the way he did and what effect their order has on the reader.
2. Discuss Brent's concept of the world as a whirligig, from the next to the last paragraph of the book, including the ways you agree and disagree with this concept.
3. Speculate on what Brent will be like when he goes back to Chicago, and how his life will continue.
4. Lea's mother said she wanted the whirligigs to spread joy. Discuss whether or not that goal was met and why or why not.

BOOKTALK IDEAS

1. Write a plot summary booktalk leading up to Mrs. Zamara's request and Brent's departure.
2. Focus your talk on one of the whirligigs—how it was built and whose lives it touched.
3. Center your talk on the idea of interconnectedness and how Brent changed the lives of people he never met.
4. Use a whirligig as a prop for your talk.

RISKS

*   Shows drunk driving.
*   Suicide is attempted.
*   Sequencing of the book may be difficult for some to follow.

STRENGTHS

*   Promotes the idea of the interconnectedness of all humanity.
*   Characters grow and gain insight.
*   Many opportunities for group discussion and individual reflection.
*   Nonsequential story line adds complexity.

AWARDS

Best Books for Young Adults, 1999 (ALA)
Booklist Editors' Choice, 1998
100 Best Books for Teens, 2000 (ALA)

REVIEWS

"Through the diversity of [the] people who never meet Brent but are somehow forever changed by his work, Fleischman proves his point: "the world itself was a whirligig, its myriad parts invisibly linked." This is a cathartic story of redemption. Brent, filled with self-doubt, guilt, and a host of worries, is a character today's adolescents will recognize and agonize with." —*Voice of Youth Advocates*, 6/98, Maura Bresnahan.

"The story as a whole and the inner sense of self that Brent achieves through his experiences are mesmerizing. The language of the whirligig stories gleams and soars a metaphor of movement, dance, laughter, and irrepressible life. . . . loss, fear, and guilt in Fleischman's story find a universally recognizable shape." —*Booklist*, 4/1/98, GraceAnne A. DeCandido.

"In an intricately structured novel, Fleischman skillfully connects the stories of several people to the evolution of his main character. . . . He is by [the book's end] fully mindful of the consequences of small actions." —*Horn Book*, 7-8/98, N.V.

📖📖📖

WHISTLE ME HOME. Wersba, Barbara. Holt, 1997. $14.95. 108p. ISBN: 0-805-04850-2. Realistic fiction. Reading level: MS. Interest level: MS, YHS. English, Psychology, Sex education.

SUBJECT AREAS
friendship; homosexuality; sex and sexuality; rites of passage; self-knowledge; family relationships; substance abuse.

CHARACTERS
Noli Brown: a thin, boyish-looking girl, she is in love with TJ
TJ Baker: he's new in Sag Harbor, in several of Noli's classes, and immediately attracted to her
Tracy: Noli's best friend since childhood
Noli's mother: she fights with Noli constantly, nagging her to clean up her room, grow out her hair, and be more feminine
Noli's father: he tries to run interference between his wife and daughter, and is a lonely and unhappy man
Walker: TJ's friend after he and Noli break up
Melissa: Noli's mentor at AA, and her friend

BOOKTALK
It's been a terrible five months. Sometimes I've felt like one of the old black-and-white movies TJ and I used to watch—all the color is gone from my life—and not just that, half my life is gone, too. I can't see him without aching, and I can't stop thinking about him. There's no one to talk to, hold hands with, hug, talk, share—there's no one, no one at all. We were soulmates from the moment we met, and now we're nothing.

No one knows the truth about what happened that night last March, just me and TJ. I can't forget what he said, or the words I screamed at him in response. Nothing makes it feel better except the vodka. It makes a warm, full place inside me. Without it, life is cold, frozen hard, like a lake in winter. Without it, I am totally alone.

Somehow I have to figure out how to put my life back together again. I can't go on this way, it hurts so much it's tearing me apart. I have to know why it all happened, who I am now, and what to do next.

Maybe if I go back to the beginning, look at all of it again, I can make it all make sense. . . .

It was September 5th, the first day of school. . . .

MAJOR IDEAS OR THEMES
• You are the only person who can define yourself.

- Homosexuality is just another way of loving someone.
- Accepting who you are, what you are, is not always easy, but it is always necessary if you are going to succeed in life. It is also an essential part of true intimacy.
- There are many different kinds of love. Make sure the person you love, loves you in the same way.
- Your future grows from your acceptance of the past and your ability to move beyond it. Focusing too completely on the past can blind you to new options, opportunities, and open doors.
- Life is tough, and you must be tough to deal with it successfully.
- Unfortunately, most of the lessons you will learn in life will be painful, because it is that pain that persuades you to change.
- When you love someone, accept that person as he or she is, without trying to change them to suit your tastes.
- Alcohol doesn't solve problems, it compounds them.
- Lying to yourself is not any more effective than lying to someone else.

BOOK REPORT IDEAS

1. Discuss how Noli and TJ's relationship might have changed if she had found out about his homosexuality in a different time and place. Were there clues that Noli ignored that might have shown her that TJ was gay?
2. Discuss what you would have done in Noli's place, including what you would have done differently, and what differences that would have made in her relationship to TJ.
3. Speculate on what will happen after the end of the book. How will Noli change in the way she sees herself and TJ? Do you think they will be able to be friends, or will Noli prefer to maintain more distance from him?
4. Examine the significance of Noli's dream, and how it changed during the course of the story.

BOOKTALK IDEAS

1. Tell the story alternately from Noli and TJ's points of view, showing how they felt about each other, and hinting at the secrets that would eventually destroy their relationship.
2. Tell the story from TJ's point of view, as he looks back on it from a perspective of four or five months, but before his last conversation with Noli. Show his hurt and confusion as well as his love for Noli.

RISKS

- Sexually active teens, both straight and homosexual.
- One of the main characters is unable to stop being homosexual even though for a time he wants to.

- One of the main characters becomes an alcoholic as a way to escape her problems.
- Realistic but vulgar language.
- Realistic portrayal of dysfunctional family and the impact that has on its members.

STRENGTHS

- Multidimensional characters who grow and mature, gaining insight during the book.
- Ending is realistic rather than idealistic.
- Positive depiction of a homosexual lifestyle.
- Positive depiction of a gay relationship.

AWARDS

Best Books for Young Adults, 1998 (ALA)
Booklist Editors' Choice, 1997

REVIEWS

"Characters are three-dimensional...teens will relate to [the] experience of falling in love and being hurt, the overwhelming joy and the sharp disappointment. . . . It is easy to empathize with both characters' dilemmas, which is why this book is so worthwhile. . . . this brief, well-written novel deals sensitively with important issues and will have a wide appeal." —*Voice of Youth Advocates*, 8/97, Jacqueline Rose.

"Wersba handles prime problem novel territory with panache. . . . letting the messages for the most part, speak for themselves. . . . uses a dispassionate omniscient narration that both underplays and underlines the story; the dialogue, while sometimes passionate, is that of two well-spoken young adults." —*Horn Book*, 5-6/97 R.S.

"A story of immense strength and honesty; Wersba gets the relationship between Noli and TJ exactly right. . . . Wersba's use of the present tense is inspired, giving an immediacy to events that, though in the past, are still crashing around in Noli's brain." —*Booklist*, 4/1/97, Ilene Cooper.

📖📖📖

THE WHITE HORSE. Grant, Cynthia. Atheneum, 1998. $16.00. 157p. ISBN: 0-689-82127-1. Aladdin, 2000. $4.99. 160p. ISBN: 0-689-83263-X. Reading level: MS. Interest level: MS, YHS, OHS. English, Creative writing.

SUBJECT AREAS

substance abuse; problem parents; adoption; school; writing; unwed mothers; sex and sexuality; teen pregnancy; love; homeless; friendship; manipulation; crime and delinquency; death and dying.

CHARACTERS

Raina: a young girl struggling to survive her bleak, drug-centered life
Margaret Johnson: Raina's teacher who reads Raina's poems and stories and
    yearns to help her
Carla: Raina's reckless drug-addicted mother
Sonny: Raina's junkie boyfriend
Kimmy, Rita, Caleb: friends of Raina and Sonny who crash at their apartment
Stevie Joe: a nice guy whose nickname is Robin Hood because he likes to help
    people out.
Raymond, Sheila, Lynette, Willie, Bobby, Brandy: Raina's half brothers and
    sisters
Granny: Carla's mother

BOOKTALK

Raina knows only abuse, poverty, drugs, and hopelessness. Peggy Johnson can hardly believe the horrors of the life Raina pours out on the papers she puts on the teacher's desk. Is there anything she can do for this lost and damaged girl?

For Raina, the most important things in life are her junkie boyfriend, Sonny, and staying in school long enough to graduate. She knows she's on her own— her angry, abusive, drug-addicted mother has kicked her out for the last time. Raina knows a bitter secret her mother wants to forget. Living on the street is never easy, and Raina does whatever she needs to do to make sure she and Sonny survive.

For Peggy, life is a series of disappointments—no children, no husband, few friends, and a dead end job, trying to teach kids almost too far gone to be rescued. She's missed out on everything she thinks, until she meets Raina, and realizes she wants more than anything to help her find a better life.

A cynical, frustrated woman and a damaged, angry, and cynical girl—can they change each other's lives?

MAJOR THEMES AND IDEAS

- If you take chances because you think you're lucky, one day you'll take just one too many. Luck runs out.
- Drug addicts care only about themselves and their addiction.
- Surviving on the street is never easy when you don't have any other place to go.
- Drugs kill, one way or another.
- You learn to do what's necessary to survive.

- It's easier to ignore the "at-risk" kids than it is the ones with wealthy parents.
- No one ever plans to be a junkie on the street. It's just that some people don't plan *not* to.
- It isn't true that having a bad man in your life is better than no man at all.
- Dreams can come true if you're willing to work hard to make them real.
- Parents are supposed to take care of their kids, not the other way around.
- Take responsibility for your own life. You're the only one who can change it.
- Sometimes the right thing to do is what makes the most sense to you, even if it's an unlikely solution to your problem.

BOOK REPORT IDEAS

1. Discuss the aspects of Raina's character and personality that allow her to survive.
2. Speculate on the relationship between Peggy and Raina after the book ends and after Raina finishes school.
3. Compare the characters of Granny, Carla, and Lyn, showing the patterns they follow and comparing their lives to Raina's.
4. There are several parents that reject their children for various reasons. Examine what effect this rejection had on them and on their children.
5. Examine the examples of drug and alcohol use and show how characters' lives spiraled downward with their increased substance abuse.
6. Discuss the various positive steps Raina takes to first make her life bearable, and then to get it back on the right track.
7. Explain your understanding of Raina's poem, "The White Horse." It is obviously about drug addiction, but what does the ending mean to you?

BOOKTALK IDEAS

1. Use Raina's stories for Miss Johnson as a prop, copying them onto notebook paper as described in the book, and reading brief excerpts from them in your talk.
2. Write your talk from two alternating perspectives, Raina's and Miss Johnson's.
3. Focus your talk on the brutality and traumas of Raina's childhood and current life, and posing the question, "Can someone with this kind of life ever do better, and rise above it?"

RISKS

- Mother portrayed as violent, rejecting, abusive, and drug-addicted.
- Teens are addicted to drugs and are sexually active.
- Shows many scenes of drug and alcohol use/abuse.
- Includes teen pregnancy and unwed mothers.

- Physically abusive relationships are portrayed.
- Language is realistic, vulgar.
- Includes sexual and child abuse.
- There are many brutal and violent characters.

STRENGTHS
- Multiple perspectives and points of view add complexity to the story.
- Typeface changes with point of view, adding visual interest to the story.
- Book is brutally honest and realistic.
- Realistic portrayal of how negative patterns are passed from one generation to another.
- Compelling portrayal of the dangers of drugs and of living on the street.
- Narrators' voices clear, distinct, and realistic.
- Teacher is an example of a positive role model, concerned about her students.
- Nonstereotypical ending offers hope without guarantees.
- Frank presentation of the problems of a teenager raising her baby on her own.
- Format and writing style accessible to teens.
- Nondidactic or sentimental presentation of a variety of negative situations.

AWARDS
Quick Picks for Reluctant Readers, 1999 (ALA)

REVIEWS
"Realistic dialogue (including profanity) and vivid descriptions make this book heartbreakingly believable. Because this story portrays the characters and action with brittle clarity, and exposes [their] foibles . . . with tempered love, teens will relate to its truthfulness. One feels as if the author had a personal stake in the outcome of the characters' lives, and this makes for compelling reading."
—*Voice of Youth Advocates*, 12/98, Colleen Harris.

"With devastating realism . . . using alternating perspectives and narratives . . . the reader is given the opportunity. . . . to better understand not only the vicious cycles of drug and emotional abuse but also how norm is a relative, personal term. Brutal, heart-breaking, occasionally shocking, yet beautifully written. . . . gives voice to the kids on the street and in school who slip through the cracks."
—*Booklist*, 10/98, Shelle Rosenfeld.

"Explores this . . . tough-as-nails territory but adds a responsible, caring adult who is not afraid to admit her own fallibility. . . . this book will open both teen and adult eyes to the unique set of issues that each may face." —Amazon, 1998 Jennifer Hubert.

"Grant creates a nightmarish world in which the few who care are nearly overwhelmed by the sick, desperate, predatory, indifferent, and damaged. She takes readers on a scary, exhausting ride, but her women are strong enough to survive, to overcome their differences, and, in the end, to try for the family they both crave." —*Kirkus Reviews*, 9/15/98.

ᗕ ᗕ ᗕ

WILDSIDE. Gould, Steven. Tor Books, 1996. $22.95. 320p. ISBN: 0-312-85473-0. Tor Books, 1997. $5.99. 316p. ISBN: 0-812-52398-9. Science fiction. Reading level: MS. Interest level: MS, YHS, OHS. English, Psychology, Sociology, Ethics, Biology, Government, Science.

SUBJECT AREAS
activism; friendship; family relationships; adventure; survival; environmental issues; ethics; homosexuality; love; rites of passage; secrets; self-knowledge; substance abuse; working; violence; justice; legal system; politics.

CHARACTERS
Charlie: he owns the ranch and discovered the tunnel
Rick Brockrash: one of Charlie's best friends, he dates Clara
Joey Maloney: another of Charlie's closest friends, he is going with Marie
Clara Prentice: she rides a motorcycle and her horse, Impossible
Marie Nguyen: she has a pilot's license and loves Joey
Captain and Mrs. Newell: Charlie's parents, he's a commercial pilot and she is
    interested in wildlife and environmental issues
Luis Cervantes: attorney for the Wildsiders
Richard Madigan: a lawyer in Austin who works for Luis Cervantes
Chris Valencia: a friend of Rick's
Mr. Bestworst: he wants to take over the tunnel
Captain Marem, Lt. Malcolm Thayer, Sargent Costner: officers commanding the
    soldiers who try to take over the tunnel

BOOKTALK
Charlie has a secret. He's found something in the back of the old barn on the ranch he inherited from his uncle, a door behind a stack of hay bales. But this door doesn't lead into the pasture behind the barn; it leads into somewhere else. Charlie isn't sure where it is, or when it is, but this place has sabertooth tigers, and mastodons, and buffalo, and too many extinct species to count. But it has no people, no pollution, no trash. It belongs only to Charlie.

What will he do with his brave new world?

MAJOR THEMES AND IDEAS

* You probably don't know your parents as well as you think you do—and vice versa.
* In a tight spot, your friends are the ones you can depend on completely.
* It is an unfortunate fact that if you have something valuable, almost always, someone else will want to take it away from you.
* Being gay isn't a choice. It's a fact of life.
* Friendship can lead to love.
* Working together toward a goal can help people forge strong bonds.
* In a violent situation, lying can be a necessary means of survival.
* Some secrets are better kept.
* In a fight for your life, nothing is off-limits.

BOOK REPORT IDEAS

1. The book has a strong environmental message. Decide whether the Wildsiders' explorations were or were not environmentally appropriate and discuss your point of view.
2. During the battle to take over the tunnel, Luis, Richard, Captain Newell, and the Wildsiders had many of their rights violated. Discuss the ones that were and explain the sources of those rights.
3. Several characters were secretive about their activities. Discuss the ethics behind keeping secrets and how those characters were or were not ethical.
4. Examine the realism of the government and army employees in the book, and explain why or why not their actions are reflective of real life.
5. The main characters all experienced their rites of passage from adolescence to adulthood. Explain for each one when you believe that happened and why.

BOOKTALK IDEAS

1. Write your talk in first person as Marie, Joey, Clara, or Rick, and focusing mainly on the scene when Charlie shows them the passenger pigeons or takes them to the Wildside for the first time.
2. Focus your talk on the idea of the Wildside—an untouched version of Earth.

RISKS

* Teens are sexually active.
* Teens are shown drinking.
* Teens defy parents.
* Language is realistic, including obscenities.
* FBI conspiracy is portrayed, including violence.

STRENGTHS

* Multidimensional characters that grow in insight.

- Teens' strengths and flaws are both shown.
- Realistic relations among teens and with their families.
- Strong portrayal of friendship and how friendships change over time.
- Strong portrayal of functional supportive families.
- Sends strong pro-environmental message.
- Ending leaves room for both group or individual reflection and speculation.

AWARDS
Best Books for Young Adults, 1997 (ALA)

REVIEWS
"Gould has written a slam-bang, riveting science fiction novel, one which is a totally teen-centered tale. . . . [characters are] incredibly resourceful individuals who are ecology-minded yet savvy entrepreneurs. . . . the plot is so intriguing and fiercely paced that readers. . . . will be compelled to press on to the final epilogue." —*Voice of Youth Advocates*, 2/97, Suzanne Manczuk.

"More than a few surprising plot developments make for compelling reading." —*Booklist*, 1997, Carl Hays.

"A splendid adventure. . . . solidly plotted and with above-average characters." —*Kirkus Reviews*, 1996.

"Suspenseful. . . . [pays] homage to Heinlein's young adult fiction. . . . will satisfy all ages." —Amazon, 1997.

📖📖📖

WRINGER. Spinelli, Jerry. HarperCollins, 1997. $14.95. 228p. ISBN: 0-060-24913-7. HarperCollins, 1998. $5.95. 228p. ISBN: 0-064-40578-8. Realistic fiction. Reading level: MS. Interest level: MS. English, Ethics, Sociology.

SUBJECT AREAS
friendship; animals; death and dying; peer pressure; self-knowledge; family relationships; manipulation; rites of passage; secrets; gangs; intimidation.

CHARACTERS
Palmer La Rue/Snots: he dreaded turning ten, because he did not want to become a wringer
Beans: he's the leader of the kids on the street, has a mean streak, and can't wait to be a wringer

Mutto, Henry: the other two members of the gang who follow Beans' lead
Dorothy Gruzik: she lives across the street from Palmer
Farquar: legendary wringer and the coolest, most feared kid in town
Mom: Palmer's mother who dislikes Palmer's gang—especially Beans
Dad: Palmer's father who was a wringer and later won the Sharpshooter Award
Nipper: Palmer's pet pigeon

BOOKTALK

For most boys in town, the summer they were ten was the most important summer of their lives. It was the summer they got to be wringers on Pigeon Day.

But Palmer LaRue isn't like most boys. He doesn't want to be a wringer. In fact, he's never wanted to be a wringer. He has dreaded turning ten ever since he can remember. Knowing he'd have to be a wringer even when he didn't want to be is something he couldn't forget. It slipped into his mind over and over, interrupting whatever he was doing. "I don't want to be a wringer." It even invaded his dreams, when he looked at his hands locked around the pigeon's feathery, gray neck, the unblinking orange eye with the black dot in its center watching him. It would take only one quick twist, and it would be over. But even in dreams, Palmer couldn't do it. He didn't want to be a wringer.

But he did want to fit in, have friends, be part of a gang. So he kept his feelings to himself, and on his ninth birthday he got what he wanted—Beans let him into his gang. Beans was the leader of all the kids on the street, and being in the gang gave Palmer a new status he'd never had before. But it made his conflict about being a wringer even worse. Beans had a mean streak, and he couldn't wait to become a wringer, so Palmer had to pretend he felt the same way.

And then, about six months before Pigeon Day, Palmer heard a tapping at his bedroom window and there he was, Nipper, a pigeon that walked, on its pink feet, right into Palmer's heart. But it's hard to have a pigeon for a pet, when your father won a sharpshooter award, when your best friends hate pigeons, and when you live in a town that shoots 5,000 of them every summer on Pigeon Day.

MAJOR THEMES AND IDEAS

- When you hurt someone you care about, you hurt yourself first.
- Someone who forces you to do what you don't want to isn't a friend, even if he says he is.
- Hiding what you believe in is more difficult than standing up for it.
- Fitting in is sometimes too high a price to pay.
- Letting go of a secret can sometimes be a relief.
- Killing anything just for the fun of it is wrong.
- Blood money is still blood money, even when it's spent on something good.
- Standing up for what you believe in is usually worth it.

- Friends are people who make you feel better about yourself, not worse.
- Secrets can rot your soul.

BOOK REPORT IDEAS
1. Discuss the ethical conflicts of paying for a city park with the profits from a mass slaughter.
2. Discuss the psychological effects of Pigeon Day on the children of Waymer, including examples from the book of how kids treated each other.
3. Describe what Nipper meant to Palmer, and what he gained in his relationship with the bird.
4. Compare the different kinds of friendships in the book and what they meant to Palmer.
5. Compare the ways Palmer and Henry responded to Beans' manipulation and what that revealed about them.

BOOKTALK IDEAS
1. Introduce Palmer by having several characters give their opinions about him, ending with Palmer describing himself. Each of these descriptions should relate to wringers or Pigeon Day.
2. Focus your talk on Pigeon Day and how Palmer learned to hate and dread it.
3. Use Palmer's relationship with Nipper as the body of your talk, revealing the horror of Pigeon Day at the very end.

RISKS
- Graphic descriptions of the casual slaughter of hundreds of birds.
- Proceeds of horrifying slaughter used for a playground and park.
- Shows manipulation and persecution of the individual who doesn't fit in.
- Encourages children to kill.
- Portrays life as worthless.
- Encourages gun use.

STRENGTHS
- Provides many options for group discussion and individual reflection.
- Powerful antiviolence message as Pigeon Day is described in almost revolting detail.
- Parents gain insight and change.
- Clear portrayal of evil in Beans and how it can be insidiously attractive.
- Strong ending shows stark contrast between Palmer's actions/ethics and those of the town.
- Shows the importance of standing up for your own beliefs.
- Includes powerful ethical dichotomies to consider.

AWARDS
Children's Notables, 1998
Booklist Editors' Choice, 1997

REVIEWS
"Characters are memorable, convincing, and both endearing and villainous; and they are involved in a plot that, from the first page, is riveting. . . . Story is told in language simple enough for young readers, yet elegant enough for adults. . . . a moral dilemma familiar to everyone; how does one stand up for one's beliefs when they will be very unpopular?" —*School Library Journal*, 9/97, Tim Rausch.

"A realistic story with the intensity of a fable. . . . The setting here is closed and externally featureless, allowing the moral drama the full stage. . . . a world of children subject to its own rules and unanswerable to adult authority is starkly captured here . . . story is honest but not without hope." —*Horn Book*, 9-10/97, R.S.

ᒪᒪᒪ

 *APPENDIXES*

📖 APPENDIX ONE 📖
Censorship: What It Is, Why It Is, and How to Deal with It

Censors. We all know they exist. We all know what they do. But why do they do it?

Censorship is a fact of life, something that affects us everyday. We censor what we say and what we do, fitting our actions to the situation. We say the tactful rather than what is absolutely true. We select one action and reject another. We decide that someone else is too young or too old to understand something, and prevent that person from seeing or hearing or having something, and by doing so, make the world a safer place—at least in our own opinion. The censor in all of us helps keep us and those we care about safe, perhaps even moral. But sometimes that censor gets out of control and decides to control the environment more than is appropriate, trying to make not just immediate surroundings safe, but trying to make the whole world safe—on its own terms. That's when the censor, in an effort to completely control its environment, moves from being a positive to a negative force.

The American Library Association defines censorship in the following way: "Censorship is the suppression of ideas and information that certain persons— individuals, groups or government officials—find objectionable or dangerous. It is no more complicated than someone saying, 'Don't let anyone read this book, or buy that magazine, or view that film, because I object to it!'"

The *ALA Intellectual Freedom Manual* states: "Although an attempt to stereotype the censor would be unfair, one generalization can be made: Regardless of the specific notices, all would-be censors share one belief—that they can recognize 'evil' and that other people must be protected from it. Censors do not necessarily believe their own morals should be protected, but they do feel compelled to save their fellows."

The psychology of censors is composed of fear, fear of loss of power and control, over themselves, their families, their children, and their situations.

Censors are not necessarily logical when they are afraid or on a moral crusade. They attempt to exert their authority over others in order to have the situation resolved the way they want. Censors are filled with fear, and use that fear to try and persuade others to think the same way they do.

Censors mask their concerns with semantics filled with emotions. Books become power tools that can turn young adults into serial killers or sex fiends. The language of censorship surrounds the protection of our young, the protection of family, and deciding what is morally appropriate for our culture. Censors want to remove all the objectionable materials so that no one else can judge for themselves whether the subject matter is appropriate or not. They don't trust young people to decide for themselves whether or not the material is harmful. Censors are afraid that exposure to the objectionable subject matter will result in the loss of control over their children or children in general. But censors who believe they are protecting children are also acting out their personal agenda. If they are against abortion, they will not want young adults reading books about teenagers grappling with the issue. If the censors are deeply religious, then any book dealing with something that is deemed inappropriate by the church will be challenged.

Censors believe that they seek the highest moral ground, and believe everyone should have the same vision of morality, removing what doesn't fit into that vision. Censors typically object to specific scenes or pages, taking them out of context and ignoring the overall message or theme of the material. They may circulate copies of these to friends or read them aloud in a meeting. Censors also assume that the librarian, library, school, or teacher endorses the entire work including what they are objecting to. In a school situation, even when alternative materials are available for children of parents who object to the work, censors want the work unilaterally banned. The most frequent reasons for banning a book are sex, violence, profanity, supernatural elements, inappropriate family values or structures, abuse of various kinds, and racist comments or slurs. Censors believe that exposing children to this subject matter will be dangerous, and confuse them about the values and ethics their parents are teaching them. The larger issue of control is masked by the idea of protecting children from the ideas expressed in books. Ideas and words are power, and censors are afraid of them.

Suzanne Fisher Staples (*ALAN Review*, Winter, 1996) speculated on why certain parents become censor zealots: "They feel helpless sending their children into a world that seems increasingly plagued with hazards over which they have no control. They see the books available to their children as an area where they can have control."

Unfortunately, parents don't realize that kids have already heard the language and experienced or been exposed to a great deal more in school and through television, radio, the Internet, and video games than parents are aware of. Furthermore, these parents are doing their children a disservice. Children develop good judgment when allowed the freedom to find and select materials for themselves. Parents who make their children aware of what behaviors are acceptable and what are not, build accountability into their children instead of fear.

Librarians and teachers do consider what is age-appropriate as they build their collections or curricula. However, the need to control and have power over individuals who have access to children is a strong force within the censor. After all, words like child, young adult, and appropriate can be defined in a wide variety of ways.

Most people agree that it is the parents who are ultimately responsible for what their children watch, read, and come into contact with. The American Library Association states that: "The primary responsibility for rearing children rests with parents. If parents want to keep certain ideas or forms of expression away from their children, they must assume the responsibility for shielding those children. Governmental institutions cannot be expected to usurp or interfere with parental obligations and responsibilities when it comes to deciding what a child may read or view."

Censors need to understand that this control extends only to their children, not all the children of the entire community. The issue of protecting all children from witchcraft, sexual issues, AIDS, obscenities, abuse, and a wide variety of other subjects in print and nonprint media should not be a governmental concern. Ideas and freedom of expression are part of the Constitution for all citizens. Parental control must stay within the family or organizational boundaries.

Some of the best reasons for young adults to read the edgy, controversial literature when it is age appropriate for them to do so is to allow them to deal with issues they face in a private, nonthreatening manner. If a child is being abused at home and afraid to tell anyone, books such as *Staying Fat for Sarah Byrnes , Dreamland, Learning to Swim,* or *Breathing Underwater* might be an outlet for their fears, and help them make a decision about their situation. If nothing else, these titles tell them that they are not the only one enduring an abusive situation.

If schools are charged with preparing students for life, then studying controversial subjects in the classroom is necessary. AIDS, drug and alcohol abuse, sexuality, homosexuality, ethics, gangs, self-reliance, anorexia nervosa/bulimia, prejudice, and self-esteem are just a few of the topics that teachers and librarians must educate students about during their time in school. Subjects like these are all controversial, "hot" subjects. They are loaded with emotions and prejudices. Parents or censors are often afraid to discuss these issues with their own children and usually do not want anyone else to do so either. If censors are afraid of the topics presented in the classroom and supported by materials in the library, a challenge is a very strong possibility.

This is a group of people who knows what is right, not only for themselves, but for everyone. They do not deal well with confrontation and when confronted, tend to dig in and defend their position even more strongly. They are ruled by fear, fear of losing power and control. When making a challenge, they may also be angry or frustrated. The library staff must be trained to deal with them effectively and positively.

For this reason, strong reconsideration and challenge policies and procedures need to be present in every library. Staff must be trained to deal with challenges and be educated about guidelines and procedures. Written policies and an educated staff form a solid foundation of support for the teacher or librarian who wants to keep the more edgy, realistic young adult fiction in their collections and in the hands of young readers.

It is important to know how to make challenges less difficult and traumatic for both the challenger and the librarian. These tips offer suggestions for what to do before a challenge occurs, how to deal with a challenger face-to-face, and what kinds of policies and procedures need to be in place to support you in facing the challenge.

The first thing to remember in dealing with challenges is to accept the fact that sooner or later someone will object to something in your collection. It may or may not be about an item that you thought would be challenged, and it may or may not be about a part of that item that you thought would be controversial—in fact, it will probably be something you never expected a challenge about. Given this, it is important to prepare ahead of time so you already know what steps to take.

Of course a written selection policy, including reconsideration procedures, is essential. This policy is a general one, covering the whole library collection. Smaller departments, especially children's and young adult departments, should have their own written policies tailored to their customers' specific needs, but the procedures and forms used should be consistent throughout the library. The general policy should first clearly define the goals and philosophy of the library and then include sections on selection of materials, intellectual freedom issues, reconsideration procedures and forms, and any curriculum guidelines that apply to the library. (Other sections not having to do with challenges have been omitted here, for brevity's sake.)

The reconsideration form should be concise, but should include several key pieces of information.

- Has the customer read the whole book or just a part?
- If the latter, how did the customer find out about that section in the book?
- Is the customer affiliated with any organization seeking to challenge the book? Has the customer read any reviews of or articles on the book?
- What action does the customer want the library to take?

The form should help the customer clarify his thoughts about the book and formalize his concerns.

The selection policy is the library's first line of defense. It should be backed up by additional "ammunition" on the titles and authors that are most likely to be challenged. This ammunition can include a wide variety of materials, for instance:

- A file of reviews, including the full text of each review and a citation to its source
- A list of honors that the book has won (the cover or dust jacket may help you get started with this)
- Articles written about the book, either by the author or critics
- A rationale supporting the book, containing bibliographic information, intended audience, a brief summary of the plot, a statement on the value of the book and how it might be used, the impact of the book, and the new perspectives it could open up, the potential problems or risks with the book and how they might be handled, and alternative titles that might be less objectionable
- A list of other challenges to the book, and information on how they were handled
- Statements from customers who support the book, especially from members of the intended audience for the book or from influential community members
- Books or Web sites on how to deal with censors
- Information on how to contact the Office for Intellectual Freedom at the American Library Association and at your state or regional library association
- And of course, this book is designed to help you defend the titles in it!

These are only a few of the kinds of ammunition you can collect about a book that you expect will be challenged. Almost anything can be grist for this mill.

A third line of defense is a well-trained library staff that knows how to handle a customer and a situation that can quickly become explosive. Training classes that include role-playing and lists of tips on how to handle customers' complaints are very helpful. Some things that are important to remember when faced with a challenge are:

- First of all, remember to breathe! Pay conscious attention to maintaining a relaxed body posture and to staying calm.
- If you are in a public area, ask the customer to go to a less public or less crowded area, so you can devote all your attention to their complaint without the distraction of other customers. This also prevents others from getting involved in the situation and helping to escalate it.
- Invite the customer to sit down with you. It's harder to maintain a high level of emotion when you are sitting rather than standing. Do not sit across the table from the customer, which is a confrontational posture. Rather, sit on the same side of the table, or at one end, while the customer sits at right angles to you.
- Make eye contact but don't stare.
- If you choose to take notes, make sure the customer can easily see what you are writing.

- Watch your body language. Your posture should be open and relaxed, your facial expression should be polite, calm, attentive, and receptive.
- Keep your voice low. The louder the customer gets, the more quietly and softly you should respond.
- Respond to what the customer is saying by nodding, and using verbal encouragers such as "I see. . . . Yes. . . . Right. . . . Um-hum. . . . I understand. . . . "
- Listen to the content of the complaint and also to the subtext behind it. "I can't believe you have this smut in the library where children can find it!" "It sounds like you really care about your kids." Work to change the interaction from a confrontation to a dialogue.
- Agree with the customer as much as you can, so that he or she doesn't have to become defensive.
- Find something positive to say, some kind of praise you can give. "It's really great to see a parent willing to go to so much trouble for their children."
- Let the customer tell the story over and over, as many times as he or she wants to. It may take several retellings before the customer has vented enough to be ready to go on to the resolution stage of the interaction. Remember, these people are angry, anxious, nervous, and need to defend themselves and their points of view and try to convince you of the rightness of their cause before thinking about how to solve the problem.
- Really listen to the customer without planning ahead what you are going to say or do. Be in the moment with the customer at all times.
- Once the customer is ready to move into the resolution stage, explain the library's policies and procedures and what the next steps will be.
- Have copies of the reconsideration form, the Library Bill of Rights, and the Freedom to Read Statement available for the customer to have.
- If necessary, or if requested by the customer, refer him or her to someone higher in authority, and when possible, take the customer to that person and introduce them, rather than just giving the customer a name and phone number. If the staff person being referred to is in another building, offer to call them for the customer and introduce them over the phone.
- Finally, follow the procedures given in the reconsideration policy if the customer wishes to continue with the challenge.

📖 APPENDIX TWO 📖
How to Write a Rationale

http://ncte.org/censorship/write_rationales.shtml
Adapted from SLATE Starter Sheet, NCTE, April 1994
Jean E. Brown, Saginaw Valley State University, Michigan
Region 4 Representative to the SLATE Steering Committee
(SLATE stands for Support for the Learning and Teaching of English, and is the
intellectual freedom network of the National Council of Teachers of English)

WHAT IS A RATIONALE?

We frequently hear the term rationale defined as a justification for doing
something. Certainly that perspective is a vital one as we explore the need for
developing rationales for books or other instructional material. Both Diane
Shugert (1979) and Margaret Sacco (1993) advocate writing and keeping a file
of rationales in advance as a defense against potential censorship. We will frame
the discussion in a broader context, describing the overriding role of rationales
in classroom planning. Teachers must make decisions about what they will teach
and how they will then teach it, decisions that will achieve their purposes and
address their students' needs. The value of developing a rationale is that it
provides a framework for this planning.

A rationale is the articulation of the reasons for using a particular literary
work, film, or teaching method. Minimally, a rationale should include: a
bibliographic citation and the intended audience, a brief summary of the work
and its educational significance, the purposes of using the work and how it will
be used, potential problems with the work and how these can be handled,
alternative works an individual student might read or view. Shugert (1979)
identifies criteria for assessing rationales. Among these guidelines are that they
are well thought out, avoid specialized technical jargon, are specific and
thorough, and are written so that they will be readily understood by teachers
who use the work. These and other components of rationales will be explored in
the section on Guidelines for Writing a Rationale.

WHY DEVELOP A RATIONALE?

Rationale development should be part of thoughtful planning for classroom instruction. If we have not reflected on the whys of what we teach, we will be unprepared to meet the needs and challenges of our students and to respond to potential complaints, either from parents or from others in the community who seek to influence the curriculum. While rationales are important in every aspect of teaching, we will focus here on the need for well-developed rationales for books used in the classroom—whether in whole-class instruction, small-group work, or classroom libraries. Teachers who make curricular decisions based upon mere expediency leave themselves vulnerable. Problems can be averted by carefully analyzing the audience (the students), the school, and the community and taking into full account the most effective means for meeting students' interests and educational needs.

HOW DO WE DEVELOP RATIONALES?

Teachers are frequently advised to have a written rationale for every book that they use. Realistically, this issue might be better addressed in a less absolute way by exploring four levels of rationale development. In an ideal situation, teachers would automatically write a rationale for every book that they teach, assign, include on a reading list, or keep in their classroom libraries. But mandating teachers to take on such a task when they are already overburdened is unrealistic and unreasonable. If teachers were required to write rationales for every book, many might simply stick to their literature anthologies and even avoid potentially controversial selections in those books. So while Shugert (1979, pp. 190-91) rightly cautions about using shortcuts to rationales, we do suggest options in the belief that the circumstances and conditions will determine what the teachers will do at any time.

1. A brief written statement of purpose for using a particular book—the "why" for using it and where it will fit in the curriculum. This is prepared by individual teachers based on the students, school, and community noted above and on curricular and instructional objectives and needs. At this level of rationale writing it is essential for teachers to have a written statement. Just thinking about the reason is not enough to demonstrate thoughtful planning if a protest should arise, nor does it provide teachers with opportunities to be reflective about their decisions.

2. The second level involves a more detailed accounting through use of forms. Pages 326-329 of this appendix show sample forms from the Connecticut Council of Teachers of English (Shugert, 1979, pp. 192-93). These samples provide two approaches—the first for an individual teacher to complete and the second for department members to fill out together. Of course, both forms can be modified to meet the needs of particular school situations.

3. The third level provides for the development of fully constituted rationales by individual teachers, departmental or district wide committees, or the district English language arts coordinator or supervisor in cooperation with teachers. These rationales include many of the elements discussed above and will be explored further in the next section.

4. The fourth level calls for the collection of existing rationales that have been developed by other teachers or by professional organizations. By their nature these rationales are often comprehensive because they are developed as a service for schools that have challenges.

GUIDELINES FOR WRITING A RATIONALE

The guidelines below will promote consistency as well as provide direction and support for writing rationales individually, in small collegial groups, or in departments. Sacco, in a paper prepared for the Assembly on Literature for Adolescents (ALAN) Intellectual Freedom Committee, and Shugert (1979) are among those who have presented systematic views of how to put together a rationale. Sacco uses a highly structured format in developing rationales with her undergraduate students; Shugert provides a more open-ended approach based on the following questions posed by Donelson (1979, p. 166):

1. For what classes is this book especially appropriate?

2. To what particular objectives, literary or psychological or pedagogical, does this book lend itself?

3. In what ways will the book be used to meet those objectives?

4. What problems of style, tone, or theme or possible grounds for censorship exist in the book?

5. How does the teacher plan to meet those problems?

6. Assuming that the objectives are met, how would students be different because of their reading of this book?

Fundamentally, Sacco, Shutgert, and Donelson concur that the role of the rationale is to provide a written statement of teachers' best professional perspective on their curriculum. The following guidelines for preparing rationales draw upon and synthesize their ideas.

1. **The bibliographic citation**. A rationale should begin with a complete bibliographic citation including author's name, complete book title, publisher, publication date, and edition.

2. **The intended audience**. The rationale should articulate the type of class and the range of grade levels at which the book will be used. The rationale should indicate whether the book is going to be used for individual study, small-group work, or whole-class study, along with an explanation of reasons for why the book is being used.

3. **A brief summary of the work**. There are a number of reasons for summarizing a book in the rationale. Writing a summary requires an in-depth look at the book. The summary provides an overview of the book

for anyone who chooses to read it, and it can also reflect aspects of a work that the teacher considers most important and aspects that relate to its educational significance.

4. **The relationship of the book to the program**. Reading a book is not an isolated educational experience; as a part of the total program, the book should be consistent with the ongoing objectives of the class. Regardless of the quality of a book, if it does not make sense within the broad goals of the program, it is an inappropriate choice in that particular classroom. Any discussion of objectives should also include an examination of how a book will be used, including the teaching methodology and methods of assessment.

5. **The impact of the book**. One of the significant arguments for any work is the ways in which it will open new perspectives to its readers. In determining the reasons for using a book, teachers should also consider the potential impact it will have on students' behavior or attitudes.

6. **Potential problems with the work**. Teachers and districts are often blindsided by complaints that they never anticipated. The reflective process of developing a rationale is an opportunity for anticipating uses of language, actions, and situations in a work that might be the source of challenges. Additionally, as teachers examine potential problems, they have the opportunity to make decisions about how to address the problems, establishing a framework that supports the book's quality and strengths. For example, a teacher might anticipate an objection to the language in Walter Dean Myers's *Fallen Angels*. The issue can be addressed within the context of the realistic portrayal of young men fighting in Vietnam; the language, while inappropriate in many settings, helps build the portrait of the war's horrors. The language quite simply adds to the book's credibility.

7. **Collection of information about the book**. It is useful to collect references about the book, especially published book reviews. Professional journals and booklists from various associations (e.g., NCTE, the International Reading Association, American Library Association), journals like *ALAN Review*, *Horn Book*, and *New Advocate*, as well as non-school sources like the *New York Times Book Review* and *Time* magazine are rich resources that can be searched via various databases for reviews of particular books. Reviews that address any controversial issues in the book are particularly helpful. These materials should be kept in a file with the rationale.

8. **Collection of supplementary information**. Teachers should collect additional materials such as biographical information about the author, especially if it includes any critical assessment of the author's work.

9. **Collection of books of rationales**. Books of rationales such as *Rationales for Commonly Challenged/Taught Books* (*Connecticut*

English Journal, Vol. 15, 1983), *Celebrating Censored Books!* (Wisconsin Council of Teachers of English, Ed. Nicholas J. Karolides), and *Hit List* (Intellectual Freedom Committee, American Library Association, 1989) are valuable as part of the teacher's individual library or as part of the English department's professional library.

10. **Alternative works an individual student might read.** For each book they use, teachers should have a list of related titles that might serve either as an alternative or as a supplement to the book. The list of alternatives is useful when parents exercise their right to choose what their child will read. Additionally, the list may be used when students are choosing books from several options, or when they want to read related works. In other words, the listing can be useful in a number of ways, not just in response to a challenge.

REFERENCES

American Library Association. Young Adult Services Division's Intellectual Freedom Committee. *Hit List: Frequently Challenged Young Adult Titles: References to Defend Them.* Chicago: ALA, 1989.

Donelson, K. "Censorship in the 1970s: Some Ways to Handle It when It Comes (and It Will.)" *Dealing with Censorship*, edited by James Davis. Urbana, IL: NCTE, 1979.

Karolides, N.J., and L. Burress, editors. *Celebrating Censored Books!* Racine: Wisconsin Council of Teachers of English, 1985.

Sacco, M.T. "Writing Rationales for Using Young Adult Literature in the Classroom" Unpublished manuscript.

Shugert, D., editor. "Rationales for Commonly Challenged/Taught Books." *Connecticut English Journal*, Vol. 15, 1983.

Shugert, D. (1979). "How to Write a Rationale in Defense of a Book." *Dealing with Censorship*, edited by James Davis. Urbana, IL: NCTE, 1979.

Teacher's Rationale Form

This form is a model that is intended for individual teachers to fill out. You may wish to print this form and make as many copies as you need or amend it to suit your own situation. It is designed to be used primarily to assist teachers with specific local situations.

School:

Teacher:

Author:

Title:

Grade or course:

Approximate date(s) a book will be used:

This book will be (check one or more):
- Studied by the whole class
- Studied by small groups
- Placed on a reading list
- Placed in a classroom library
- Recommended to individual students

Part of a larger study of (explain):

Other (explain):

Ways in which the book is especially appropriate for students in this class:

Ways in which the book is especially pertinent to the objectives of this course or unit:

Special problems that might arise in relation to the book and some planned activities which handle this problem:

Some other appropriate books an individual student might read in place of this book:

English Department Rationale Form

This form is a model that is intended for department members to fill out together. You may wish to print this form and make as many copies as you need or amend it to suit your own situation. It is designed to be used primarily to assist departments with specific local situations.

Submitted by:

Email:

School:

Title:

Author Name:

Recommended grade(s) or course(s):

Ways in which the book is appropriate for students in this school:

Ways in which the book is pertinent to the objectives of this curriculum:

Special problems that might arise in relation to the book:

Ways that a teacher might handle those problems:

Some other appropriate books an individual student might read in place of this book:

📖 APPENDIX THREE 📖
Sources of Support for Resisting Censorship

Organizations and Web sites

Office for Intellectual Freedom, American Library Association. 312 280-4223.
www.ala.org/alaorg/oif/index.html
- Coping with Challenges: Kids and Libraries
  www.ala.org/alaorg/oif/kidsandlibraries.html
- Coping with Challenges: Strategies and Tips
  www.ala.org/alaorg/oif/coping
- Top 100 Banned or Challenged Books of 1990-1999
  www.ala.org/alaorg/oif/top100 bannedbooks.html

National Council of Teachers of English (Standing Committee Against
Censorship, SLATE—Support for the Learning and Teaching of English)
800-369-6283. www.NCTE.org/censorship/

Joint Task Force on Intellectual Freedom of the National Council of Teachers of
English and the International Reading Association. 800-336-READ.
www.reading.org

Peacefire: Youth Alliance Against Internet Censorship
http://www.peacefire.org/

Cyberliberties: Teens Affected by Online Censorship Speak Out
http://www.aclu.org/issues/cyber/trial/teens.html

Banned Books and Censorship
http://www.booksatoz.com/censorship/banned.htm

Anti-Censorship Home Page
http://www.best.com/~cgd/home/anticens.htm

National Coalition Against Censorship
http://www.wlma.org/intfree/first.htm

Archive of [Censorship] Cases
  (sorted by date, location, medium, and grounds for censorship)
  http://fileroom.aaup.uic.edu/FileRoom/documents/CategoryHomePage.
  html
Censorship and Intellectual Freedom Page
  http://ezinfo.ucs.indiana.edu/~quinnjf/censor.html
Censorship in the Library?
  http://www.rightnow.org/censorship.html
Free Expression Clearinghouse
  http://www.FreeExpression.org/
Free Expression (American Booksellers Association)
  http://www.ambook.org/abffe/
Freedom, Discipline, and Censorship
  http://www.cudenver.edu/~mryder/itc_data/censorship.html
Freedoms Under Fire
  http://www.uniontrib.com/reports/bill_of_rights/bill_of_rights_1st.html
Index on Censorship
  http://www.oneworld.org/index_oc/index.html
Know Your Enemies
  http://www.eff.org/pub/Groups/BCFE/bcfenatl.html
Outpost Culture
  http://www.coolbooks.com/~outpost/
ProjectCensored
  http://censored.sonoma.edu/ProjectCensored/
See/Hear/Speak No Evil
  http://www.xnet.com/~paigeone/noevil/noevil.html
Banned Books and Censorship: Information and Resources
  http://www.luc.edu/libraries/banned/
Banned Books on the Internet
  http://www.lhup.edu/~rparker/advcomp/papers/bressle.htm
Banned Books Online
  http://www.cs.cmu.edu/Web/People/spok/banned-books.html
Book Banning, Burning, and Censorship
  http://www.banned.books.com/
The File Room's Exhibit of Banned Books
  http://fileroom.aaup.uic.edu/FileRoom/documents/Mliterature.html

Journals
Newsletter on Intellectual Freedom. ALA.

Books
Intellectual Freedom Manual. American Library Association, Fifth ed., 1996.

The Hit List II: Frequently Challenged Books for Young Adults. American Library Association, Second ed.,1996.

Dealing with Censorship in the 21st Century: A Guide for Librarians and Teachers, by Eliza Dresang and John Simmons. Greenwood Press, 2000.

Rationales for Teaching Young Adult Literature, edited by Louann Reid. Calendar Islands, 1999.

Pamphlets

Intellectual Freedom Packet. American Library Association/Association for Library Service to Children.

Censorship: Don't Let It Become an Issue in Your Schools. National Council of Teachers of English (NCTE).

The Student's Right to Know. NCTE.

The Student's Right to Read. NCTE.

Guidelines for Dealing with Censorship. NCTE.

Common Ground. Joint Task Force of NCTE and International Reading Association.

CD-Rom

Rationales for Challenged Books. Joint Task Force of NCTE and IRA, 1998.

📖 APPENDIX FOUR 📖
Bibliography

Aronson, Marc. "The Challenge and the Glory of Young Adult Literature." *Booklist* (April 15, 1997).

Aronson, Marc. "Puff the Magic Dragon: How the Newest Young Adult Fiction Grapples with a World in Upheaval." *Los Angeles Times*, 1999.

Brown, Jennifer M., and Cindi Di Marzo. "Why So Grim? Awards and Controversy Focus Attention on a Recent Burst of Dark-Themed Fiction for Teens." *Publishers Weekly* (February, 16, 1998).

Campbell, Patty. "Rescuing Young Adult Literature." *Horn Book* (May-June 1997).

Cole, Brock. "Children Braving an Adult World." *Publishers Weekly* (February 17, 1997).

Cruz, Clarissa. "No Kidding: Think All Teen Books Are Cute and Lightweight? Think Again." *Entertainment Weekly* (October 15, 1997).

Curry, A. *The Limits of Tolerance: Censorship and Intellectual Freedom in Public Libraries.* Lanham, MD.: Scarecrow Press, 1996.

Fine, Sara. "How the Mind of a Censor Works: The Psychology of Censorship." *School Library Journal* (January 1996).

Frederick, Heather Vogel. "What's Known Can't Be Unknown: An Interview with Chris Crutcher." *Publishers Weekly* (February 20, 1995).

Howard, Elise. "Making YA Cool for Teens." *Publishers Weekly* (June 1, 1998).

Jackson, Richard. "The Beasts Within." *Booklist* (August 1998).

Maughan, Shannon. "Books: Market for Young Adult Literature Has Many Possibilities." *Publishers Weekly* (October 18, 1999).

November, Sharyn. "We're Not "Young Adults"—We're Prisoners of Life." *Voice of Youth Advocates* (August 1997).

Reid, Suzanne, and Sharon Stringer. "The Psychological Impact of Troubling YA Literature on Adolescent Readers in the Classroom: Ethical Dilemmas in Teaching Problem Novels." *ALAN Review* (Winter 1997).

Spitz, David. "Reads Like Teen Spirit: Edgy Fiction Is Making Literature 'Cool' Again." *Time* (July 19, 1999).

Suhor, Charles. "Censorship—When Things Get Hazy." *English Journal* (February 1997).

Werlin, Nancy. "Experimental YA Fiction." *Booklist* (October 1, 1998).

 **INDEXES**

📖 AUTHOR INDEX 📖

📖 READING LEVEL AND AGE/INTEREST LEVEL INDEX 📖

📖 CURRICULUM AREAS INDEX 📖

Film

Foreign Language

Geography

Government

📖 GENRE INDEX 📖

Satire

Science fiction

Short story collections

Verse novels

📖 SUBJECT INDEX 📖

This index contains a more complete listing of subject areas
than those given in individual entries.

Divorce and Separation

Dysfunctional Families

Fear

Friendship

Rites of passage

Self-Knowledge

School

Sex and Sexuality

Short Stories

Sports

Stepparents

Writing

📖 ABOUT THE AUTHOR 📖

Internationally known as an author, lecturer, and workshop leader on booktalking and young adult literature and services, Joni Richards Bodart has been active in the ALA Young Adult Library Services Association since the 1970s. Formerly assistant professor at Emporia State University in the School of Library and Information Management, she is now on the faculty of the Division of Library and Information Science, College of Education, University of Denver. She lives in Colorado, where, in addition to teaching, she works as a writer, a consultant to public and school libraries, and a part-time YA/reference librarian for Denver Public Library. She is currently working on *The Booktalkers' Bible*, a revision of her *Booktalk!2*, widely considered to be the standard on the subject.